THE ELECT AND THE HOLY

SUPPLEMENTS
TO
NOVUM TESTAMENTUM

VOLUME XII

THE ELECT AND THE HOLY

AN EXEGETICAL EXAMINATION OF I PETER 2:4–10 AND THE PHRASE

βασίλειον ἱεράτευμα

BY

JOHN HALL ELLIOTT

Dr. Theol.
Assistant Professor of Exegetical Theology
Concordia Seminary, St. Louis, Missouri
U.S.A.

Wipf & Stock
PUBLISHERS
Eugene, Oregon

Wipf and Stock Publishers
199 W 8th Ave, Suite 3
Eugene, OR 97401

The Elect And The Holy
An Exegetical Examination of 1 Peter 2:4-10 and the Phrase of 'basileion hierateuma'
By Elliott, John H.

ISBN: 1-59752-410-7
Publication date 10/1/2005
Previously published by E. J. Brill, 1966

TABLE OF CONTENTS

Errata

PAGE	
xv	last para: read Board for Higher…
9	6th line from bottom: read "is" in place of "are."
12	Note 3, last para, referring to Cross, *I Peter* read "1954; 2d ed. 1957" in place of "1934"
18	under Group B: right hand column read "5d theô… "5d pneumatikas…in place of "5a"
33	4th line from bottom: read "Philipp" in place of "Phillip"
44	Note 4: read "Selwyn", in place of "Selwin"
46	3d line from top: read ta\ e1qnh in place of *hoi ethnoi*
55	Note 3 insert qamets under resh in place of patakh in)rq
71	Note 4: read "Dan . 5:1, 6:19" in place of "6:9"
97	3d line from top: add smooth breathing and read: o0ikodo/mhma
98	2d line of Greek under 2. De Abrahamo 56: read i9era/teuma (replacing m for n)
144	Note 1, line 3. read "cf. Lk. 9:35" replacing "cp…."
144	Note 2 2d line: read "Apoc. 2:27, 12:5, 19:15" in place of" 2:7… 19:5"
146	3d para: read "depiction" for "depicture"
157	Note 2. read "Mk. 11:17" in place of "Mark 11:37"
158	Last para., 3d line: read "in" in place of "is" (in this sense…)
159	last para before section 3: Remove comma after "Spirit" and replace with period.
160	Note 2, 4th last line: read "(42 occurrences)" for (39…)
161	2d line . Capitalize chi in Xristou
170	Note 4. Read "Hebräerbrief" (adding an e)
171	Note 8, last word: read "here" (adding h).
172	4th line from top. Capitalize chi in Xristou
173	2d last para. Capitalize chi in Xristou
179	1st para of Excursus 5: delete "3:11" and close parens after "16". 2d last line: read a0nastrofnh/ (replacing theta with phi)
180	2d para from top. read "(1:14)." replacing "1:13." Note 8 read "Brandt, op. cit., p. 25" replacing "Brandt, *ibid*…."
181	Note 6. Following "Bigg, op. cit.: add "p. 128."
202	1st para. Read "1:13-25" replacing "1:13-15." same para: Read "Is. 40:8" replacing Is. 40:7. last para., 2d line. Read "13-25" replacing "13-24"

203	Note 4, 1st line: following “I Cor 3:1f” add comma and “Heb 5:12,”
204	2-3 lines from top: Read lo/goj zw~n kai\ me/nwn (1:23) replacing zwntoj menontoj0
206	Note 1, lst line: read “Hebräer” (omitting s)
211	first line: revise to read: “I P, and the comparison of the texts of the two section make this theory most unlikely.” (adding comparison of the and deleting “compared”
212	first para, 4th line: read “irreconcilable” replacing “non-reconcilable”
	first para, 7th line from top: read “reference” to replace “allusion”
217	4th line from bottom: read “2:11ff.” replacing “2:12ff.”
223	2d para. Read “inadmissible” replacing “inadmissable.”
224	last para. Read “inadmissible” replacing “inadmissable.”
227	re. FRLANT read: “Forschungen… (adding –en)
228	re KJV read: “Authorized Version” (with capitalized V)
234	Büchsel…. Read a0nagenna/w replacing a0rtigenna/w
235	Cullmann….Read *Urchristentum und Gottesdienst* (correcting erroneous letter division)
237	Hort… read: “*The First Epistle of St. Peter I:1-II:17*.” (entirety italicized and numbers corrected)
238	Lohse…Read “(1954), 68-89.” replacing (1945), 68-69.
241	Thornton…add question mark after “Liturgy” and read: “a Paschal Liturgy?” ”

FOREWORD

The publications of the School for Graduate Studies of Concordia Seminary, St. Louis, are products of the members of the staff of Concordia Seminary or works prepared within the School.

Dr. Elliott's *The Elect and The Holy* was written, as the acknowledgments show, as a dissertation for the Evangelical Theological Faculty of the Wilhelms University in Münster. He was appointed as assistant professor of Exegetical Theology at Concordia Seminary in 1964. His services have been utilized also by the School for Graduate Studies. His intensive study of a significant theological topic deserves to be disseminated. The Council for Graduate Studies was happy for the opportunity to publish this scholarly contribution by a member of the faculty of Concordia Seminary as Graduate Study Number VII. We are grateful, too, to the Aid Association for Lutherans of Appleton, Wisconsin, for the financial help given to the Publication Fund of the School for Graduate Studies. The continued support of this group for various scholarly enterprises has been of great value to The Lutheran Church--Missouri Synod.

It is not supposed that all readers will fully concur with all of the findings of the author. They will acknowledge his rigorous *wissenschaftliche Untersuchungen*, his great care in documentation, and his precise statement of his findings. We ask them to weigh these findings carefully in the light of the new evidence the author presents.

CARL S. MEYER, DIRECTOR
School for Graduate Studies
Concordia Seminary, St. Louis

Meiner lieben Frau Linde, die die liebenswertesten Eigenschaften des Volkes und die teuerste Verbindung mit dem Lande verkörpert, in dem diese Arbeit entstanden ist.

FOREWORD

"The danger for us is not the theological problems but rather the untheological slogans," one of Germany's outstanding theologians has perceptively observed.* The danger is that convenient slogans and generalizing labels not only hinder the accurate treatment of theological issues; even worse, their very presence and use often implies a consensus of opinion which, in turn, denies that certain problems even exist.

Such is the case with the Biblical pericope 1 Peter 2:4-10 and the slogan "the universal (or royal) priesthood of believers." For centuries, but particularly since the Reformation, theologians have found the import of this text to be an affirmation of the priestly character of all believers and of their royal and sacerdotal perogatives. Not only does this apply to scholars of the historic churches of the Reformation but in more recent time, though with varying accent, to Roman Catholic theologians as well. In view of the increased emphasis laid upon this text among all communions engaged in the ecumenical dialogue, the question regarding the accuracy of this popular interpretation becomes an urgent one. From the surprisingly few exegetical investigations ever devoted to this question it becomes apparent that for the most part the *popularity* of this explanation has provided the chief canon of acceptance. Such a situation suggests the stifling influence of a theological slogan and a less than critical reception of an assumed *opinio communis*.

To raise the question regarding the accuracy of a current trend in the interpretation of 1 Peter 2:4-10 and from this point of departure to subject the text to critical scrutiny—and thus to dig at the roots of this particular slogan—is the purpose of this present undertaking. Its prime concern, therefore, involves the structure, content, and import of this pericope. The analysis attempts to be strictly exegetical throughout. The relatively few references to the "universal priesthood of believers" in this study indicate that this theme, though the original stimulus of this investigation, proved insignificant, if not altogether useless, in the specific exegesis of the

* Ernst Käsemann, "Eine Apologie der urchristlichen Eschatologie," *Zeitschrift für Theologie und Kirche*, 49 (1952), p. 296.

text. Since the most important characteristics of this theme are treated individually throughout the book, it has been considered unnecessary, except for a final reference in the Conclusion, to discuss the topic at any additional length. Though a possible rethinking of the essence of the "universal priesthood of believers" idea on the basis of the conclusions made in this study would be most profitable, such an undertaking would fall outside the purview of an exegetical examination and for this reason such has been omitted here.

Nevertheless, it is sincerely hoped that should this investigation be judged in any manner contributive, its contribution pertain not only to the Biblical text treated but also to the topic which stimulated this study in the first place. If this should be the case, then progress perhaps has been made not merely in the elimination of a theological slogan and identification of a theological problem, but also possibly in the advance from the real problem to a valid solution.

ACKNOWLEDGEMENTS

This study constitutes, in the main, the inaugural dissertation submitted to the Evangelisch-Theologische Fakultät of the Wilhelms-Universität in Münster, Westfalen, Germany, in the fall of 1963. Revisions made subsequent to this time involve corrections in the interests of greater clarity, the addition of further pertinent literature and the concluding indices.

To all who have contributed to this work, be it through theological stimulation, personal encouragement, or through practical assistance in the preparation of the end product, I express my profound gratitude.

For my esteemed advisor, Professor D. Dr. Karl Heinrich Rengstorf, this book reflects in but small part the bond of respect and appreciation which had its beginning during my years at Münster, a bond which transcends the realm of academic dissertation. To Professor D. Franz Hesse, the thesis' Korreferent, and the other members of the Evangelisch-Theologische Fakultät I express the wish that this study in some way convey the pride and honor I consider it to have studied under their tutelage and now in the United States to be a representative of this distinguished German university.

In August 1962 I had the privilege and pleasure of discussing at length the subject of this work with Dr. Josef Blinzler whose article on 1 Peter is cited frequently throughout the book. Dr. Blinzler welcomed this study most cordially and his friendliness and encouragement were most appreciated. If occurrences of differences of opinion between Dr. Blinzler and myself seem abundant, this is witness only to the *Gründlichkeit* and comprehensiveness of his brief but significant contribution to the understanding of 1 Peter 2.

The Bibliothek der Westfälischen Wilhelms-Universität was most helpful in the obtaining of much material unavailable in Münster and the Institutum Judaicum Delitzschianum in Münster, beside providing certain Rabbinic materials, offered an atmosphere of stimulation for which I am most grateful.

Through the generosity of the Ev.-luth. Zentralverein für Mission unter Israel and the Board fof Higher Education of the Lutheran Church-Missouri Synod I received the financial support necessary to complete this project in Germany.

To my former instructor and present colleague, Professor Dr. Arthur Carl Piepkorn, I am grateful for a careful proof-reading of the manuscript and for the many valuable suggestions he offered for a clearer presentation. I am indebted also to Mrs. Lucille Meyer for her painstaking work in the final typing, to seminarians Arthur Giger, Bruce Dahms, Gary Pence, and Gary Stansell for their assistance in the tedious compilation of the indices, and above all to Concordia Seminary and particularly the School for Graduate Studies for their most generous financial support and subsidization of this publication.

Finally, my sincere thanks are extended to Mr. E. J. Brill, the publisher, and to the editorial board of *Novum Testamentum* for receiving this study as a supplement to this distinguished journal.

If despite all such generous assistance the work still admits of errors and faults, then they can be charged only to the oversight of the author.

JOHN H. ELLIOTT

The Festival of St. Michael and All Angels
St. Louis 1964

INTRODUCTION

The Need of an Examination

"The doctrine of the universal priesthood is one of the basic truths of Catholic ecclesiology." It is no insignificant matter that these are the recent words of a Roman Catholic scholar, the renowned professor of Fundamental Theology at the University of Tübingen, Hans Küng.[1] Less than two decades ago this same doctrine was described by the Anglican Bishop of Oxford, Kenneth E. Kirk, as "the decisive formula of all non-episcopal Christendom."[2] In their inclusiveness these two statements spotlight a concern which embraces the totality of the Church Catholic.

In the ecumenical conversation of the post World War II years the significance of the priestly character of the Church has received, and continues to receive, increasing accentuation. This, of course, is a logical consequence of the interdenominational dialogue which has concentrated more and more upon the ecclesiological question—the nature and function of the Church. In view of the host of recent literature which has appeared treating the question of the Church's priesthood under such various aspects as universal priesthood, priesthood, priesthood and ministry, laity and hierarchy, and lay apostolate, it is not surprising that precisely this concern has been labeled "perhaps the major theological problem of the twentieth century."

Certainly the excited echo stimulated by the important contributions of the French Dominican scholar Yves M.-J. Congar, *Jalons pour une théologie du laicat*[3] and the Dutch Reformed theologian

---

[1] Formerly a Privatdozent at the University of Münster, Küng made this point during his inaugural address at the University of Tübingen, November 24, 1960. The statement is taken from the English translation of the same, which appeared in *Dialog* 1/3 (Summer 1962), pp. 40-49, under the title, "The Ecumenical Council in Theological Perspective" (translation by J. W. Kleiner), p. 46.

[2] "The Apostolic Ministry," *The Apostolic Ministry*, Essays on the History and the Doctrine of Episcopacy, ed. K. E. Kirk, London, 1946, p. 48.

[3] *Jalons pour une théologie du laicat*, Paris, 1952 (2nd ed. 1954). German translation from the original French by the Gemeinschaft der Dominikaner in Walberberg: *Der Laie*, Entwurf einer Theologie des Laientums, Stuttgart, 1957. English translation from the original French by Donald Attwater:

Hendrik Kraemer, *A Theology of Laity,*[1] is representative of the enthusiasm with which this emphasis upon the charge and mission of the priestly *ecclesia in toto* has been received. Moreover, the attention which is being focused upon the idea of the priesthood of all believers in the current Vatican Council II[2] is nothing short of historical moment.[3]

The Biblical text which is consistently cited in this connection, the passage which has come to be regarded as the "*locus classicus*" for the idea of a "universal priesthood" or a "priesthood of all believers," is 1 P 2:4-10, specifically, vv. 5 and 9. Supremely influential in this identification was Dr. Martin Luther and the reform movement of the sixteenth century. Over against the then current conception of the priesthood as representing a special religious class, a "geistlicher Stand" imbued with a *character indelebilis* in contrast to the "weltlicher Stand" of the laity, Luther, pointing to 1 P 2(:9) and Apoc. (5:10), rejected this differentiation and *character indelebilis* on the basis that Christians are "allesampt durch die tauff zu priestern geweyhet."[4] According to Luther, the function of this priesthood is precisely that of the ministry or *Amt*—the proclamation and administration of the *media gratiae*. This identity was seen as a result of the fact that both priesthood and ministry devolve from participation in the priesthood of Christ. The ministerial office, according to Luther, itself a divine institution, is responsible for the public exercise of this priestly task within the congregation.[5]

Lay People in the Church, A Study for a Theology of Laity, London, 1957. Citations of this book in this study, unless otherwise stated, are made according to the English translation.

[1] *Theology of Laity*, London, 1958.

[2] Cf. e.g. Küng, *op. cit.* On Nov. 6, 1962 in Rome, Père Jérôme Hamer, O.P., delivered a lecture entitled "The Relation between Priesthood and Laity" before the delegated observers to the Council. Père Hamer has kindly advised this author that the essence of this lecture is to be found in Ch. V, esp. § 2, of his recent publication, *L'Eglise est une communion* (*Unam Sanctam* 40), Paris, 1962.

[3] For further Roman Catholic treatments of this subject cf. P. Dabin, S.J., *Le Sacerdoce Royal des Fideles dans la tradition ancienne et moderne*, Paris, 1950; Congar, *op. cit.*; and the unpublished Leipzig Dissertation of Ch. M. Haufe, *Das Allgemeine Priestertum im Katholizismus der Gegenwart*, 1961.

[4] *WA* 6, 407, 22-25. Cf. also 6, 564, 6f.

[5] For these thoughts cf. *WA* 6, 408, 32-35 where in connection with 1 P 2:9 Luther states "das wir alle ein corper sein des heubts Jesu Christi, ein yglicher des andern glidmasz. Christus hat mit zwey noch zweyerley Art corper, einen weltlich, den andern geistlich. Ein heubt und einen corper hat er." *WA* 6, 564, 6-13: "Qui si cogerentur admittere, nos omnes esse aequaliter

Of course, the associations made between these verses of 1 P and Holy Baptism, the priesthood of Christ, and the ministerial office by no means originate with Luther but reflect the thinking of the Church from the Early Fathers onward.[1] However, it was Luther's co-ordination of these associations to meet a crisis of the moment which enabled his formulation to leave a profound and indelible imprint upon subsequent thinking concerning the nature of the Church and her priestly character.[2] It was from this point onward that the idea of a priesthood in which all believers shared began to assume pre-eminent significance for the Church's self-image—at least among the churches of the Reformation. In fact, Cyril Eastwood in his recent study, *The Priesthood of All Believers*, goes so far as to maintain that "the history of the Reformation, the History of Puritanism, and the History of the Evangelical Revival, are the story of the extent to which Christians have understood and applied the doctrine of the priesthood of all believers."[3]

So it was destined that also Luther's interpretation of 1 P 2:5,9 was to figure determinatively in all subsequent evaluation of these verses—even up to the very present. Yet, as is evident in all too numerous *"loci classici"* used as bludgeons or swords in the inter-

---

sacerdotes, quotquot baptisati sumus, sicut revera sumus, illisque solum ministerium, nostro tamen consensu commissum, scirent simul, nullum eis esse super nos ius imperii, nisi quantum nos sponte nostra admitteremus. Sic enim 1 Pet. ii dicitur: Vos estis genus electum, regale sacerdotium et sacerdotale regnum. Quare omnes sumus sacerdotes, quotquot Christiani sumus. Sacerdotes vero quos vocamus ministri sunt ex nobis electi, qui nostro nomine omnia faciant, et Sacerdotium aliud nihil est quam ministerium." *WA* 12, 180, 1-4: "Sunt autem sacerdotalia officia ferme haec: docere, praedicare annunciareque verbum dei, baptisare, consecrare seu Eucharistiam ministrare, ligare et salvare peccata, orare pro aliis, sacrificare et iudicare de omnium doctrinis et spiritibus." Cf. further *WA* 6, 370; 407, 13ff.; cf. 408, 2ff.; 409, 7; 440, 30ff.; 561ff.; 7, 27, 17-23; 8, 486, 27; 11, 411, 31-413, 2; 12, 178, 26-179, 39f.; 180, 17-23; 18, 202; 30, 2, 526-30; 554, 2; 38, 230, 13; 299, 19; 41, 207, 37; 50, 632, 35-634, 15.

[1] Cf. Dabin, *Sacerdoce . . . moderne* and *infra*, p. 14, n. 2.

[2] For discussions of Luther's interpretation of the idea of a priesthood of all believers cf. recently H. Storck, *Das allgemeine Priestertum bei Luther* (*ThEx* 37), 1953; W. Brunotte, *Das geistliche Amt bei Luther*, Berlin, 1959; R. Prenter, "Die göttliche Einsetzung des Predigtamtes und das allgemeine Priestertum bei Luther," *ThLZ* 86/5 (1961), 321-32; B. Lohse, *RGG* V, 578-81; R. Prenter, *ibid.*, 581f.; W. Joest, "Allgemeines Priestertum der Gläubigen," *EKL* III, 330-32. Further Protestant literature on the subject of universal priesthood is also offered in the above-mentioned works.

[3] C. Eastwood, *The Priesthood of All Believers*, An Examination of the Doctrine from the Reformation to the Present Day, London, 1960, p. 241.

Churchly and denominational battles which marked Reformation and post-Reformation history, the primary content and intent of Biblical texts were often misconstrued, misrepresented, and misapplied in the rush for *dicta probantia* intended to strengthen the bulwarks of hierarchical station or to sharpen the wedge of congregational or individual supremacy.

If, in this new and positive atmosphere of inner-Churchly dialogue, there is "need and room for a thorough examination of the basis, meaning and development of the doctrine of the Priesthood of all Believers,"[1] then this need includes not only historical-systematical surveys, but also an exegetical examination of the assumed NT basis of this idea, namely 1 P 2:4-10.

Yet it is an irony of modern scholarship that though systematic or historical investigations of the idea of a priesthood of believers are numerous enough to fill a library shelf, all the exegetical examinations of the Scriptural basis of this doctrine, when taken together, would not fill the first hundred pages of a single book! No less ironical is the fact that of the few exegetical studies devoted to the "*locus classicus*" of the doctrine which until recent time has been regarded as so characteristic of Protestant theology, the majority have been authored by Roman Catholic scholars.

To be sure, references to 1 P 2:4-10 are frequent among Biblical studies of a more general nature treating such themes as "royal or universal priesthood," "priesthood and ministry," or "priesthood and sacrifice."[2] However, such investigations, seeking as they do a comprehensive Biblical or NT conception of priesthood, on the whole are operating with presuppositions with which 1 P 2:4-10 does not necessarily concur. Presupposed is the notion that the NT presents a uniform or a unified conception of Christian priesthood.

---

[1] *Ibid.*, p. ix.

[2] Cf. e.g. E. Niebecker, *Das Priestertum der Gläubigen*, Paderborn, 1936; H. Asmussen, *Das Priestertum aller Gläubigen*, Stuttgart, 1946, esp. pp. 20-27; E. Kinder, "Allgemeines Priestertum im Neuen Testament," (*Schriften des Theologischen Konvents Augsburgischen Bekenntnisses*, Nr. 5), Berlin, 1953, pp. 5-23; T. F. Torrance, *Royal Priesthood* (*SJT Occasional Papers* 3), Edinburgh/London, 1955; V. Ordonez, "El Sacerdocio de los Fieles," *Revista Espanola de Teologia* 64 (Madrid 1956), 359-79; T. W. Manson, *Ministry and Priesthood, Christ's and Ours*, London/Richmond, 1959; E. Schweizer, *Gemeinde und Gemeindeordnung im Neuen Testament*, Zürich, 1959 cited here according to the English translation by Frank Clarke: *Church Order in the New Testament* (*SBT* 32), London, 1961, esp. Ch. 23; E. Best, "Spiritual Sacrifice, General Priesthood in the New Testament," *Interpretation* 14/3 (1960), 273-99.

Hence it is considered justifiable to equate individual statements on priesthood or those connoting a notion of priesthood. 1 P is compared with and interpreted in the light of certain passages from the Ep. Hebrews or the Apocalypse, for instance. However, it has never been demonstrated that this presupposition is valid. It simply is universally taken for granted. Again, presupposed is the idea that Christian priesthood necessarily derives from the priesthood of Jesus Christ. On the basis of a theory of the *Soma Christou* the Church is assumed to participate in the priesthood of her Head. Is this assumption valid *a limine* in 1 P also, even though no such theory of incorporation has been employed? Popular also is the notion, reminiscent of Luther and the early Fathers, that 1 P 2:9 relates directly to baptism as the source and to the ministry as the exercise of the "priesthood" described here. Despite the wide acceptance of these associations, however, they have never been proved—unless Luther is regarded as the final court of appeal.

The danger always embodied in topical approaches to the NT or in studies seeking a comprehensive NT view on a certain subject is that of overgeneralization and oversimplification. The *specifics* of individual texts are often neglected and the oversight of particular nuances is frequently the price paid for the construction of an all-inclusive conception.

To avoid these pitfalls and the temptation of accommodating the statements of 1 P 2:4-10 to pre-conceived ideas concerning a priesthood of the Church, it would seem advisable—if not imperative—that a study of these verses begin not with a general treatment of such subjects as "sacrifice" or "Jewish priesthood" or "ministry and office in the Early Church," but rather with this text alone. Comparison with other NT statements would be made only after the particular nuance of this section had been determined. In this process attention would be concentrated primarily upon the context of 1 P, and the *specific import* of this text, the peculiar rather than the common characteristics, would be spotlighted.

Aside from the commentaries on 1 P, the only significant analysis of 1 P 2:4-10, or a part thereof, which has taken this approach is the brief but instructive article of the Roman Catholic New Testament scholar, Josef Blinzler, "IEPATEYMA, Zur Exegese von 1 Petr 2,5 u. 9."[1] Two important contributions preceded Blinzler's study,

[1] Published in *Episcopus, Festschrift für Kardinal Michael von Faulhaber*, Regensburg, 1949, pp. 49-65. The polemical thrust of P. Ketter's study,

however, and provided the foundation upon which he built. It is with these two investigations that we commence our review of the present position of research concerning 1 P 2:4-10.

The Present Position of Research

In 1938 appeared an article by Gottlob Schrenk in the *TWNT* on one of the most important words of this pericope, ἱεράτευμα.[1] Schrenk pointed out the rarity of this word and its occurrence only in the Biblical literature or closely related writings. The particular contribution of this brief three page article is the collection of the majority of the occurrences of this term and the notation of its constant relationship to Ex. 19:6 (LXX).

One year later Monseigneur Lucien Cerfaux of Louvain University published his study, "Regale Sacerdotium."[2] Taking account of the texts assembled by Schrenk, Cerfaux attempted to sketch the various emphases which the ideas of the kingship and the priesthood of God's people received in connection with the transmission of and allusion to Ex. 19:6. From the period between the MT Ex. 19:6 and its allusions in the NT he found three main types of interpretation and two variations of emphasis.

Cerfaux saw an emphasis falling on either the *royalty* or the *priesthood* of God's folk. Determinative for the accent upon *royalty*, he felt, was the messianic hope and those periods of history when this hope was especially alive. This emphasis he held to be a characteristic of Palestinian exegesis. The idea of *priesthood*, on the other hand, he found stressed in the "spiritualistic" exegesis of Alexandrian Judaism and the apocalyptic idealizations of the Law and cultus.

1 P, according to Cerfaux, stands in line with Philo and the "spiritualistic" exegesis of Alexandria. This means that especially v. 5 describes, in contrast to the institutional conception of temple, priesthood, and sacrifice, the "culte interieur" of the pious soul.[3]

"Das Allgemeine Priestertum der Gläubigen nach dem 1. Pbrf," *TThZ* 56 (1947), 43-51, makes it difficult to reckon this work as a strictly exegetical undertaking. The concern of W. Arndt, "A Royal Priesthood," *CTM* 19 (1948), 241-49, is other than that of a comprehensive analysis of 1 P 2:4-10.

[1] *TWNT* III, 249-52.

[2] Published in *RSPhTh* 28 (1939), 5-39 [reprinted in *Recueil Lucien Cerfaux* II (*Bibliotheca Ephemeridum Theologicarum Lovaniensum* 6/7), Gembloux, 1954, 283-315].

[3] *Ibid.*, pp. 25f. 1 P is treated on pp. 21-26.

Ch. 2:4-10, he maintained, must be seen in its paraenetic setting[1] and the allusion to Ex. 19:6, in turn, is not to be isolated from the other social and corporative expressions of the "prérogatives et la dignité de l'Eglise, le peuple de Dieu."[2]

Criticizing the Reformers' interpretation of 1 P and other NT texts pertaining to priesthood, he argued that they were too dependent upon certain writings of the Church Fathers which were very anti-traditional. In his conclusion Cerfaux found the significance and relevance of the Exodus Formula (Ex. 19:6) not primarily in connection with the Eucharist but in the realization of the dignity, honor, and obligation of the Christian calling:

> Un autre champ, très vaste, reste pour enseigner aux fidèles qu'ils sont rois et prêtres. Lorsqu'il s'agira de leur donner le sens de leur dignité de chrétiens, de l'honneur de leur baptême, de leurs obligations et du 'service' religieux auxquels ils sont appelés, notre formule sera merveilleusement à sa place et, en troupeau serré, des développements parénétiques accourront de tous les horizons de la tradition.[3]

Two years later, in 1941, appeared *Le Sacerdoce Royal des Fideles dans les Livres Saints*,[4] the ambitious undertaking of the French Jesuit, Paul Dabin. This work contains two major sections: a less exegetical, more systematical treatment of the concept of "royal priesthood" in the OT and NT, and a systematical-theological coordination of the idea of a "royal priesthood" with the sacramental life of the Church which composes the second half of this almost 500 page work. As Blinzler has noted, however, Dabin's work does not pursue a specifically exegetical goal[5] and therefore does not figure significantly in the course of modern exegesis of 1 P 2:4-10.[6]

Then in 1949 Blinzler offered his exegesis of 1 P 2:5 and 9. This study composes two parts: an interpretation of vv. 4f and 9, and a survey of the references to Ex. 19:6 previous to 1 P, including an evaluation of the various interpretations given this passage and an analysis of its textual form of transmission.

Blinzler built upon the conclusions of his predecessors but also corrected and progressed beyond them. Of prime importance is his

---

[1] *Ibid.*, pp. 24f.
[2] *Ibid.*, p. 6.
[3] *Ibid.*, p. 38.
[4] *Le Sacerdoce Royal des Fideles dans les Livres Saints*, Paris, 1941.
[5] Blinzler, *op. cit.*, p. 50, n. 3.
[6] For Dabin's treatment of 1 P cf. pp. 179-97.

recognition of the basic concern of this pericope: a demonstration of "was die Lesser an ihrer Erwählung haben."[1] He rejected the theory of a "spiritualistic" interpretation as suggested by Cerfaux and others,[2] and demonstrated that 1 P's relationship to Philo centered about an entirely different factor. His review of the Ex. 19:6 occurrences pointed out variations of emphasis given the Exodus passage and the influence which the LXX exerted upon subsequent text-forms of this verse.[3] Over against a comparison or equation of 1 P 2 with other NT texts Blinzler emphasized that the meaning of this section, including ἱεράτευμα, must be determined primarily within its own context.

Discussing in his conclusion the relevance of the results of this exegesis to the thought of the universal priesthood,[4] Blinzler called attention to the dynamic aspect of the Church's priestly character. The correlation between "Priesterschaft und Opfer" was noted, but it was stressed that neither the idea of the Eucharistic sacrifice nor the connection of ἱεράτευμα and ministerial function is to be found here. Indeed, according to Blinzler, it is questionable if this text is at all appropriate as a basis of the views commonly associated with the idea of the universal priesthood. Both the Reformers, he maintained, with their idea that all baptized believers possess priestly authority and those who defend the thought that believers are priests—not in an official but nevertheless real sense—incorrectly allude to 1 P. "Zur Rechtfertigung der Ansicht von einem wahren Priestertum aller Gläubigen. . . hat man sich anderer Beweismittel zu bedienen."[5]

The accent upon the dynamic character of the Church of 1 P made by both Cerfaux and Blinzler has been further developed in one of the most recent discussions of 1 P 2:4-10, "Het Koning- en Priesterschap der Gelovigen in Het Nieuwe Testament" an article written in 1958 by the Leiden University scholar Gerhard Sevenster.[6] He has found both in the references to Ex. 19:6 and in 1 P, as well as in the rest of the NT, the thought of *priestly service and witness to the world.*[7] Calling attention to the idea of the holy life and of witness

[1] Blinzler, *op. cit.*, p. 51.
[2] *Ibid.*, p. 55.
[3] *Ibid.*, pp. 58-62.
[4] *Ibid.*, pp. 63-65.
[5] *Ibid.*, p. 64.
[6] Published in *NThT* 13 (1958), 301-17.
[7] The Ex. 19:6 texts and 1 P are discussed on pp. 403-07.

which occupies such a central position in the paraenesis of 1 P, Sevenster found these thoughts determinative for the connotation of the term ἱεράτευμα and the priestly task of sacrifice. Similar to Blinzler, he objected to Cerfaux's overemphasis of the "spiritualistic" character of the statements in 1 P 2 and suggested that Cerfaux was possibly polemicizing against various concepts of ministerial office.[1]

Considering also other NT passages describing the activity of Christians in cultic or priestly categories, he arrived at two main lines of thought coloring the whole NT idea of priesthood: (1) the priesthood of believers is seen as a worship (*eredienst*) with one's life; (2) "to-be-a-priest" (*priester-zijn*) above all conveyed the thought of the splendor from and a voluntary approach to the God of redemption.[2]

Though Sevenster's analysis is not specifically exegetical and though the connection he draws between 1 P and other NT texts is open to debate, the worldly orientation of the priestly task which he has seen outlined in 1 P 2:4-10 marks his study as a contribution to the understanding of this pericope and suggests the path which further analysis of this text might take.

Finally, in the light of the attention which it has aroused in English speaking circles, perhaps Cyril Eastwood's *The Royal Priesthood of the Faithful*, published recently in 1963,[3] deserves mention. Presented as a companion volume to his earlier work cited above,[4] this book, as a subtitle indicates, is meant to be "An Investigation of the Doctrine [of the royal priesthood] from Biblical Times to the Reformation." However, the Biblical material, which is examined in the first two chapters, is treated only with broad, superficial, and frequently unfounded generalizations. None of the pertinent texts, including 1 P 2:4-10, are subjected to careful exegetical scrutiny; nor has any reference to or analysis of the relevant literature been made. Though the author recognizes the importance of the election and holiness themes in the OT, he is unable to demonstrate how these motifs were continued and interpreted in the NT passages. Most unfortunately, there is nothing here which

---

[1] *Ibid.*, p. 416.

[2] *Ibid.*, p. 415.

[3] *The Royal Priesthood of the Faithful*, An Investigation of the Doctrine from Biblical Times to the Reformation, Minneapolis, 1963.

[4] Cf. *supra*, p. 3.

represents a step forward in the position of exegetical research.

In view of the fact that a sizable portion of 1 P 2:4-10 also involves, beside Ex. 19:6, OT passages pertaining to a "stone" or "λίθος" analogy, mention might also be made of the investigations dealing with this NT image. Since, however, this would entail the enumeration of a vast amount of literature not directly related to our text, and since this element heretofore has played a relatively minor role in the exegesis of this pericope, we shall reserve a discussion of these studies for a more pertinent point in our investigation.[1]

The *Commentaries and NT Introductions*, responsible for ascertaining the function of ch. 2:4-10 within the total context of 1 P, generally include it with the foregoing section (1:13ff) under the caption of "general admonitions to holiness and love,"[2] take section ch. 2:1-10 as a description of the "nature of the Church and her priestly function"[3] or of the community's "Anschluss an Christus,"[4] or treat the pericope alone as a statement on the "new worship."[5]

Since the majority of commentaries appeared earlier than the above mentioned studies, they were prepared without the benefit of the insights of these later analyses. Especially in the explanation of vv. 5 and 9 commentators have tended to follow or even defend their own ecclesiastical viewpoint. A broad expanse of interpre-

---

[1] Cf. *infra*, pp. 23ff.

[2] F. J. A. Hort, *The First Epistle of St. Peter I. I-II.* 17, London, 1898; A. Jülicher, *Einleitung in das Neue Testament*, 7. Aufl. neubearbeitet von E. Fascher, Tübingen, 1931, p. 190; H. Windisch, *Die Katholischen Briefe* (*HNT* 15), dritte, stark umgearbeitete Auflage von H. Preisker, Tübingen, 1951, p. 58; F. W. Beare, *The First Epistle of Peter*, 2nd rev. ed., Oxford, 1958, p. 52; J. Schneider, *Die Briefe des Jakobus, Petrus, Judas und Johannes* (*NTD* 10), 9. Aufl., Göttingen, 1961, p. 50; A. Wikenhauser, *Einleitung in das Neue Testament*, 4. Aufl., Freiburg i. Br., 1961, pp. 357f.; P. Feine-J. Behm, *Einleitung in das Neue Testament*, 12. völlig neu bearbeitete Auflage von W. G. Kümmel, Heidelberg, 1963, p. 303.

[3] E. G. Selwyn, *The First Epistle of St. Peter*, 2nd ed., London/New York, 1955, pp. 153ff.; C. E. B. Cranfield, *The First Epistle of Peter*, London, 1950, pp. 43ff.; K. H. Schelkle, *Die Petrusbriefe, Der Judasbrief* (*HTKNT* 13), Freiburg, 1961, p. 4.

[4] P. Ketter, *Der erste Petrusbrief* (*Die Heilige Schrift für das Leben erklärt - Herders Bibelkommentar* 16/1), Freiburg i. Br., 1950, pp. 221ff.; J. Reuss, *I. u. II. Timotheus, Titus, Philemon, Hebräer, Die Katholischen Briefe* (*EB* 3), Würzburg, 1959, pp. 96f.; cf. also Feine-Behm-Kümmel, *loc. cit.*

[5] A. Schlatter, *Petrus und Paulus nach dem 1. Petrusbrief*, Stuttgart, 1937, pp. 92ff.

tations is at hand—from those who would find here a *Grundschrift* for ecclesiastical organization, a democratic *Magna Charta* insuring the freedom of the individual from hierarchical representation or domination, to those discovering a cultic coloration and the institution of a "neo-Levitical community."

That these variations are by no means typical only of earlier works can be seen in the comparison of two of the most recent treatments of 1 P. On the one hand, the Roman Catholic scholar Joseph Reuss of Regensburg considers it necessary to emphasize in connection with 2:4ff that "wie die allgemeine priesterliche Würde der Israeliten nicht das Dasein einer besonderern Klasse von Priestern ausschloss, so steht auch im NT das allgemeine Priestertum der Christen nicht im Gegensatz zum Weihepriestertum."[1] On the other hand, the Baptist New Testament exegete Johannes Schneider of Berlin stresses that "vom einem exklusiven Priesterstand ist nicht mehr die Rede. . . Jeder einzelne hat die Stellung und das Recht eines Priesters."[2]

Though on the meaning and significance of ἱεράτευμα exegetes seem to have reached a regrettable stalemate—to no small extent the product of denominational polemic, appreciable progress has been made in the form-analysis of this document, and this has shed new light on the complexes figuring in the composition of 1 P 2:4-10. Influential in this progress have been the impressive work of the late Dean of Winchester, Edward Gordon Selwyn, and the provocative analysis of Herbert Preisker, the late professor of NT at Jena University.

Selwyn, developing an earlier theory,[3] amassed a wealth of material in the form of comparative tables and texts to support the hypothesis that the author of 1 P (Selwyn: Silvanus) composed his epistle with the help of catechetical material centering about an early Christian Holiness Code.[4] The intention, according to Selwyn, was to depict the Church as a "neo-Levitical community" and this

---

[1] Reuss, *op. cit.*, pp. 96ff. Cf. sim., e.g., Niebecker, *op. cit.*, pp. 73, 143f.; Ketter, *Priestertum*, pp. 47f., 51, *Petrusbrief*, pp. 228-30; Schelkle, *op. cit.*, p. 65, n. 1.

[2] Schneider, *Petrus*, pp. 60, 62; cf. sim. Beare, *op. cit.*, p. 104.

[3] Ph. Carrington, *The Primitive Christian Catechism*, Cambridge, 1940. Cf. also A. Seeberg, *Der Katechismus der Urchristenheit*, Leipzig, 1905; G. Klein, *Der Älteste Christliche Katechismus und die Jüdische Propaganda-Literatur*, Berlin, 1909.

[4] Cf. esp. Essay II, pp. 365-466.

image, he maintained, received its clearest expression in ch. 2:4-10, a section influenced by an early Christian hymn.[1]

Preisker, author of the latest edition of Hans Windisch's commentary, *Die Katholischen Briefe*, would also find in 1 P 2 a hymn which, however, he considered to have been a part of a baptismal liturgy reflected in 1:3-4:11.[2] The isagogical problem involved in this theory of a baptismal liturgy or of the incorporation of a baptismal homily is a knotty one and the opinion of scholars is divided.[3] In its

---

[1] Cf. pp. 268-98, 388-406, 459f.

[2] Windisch-Preisker, *op. cit.*, pp. 156-60.

[3] Preisker's position represents an advanced state of a theory originating with Richard Perdelwitz several decades earlier (*Die Mysterienreligion und das Problem des ersten Petrusbriefes*, [*Religionsgeschichtliche Versuche und Vorarbeiten* 11/3], Giessen, 1911). Noting the letter's paraenetic tone, baptismal allusions, and epistolary irregularity (marked by the apparent caesura between 4:11 and 12), Perdelwitz concluded that 1 P 1:3-4:11 was a discourse directed to Christian neophytes at the occasion of their baptism (pp. 95ff.). 1:1-2, 4:12-5:14 represented a brief letter of consolation ("Ermunterungsschreiben") of the same author to the same congregation, which was appended to the discourse and sent at a time when the previously threatening persecution had become reality. The writer was not St. Peter the Apostle but someone of the early second century strongly under the influence of the cult of Cybele. With varying types of modification this thesis of 1 P as a baptismal homily appended by a "Trostbrief" found wide acceptance among later scholars. Cf. e.g. W. Bornemann, "Der erste Petrusbrief - eine Taufrede des Silvanus?" *ZNW* 19 (1919/20), 143-65; B. H. Streeter, *The Primitive Church*, New York, 1929, pp. 129-34; Jülicher-Fascher, *op. cit.*, pp. 199f.; Windisch, *op. cit.*, 2. Aufl., 1930, p. 82; F. Hauck, *Die Katholischen Briefe* (*NTD* 3/2) Göttingen, 1933, pp. 35f. (8. Aufl. 1958, pp. 35ff.); Beare, *op. cit.*, pp. 6-9; E. Fascher, *RGG* I, 1414 (but cp. *ibid.*, *RGG* V, 259!); I. Fransen, "Une homélie chrétienne la première Epître de Pierre," *Bible et Vie Chrétienne* (1960), pp. 28-38; Schneider, *Petrus*, pp. 41, 90.

Proceeding from this baptismal Sitz im Leben, Preisker proposed that 1 P did not simply contain a baptismal homily but that the document as a whole portrays a baptismal liturgy, and is "das älteste Dokument eines urchristlichen Gottesdienstes" (*op. cit.*, p. 157). F. L. Cross, *1 Peter: A Paschal Liturgy*, London, 1934, supported this hypothesis and on the basis of a comparison of 2-3 century Christian rites suggested that 1 P reflected the celebrant's part of a baptismal Eucharist occurring in the Paschal Vigil. Earlier J. Danielou, *Sacramentum Futuri*, Paris, 1950, p. 141, who favors the theory of a baptismal homily, also ventured locating this address in the Easter Week. Cf. sim. Ph. Carrington, *The Early Christian Church*, Cambridge, 1957 I, 207ff.; E. M. Llopart, "La Protovetlla Pasqual Apostólica," *Liturgica* I, Montserrat, 1956, 387-524; A. Strobel, *NTS* 4 (1957/58), 211, n, 2 (1 P = a circular letter at the occasion of the Pasch). M. E. Boismard, in his studies "une liturgie baptismale dans la Prima Petri (son influence sur Tit., 1 Jn., Col., Jac.)," *RB* 63 (1956), pp. 182-208 and 64 (1957), pp. 161-83, and *Quatre Hymnes baptismales dans la première épître de Pierre* (*Lectio Divina* 30), Paris, 1961, has attempted to reconstruct the baptism-liturgy fragments

entirety this question has little relevance for an exegesis of ch. 2:4-10. The main related concern which must be handled in a discussion of these verses is the proposed hymnic character of this section.

Likewise, the questions of dating, addressees and authorship will not concern us to any extent. For convenience sake the author of this document will be referred to simply as Peter, though in the light of weighty arguments against Apostolic authorship this designation is not necessarily to be equated with St. Peter the Apostle.

---

upon which 1 P was assumedly dependent. Cf. also G. Braumann, "Zum traditionsgeschichtlichen Problem der Seligpreisungen Mt V 3-12 *NovTest* 4 (1960), 253-260, who, in comparing a number of thoughts in 1 P and the Beatitudes of Mt 5, suggests that "zunächst die Tauftheologie der urchristlichen Gemeinde" provides the *Sitz im Leben* for the common Christian tradition upon which both 1 P and Mt were apparently dependent.

Not all scholars agree, however, with the thesis of a baptismal homily, let alone that of a liturgy. Selwyn, e.g., though finding 1 P "supremely appropriate" for the "celebration of the Pascha or Feast of Redemption" (*op. cit.*, p. 62f.), dismissed the idea of a baptismal homily (*ibid.*, pp. 41f., 62). Likewise, E. Lohse, *op. cit.*, pp. 69ff., C. F. D. Moule "The Nature and Purpose of 1 Peter," *NTS* 3/1 (1956), 1-11, and W. Bieder, *Grund und Kraft der Mission nach dem ersten Petrusbrief* (*Theologische Studien* 29), 1950, insist that the act or concept of baptism does not occupy a central position in this document. Against the proponents of a baptismal liturgy have been leveled accusations of fantasy and exegetical gymnastics. Cf. in addition to E. Lohse and Moule, E. Käsemann, *Verkündigung und Forschung*, 1949-50, p. 192; W. C. van Unnik, "Christianity according to 1 Peter," *ExpT* 68/3 (1956/57) 79f.; D. Schroeder, *Die Haustafeln des Neuen Testaments* (Dissertation, Hamburg), 1959, pp. 6f. and note; T. C. G. Thornton, "I Peter, A Paschal Liturgy," *JTS* 12/1 (1961), 14-26; Schelkle, *op. cit.*, pp. 4-7.

On the whole, three main camps of thought can be distinguished: (1) the theory that 1 P represents a baptismal liturgy; (2) or that it is a baptismal homily with an appended note—or a homily incorporated into a genuine epistle; (3) or the conviction that 1 P is a genuine epistle which made use of a variety of liturgical-cultic and paraenetic traditions and fragments.

The cautious position concerning liturgical reconstructions which recent scholars have taken is perhaps best illustrated in Wikenhauser's respectful but reserved evaluation of Boismard's analyses: "Die Untersuchungen von Boismard haben ohne Zweifel erwiesen, dass in 1 P (wie in anderen Briefen) in erheblichem Umfang überliefertes Gut verarbeitet ist, das mit der Tauffeier in Zusammenhang steht (Tauftheologie, Taufparänese, Lieder). Da aber die urchristliche Taufliturgie noch nicht genügend bekannt ist, kann kaum Genaueres gesagt werden" (*op. cit.*, p. 446).

For more comprehensive discussions of the position of scholarship on this question cf. Moule, *op. cit.*; Beare, *op. cit.*, Supplement: First Peter in Recent Criticism, pp. 185-202; R. P. Martin, "The Composition of 1 Peter in Recent Study," *Vox Evangelica*, ed. R. P. Martin, London, 1962, pp. 29-42.

The Problem

In summary, this representation of literature indicates that the present position of research on our pericope is by no means a unified one. Though individual studies have made noteworthy advance in the clarification of specific verses and their underlying sources, these contributions are fragmentary and remain to be fit together into an integrated picture. The most important exegetical monograph on this section has treated only vv. 4f. and 9. An exegesis is required which takes into consideration the entire span of vv. 4-10. Furthermore, important differences of opinion exist—not only among the commentaries but also among the briefer analyses—regarding both Peter's relationship to his sources and the total thrust and import of these verses. In particular, a clearer definition of the term ἱεράτευμα and its function of offering is still to be sought. A popular interpretation of this term, much influenced by Luther's exegesis, includes immediate connections made to Holy Baptism, the priesthood of Christ, the ministerial office, and the Eucharistic sacrifice. That no small number of contemporary Roman Catholic scholars[1] are also suggesting some of these associations is not necessarily indicative of an indebtedness to Luther but rather evincive of a tradition of associations ever alive in the Church since the formulations of the Early Fathers. One question, however, deserves much closer attention than has been granted heretofore: how accurately and faithfully do even the Early Church Fathers represent the position of the New Testament, specifically 1 P?[2] Striking over

[1] E.g. Congar, Dabin, Niebecker.

[2] Cerfaux, *op. cit.*, pp. 32-37, Dabin, *Sacerdoce . . . moderne*, and B. Lohse, *RGG* V, 578ff. have gathered many of the most relevant passages of the early Patristic writings; a careful examination would have to begin where they left off. Several second century references would deserve close scrutiny: Justin Martyr, *Dialogue*, 116, 3; Irenaeus, *Adv. Haereses* IV, 8; Tertullian, *De oratione* 28, *De baptismo* 17, *De exhortatione castitatis* 7. 3, *De monogamia* 12. The recent English attempt to deal with these materials, Eastwood's *Royal Priesthood*, esp. ch. 3, pp. 56-90, is extremely inadequate. His failure to subject each passage to an exacting exegesis and his failure to compare these sections carefully with a precise definition of the NT position on the significance of the priesthood of the Church has produced little more than a superficial overview in sore need of supplementation. This present examination, while not directly concerned with the position of the post-Apostolic Church regarding the Church's priestly character, has as its goal a clarification of position espoused by the author of 1 P. And such a clarification is necessary if ultimately the continuity between Apostolic and post-Apostolic ages is to be traced.

against the systematic reviews of the "Biblical idea of priesthood" is the caution and hesitancy shown by some exegetes to make these same associations. Could this discrepancy perhaps be indicative of a widespread and basic misinterpretation of this text? Finally, Blinzler, for one, with his rejection of 1 P 2:4ff. as the basis of the common version of the priesthood of believers has put his finger on a question concerning the very core and essence of this pericope, a question which in the interests of sober exegesis and sound systematical correlation can no longer be circumvented.

It is these problems and this task to which the present investigation addresses itself. The method of approach chosen for this analysis is an attempt to meet the need of an exegesis of the accepted *locus classicus* of the idea of a priesthood of all believers as well as to find an exit from the dead end at which interpretation of this text currently finds itself.

CHAPTER ONE

THE STRUCTURE AND CONSTRUCTION OF 1 P 2:4-10

The text at the basis of our study is 1 P 2:4-10. These verses occur at the end of the first paraenetic section of 1 P commencing at 1:13 and ending at 2:10. 'Αγαπητοί, παρακαλῶ (2:11), while continuing the exhortatory mood of 1:13ff., begin a new division of thought. 2:4-10, though connected immediately to the preceding v. 3 by the introductory phrase πρὸς ὃν προσερχόμενοι of v. 4a (ὃν refers to ὁ κύριος, v. 3), presents a self-contained unit extending from vv. 4b-10. This is seen in the double allusions to Ps. 118(117):22 and Is. 28:16 in v. 4 and vv. 6-7, and to Ex. 19:6 in vv. 5 and 9. The content of this section is provided mainly by the catena of OT allusions occurring in the latter five verses, 6-10.

In contrast to 2:1f. the mood is indicative throughout. Analogous to 1:18-21, 1:23-25, 2:21-25, and 3:18-22, this section explicates and substantiates foregoing exhortation. The descriptive character of these verses indicates that the two initial verbs προσερχόμενοι (v. 4a) and οἰκοδομεῖσθε (v. 5a) are to be understood as indicatives rather than imperatives.[1]

---

[1] From (1) the participial imperative ἀποθέμενοι (2:1), (2) the similarity of sentence structure in vv. 1f. and 4f. (ἀποθέμενοι . . . ὡς ἀρτιγέννητα βρέφη . . . ἐπιποθήσατε followed by a final ἵνα / προσερχόμενοι . . . ὡς λίθοι ζῶντες . . . οἰκοσομεῖσθε followed by a final infinitive), and (3) the position of vv. 4-10 within preceding and succeeding paraenesis one might assume that both verbs should be treated as imperatives (so R. Knopf, *Die Briefe Petri und Judä* (KEK 17), 7. Aufl., Göttingen, 1912, pp. 88f.; H. Gunkel, *Der erste Brief des Petrus* (*Schriften des NT* 3) 3. Aufl., Göttingen, 1917, p. 266; Hauck, *op. cit.*, p. 49; J. Jeremias, *TWNT* IV, 280; Cerfaux, *op. cit.*, p. 25; Windisch-Preisker, *op. cit.*, pp. 58ff.; BAG, *s. v.*).

Nevertheless, the description of Jesus and the believers unfolded here requires the indicative (so G. Wohlenberg, *Der erste und der zweite Petrusbrief und der Judasbrief* (*ZKNT* 15), 3. Aufl., Leipzig/Erlangen, 1929, p. 54 (extensive discussion); U. Holzmeister, *Commentarius in Epistulas SS. Petri et Judae Apostolorum* 1 (*Cursus Scripturae Sacrae* 3/13), Paris, 1937, p. 242; Dabin, *op. cit.*, p. 188; Selwyn, *op. cit.*, pp. 157ff.; Blinzler, *op. cit.*, p. 51; Beare, *op. cit.*, pp. 92ff.). προσερχόμενοι cannot be compared to other participles serving as imperatives (cf. 1:14, 2:18, 3:1, 7-9, 4:7-10) because it does not express a general rule or direction, and this is the necessary characteristic of all participles which function as imperatives (cf. D. Daube, "Participle and Imperative in 1 Peter," an appended note in Selwyn, *op. cit.*, pp. 467-88, esp.

Most commentators dealing with this pericope have followed the customary course of beginning with v. 4 and continuing through v. 10, taking the OT allusions in vv. 6-10 as secondary material suggested by the formulation of vv. 4-5. However, when the structure of vv. 4-10 is subjected to precise analysis, this method of procedure becomes questionable. For this structure suggests that we are dealing here with a type of parallelism in which vv.4-5 were accommodated to the formulation of the passages in vv. 6-10 and not vice versa.

If this is in fact demonstrable, then an interpretation of this section will have to take this phenomenon into account. This would also imply that certain elements such as βασίλειον ἱεράτευμα would then appear in a totally new light. Our first step, therefore, is an analysis of the *formal structure* of vv. 4-10.

At first glance one of the most striking factors of this pericope is the unusually long list of OT[1] quotations or allusions contained in vv. 6-10 and introduced with the words διότι περιέχει ἐν γραφῇ (v. 6a). In fact, this cento of passages is one of the largest in the entire NT literature! The passages in order of appearance are: Is. 28:16 (v. 6b), Ps. 118(117):22 (v. 7b), Is. 8:14 (v. 8a), Is. 43:20f. (v. 9a, 9c-d), Ex. 19:6 (v. 9a,b), Hos. 1:6,9,2:3,25 (v. 10a-b).

A. The Structure of vv. 4-10

This collation of OT passages appears to be contained only in vv. 6-10. Nevertheless certain terms from Ps. 118 (117):22, Is. 28:16, and Ex. 19:6 do occur also in the first two verses, vv. 4-5. This multiple occurrence of particular words is a phenomenon which marks the entire pericope to such an extent, in fact, that these recurrences deserve closer attention.

Aside from the usual conjunctions, prepositions, and other particles, the major recurrences can be seen in the following table:

Group A

1. 2:4b	λίθον . . . ὑπὸ ἀνθρώπων μὲν ἀποδεδοκιμασμένον	7b	λίθος . . . ὃν ἀπεδοκίμασαν οἱ οἰκοδομοῦντες

480-84). Furthermore, v. 4 is not an imperative sentence next to vv. 1-3 but, as a relative clause, continues the indicative mood of v. 3: "since you have tasted that the Lord is good." For further discussion cf. *infra*, pp. 148ff.

[1] With few exceptions the LXX is followed.

2.	4b	παρὰ δὲ θεῷ ἐκλεκτὸν ἔντιμον	6b	ἰδοὺ τίθημι ἐν Σιὼν λίθον ἐκλεκτὸν ἀκρογωνιαῖον ἔντιμον
3.	5b	εἰς ἱεράτευμα ἅγιον	9b	ἱεράτευμα, ἔθνος ἅγιον
4.	5b	οἶκος πνευματικός	9b	βασίλειον

Group B

5.	4b	λίθον ζῶντα	5a	λίθοι ζῶντες
6.	4b	θεῷ	5a	θεῷ
7.	5b	οἶκος πνευματικὸς	5a	πνευματικὰς θυσίας
8.	6b	λίθον ἐκλεκτὸν	7b	λίθος ὃν ἀπεδοκίμασαν οἱ οἰκοδομοῦντες, οὗτος ἐγενήθη εἰς κεφαλὴν
		ἀκρογωνιαῖον ἔντιμον		γωνίας
			8a	λίθος προσκόμματος
9.	9c	λαὸς εἰς περιποίησιν	10a	οὐ λαός . . . λαὸς θεοῦ

Group C

10.	6b	τίθημι	8c	ἐτέθησαν
11.	6b	ἔντιμον	7a	ἡ τιμὴ
12.	6c	ὁ πιστεύων	7a	τοῖς πιστεύουσιν
			7b	ἀπιστοῦσιν
13.	8a	λίθος προσκόμματος	8b	οἱ προσκόπτουσιν
14.	9a	ὑμᾶς	9b	ὑμᾶς
			7a	ὑμῖν
15.	10aα	οἵ ποτε οὐ λαός	10aβ	νῦν δὲ λαὸς θεοῦ
16.	10bα	οἱ οὐκ ἠλεημένοι	10bβ	νῦν δὲ ἐλεηθέντες

Upon close observation it becomes evident that these repetitions occur by no means haphazardly but rather follow a certain scheme. The following pattern is evident:

(1) In occurrences 1-4 the recurrent words or phrases occur once in either v. 4 or 5 and then once again in vv. 6-10. For convenience sake we may call nos. 1-4 Group A.

(2) The next group of five, nos. 5-9, show a different relationship. This Group B includes words which occur in close proximity. Whereas Group A shows a relation between vv. 4f. and 6-10, Group B involves words which fall within pairs or a triad of verses. This yields the subsections vv. 4f., 6-8, 9-10.

(3) Still a different factor characterizes a third group. The final

seven instances, Group C, are similar in nature to Group B. Here again for the most part are words occurring in close connection. Nevertheless there are two important differences: (a) These terms are found only in vv. 6-10, not in vv. 4f. (b) The word in common never appears twice in exactly the same form. (c) A third factor which best explains these two differences is that in every instance the first occurrence of the common word involves an OT passage; the second member appears to be a reformulation of, and thus dependent upon and secondary to, the first member. In this respect Group C bears a close resemblance to vv. 4f. where inexact recurrence also appears.

Together these three groups demonstrate the inner unity of vv. 4-10. On the other hand, they also indicate the pattern through which this unity was effected. Group A reveals a certain correspondence between vv. 4-5 and 6-10; more specifically, between v. 4 and vv. 6-8, v. 5 and v. 9(f.). This is obvious (1) in the combination of phrases from v. 6b and v. 7b which is found in v. 4b; and (2) in the appearance of ἱεράτευμα in v. 5 and v. 9. Ordinarily a word's double occurrence within a given pericope is nothing unusual. However, since these two appearances of ἱεράτευμα are the only two in the entire NT, this recurrence assumes special weight.

In v. 4 and v. 5 the formulation is slightly modified from that of vv. 6-7 and v. 9. The expressions in vv. 6-7 appear in v. 4 in a shorter combined form. Some words have been omitted.[1] Others have been modified in form or have been replaced.[2] Finally, some words have been added.[3] Together these modifications leave no doubt that v. 4 contains a condensation and reformulation of longer, more original[4] material contained in vv. 6-7. This material incorporated in vv. 6-7 has been reproduced in inverted, chiastic form in v. 4b.

Verse 5 shows a similar relationship to v. 9 and, accordingly, properties similar to those of v. 4. For one thing, the rare word ἱεράτευμα is common to both verses. ἱεράτευμα occurs in v. 5 not in

---

[1] ἰδοὺ τίθημι ἐν Σιὼν . . . ἀκρογωνιαῖον . . . καὶ ὁ πιστεύων ἐπ' αὐτῷ οὐ μὴ καταισχυνθῇ (v. 6b); (λίθος) ὃν . . . οὗτος ἐγενήθη εἰς κεφαλὴν γωνίας (v. 7b).

[2] ἀποδεδοκιμασμένον (v. 4b) = ἀπεδοκίμασαν (v. 7b); ἀνθρώπων (v. 4b) = οἱ οἰκοδομοῦντες (v. 7b).

[3] ζῶντα, θεῷ and the prepositions and particles used to create the antithetical construction in v. 4b: ὑπὸ ἀνθρώπων μὲν ἀποδεδοκιμασμένον / παρὰ δὲ θεῷ ἐκλεκτὸν ἔντιμον.

[4] Insofar as vv. 6-7 reproduce more closely the LXX text.

the nominative case as in v. 9, however, but in the accusative as object of the preposition εἰς and is modified by the epexegetical infinitive ἀνενέγκαι (v. 5d). As in the case of v. 4, the word which v. 5 and v. 9 have in common is contained in an OT allusion—in this case in v. 9. As v. 4, v. 5 condenses and modifies. The entire phrase of v. 9b does not occur explicitly in v. 5. Only ἱεράτευμα and ἅγιον are exact repetitions. As later examination shall show,[1] however, οἶκος πνευματικός also comes into consideration. The formulation of v. 5 does not betray direct dependence upon the LXX text. The latter is represented exactly in v. 9,[2] from which v. 5 shows appreciable differences. Rather, similar to the relationship between v. 4 and vv. 6-7, v. 5 is a condensation and a modification of v. 9. Verse 5 appears to be dependent upon and secondary to v. 9.

These factors of relationship between vv. 4,5 and vv. 6-7, 9 are described best with the term *parallelism*. The pattern of this parallelism, moreover, shows not merely a correspondence of terminology but dependence—a dependence of the formulation in vv. 4f. upon that of vv. 6-7 and 9. For two strata of formulation are evident whereby vv. 6-7(8) and 9(10) represent a primary layer closer to the wording of the OT and vv. 4f., a secondary stage of reflected reformulation. That is, vv. 4-5 offer an *interpretation* of the OT passages adduced in vv. 6-7 and 9.

The instances referred to as Group B substantiate these conclusions while also providing evidence for the probable partition of the pericope. The several word parallels of this group indicate the coherence of vv. 4-5, 6-8 and 9-10. Nos. five and six demonstrate the connection of vv. 4 and 5 through the parallel formulations λίθον ζῶντα / λίθοι ζῶντες, and the double dative θεῷ. And of course the conjunction καί leaves no doubt as to their connection.

The next subsection, according to no. 7, includes vv. 6, 7 and 8. The coherence of these verses is suggested by the recurring term λίθος. Already noted is the connection of vv. 6 and 7 which is mirrored in v. 4. The common term γωνία (ἀκρογωνιαῖον, v. 6b; κεφαλὴν γωνίας, v. 7b) also underlines this relatedness. However, that which unites these two passages with v. 8a is the term λίθος. As vv. 4b-5a show, this is the word which provided the point of contact and the springboard for the reformulation and interpretation in this

[1] οἶκος πνευματικὸς relates to βασίλειον, cf. *infra* pp. 149ff.

[2] Except for the omission of a καί joining ἱεράτευμα and ἔθνος in LXX Ex. 19:6.

first section. It is worth noting, though, that not all of this section (vv. 6-8) is treated in vv. 4b-5a; v. 8 receives no mention.

No. 8 indicates that the final section of this threefold partition involves the last two verses, 9 and 10. This is seen in the term λαός common to both verses. Again we note that, as v. 4 relates to the section vv. 6-8, so v. 5 relates to vv. 9-10. Not all elements of vv. 9-10 recur in v. 5. Verse 10 receives no explicit mention.

The fact that both vv. 6-8 and vv. 9-10 appear to have received their coherence via a particular terminus or *Stichwort* accordingly has led to their description as a "λίθος complex" and a "λαός complex," respectively.[1] At this point, however, a word of caution is in order. Very seldom are external elements of form or terminology sufficient evidence for the coherence of sentences or sections. As E. Earle Ellis has aptly remarked concerning similar combinations of passages appearing in the Pauline literature, "although a number of Pauline citations appear to be united under a Stichwort, the significance is far deeper than a verbal congruence. The recurrence of the Stichwort is perhaps a designed mnemonic, but at times it is only a natural coincidence in the subject matter."[2] Thus we may speak provisionally of two "complexes"; however, the accuracy of this designation remains to be demonstrated by an examination of content. This *caveat* applies equally to all the observations made in this initial formal analysis of vv. 4-10.

The distinctiveness of each of these three sections is seen in their peculiar character. Verses 4-5 are distinct from vv. 6-10 insofar as the latter are composed mainly of OT references whereas the former are secondary reflections of the same. Furthermore, the obvious difference between vv. 6-8 and 9-10 is that the two sections have nothing in common content-wise. The former section treats the term λίθος in the third person singular; the latter features a variety of predicates for the *Gottesvolk* applied to the hearers/readers in the second person plural.

The instances of Group B point to three distinct subsections within vv. 4-10: two complexes involving the words λίθος (vv. 6-8) and λαός (vv. 9f.) and a pair of verses which in corresponding order apply to elements of both these complexes reformulation and interpretation (vv. 4-5).

---

[1] Cerfaux, *op. cit.*, pp. 22f.

[2] *Paul's Use of the Old Testament*, Edinburgh/London, 1957, p. 50.

Finally Group C, though limited to vv. 6-10, composes words which are similar in function to vv. 4-5. Selwyn's description of some of these terms as "midrashic" applies well.[1] Interspersed among the OT verses they appear to provide a kind of running integrating commentary. As interpretation, then, they resemble vv. 4f.

In *summary*, an initial examination of the formal structure of 1 P 2:4-10 has yielded the following points:

(1) Verses 4-10 divide broadly into two main sections, vv. 4f. then followed by a cento of OT allusions composing vv. 6-10.

(2) Within these two sections a recurrence of particular words and phrases is evident.

(3) These recurrences are neither repetitions for the sake of emphasis nor haphazard redundancies but products of a pattern of parallelism.

(4) They order themselves into three groups which reveal both the unity of the pericope as well as the scheme through which this unity was effected:

(a) The instances of Group A manifest a distinct parallelism between vv. 4-5 and vv. 6-10. Through this parallelism vv. 4 and 5 relate to and interpret vv. 6-7 and 9, respectively.

(b) Group B shows that vv. 6-10 divide further into vv. 6-8 and 9-10. Verses 4-5 also belong together. Thus three subsections of the pericope are identifiable: a cento of OT allusions includes two sections provisionally called a "λίθος complex" (vv. 6-8) and a "λαός complex" (vv. 9-10). An initial pair of verses contains reference to elements of both these complexes, in parallel form, corresponding order, and of interpretative nature (vv. 4-5).

(c) Group C includes words or phrases in vv. 6-10 serving as midrashic commentary upon the OT citations contained here.

(5) According to these facts two strata of material are evident: the OT references and the commentary upon these texts (vv. 4f. and the midrash within vv. 6-10). Whereas the former are passages close to the LXX in formulation, the latter are reformulations and reflections upon the same, dependent upon and secondary to the former. These reformulations are specifically Petrine, that is, from

[1] Selwyn, *op. cit.*, pp. 164, 269. Sim. J. Danielou, *Théologie du Judéo-christianisme (avant Nicée)*, Tournai, 1958, pp. 102ff., who finds here an example of "Targumim Judeo-chretiens."

the hand of the author of 1 P, and hint that herein lies the clue to the intent and purpose of this pericope.

B. The OT Passages in vv. 6-8

From these results based upon observations of form we now proceed to an analysis of content. Since vv. 4-5 give evidence of being formulated with a view to the OT material assembled in vv. 6-10, it will be profitable to commence with the primary material beginning at v. 6. The main questions are: under what aspect were these OT texts combined here and what is their relationship to the initial two verses, 4 and 5?

The term λίθος is common to the three OT passages contained in vv. 6-8; Is. 28:16, Ps. 118(117):22, Is. 8:14b.[1] According to Is. 28:16 in its original context, a λίθος is being established in Zion as a solace and a surety for those who believe. To the godless rulers of Israel (v. 14) this is not a word of comfort but one of warning before impending judgment and doom (vv. 17ff.). The wording in 1 P 2:6 varies from that of the LXX. This might suggest that Peter was not citing from the LXX but from another Greek version or source. One significant point in which they do agree, however, is the phrase ἐπ' αὐτῷ which is a later interpolation absent from both the MT and the LXX Codex Vaticanus. Over against the MT where the participle, "those who believe" (הַמַּאֲמִין) receives no direct object, Codex Alexandrinus and 1 P 2:6 (and Rom. 9:33b) read: "and he who believes upon it (the λίθος) . . . ." That is, belief is directed to the stone as object. According to Joachim Jeremias, in Codex Alexandrinus we have "den ältesten Beleg für die messianische Deutung einer alttestamentlichen Steinaussage."[2] Its importance for the NT and 1 P we shall soon discover.

In Ps. 118(117):22 λίθος occurs within a song of praise for the

---

[1] Is. 28:16 Ἰδοὺ ἐγὼ ἐμβαλῶ εἰς τὰ θεμέλια Σιων λίθον πολυτελῆ ἐκλεκτὸν ἀκρογωνιαῖον ἔντιμον εἰς τὰ θεμέλια αὐτῆς, καὶ ὁ πιστεύων ἐπ' αὐτῷ οὐ μὴ καταισχυνθῇ.
ψ 117:22 λίθον, ὃν ἀπεδοκίμασαν οἱ οἰκοδομοῦντες οὗτος ἐγενήθη εἰς κεφαλὴν γωνίας.
23 παρὰ κυρίου ἐγένετο αὕτη καὶ ἔστιν θαυμαστὴ ἐν ὀφθαλμοῖς ἡμῶν.
Is. 8:14 καὶ ἐὰν ἐπ' αὐτῷ πεποιθὼς ἦς, ἔσται σοι εἰς ἁγίασμα, καὶ οὐχ ὡς λίθου προσκόμματι συναντήσεσθε αὐτῷ οὐδὲ ὡς πέτρας πτώματι· ὁ δὲ οἶκος Ιακωβ ἐν παγίδι, καὶ ἐν κοιλάσματι ἐγκαθήμενοι ἐν Ιερουσαλημ.

[2] Jeremias, *TWNT* IV, 276.

assured experience of divine deliverence. The psalm's central theme is the great reversal of fortune which the psalmist calls σωτηρία (ψ 117:21), which is θαυμαστή (v. 23). This reversal of fortune is depicted in the image of a stone which had been rejected as useless now becoming the cornerstone which can be understood as either "foundation-stone" or "copestone". Jeremias in a number of publications has argued energetically that the meaning of ἀκρογωνιαῖος is not "foundation-stone" (*Grundstein*) but "copestone" (*Schlussstein*).[1] This stone, according to Jeremias, probably has its place above the portal. Regarding both Is. 28:16 and ψ 117:22 he suggests that they spoke "schon ursprünglich beide vom Tempelschlussstein; auf jeden Fall wurden sie schon von der griechischen Übersetzung des AT und dann von den urchristlichen Schriftstellern so verstanden."[2]

This explanation has won the favor of a number of scholars[3] and well accounts for the meaning in LXX Is. 28:16 and ψ 117:22. In the NT, however, it is questionable if this denotation was consistently retained. In respect to Eph. 2:20 such a meaning has recently been firmly rejected and it is possible that it is as unlikely for I P 2:6-7 as well.[4] Jeremias himself, in fact, has dismissed the meaning "copestone" for κεφαλὴν γωνίας of ψ 177:22 in v. 7. Here he sees the psalm interpreted in view of Is. 8:14. Thus he feels inference is made "auf einem spitzen Stein an der Ecke des Gebäudes an dem man sich stösst und zu Fall kommt."[5]

In point of fact, it is obvious from I P 2:4 (exaltation motif), v. 5 (foundation stone and building motif), and v. 8 (stumbling motif)

---

[1] J. Jeremias, "Der Eckstein," *Angelos* I (1925), 65-70; "Golgotha," *Angelos* I (1926), 79, n. 2; *Jesus als Weltvollender*, 1930, pp. 79f.; *ZNW* 29 (1930), 264-80; *ZNW* 36 (1937), 154-57; *TWNT* I, 792f.; *TWNT* IV, 274-83.

[2] *Angelos* I (1926), 79, n. 2.

[3] Among others, M. Dibelius, *An die Kolosser, Epheser, an Philemon* (*HNT* 12), 3. Aufl. von H. Greeven, Tübingen, 1953, p. 72; H. Schlier, *Der Brief an die Epheser*, 2. Aufl., Düsseldorf, 1958, p. 142, n. 3 where a list of further literature is offered.

[4] R. J. McKelvey, "Christ the Cornerstone," *NTS* 8 (1961/62), 352-59. On the basis of philology and the context of Eph. 2:20 he has argued convincingly that ἀκρογωνιαῖος designates "a stone connected to the foundation of the building, which was located at one of the corners (probably the determinative corner) and bound together the walls and the foundation" (p. 359). Pointing to the context of I P 2:4-8 (particularly λίθος προσκόμματος) he notes that this meaning might also be implied here.

[5] *TWNT* I, 793. Cf. also P. Vielhauer, *Oikodome*, Das Bild vom Bau in der Christlichen Literatur vom NT bis Clemens Alexandrinus, Karlsruhe, 1940, p. 149; Blinzler, *op. cit.*, p. 53.

that all three connotations are possible in 1 P. Verse 4, however, indicates that Peter's particular concern was the exaltation-election motif. What function this stone had or theoretically what position it might have assumed in a building are questions irrelevant here. Primarily important was the fact that this stone was the *elect* stone. Thus ἀκρογωνιαῖον (v. 6b) and κεφαλὴν γωνίας (v. 7c) were omitted in the commentary of vv. 4b-5a as superfluous.

A lengthier discussion of the precise function or position of the λίθος in LXX Is. 28:16 or ψ 117:22 is unnecessary here. Important is the fact that the psalmist used this picture of the exaltation of a rejected stone to describe the impending defeat and surprising victory of Israel.[1] Thus, as in Is. 28:16, a stone image is used to depict the fate of the people of God.

The text and meaning of Is. 8:14 varies in the MT and the LXX and 1 P 2:8a appears closer to the sense of the original Hebrew. Whereas the LXX reads: καὶ ἐὰν ἐπ' αὐτῷ πεποιθῶς ἦς, ἔσται σοι ἐις ἁγίασμα καὶ οὐχ ὡς λίθον προσκόμματι συναντήσεσθε αὐτῷ οὐδὲ ὡς πέτρας πτώματι, 1 P 2:8a omits the negative particles οὐχ and οὐδέ and reads λίθος προσκόμματος καὶ πέτρα σκανδάλου. This reflects the sense of the Hebrew text where the negative particles are also absent: וְהָיָה לְמִקְדָּשׁ וּלְאֶבֶן נֶגֶף וּלְצוּר מִכְשׁוֹל. Whereas the MT and 1 P *affirm* that the stone will be a stumbling-stone and a rock of offense, the LXX *denies* the same.[2]

---

[1] Verses 19ff. suggest a liturgical procession to the temple (esp. vv. 19, 20, 24, 26, 27). A. Cohen, *Psalms* (*Soncino Books of the Bible*, ed. A. Cohen), London, 1945, pp. 389-93, associates this psalm with the feast of Tabernacles, one of the three pilgrim festivals. Could this passage possibly have referred to a "rejection" or destruction of the temple which represented the Israelite nation? Y. M.-J. Congar, *The Mystery of the Temple*, Westminster, 1962, pp. 139f. lists two situations to which Ps. 118(117) could have alluded: (1) the destruction of Jerusalem in B. C. 587 or 538; (2) the profanation and purification of the temple in B. C. 168-65. In any event Congar concludes that the psalm concerns "a reconstruction of Sion and the Temple after a period of trial equivalent to death and from which Yahweh has delivered his people" (p. 140).

[2] Important is the interpolation in LXX Is. 8:14a "and if you put your trust in Him . . ." which explains how the interpolator can then further add the negating particles: "He shall be to you . . . *not* as a stumbling-stone and you shall *not* stumble upon Him as upon a stumbling-stone *nor* as a rock of offense." T. Jonathan, apparently also attempting to clarify Is. 8:14, reverses the procedure of the LXX by putting the introductory conditional clause in the negative: "And if you are not obedient, His word will be against you as an avenging and as a rock of destruction" (ואם לא תקבלון ויהי מימריה בכון לפורען ולאבן מחי [text according to A. Sperber, *The Bible in Aramaic, III: The Latter Prophets according to Targum Jonathan*, Leiden, 1962, p. 17]).

The more original meaning, which 1 P 2:8a reflects (cf. also Rom. 9:33a), is that God has spoken to His prophet warning him not to join with the conspirators and in view of the approaching Assyrian hoard not to fear what they fear (v. 13). Rather he is to fear JHWH Who "will become a sanctuary, a stumbling-stone, and a rock of offense to both houses of Israel and many shall stumble thereon" (vv. 14f). The warning is one of judgment against those who put their fear in anything other than the Lord (v. 13).

Under what aspect were these three OT texts correlated? A common theme is difficult to find. While Is. 8:14 is negative in tone, Is. 28:16 and Ps. 118(117):22 offer a positive hope to those who believe. Whereas Is. 8:14 and 28:16 fall within contexts of admonition and warning, Ps. 118(117):22 is part of a joyous processional liturgy. While according to Is. 28:16 God is setting a stone in Zion, Ps. 118(117):22 seems to identify this stone directly with Israel (or her temple). In Is. 8:14, however, it is God Himself who is the λίθος. Could a mere verbal congruence have been the sole factor responsible for the combination of these verses or is there yet another alternative?

As a matter of fact, certain Qumranic and Rabbinic sources do point to another possibility. These sources indicate a pre-Christian, Jewish tradition of interpretation which figured formatively in the eventual combination of these passages.

Excursus 1

A λίθος Tradition

1. *The Qumran Literature*

Within the literature found at Qumran there are a number of texts which allude either explicitly or implicitly to at least one of our three passages, Is. 28:16.[1] We might mention 1QS V,5, VII,17f., VIII,7f. (5-10); 1QH VI, 25f., VII,17f.; 4QpIs.d. The significant element in all these passages is that the image of stone and/or building is applied to the community as the eschatological congregation of the Last Day.[2] Johannes Maier has pointed out that this

[1] A "reminiscence" of Ps. 118(117):22 may be present in 2Q 23:6 according to M. Baillet, *Discoveries in the Judean Desert*, Oxford, 1962, III, 83. The fragmentary condition of the text offers little information concerning the context, however.

[2] Cf. J. Maier, *Die Texte vom Toten Meer*, München/Basel, 1960, II, 93.

interpretation of Is. 28:16 is intimately bound with the process of entrance into the community.[1] The laying of the foundation is effected through the formation of the community.[2]

Maier supposes that the picture of the building of the community derives from the construction of the "city" or "wall," pointing to 4QpPs.37 II, 16 and Mt. 16:18. Be that as it may, the significance of this interpretation is obvious enough. The λίθος image of Is. 28:16 was identified with an eschatological event and applied to entrance into and maintenance of the holy congregation.[3]

2. *The Targumim and Early Synagogue*

The *Targumim* and Rabbinic literature show an inclination to interpret these "stone" texts in a similar light. Here the *messianic hope* was given firm emphasis. The Isaiah Targum at 28:16 reads: "Behold, I am establishing in Zion a king, a king mighty and strong" (האבן ממנא בציון מלךְ מלךְ תקיף גיבר). In place of אֶבֶן (= λίθος) appears the *interprementum* מֶלֶךְ, "king."[4] Similarly, the Targum of Ps. 118:22ff. states: "The builders abandoned a youth; he was among the sons of Jesse and was entitled to be appointed king and ruler (ביני בניא דישי וזכאה לאתמנאה למליךְ ושולטן טליא שׁביקו ארדיכליה הוה).[5] Here "stone" is replaced with "youth" and "cornerstone," with "king and ruler." In the Talmud this messianic interpretation is also to be found. Sanh. 38a records a conversation between Rabbi Judah Hanasi (ca. A. D. 200), and the two sons of R. Chiyya, Judah and

---

[1] *Ibid.*

[2] Cf. 4QpIs.d.2; 1QS I, 1b;V, 5.

[3] So also O. Betz, "Felsenmann und Felsengemeinde (Parall. zu Mt. 16:17-19 in den Qumranpsalmen)," *ZNW* 48 (1957), 51. For a discussion of Is. 28:16 as found in Qumran cf. Maier's excursus (*op. cit.*, pp. 93f.), "Die Gemeinde als 'Bau.'" For further literature treating the interpretation of Is. 28:16 (and related to OT and NT passages) cf. P. Wernberg-Møller, "Reflections on the Biblical Material in the Manual of Discipline," *StTh* 9 (1955), 40-66; O. Betz, "Felsenmann und Felsengemeinde," *ZNW* 48 (1957), 49-77; "Die Proselytentaufe der Qumransekte und die Taufe im Neuen Testament, *RQ* 1 (1958/9), 213-34. D. Flusser, "The Dead Sea Sect and Pre-Pauline Christianity," *Scripta Hierosolymitana* 4, 215-66. Betz and Flusser as well as E. Lohse, *op. cit.*, p. 79 and K. H. Schelkle, *Die Gemeinde von Qumran und die Kirche des NT.*, Düsseldorf, 1960, p. 77; *Petrusbriefe*, pp. 61f., make particular reference to 1 P 2:4ff. and the above-mentioned Qumran texts.

[4] האנא ממני בציון מלך מלך חקיף גיבר (text according to Sperber, *op. cit.*, p. 54). Cf. also *Str.-B* III, 276.

[5] Text according to *Biblia sacra polyglotta*, ed. B. Walton, III, London, 1653-57, *ad loc. Str-B* I, 876, suggests that king David was implied: "Einen Jüngling (gemeint wird David) liessen die Baumeister (d. h. Samuel und sein Gerichtshof) dahinten; er war unter . . . den Söhnen Isais und er erlangte es, zum König und Herrscher (Wiedergabe von ראש פנה) ernannt zu werden." Cf. also Pes. 119a and Midr. Qol. 3:8(17b).

Hezekiah, where the sons relate Is. 8:14 to the coming of the Son of David and the entrance of the Messianic Age.[1] Later, Rashi (ad Micah 5:1) likewise applies Ps. 118(117):22 to the Messiah, the Son of David.[2]

Thus there is a string of evidence for the fact that as early as the writings found at Qumran there was a tradition of interpretation within late Judaism and the early Synagogue wherein certain "stone" texts (including the three cited in 1 P 2:6-8) were singled out and applied to the Messiah and the coming eschatological Messianic Age.[3]

3. *The* λίθος *Image in the NT*

It is no wonder therefore that in the NT these texts appear with exactly this messianic/eschatological connotation. The image had already been prepared; the Church simply had to make the application.

An examination of the NT material shows that Peter was only one of many Christian authors who made allusion to these passages. Neither his choice of references nor their combination are uniquely Petrine. The significance of this fact for the complex in vv. 6-8 is best demonstrated by a brief review of those other NT passages containing reference to these texts: Mk. 12:10f. and pll. (Mt. 21:42ff., Lk. 20:17), Act. 4:11, Rom. 9:32f., Eph. 2:20.[4]

In every case, without exception, the λίθος image has been applied to Jesus as the Messiah. Thus the messianic/eschatological interpretation begun in pre-Christian Judaism reaches its culmination in its application to Jesus as the Bringer of the Messianic Age, the Last Aeon. Interpretation is not limited to a simple identification of the λίθος with Jesus, however. Other motifs enter the picture. As we can see, these motifs vary.

In the Synoptic parallels, Ps. 118(117):22[5] occurs in all three instances at the conclusion of the parable of the Wicked Husbandmen (Mt. 21:33-46, Mk. 12:1-12, Lk. 20:9-19). Further, all three Evangelists attribute this Psalm reference to a word of Jesus. In Mk. the significance of the allusion is to be determined only from the sense of the parable; namely, the rejection of the ὑιὸς ἀγαπητός (12:6) by the "builders" and his exaltation by God. Both Mt. and Lk. add a further note, addressing their hearers more explicitly. Mt. 21:43 interprets in the light of a universalistic/polemical motif: "The kingdom of God will be taken away from you and given to a

---

[1] Cf. Seder Nezikin V, Sanh. 38a, ed. Soncino, p. 238; *Str-B* II, 139f.

[2] Cf. *Str-B* I, 876. For further texts cf. Jeremias, *TWNT* IV, 277.

[3] Sim. Schelkle, *op. cit.*, pp. 61f.

[4] A less direct influence might be seen in Mk. 8:3 and pll. (Lk. 9:22, cf. 17:25) and Lk. 2:34.

[5] Mk. 12:11 and Mt. 21:42b include v. 23 of Ps. 118(117).

nation (ἔθνει) producing the fruits of it." The implications of the rejection are thereby applied directly to the hearers.[1]

In Lk. 20:17f.[2] the λίθος remains more the center of attention. Verse 18 (whose parallel is in Mt. 21:44) represents a thought formulated according to Is. 8:14 and Dan. 2:34-45: "Everyone who falls on that stone will be broken to pieces; but when it falls on anyone it will crush him." The first clause, v. 18a, is similar to Lk. 2:34. The judgment theme, the image of falling over a stone, and the terminology recall Is. 8:16.[3] The second clause no doubt has been determined by the concept of the Stone of Judgment and the eschatological Kingdom of God as portrayed in Dan. 2:44f. This, by the way, offers another link in the chain of the messianic/eschatological interpretation of the "stone" image in the Judaic pre-Christian period. It is one of the sources which provided the apocalyptic tone accompanying this messianic interpretation.[4]

St. Peter's address before the Jewish rulers, elders, and scribes, Act. 4:8-12, specifically describes "Jesus Christ of Nazareth" with words of Ps. 118(117):22.[5] Here again the rejection/exaltation motif dominates the scene.[6] However, the direct identification of the hearers as the "builders" through the interpolation ὑφ' ὑμῶν τῶν οἰκοδόμων is similar to the polemical tone of Mt. 21:43. The text of Ps. 118(117):22 is recalled quite freely; direct quotation of the LXX is unlikely. Similar to Lk. 20:17 and 1 P 2:7b, only v. 22 and not v. 23 has been cited.

Two other texts which belong to this λίθος complex, Is. 28:16 and 8:14, are found combined in Rom. 9:33, likewise colored with the motifs of rejection and judgment. Paul is discussing the relation of the Old Israel to the New Israel, and Jesus is implicitly identified as the "stone that will make men stumble." Righteousness has as its correlate faith, not meritorious deed. Therefore righteousness was received by the ἔθνη as a gift. Israel, on the other hand, because they sought righteousness not through faith but through obedience to the Law, "they stumbled over the stumbling-stone" (vv. 30-32). Thereupon follows Paul's conflation of Is. 28:16 and 8:14: ἰδοὺ τίθημι ἐν Σιὼν λίθον προσκόμματος καὶ πέτραν σκανδάλου, καὶ ὁ πιστεύ-

---

[1] Mt. 21:44 was possibly added under the influence of Lk. 20:18.

[2] Lk. 20:17 is the Synoptic text bearing the closest formal similarity to 1 P 2:7b; both limit their citation to Ps. 118(117):22.

[3] Cp. Lk. 2:34b: ἰδοὺ οὗτος κεῖται εἰς πτῶσιν . . . with Is. 8:14: πέτρας πτώματι.

[4] Cf. Josephus, *Ant. Jud.* 10.195 (cf. 10.10.2), where the λίθος of Dan. 2 is also understood as messianic.

[5] Act. 4:10-12: "Be it known to you all and to all the people of Israel that by the name of Jesus Christ of Nazareth, whom you crucified, whom God raised from the dead, by him this man (the healed cripple) is standing before you well. He is the stone which was rejected by you builders but which has become the head of the corner. And there is salvation in no one else . . . ."

[6] Cp. Lk. 9:22.

ων ἐπ' αὐτῷ οὐ καταισχυνθήσεται. The form of this conflation is unusual. The wording λίθον προσκόμματος καὶ πέτραν σκανδάλου does not follow the LXX but joins 1 P 2:8a in agreement with the MT. Secondly, v. 33 contains no mere combination of Is. 28:16 with 8:14, Rather the words from 8:14b, προσκόμματος καὶ πέτραν σκανδάλου have been inserted into the statement from Is. 28:16, attaching to λίθον. Is. 28:16 is cited in adumbrated form. No mention is made of Ps. 118(117):22.

The peculiar arrangement of this conflation is best attributed to the author's intention.[1] The reversal of fortune and exaltation motif of Is. 28:16 ("cornerstone," "elect," "precious") and Ps. 118(117):22 ("cornerstone") did not relate to his emphasis upon the rejection of the unbelievers, so he omitted the irrelevant words or phrases. According to Paul's point (v. 32b), the aspect of stumbling controls the context. Therefore the λίθος is identified exclusively as the λίθον προσκόμματος καὶ πέτραν σκανδάλου to emphasize the σκάνδαλου τοῦ σταυροῦ and the factor of πίστις in Jesus Christ as the element determinative of δικαιωσύνη.

Finally, an echo of this complex is found in Eph. 2:20. Again, the interpretation is Christological. The ἀκρογωνιαῖος of Is. 28:16 (cp. ψ117:22: εἰς κεφαλὴν γωνίας) as in 1 P (and sim. in the Syn. and Act.) has been applied to Christ Jesus: ὄντος ἀκρογωνιάιου αὐτοῦ Χριστοῦ Ἰησοῦ. Similar to 1 P also is the combination of the λίθος image with the picture of the Church as οἶκος (οἰκοδομή) and the utilization of both within a paraenetic context. The word λίθος, however, does not appear in the Eph. context.

1 P 2:6-8 presents this body of λίθος passages in its fullest NT

---

[1] There is no need to see here with Beare, *op. cit.*, p. 95, an erroneous quotation "evidently translating the Hebrew from memory."

[2] C. H. Dodd, *According to the Scriptures*, London, 1952, in his discussion of the use of the OT in the NT, among other passages has treated Is. 8:14 and 28:16 and concluded that they formed a "two-fold testimonium" of which Paul and the author of 1 P made use (p. 43). However, he failed to see the relation of the Syn. pll. and Act. to this complex. Hence his "twofold" source must be enlarged to include Ps. 118(117):22(f.) also. If the complex were twofold, then the presence of Ps. 118(117):22 in 1 P 2:7b must have been added by Peter. However, it would have been no mere addition but an interpolation interrupting the continuity of the two Isaianic passages. It might be argued that this is entirely possible, for the author would have found the κεφαλὴν γωνίας (ψ 117:22) attracted to the ἀκρογωνιαῖον of Is. 28:16. Yet it is just this adjective which together with ἐκλεκτόν and ἔντιμον is absent in Rom. 9:33. If we assume that Paul records the original form of the complex, then we have eliminated the reason for Peter's "interpolation." The difference between Rom. and 1 P is much better explained when 1 P is assumed to represent the fuller complex which Paul abbreviates and revises according to his purpose. Barn. 6:2-4 would also substantiate this conclusion.

Likewise, in view of the significance which Is. 28:16 received not only in 1 P but also in Targumic, Qumranic, and Rabbinic interpretation, Dodd's remark (p. 72, cp. p. 83) that Is. 28:16 "appears chiefly in explication of Is. 8:14" is to be questioned.

form,[1] containing all three texts: Is. 28:16, Ps. 118(117):22, and Is. 8:14. As in all the other NT passages, the complex appears messianic/eschatological in tone and the λίθος is identified with Jesus. The midrashic phrases in vv. 7-8, however, also make an application of these texts to the believers and unbelievers. Over against the other NT pss. 1 P lays primary weight on Is. 28:16 and the exaltation-election theme. This can be deduced from the primary position which the author gives Is. 28:16 as the verse introducing this λίθος complex and from the particular emphasis which the ἐκλεκτός and ἔντιμος λίθος receives in v. 4b.

What conclusion may be drawn from these observations? First, these seven NT passages demonstrate the secure position which the λίθος image together with its messianic/eschatological interpretation assumed in the early Christian community.[1] In every case the λίθος has been applied to the person of Jesus either explicitly or implicitly. Furthermore, similarities may be seen among the NT passages. The Syn. are similar to Act. in that both concentrate upon Ps. 118(117): 22(f.). On the other hand, Rom. and 1 P show close affinity in their common citation of Is. 28:16 and 8:14 and their mutual variation from the reading of the LXX. Again, there is a resemblance of context between 1 P and Eph.

Just as there are similarities so there are also differences. The OT texts have been quoted at different lengths, combined differently, introduced to differing contexts, and given different interpretations. Even allusions to the same OT verse have been found to vary in text. An application to Jesus as the Messiah seems to be the one factor common to all seven texts. A common theme cannot be seen. The universalistic motif expressed in Mt. is absent in Mk. The polemic of Act. is not identifiable with the intent of 1 P. The edification motif of Eph. is absent from Rom. The stress upon the λίθος προσκόμματος in Rom. is different from the emphasis given to Is. 28:16 and the exaltation-election theme of the 1 P 2:4. Likewise, the method of citation varies from a relatively faithful reflection of the LXX text (Syn.) or a reference interspersed with commentary (Act.) to mutual disagreement with the LXX version (Rom., 1 P).

These similarities and variances are not to be accounted for by the assumption of independent originality on the part of seven different authors. The hypothesis of direct literary dependence fails just as badly. In the case of 1 P 2:4ff. and Rom. 9:32f., for instance, Beare would find a literary dependence of 1 P upon Paul.[2] Both Selwyn[3] and Dodd,[4] however, have demonstrated convincingly the improbability of such a theory. According to Dodd, "that the author

[1] Cf. further Barn. 6:2-4, 16:6-10; P. Hermas, *Vis.* 3, *Sim.* 9.

[2] Beare, *op. cit.*, p. 95.

[3] Selwyn, *op. cit.*, pp. 269-73.

[4] Dodd, *op. cit.*, pp. 41-43. Dodd's conclusions are cited approvingly also by Ellis, *op. cit.*, p. 89.

of 1 P borrowed from Romans could be maintained only on the rather unlikely assumption that he first disentangled with parts of Is. 28:16 which Paul had omitted, and yet he did not supplement them out of the LXX, since his version does not entirely agree with the LXX even where there is no Pauline parallel."[1]

When both the alternatives of independent exegesis and literary dependence are ruled out, then the most likely explanation for the phenomena connected with the λίθος image in the NT is that of a *common Christian tradition.*[2] To this conclusion the evidence from the Judaic sources discussed lend the greatest amount of probability. The flexibility of this complex and the freedom with which its contents were adapted and interpreted argue against the existence of a written source and suggest rather *oral transmission.*

In *summary*, the late Judaic and NT documents show the existence of a tradition revolving about the image of a stone (אֶבֶן/λίθος). This image traces its origin to the OT, especially the Psalms, prophetic, and apocalyptic literature. Early LXX, apocalyptic, Qumranic, Targumic and Rabbinic interpretation point to the pre-Christian origin of its messianic-eschatological associations. Its use within Christian circles and its application to Jesus are possibly traceable to a *verbum Christi.*[3] The one constant factor in the NT is the application of this image to Jesus. Further interpretation exploits the possibilities of various motifs and implications for the believers and non-believers as well.[4] These numerous emphases show that the complex was employed in the service of the Apostolic kerygma, apologetic, and paraenesis.[5] This complex had no fixed or rigid form but was more a loose group of related passages variously adopted by Christian authors according to the motifs they found aiding their proclamation and illuminating the particular points

---

[1] *Ibid.*, p. 43.

[2] So Selwyn, *ibid.*, pp. 272ff.; Dodd, *ibid.*, p. 43; Ellis, *ibid.*, Schelkle, *op. cit.*, p. 62, among many others.

[3] So Selwyn, *op. cit.*, p. 269; Dodd, *op. cit.*, p. 110; Ellis, *ibid.*; G. Delling, *Der Gottesdienst im Neuen Testament*, Berlin, 1952, p. 24. Vielhauer, *op. cit.*, p. 60 sees 117:22(f.) put in Jesus' mouth by the early Church. C. F. D. Moule, "Some Reflections on the 'Stone' Testimonia in Relation to the Name Peter," NTS 2(1955/56), 56-59 attempts to show the connection of the person Peter with the stone imagery of 1 P 2:4-8, 1 Cor. 3:11, Jn. 1:42, Mt. 16:18.

[4] Encountered are a *universalistic* motif (Mt. 21:43; Rom. 9:33) which in turn is related closely to a *rejection/polemical* motif; cf. O. Michel, *Der Brief an die Römer* (*KEK* 4), 12. Aufl., Göttingen, 1962, pp. 220f. Also related is a *rejection/eschatological judgment* motif (Mt. 21:44, Lk. 20:18) and an antithetical *rejection/exaltation* motif (Act. 4:11, cp. 1 P 2:4); cf. Jeremias, *TWNT* IV, 278. Eph. 2:20 involves an *ecclesiological/edification* motif.

[5] Cf. R. Harris, *Testimonies*, Cambridge, 1916-20, I, 18f., 26f.; II, 89ff.; Cerfaux, *op. cit.*, pp. 22f.; Vielhauer, *op. cit.*, p. 145; N. A. Dahl, *Das Volk Gottes*, Oslo, 1941, p. 210; Selwyn, *op. cit.*, p. 269; Dodd, *op. cit.*, pp. 126ff.; Congar, *Temple*, p. 135, n. 4.

they wished to emphasize. Within the NT this complex finds its fullest presentation in 1 P 2:6-8.

C. Verses 4-8 and the λίθος Complex

What significance do these facts have for 1 P? First, it is obvious that the group of OT pss. in 1 P 2:6-8 reflect dependence upon a common Christian tradition. The textual deviations of these verses from the wording of the LXX and their similarities to another NT document (Rom. 9:33) indicate that also the form of the text was not the product of direct LXX quotation but of probable reliance upon a common oral source. Furthermore, the differing NT interpretations of this λίθος image suggest that the significance which this complex assumed in 1 P 2 will be ascertainable not from the search for one common λίθος motif but from the context of 1 P itself.

Therefore we turn now to 1 P 2:4-5 and those words and phrases within vv. 6-8 offering an explanation of this image.

The NT evidence concerning a λίθος complex tradition confirms from a different angle the conclusion concerning the structure of vv. 4-10 made above: (1) the verses 6-8 form a complex or subsection within vv. 4-10; (2) reflecting a pre-Petrine tradition, vv. 6-8 could not have been assembled in correspondence to vv. 4b-5a but vice versa: this complex provided the terms and the formulation for vv. 4b-5a. For this reason the Petrine interpretation of vv. 6-8 is to be sought in vv. 4-5.

The similarity between v. 4 and v. 7 had already caught the attention of J. A. Bengel.[1] The relation of vv. 4-5 to vv. 6-10 also has been emphasized by more than one authority dealing with this pericope or related subject matter. Cerfaux, for instance, has distinguished between the essentially "paraenetic" vv. 4-5, and the biblical citations reflected in vv. 6-10 upon which, according to Cerfaux, vv. 4-5 are dependent.[2] Phillip Vielhauer,[3] Selwyn,[4] and Blinzler[5] have added further weight to this conclusion. Its significance for the Petrine interpretation, however, might be made still more fruitful.

---

[1] J. A. Bengel, *Gnomon Novi Testamenti*, 3rd. ed., Tübingen, 1773, *s.l.*
[2] Cerfaux, *op. cit.*, pp. 22ff.
[3] Vielhauer, *op. cit.*, p. 145.
[4] Selwyn, *op. cit.*, p. 269.
[5] Blinzler, *op. cit.*, p. 52.

Verse 4 begins: "To whom you are approaching . . .," the relative pronoun ὃν referring to the last word of the previous sentence, ὁ κύριος. The author continues by placing as an appositive to the pronoun an allusion to the λίθος complex: λίθον ζῶντα, ὑπὸ ἀνθρώπων μὲν ἀποδεδοκιμασμένον παρά δὲ θεῷ ἐκλεκτὸν ἔντιμον. A comparison with vv. 6-7 has shown that the words ζῶντα, ὑπὸ ἀνθρώπων μὲν ἀποδεδοκιμασμένον παρὰ δὲ θεῷ, as reformulations of or additions to the statements in vv. 6-7, represent the interpretation of the author.

ζῶντα describes the stone as the "living" stone. This adjective does not connote allegorical[1] or mythical,[2] mystical[3] or polemical[4] associations but primarily the result of God's election and favor, that is, resurrection. "*Living* stone" designates the crucified Jesus of Nazareth as resurrected.[5] That is, λίθον ζῶντα depicts Jesus Christ as the resurrected Messiah (cf. 2:3,5: 1:21).[6]

The antithetical formulation: "by men, rejected; before God, elected, precious" is the next Petrine *interprementum*. In no part of the NT λίθος tradition is exactly this contrast to be found. Through this antithesis Jesus as λίθος is posited as the point where the discrepancy between man and God comes to clearest focus. Mankind has rejected him; God has elected him and found him precious. The contrast is not between the Church and the Synagogue but more inclusively between all those who believe and all those who disbelieve.[7]

---

[1] Windisch-Preisker, *op. cit.*, p. 60.

[2] Knopf, *op. cit.*, p. 89; Gunkel, *op. cit.*, p. 226; Dabin, *op. cit.*, p. 185.

[3] Perdelwitz, *op. cit.*, pp. 69f.

[4] Vielhauer, *op. cit.*, p. 149; Windisch-Preisker, *ibid.*

[5] Cp. Act. 4:10f. and Jeremias, *TWNT* IV, 278: "So wird Ps. 118:22 zu einem der urchristlichen Schriftbelege für Tod und Auferstehung (Jesu)." Thus ζῶντα in 1 P 2:4 offers an equivalent to the relative clause of Act 4:10: "(Jesus of Nazareth) Whom you crucified, Whom God raised from the dead"; cf. Mk. 8:31 and pll., Lk. 9:22.

[6] So Vielhauer, *op. cit.*, p. 148; Blinzler, *op. cit.*, p. 52; Schelkle, *op. cit.*, p. 57; earlier, Schlatter, Spörri.

[7] It has been proposed by a number of commentators, primarily those accepting the theory of a "Testimony Book" as propounded by J. R. Harris (cf. *infra* pp. 130ff.), that v. 4 as well as the entire pericope is anti-Jewish in tone and polemical in intent. The substitution of ἄνθρωποι (a more general and inclusive term: "people, mankind") in v. 4b for the equivalent subject of the verb in v. 7a ἀπεδοκίμασαν οἱ οἰκοδομοῦντες contradicts this supposition however. Cp. Mk. 8:31.

As we know from Rabbinic sources (p. Yoma 3,40c, 26; b. Shab. 114a; Midr. r. Cant. 1:5; cf. *Str-B* I, 876), "builders" (οἱ οἰκοδομοῦντες = בַּנָּיִין) in its transferred sense was used to designate the teachers of Judaism, the Rabbis,

A further point shedding light on the intention which determined the author's method of interpretation concerns the manner in which allusions to ψ 117:22 and Is. 28:16 are combined in v. 4b. Important is the order of combination: ψ 117:22 followed by Is. 28:16. In vv. 6-7 the order is reversed.[1] This inversion in v. 4b suggests a particular purpose. This intention may be found in the emphasis which has been given to the latter positive member of the antithesis, "before God, elect, precious." A comparison with other negative-positive antitheses in 1 P reveals this arrangement to be a characteristic of Petrine formation.[2] The *membrum positivum* always follows the *membrum negativum* and thereby always receives the emphasis. Thus in v. 4b the supremacy and sovereignty of the Divine will and plan receives stress (cf. 1:2). Or stated differently: Divine election is the overwhelming counter to human rejection. Men have rejected the λίθος Jesus but in God's sight he is elect and precious. In this formation the author has used ψ 117:22 (actually, only elements thereof) to create only the antithesis. The significance of the λίθος complex, as seen by Peter, is expressed through Is. 28:16 and the theme of election/exaltation.

Verse 5 is joined to the preceding verse through the corresponding

---

their students, or the Sanhedrin. The thought was that through the teaching and propagation of the Torah these men were effective in the "building up" or edification of the world.

Should Peter have been concerned with an anti-Jewish polemic, then no word would have been more suitable to his purpose than this one (assuming that this identification ["builders" = Rabbis] is as old or older than 1 P). In fact, Act. 4:11, which shows the early age at which this title was applied to the leaders of Israel, specifically indicates how such a text might be employed polemically. Here the hearers are explicitly identified as "the rejecting builders," whereby the honorific title is transformed into a word of disdain. Yet Peter deliberately replaces this "polemically packed" term with one of more inclusive nature: "mankind." (For similar "God/man" contrasts cf. Mt. 10:32f., 19:6; Mk. 10:9; Gal. 1:10; 1 Th. 2:13; and esp. Heb. 13:6 where Ps. 118(117):6 [!] is cited.) This involves not merely the Jews but all men who disobey the word (v. 8b), who reject, who refuse belief in Jesus as the Christ (vv. 6-7). This substitution hardly coincides with the proposed intention of an anti-Jewish polemic!

[1] This arrangement in v. 4 is added demonstration of the fact that vv. 6-7 provided the terminology for vv. 4f. If the author were quoting Is. 28:16 and ψ 117:22 to support v. 4, then their order of appearance in vv. 6f. would have been first ψ 117:22 and then Is. 28:16.

[2] Cf. 1:8a α/β, b α/β; 1:14/15; 1:18/19; 1:23a/b; 2:9 (σκότος/φῶς); 2:10a α/β, b α/β; 2:16b α/β; 2:18b α/β; 2:20a/b; 2:23a-b/c; 2:25b/c; 3:3/4; 3:9a/b; 3:14/15; 3:21b α/β; 4:2a/b; (4:6); 4:12/13; 4:16b/c; 5:2b α/β; c α/β, d α/β. Cf. Holzmeister, *op. cit.*, p. 100.

formulation καὶ αὐτοὶ ὡς λίθοι ζῶντες (cp. λίθον ζῶντα v. 4). Through this parallelism the author makes the foregoing statement concerning Jesus as the λίθος relevant to his hearers/readers. At the same time, through the continuation of the λίθος analogy, he prepares for the related analogy of building (οἰκοσομεῖσθε).

As Jesus is the "living stone", so those who believe in him (v. 6c) are designated as the "living stones". As Jesus is the stone who has been given life, so they too who confess him as *Kyrios* have been reborn from death to life (cf. 1:3, 23; 2:2). The particle ὡς is not to be pressed in the sense of "similar (to Jesus) but not quite equal to."[1] It is not introduced to distinguish between Jesus and the believers[2] but to indicate that they are "participes vitae ipsius;"[3] "as" implies not a double metaphor[4] but rather a fact.[5] Verse 5 thus leads from a description of Jesus as the stone and the λίθος complex from which this image derived to a description of the addressed believers and the OT allusions concerned with the People of God (vv. 9f.).

Thus in v. 5a begins the connection made between Jesus and the believers. A transition begins through which a description of Jesus as the stone is united with a description of the believers as the People of God. Preparation is thereby made for the transition from the λίθος complex in vv. 6-8 to the complex of OT passages in vv. 9-10.

D. Verses 6-8 and the Midrashic Notes

Before we leave vv. 6-8 one further factor remains to be considered. This is the body of phrases or words designated above as Group C. Included here are terms which were not part of the OT passages but which served as a type of midrashic commentary upon the same. The words referred to include ὑμῖν οὖν ἡ τιμὴ τοῖς πιστεύουσιν (v. 7a), ἀπιστοῦσιν δὲ (v. 7bα), οἱ προσκόπτουσιν τῷ λόγῳ ἀπειθοῦντες, εἰς ὁ καὶ ἐτέθησαν (v. 8b-c).

---

[1] As Selwyn, *op. cit.*, p. 159 seems to imply.

[2] ὡς does not introduce a mere comparison but is regularly employed to identify the hearers themselves from a certain point of view: "as newly-born babies" (2:2), "as aliens and exiles" (2:11). The particle is characteristic of the author of 1 P, occurring 26 times in the epistle. Peter even interpolates it into his quotations (cf. 1:25).

[3] Holzmeister, *op. cit.*, p. 241.

[4] Selwyn, *ibid.*

[5] Holzmeister, *ibid.*: "ὡς: *reale = de facto.*"

That which primarily characterizes these phrases is their *interpretative function.* Through a verbal parallelism these words connect directly to the OT passages in such a way that they explain, apply, and expand. Relationship to this stone is explained as either belief or unbelief (v. 7ab). This relationship is applied to the author's hearers/readers (v. 7a) as well as to the "unbelievers" (v. 7b) and "disobedient" (v. 8b). In v. 7a ἡ τιμή ("preciousness, honor") corresponds to ἔντιμον of the preceding Is. passage cited in v. 6b-c and is ascribed to the readers (ὑμῖν) because they believe (τοῖς πιστεύουσιν = ὁ πιστεύων ἐπ' αὐτῷ, Is. 28:16/v. 6c) in this "precious stone." Those who disbelieve, on the other hand (ἀπιστοῦσιν δὲ, v. 7bα), have rejected (ἀπεδοκίμασαν, v. 7bβ) the stone. For such rejectors the stone has become a stumbling-stone. They stumble (οἱ προσκόπτουσιν) because they have not believed[1] the word (τῷ λόγῳ ἀπειθοῦντες, v. 8c). Thereby the stone analogy is expanded to explicate the relationship with the word. This expansion includes v. 8c which is best understood as a "reverential periphrasis"[2] stating that this stumbling is the will of God for those who refuse to believe.

This singleness of purpose, namely interpretation of the OT λίθος expressions in the light of belief or disbelief in Jesus, is accompanied and supported by a unity of form.

There are three midrashic notes. Each attaches to one of the three members of the λίθος complex. Further, these applications are so arranged as to provide a logical sequence from one OT passage to the next. Verse 7a attaches to the first member of the λίθος complex in v. 6 (Is. 28:16) and simultaneously prepares the antithesis to v. 7b. Verse 7bα presents the negative pole of the antithesis and introduces the second member of the λίθος complex (ψ 117:22). The conjunction καί joining ψ 117:22 and Is. 8:14 (v. 8a) either could have belonged to the pre-Petrine tradition or could have been added by Peter. In the light of Mk. 12:10 and pll., Act. 4:11, and Rom. 9:33 the latter alternative appears more likely.[3] Finally, v. 8b, as v. 7a, explains the preceding OT reference, applying its content to the unbelievers whose unbelief is pictured as "stumbling", in

---

[1] πείθειν = πιστεύειν cf. 3:1.

[2] This is a trace of customary pious Jewish practice of substituting a passive to avoid utterance of the Divine Name.

[3] According to v. 4b Peter understood ψ117:22 negatively; καί would thus represent his combination of both passages sharing the common rejection theme.

faithfulness to the stumbling-stone analogy. This stumbling, says the author, is disbelief of or disobedience to the word. Thereby he so interprets his source as to relate it thematically to the preceding discourse on the rebirth through the word (1:23-2:3).

Thus v. 7bβ and its commentary, v. 8b, present a direct parallel in both form and content to v. 6 and its commentary, v. 7a.[1] Further, ἐτέθησαν in v. 8c corresponds to τίθημι in v. 6b.[2] The ultimate subject of this verb in both cases is God. Thus an act of God as mentioned in the source (v. 6b) is matched by a similar act of God in the midrash (v. 8c). Together these two forms of the same verb form the opening and close to the section, vv. 6-8.

Finally, we note that these interjected interpretative notes alter the object of concern. As in every other NT occurrence of the λίθος complex, the underlying theme is Christological. However, through the midrash the believers and unbelievers are brought to the center of attention. The original Christological thrust has been channeled into a soteriological statement.[3] This corresponds with the intention of v. 5. The λίθος complex has not been cited merely to make a Christological statement but to provide the basis for a description of the believing community.

In summary, this secondary strata of midrashic material serves to explain, apply, and expand upon the λίθος complex, relating it to the factor of belief and/or unbelief in the Stone and the word. Thus it infuses an originally Christological complex with soteriological significance. This unity of function and form is attributable to the designing hand of the author of 1 P.[4]

E. Verses 9-10 and the Epithets for Israel

The antithesis of believers over against non-believers and the concern for the addressees evident in both vv. 6-8 and v. 5 leads

---

[1] Verse 7bα functions more to establish parallelism and antithesis than as commentary. The actual interpretation corresponding to v. 7a begins first in v. 8b.

[2] So F. J. A. Hort, *op. cit.*, *s.l.* cited approvingly by Selwyn, *op. cit.*, p. 165.

[3] Cp. the similar procedure by Paul in Rom. 9:30-33.

[4] The recurring "word" theme in v. 8 (cf. 2:2, 1:23ff.), the synonomous use of πείθειν and πιστεύειν (cf. 3:1), and the syntactical construction of εἰς ὅ (cf. the similar ambiguous formulation in 1:6 and the preference for εἰς constructions in 1 P—38 occurrences!), all represent Petrine characteristics.

directly to vv. 9-10. In these last two verses the *characteristics and attributes of the believing community* come to clearest expression.

As in vv. 6-8, we have here a conflation of OT allusions. These were most likely included with the foregoing allusions under the introductory formula "as it is contained in Scripture" (v. 6a).

That which distinguishes this cento of passages from the previous complex is that these focus upon a different object—the People of God. Whereas the λίθος complex is originally Christological in nature, it is the *ecclesia Dei*[1] to which these expressions apply. The conflation is not a combination of complete OT verses or longer fragments thereof as in vv. 6-8 but rather a collation of *epithets*, "*Ehrenprädikate*" ascribed in the OT to Israel as "das auserwählte Gottesvolk," "*the elected People of God.*"[2]

The opening words ὑμεῖς δὲ (v. 9aα) together with βασίλειον ἱεράτευμα, ἔθνος ἅγιον (v. 9b), derive from the LXX version of Ex. 19:6: ὑμεῖς δὲ ἔσεσθέ μοι βασίλειον ἱεράτευμα καὶ ἔθνος ἅγιον. This verse originally formed part of the Covenant Formula Ex. 19:3b-6. Inasmuch as this pericope represents the origin of Israel's proclamation of herself as the elect and chosen nation of God, Ex. 19:3bff. has been described one of the most dominant, central expressions of Israel's theology and faith in the entire OT.[3]

The second OT allusion with which this Ex. passage has been interwoven is from Is. 43:20f.: ὅτι ἔδωκα ἐν τῇ ἐρήμῳ ὕδωρ καὶ ποταμοὺς ἐν τῇ ἀνύδρῳ ποτίσαι τὸ γένος μου τὸ ἐκλεκτόν, λαόν μου, ὃν περιεποιησάμην τὰς ἀρετάς μου διηγεῖσθαι. The original context of this text involves JHWH's promise of Israel's redemption and liberation from her Babylonian captivity (43:14ff.; cf. 42:1ff.). The predominant theme is the imminence of salvation for the Chosen of the Lord.[4] Recalling the Exodus as the event through which JHWH

---

[1] The *eschatological* People of God. Since the exile these terms had become descriptions of God's People of the Last Time; cf. Dahl, *op. cit.*, p. 38.

[2] Holzmeister, *op. cit.*, p. 247; Blinzler, *op. cit.*, p. 58; Schelkle, *op. cit.*, pp. 64f.

[3] Cf. *infra* pp. 50 ff.

[4] Liberation is spoken of as "salvation," "redemption" (43:1, 12, 14). It is likened to *the* great saving act of God in Israel's history, the Exodus (43:16-18; 43:2) and described as a "new thing" (43:19; 42:9; cp. 43:9). He Who does these things is the "Holy One, your Savior" (43:3), "your Redeemer, the Holy One of Israel" (43:14), "the Lord, your Holy One, the Creator of Israel, your King" (43:15). Those whom JHWH saves are "My chosen people," "My chosen" (42:6), those whom JHWH has "called" in righteousness . . . whom He has given "as a covenant to the people, a light to the nations" (42:6).

first chose and elected His people, the prophet identifies salvation with Israel's election[1] and portrays this redemption as a ratification of the same. He Who has called Israel now gives them as a covenant to the heathen. The concept of election is correlative to that of redemption.[2]

Τὸ γένος μου τὸ ἐκλεκτόν identifies Israel as the "elect nation" among all the nations. This title characterizing Israel's electedness is quoted in anarthrous form and deliberately placed first in the series of honorific predicates in vv. 9f.[3] The original phrasing λαόν μου, ὃν περιεποιησάμην ("My people whom I have made My special possession," Is. 43:21) has been abbreviated in 1 P 2:9c to λαὸς εἰς περιπόιησιν ("a people for [God's] private possession," "a people which finds the end of its existence in its possession by God").[4] Λαός in the language of the LXX became the terminus par excellence for the People of God.[5] In very broad terms the significance of λαός can be described as twofold:[6] semantically it served as the ethnic designation for Israel; theologically there was implied, in addition, the religious character of Israel, her election and covenantal status with JHWH, her holiness, and her redemption. In the NT the same twofold manner of application of λαός was retained as an ethnic designation for Jewish Israel and as a title for the true people of God.[7] In the latter instance where the religious element of the

---

[1] Dahl, *op. cit.*, p. 38.

[2] Similarities in both conception and terminology with the Covenant Formula of Dt. 7:6 and its context show the centrality of the election theme common to both and point to Dt. rather than Ex. 19:6 as the nearest parallel of the Is. text. Cf. (1) the use of the term "elect": Is. 43:20: בְּחִירִי = ἐκλεκτόν/ Dt. 7:7: וַיִּבְחַר = ἐξελέξατο; (2) The omission of מַמְלֶכֶת כֹּהֲנִים = βασίλειον ἱεράτευμα in both Is. and Dt.; (3) the absence of וְגוֹי = καὶ ἔθνος in both; Is. omits entirely, Dt. 7:6 substitutes עַם = λαός for גּוֹי = ἔθνος; (4) Common reference to the Exodus: Is. 43:8, Dt. 7:8, cf. 6:21, 23; (5) Common conception of release as "redemption": Is. 43:14: גֹּאַלְכֶם, Dt. 7:8: יִּפְדְּךָ —in the LXX the verb λυτροῦν is used in both passages: ὁ λυτρούμενος (Is.), ἐλυτρώσατε (Dt.).

Significant is the fact that although Is. 43:20f. shows greater affinity to Dt. 7:6 and its context than to Ex. 19:3bff., not Dt. but the Ex. version of the Sinaitic Covenant Formula is the text with which Is. 43:20f. is here combined.

[3] Cf. *infra*, pp. 142f. for the purpose behind this arrangement.

[4] Beare, *op. cit.*, p. 105. For similar formulation cf. Mal. 3:17: καὶ ἔσονταί μοι . . . εἰς ἡμέραν ἣν ἐγὼ ποιῶ, εἰς περιπόιησιν.

[5] Cf. the study by H. Strathmann and R. Meyer in *TWNT* IV, 29-58.

[6] Cf. Strathmann, *ibid.*, p. 55, pp. 35ff.

[7] Strathmann, *ibid.*, p. 55, pp. 49ff.

legitimate Israel came to expression the same three major implications can be noted.[1] As in the OT, these concepts both intercross and overlap: the covenant implies holiness and vice versa; redemption occurs within the framework of the covenant as a liberation to live the holy life. The characteristic of the Christian message, however, is the supersedure of ethnic boundaries. It is not Jewish Israel alone which is the λαὸς τοῦ θεοῦ but every nation and tongue which confesses Jesus as *Kyrios*. Prerequisites for belonging to the eschatological λαός[2] are no longer genetic or historical but purely religious: belief in Jesus as the Christ.

Is. 43:20f. does not merely offer attributes for the Elected Ones but also describes their task: "that they might declare My praise" (v. 21b). The author of 1 P, after combining the predicates received from Is. 43 with those of Ex. 19:6, has used an adaptation of this clause to complete the statement of v. 9: "that you might proclaim the mighty acts of Him Who called you out of darkness into His marvelous light" (ὅπως τὰς ἀρετὰς ἐξαγγείλητε τοῦ ἐκ σκότους ὑμᾶς καλέσαντος εἰς τὸ θαυμαστὸν αὐτοῦ φῶς).

This final clause does not reproduce one particular OT passage but represents a combination of adaptations of Is. 43:21b and its previous context, 42:6-9.[3]

Ἐξαγγείλητε has been substituted for the original infinitive διηγεῖσθαι as the more emphatic of the two near synonyms: "you

---

[1] E.g. Mt. 1:21; Lk. 1:68, 77, 2:32, 7:16; Rom. 9:25-26; 2 Cor. 6:16, 18; Tit. 2:14; Apoc. 18:4, 21:3; cf. 1 Cl. 59:4.

[2] The different formulations of λαός with περιούσιος and cognates suggest that since the LXX this phrase had begun to form a Greek *terminus technicus* for "God's chosen private property." περιούσιος as well as περιποίησις is the LXX rendering for the Hebrew סְגֻלָּה "a private possession"; cf. Ex. 19:5, 23:22; Dt. 7:6, 14:2, 26:18; cp. ψ 134:4, Eccl. 2:6, Jub. 33:20. Is. 43:22 (LXX) renders the Hebrew עַם־זוּ יָצַרְתִּי לִי, "the people whom I have formed for myself," also with the verb περιεποιησάμην (possibly because the translater judged that this verb fit better in the election concept?)

In the NT, Tit. 2:14 (recalling Dt. 7:6 and pll.) and Eph. 1:14 both depicted the process of becoming "the people of God's possession" as a correlate of redemption; Act. 20:28, as a result of the shedding of God's own blood. I Cl. 64:1 expressly identifies the λαὸς τοῦ θεοῦ as the people whom God has chosen through Jesus Christ: ". . . ὁ πανεπόπτης θεὸς . . . ὁ ἐλεξάμενος τὸν κύριον Ἰησοῦν Χριστὸν καὶ ἡμᾶς δι' αὐτοῦ εἰς λαὸν περιούσιον. Cf. J. Dupont, "ΛΑΟΣ ΕΞ ΕΘΝΩΝ (Act. 15:14)," *NTS* 3 (1956/57), 47-50.

[3] Cp. 42:6: ἐγὼ κύριος ὁ θεὸς ἐκάλεσά σε (cp. 43:22a: οὐ νῦν ἐκάλεσά σε) . . . καὶ ἔδωκά σε εἰς διαθήκην γένους, εἰς φῶς ἐθνῶν (cf. 8:22-9:2, 60:1); 42:7: . . . ἐξαγαγεῖν . . . καθημένους ἐν σκότει; 42:8: τὴν δόξαν μου ἑτέρῳ οὐ δώσω οὐδὲ τὰς ἀρετάς μου τοῖς γλύπτοις.

proclaim (widely, publically)."[1] The Christian connotations associated with the "proclaiming the mighty acts of God" might have occasioned this substitution.[2] Thus it might be justified to render this term "to preach" in the sense of the "Verkündigung der Heilstaten Gottes."[3] There is no justification for Selwyn's remark, however, that ἐξαγγέλλειν was substituted because of its poetic quality; the Psalter adequately shows that *both* terms were suited to poetic contexts.[4]

The object of this proclamation is His ἀρεταί Who calls from darkness to light. The ἀρεταί are not "virtues" or "excellencies" or "praises" but the "mighty deeds," the "saving acts" of God.[5] According to Is. 43:1ff. and 63:7-9, *the* ἀρετὴ τοῦ θεοῦ, *the* saving deed of JHWH which liberation from the Babylonian captivity simulated was the Exodus. In this Divine act of redemption par excellence lay the roots for Israel's election. The proclamation of this manifestation of Divine power composed one of the earliest

---

[1] The words are practically synonymous: διηγεῖσθαι "to relate, recount," ἐξαγγέλλειν "to proclaim, report"; cf. *BAG*, *s.v.* The latter Bauer, *WNT*, *s.v.*, renders: "weithinaus verkünden," sim. J. Schniewind, *TWNT* I, 68. In the LXX διηγεῖσθαι occurs more often (65 times) than ἐξαγγέλλειν (12 times). Synonymous use is seen particularly in the parallelism of Sir. 39:10 and 44:15; cf. also ψ 9:2/15, 49:16, 70:15, 73:3. Both words are employed in conjunction with recounting the praises or deeds of God. Cp. Sir. 36:7, 13 with 1 P 2:9d.

[2] In the NT διηγεῖσθαι appears 8 times; ἐξαγγέλλειν, only in 1 P 2:9 and the *conclusio brevior* of Mk. 16. Its use in this conclusion might indicate the particular association with the "mighty act of salvation" which it received in the Apostolic and post-Apostolic age: "But they reported (ἐξήγγειλαν) briefly to Peter and those with him all that they had been told. And after this, Jesus Himself sent out by means of them, from east to west, the sacred and imperishable proclamation of eternal salvation."

[3] Delling, *op. cit.*, p. 95, n. 47.

[4] Selwyn, *op. cit.*, p. 278. According to *H-R*, διηγεῖσθαι occurs twenty times in the Psalter; ἐξαγγέλλειν occurs eight times.

[5] Cf. Schlatter, *Petrus und Paulus nach dem 1 Petrusbrief*, Stuttgart, 1937, p. 100; Dabin, *op. cit.*, p. 196; Beare, *op. cit.*, p. 105. In the LXX ἀρετή translates both הוד "glory" (Hab. 3:3, Zach. 6:13) and תְּהִלָּה "praise" (Is. 43:21). According to the juxtaposition of δόξα and ἀρετή (Is. 42:8, 12; cp. Sir. 36:13), these terms were regarded as synonyms; so *BAG*, *sub* ἀρετή, who also suggest for 1 P 2:9 the meaning "manifestation of divine power." This coincides with Schlatter, *loc. cit.*: "Die ἀρεταί eines Gottes sind nicht ihm anhaftende Eigenschaften, sondern seine mächtigen Taten und Hilfe schaffenden Leistungen. Die ἀρεταλογία eines Gottes verkündet was in seinem Tempel als wunderbare Hilfe erlebt worden ist. An diesem Sprachgebrauch war die griechische Fassung der jesajanischen Sprüche 43:12, 48:12, 63:7 entstanden."

elements of Hebrew tradition, the Song of Deliverance at the Reed Sea (Judg. 5 and Ex. 15:1-21).[1]

In this sense ἐξαγγέλλειν involves looking back upon and recounting a former event. Yet the phrase ἐξαγγείλητε τὰς ἀρετάς precludes mere preoccupation with the past. The evidences of the manifestation of Divine power—salvation, election, the holy life, hope—are present and obvious. The Christians are called upon to proclaim not a reminiscence but a present enduring reality. Thus this formulation cannot be taken for a mere accommodation to poetical diction or alteration of synonyms. These two words belong together as a *terminus technicus* for the obligatory acknowledgement of and testimony to an epiphanic manifestation of Divine grace and power.[2]

In v. 9d the author describes these "mighty deeds" as those "of Him Who called you out of darkness into His marvelous light." These words suggest an Isaianic origin, though the terms "to call" and "light" in the NT era had developed into such common images for election and salvation that we would do best here to think of a common Christian parlence.[3]

Φῶς is a metaphorical figure for the Messianic salvation. This identification had already been made in Judaism[4] and in the NT period it was applied to Jesus and those who confessed Him as Messiah. As Jesus is the Light,[5] so those who call Him Lord enter

---

[1] Cf. Holzmeister, *op. cit.*, p. 252. For the antiquity of this poetic element, or parts thereof, cf. M. Noth, *Das zweite Buch Mose: Exodus* (*ATD* 5), Göttingen, 1961, pp. 95-100; G. von Rad, *Old Testament Theology*, Edinburgh/London, 1962, I, 356f. Dabin, *ibid.*, notes the recitation of the mighty act of the Exodus in the Paschal liturgy and sees an implication in 1 P 2:9.

[2] E. Käsemann, "Amt und Gemeinde im Neuen Testament," *Exegetische Versuche und Besinnungen*, 2. Aufl., Göttingen, 1960, I, 123: ". . . τὰς ἀρετὰς ἐξαγγέλλειν technischer Terminus jener Exhomologese ist, mit welcher der Geheilte oder Errettete oder der, dem Schuld vergeben ward, pflichtgemäss und öffentlich die gnädige Macht der Gottheit in einer Epiphanie als von sich erfahren bekennt. Ein Vorgang heiligen Rechtes bildet also die Antwort des Menschen auf göttliche Manifestation . . . ."

[3] So W. C. van Unnik, *De verlossing I Petrus* 1:18-19 *en het problem van de eersten Petrusbrief* (*Mededelingen der Nederlandsche Akademie van Wetenschappen*, afd. Letterkunde, NR. 5/1), Amsterdam 1942, p. 72, who finds the phrase intrusive within the thought of 1 P 2:9-10, however. The thought is in place here, according to van Unnik, but the image is not.

[4] Cf. *Str-B* I, 151, 161; S. Aalen, *Die Begriffe 'Licht' und 'Finsternis' im Alten Testament, Spätjudentum und im Rabbinismus*, Oslo, 1951, pp. 304f. The community at Qumran also interpreted this concept eschatologically; cf. esp. 1QM.

[5] Cf. Jn. 1:4f., 8f., 8:12b.

and walk in the eschatological light.[1] The metaphor of light[2] and illumination served particularly as an expression for the activity of *baptism* and was intimately connected with the motif of *metabasis*.[3] This metaphor formed a part of early Christian paraenesis and baptismal instruction.[4]

The verb καλεῖν both in the LXX and NT also came to be associated with Divine salvation and election.[5] It is so employed in 1 P (2:21, 3:9, 5:10) where God is He Who calls.[6] Especially the absolute use of this verb in the NT[7] and its passive form[8] indicate that this word had become a *terminus technicus* for the process of election and salvation.[9]

It is apparent that Peter knew and made use of these traditional elements in order to graphically describe the Divine ἀρεταί from which the addressees derive both their new status and their task of proclamation. The One Who called from darkness to light is not named explicitly in 2:9. The subject however is inferable from 2:21, 3:9 (passive reverential periphrasis for the Divine Name) and 5:10 as "the God of all grace, Who has called you to His eternal glory in Christ" (5:10b). These verses also indicate that though use was made of traditional terminology the specific arrangement is typical of the author of 1 P.

1 P 2:10 presents a collation of Hosean texts (1:6, 1:9, 2:3 [MT:2:1], 2:25). The context in which these passages occur describes the birth and naming of Hosea's three children *Jezreel*, *Lo-ruḥamah*, and *Lo-ammi*, an incident which served as symbol

---

[1] Mt. 5:14; Jn. 12:36c; Act. 13:47 (= Is. 42:6), 26:18, 23; 1 Th. 5:5; Eph. 5:8b, 13f.; Col. 1:12; Heb. 6:4, 10:32; also I Cl. 36:2, 59:2; Barn. 14:6; Justin, *Apol.* I, 61.12f., *Dial.* 121.4f., 122.1.

[2] Selwyn, *op. cit.*, p. 280, holds that "the belief that Christians belonged to the light rested upon *verba Christi* . . . and these in turn marked the fulfillment of prophecy (Is. 9:1)."

[3] Cf. Act. 26:18; Rom. 6:4f., 8:29f.; Col. 1:13, I Jn. 3:14; E. Käsemann, *RGG* II, 994.

[4] Cf. Carrington, *op. cit.*, pp. 80ff.; Selwin, *op. cit.*, pp. 379-82, 392; E. Lohse, *op. cit.*, p. 79.

[5] *BAG*, *s.v.*

[6] Cp. Gal. 1:15; 1 Cor. 1:9; 2 Th. 2:14; 1 Tim. 6:12.

[7] Cf. Rom. 8:30, 9:12, 24; I Cor. 7:17f., 20-22, 24; Eph. 4:1; 2 Tim. 1:9; cf. 2 Cl. 9:5, 10:1.

[8] Heb. 9:15; cf. 1 Cl. 65:2.

[9] Cf. I Cl. 59:2: "we . . . will pray . . . that the Creator of the universe may guard unhurt the number of His elect that has been numbered in all the world through His beloved Child, Jesus Christ, through Whom He called us from darkness to light (δι' οὗ ἐκάλεσεν ἡμᾶς ἀπὸ σκότους εἰς φῶς).

for God's dealing with His people Israel. The Divine promise is voiced here that in the Coming Day the people called "Not pitied" (Οὐκ-ἠλεημένη, 1:6) and "Not my people" ('Ου-λαός-μου, 1:9) will receive pity (2:25) and the names "The Pitied One" ('Ηλεημένη, 2:3), "My people" (Λαός-μου, 2:25, 3) and "Sons of the living God" (υἱοὶ θεοῦ ζῶντος, 2:1).

This conflation is found elsewhere in the NT[1] and Rabbinic literature.[2] In Rom. 9:25f. (a longer, more complete reference than 1 P 2:10), explicit mention is made of the prophet in the introductory formula: καὶ ἐν τῷ 'Ωσηὲ λέγει (v. 25a). As Billerbeck has observed, these verses were cited as though they formed a single passage in the original text.[3] This is identical with the Rabbinic manner of citation.

Selwyn[4] and Dodd[5] have demonstrated that 1 P 2:10 is not dependent upon Paul's quotation[6] but upon a previously formed tradition. Paul's reference to Hosea reflects the LXX text with little deviation.[7] Peter did not quote, as did Paul, but took certain formulations: υἱοὶ θεοῦ ζῶντος . . . Οὐ-λαός-μου . . . Λαός-μου . . . Οὐκ-ἠλεημένη (adapted to οὐκ ἠγαπημένη). Even the wording differs. Whereas in Rom. the keywords are λαός and ἀγαπᾶσθαι (Hos. 2:25 - Cod. Vaticanus), in 1 P the keywords are λαός and ἐλεεῖσθαι.[8] There is also a difference in purpose. Paul applied this episode of rejection and acceptance to the Gentiles (9:24). Peter made no such specific application. His emphasis is on the difference between the "former time" (ποτε, v. 10a) and "now" (νῦν, v. 10a, 10b). Paul was arguing; Peter was not.[9]

That which best accounts for both similarities and differences is the use of common Christian tradition.[10] According to this tradition incorporating the eschatological aspect of the Hosean symbolism

---

[1] Rom. 9:25f.

[2] NuR 2; Midr. Ps. 22:7.

[3] *Str-B* III, 274.

[4] Selwyn, *op. cit.*, pp. 280f.

[5] Dodd, *op. cit.*, p. 75.

[6] So Beare, *op. cit.*, pp. 106f., following Hort and the opinion of older commentaries.

[7] Inversion of the order of appearance of son and daughter occurs in Rom. 9:25 (cf. Hos. 2:25).

[8] Dodd, *loc. cit.*

[9] Dodd, *ibid.*, p. 22.

[10] In addition to Selwyn and Dodd (cf. *supra*, nn. 4, 5), so also Michel, *op. cit.*, pp. 215ff.

Paul developed an univeralistic motif; Peter, an emphasis upon the eschatological "now." Significant is the fact that whereas in Rom. 9:24ff. οὐ λαός is meant to designate the former situation of the οἱ ἔθνοι, in the Hosean episode it is Israel and only Israel implicated in both titles Οὐ-λαός-μου and Λαός μου. That is, Israel, formerly the λαός θεοῦ, then rejected as the Οὐ-λαός-θεοῦ, once again was to receive mercy and adoption as "sons of the living God." Therefore οὐ λαός cannot be used as proof that this statement in 1 P 2:9f. was directed to the Gentiles and contained a universalistic or anti-Judaic polemical motif. Those who take οὐ λαός as an exclusive designation for non-Israel overlook the fact that in the passage of Hosea to which Peter was referring Israel and not the Goiim was called "Not-My-people." The interpretation of Paul cannot be equated *a priori* with that of Peter. Variation in their treatment of common material has been seen in their use of the λίθος complex as well. The emphasis upon the eschatological promise and the differentiation between past, present, and future is the import of 1 P 2:10.

In v. 10 this implied antithesis becomes explicit through parallel form and the antithetical adverbs ποτε and νῦν δέ. Verse 10aβ offers a positive antithesis to v. 10aα; v. 10bβ is the *positivum* to v. 10bα. Similar to the commentary in vv. 6-8, the first member of the parallel is an OT allusion; the second, a secondary adaptation. This antithetical arrangement of *negativum/positivum* has been seen to be a characteristic of Petrine style.[1] The formulation ποτε . . . νῦν and/or τοτε . . . νῦν[2] as well as the terms νῦν, νῦν δέ, νυνί δέ[3] enjoyed wide usage in Christian parlence for designating the "eschatological now," the occurrence of the Messianic Age of salvation, in contrast to the former age of sin, darkness, and alienation from God. Their occurrence in 1 P does not suggest use of any particular written source[4] nor is the parallelism here "distinct from our author's normal style."[5] Judging from the variations between Rom. 9 and 1 P 2 in both mode of citation and interpretation, the tradition was

---

[1] Cf. *supra*, p. 35, n. 2.

[2] Cf. Rom. 11:30-31, Eph. 5:8 (both of which show definite points of contact with 1 P 2:9; Rom. 6:21, Gal. 4:8-9.

[3] Cf. Rom. 3:21, 7:6, 16:26; 1 Cor. 15:20; 2 Cor. 6:2; Gal. 2:20; Eph. 2:13; 2 Tim. 1:10 and NT *passim*.

[4] Contra Selwyn, *op. cit.*, pp. 280f.

[5] Selwyn, *ibid.* Cf. 1:12, 2:25, 3:21 and the occurrences of antithetical constructions listed *supra*, p. 35, n. 2.

flexible in form, more likely oral than written, and open to more than one type of Christian application.

The statement of vv. 9-10 is, on the whole, a compilation, application and interpretation of OT material from Exodus, Isaiah and Hosea. The honorific predicates included here are attributes peculiar to the Chosen People of God. The term λαός and the concept of election are the points of mutual contact. The author has applied these predicates to the recipients of this letter. Though the Gentile component of his audience might suggest the implication of an anti-Jewish polemic, the form and content of these verses point in a different direction. These honorific predicates have been applied in the light of the "eschatological now," the salvation-filled present (v. 10). Insofar these worthy titles receive even greater significance; the elective and salvific grace and mercy of God appear in a new dimension. The context into which these concepts have been introduced and the Christological tradition with which they have been united (vv. 6-8) indicate a direct and essential relationship between them and the foregoing Christological statements. That is, those people are God's elected race, His kingdom and body of priests and holy nation, His very own λαός, who have believed on the λίθος whom He has elected. According to that which precedes v. 10, it is Jesus Christ and the bond of faith which determine and acknowledge the eschatological present and the ascription of titles of election.

Thus vv. 9-10 are not as unrelated to vv. 6-8 as might first appear. Though the subject of this complex, "the people of God," differs from that of the original λίθος complex, points of similarity are nevertheless evident. Again three OT passages or contexts have been cited: Ex. 19:6, Is. 43:20f. (and context) and the Hosean *Lo-ammi—Lo-ruḥamah* episode. Again the arranging and interpreting hand of Peter is evident. Again a complex is introduced with a verse laying emphasis upon the concept of election. Again a complex of OT passages finds a parallel formulation in vv. 4-5.

The implication of these similarities, the relationship between vv. 6-8 and 9-10, and, in turn, their relation to vv. 4-5, remains to be demonstrated. The midrashic elements within vv. 6-8 show points of contact with vv. 4-5. Further, vv. 4-5 seem to relate to vv. 6-10 as to one entity, one group of texts. Insofar, vv. 4-5 appear to hold the key to the interpretation of this pericope. This becomes all the more evident when the relation between v. 9 and v. 5 is appreciated. For in v. 5 both the qualitative (the epithets) and the dynamic (the proclamation) aspects of vv. 9f. find a parallel. This double aspect appears to depend directly upon the phrase "kingdom, body of priests, holy nation" (v. 9b). According to vv. 4-5 this phrase figured centrally not only in vv. 9f. but for the significance of the entire pericope. Therefore it is to this phrase that we must direct our attention.

Summary

We summarize. An analysis of the form of 1 P 2:4-10, substantiated by an examination of content, has found

(1) a coincidence of terminology and formulation between certain words, verses and sections of vv. 4-10.

(2) Such similarities are evident between vv. 4-5 and 6-10; more specifically, between v. 4b-5a and 6-8, 5b-d and 9-10.

(3) These concurrences are products of a parallelistic structure.

(4) This structure implies three major segments of material: vv. 4-5, 6-8, 9-10.

(5) Vv. 6-8 and 9-10 are conflations of OT passages centering in the concepts λίθος and the elected λαὸς τοῦ θεοῦ, respectively.

(6) The OT passages of both sections are reflected elsewhere in early Christian literature. Christian and pre-Christian interpretation show the existence of a λίθος tradition and account for the formation of a λίθος complex. The fullest NT presentation of this complex is here in 1 P. The characteristics of the OT allusions in vv. 9-10 are less those of a specific tradition or complex.

(7) The relationship of vv. 4-5 to vv. 6-8 and 9-10 is that of secondary reformulation and interpretation of a primary source. That is, the OT passages of vv. 6-10 were not occasioned by the similar phraseology of vv. 4-5 and then added for substantiation; rather these OT verses provided the terminology and the thought for vv. 4-5.

(8) Other words and phrases within vv. 6-10 serve as midrash-like commentary on the original OT passages. Their function is to make an application to the epistle's recipients, to explain, to expand and to form a transition from vv. 6-8 to 9-10. Through this transition they unite both sections and maintain the unity reflected in vv. 4-5.

(9) Both this midrash and vv. 4f. are characteristic of the hand of the author of 1 P in contrast to the conflations in vv. 6-10 which are, in part, pre-Petrine in origin.

(10) The weight of the Petrine interpretation of the material contained in vv. 6-10 is most likely to be found in vv. 4-5, which also link this pericope directly with the foregoing section. The structure of these verses, as that of vv. 6-10, is by no means fortuitous; for through the deliberate arrangement of texts one concept seems to have been accorded special prominence—the concept of election.

This prominence is evident in v. 6 (λίθον ἐκλεκτὸν), v. 9 (γένος ἐκλεκτόν), v. 4 (παρὰ δὲ θεῷ ἐκλεκτὸν ἔντιμον) and the "election epithets" of v. 5.

(11) The significance which the Covenant Formula Ex. 19:6 assumes in this context is to be seen in v. 9b and its explication, v. 5b-d.

This formula from the book of Exodus, when spoken or heard by a Jew, had a special sound. It was a specialty conditioned not only by tradition of interpretation but also by the creation and transmission of a *terminus sui generis* (ἱεράτευμα) within that tradition. As the author of 1 P cited these words they already had behind them a distinguished history. To trace the stages of this history is for the clarification of 1 P 2:5 and 9 a profitable undertaking.

CHAPTER TWO

EX. 19:6: THE HISTORY OF ITS TRANSMISSION AND INTERPRETATION (OT–NT)

A. The Hebrew Old Testament

1. *Exodus* 19:6

The formulation of 1 P 2:9b leaves no doubt as to its origin, namely LXX Ex. 19:6.[1] Implied, of course, is the *literary* source of the Greek terminology. Historically, the primary source is the Hebrew text.[2] It is particularly important in our case to differentiate; for in this passage the LXX's character as not only a translation but also an *interpraetatio Graeca* is especially evident. To establish the original import and nuance of this verse we begin, therefore, with the earliest text, MT. Ex. 19:6:[3]

וְאַתֶּם תִּהְיוּ־לִי מַמְלֶכֶת כֹּהֲנִים וְגוֹי קָדוֹשׁ

This passage falls within the larger literary unit, Ex. 19:3b-6. This section occurs at the beginning of the larger so-called "Sinai-tradition" extending from Ex. 19 to Num. 10. Introducing the first portion of this tradition, the experience or the appearance of God

---

[1] A fact acknowledged by all commentators.

[2] This brief investigation of the source or sources of 1 P 2:9b will restrict itself to an examination of those texts alone which show a *textual* affinity to 1 P 2:9b or Ex. 19:6. The "kingship" or the "priesthood" of Israel as a *concept* will not concern us here.

[3] For studies devoted specifically to Ex. 19:3bff. cf. W. Caspari, "Das priesterliche Königsreich," *ThBl* 8 (1929), 105-110; H. Junker, "Das allgemeine Priestertum des Volkes Israel nach Ex. 19:6," *TThZ* 56 (1947), 10-15; R. B. Y. Scott, "A Kingdom of Priests (Ex. 19:6)," *OTS* 8 (1950), 213-19; J. B. Bauer, "Könige und Priester, ein heiliges Volk," *BZ NF* 2 (1958), 283-86. W. L. Moran, "A Kingdom of Priests," *The Bible in Current Catholic Thought*, ed. J. L. McKenzie, New York, 1962, pp. 7-20. For further literature treating this text cf. G. von Rad, *Das formgeschichtliche Problem des Hexateuch*, Stuttgart, 1938, pp. 1-72 [reprinted in *Gesammelte Studien zum Alten Testament* (*Theologische Bücherei* 8), München, 1961, pp. 9-86], esp. 25, 29f., 35f.; J. Muilenburg, "Covenantal Formulations," *VT* 9 (1959), 343-65, esp. pp. 351-57. K. Baltzer, *Das Bundesformular* (*WMANT* 4), Neukirchen, 1960, pp. 37f.; H. Wildberger, *Jahwes Eigentumsvolk*, Zürich, 1960; W. Beyerlin, *Herkunft und Geschichte der ältesten Sinaitraditionen*, Tübingen, 1961, pp. 78-90, cf. also pp. 10-16.

(Ex. 19:1-25), these verses portray God addressing the assembled folk through His mediator Moses, preparing them for the pronouncement of the Decalog (Ex. 20) and the entering of a covenant, the ratification of which is described in Ex. 24. The role which this Sinai pericope played in Israel's religious life was essentially a cultic one. It has been demonstrated that with great probability its *Sitz im Leben* was a major cultic celebration, the ancient festival of the Covenant-renewal.[1]

The *literary source* of this unit is not easily discernable and the opinion of scholarship varies appreciably.[2] Gerhard von Rad and Martin Noth both emphasize the complex interweaving of redactions here and despair of a solution of the source problem in the near future.[3] This complexity, according to Noth, is further proof of the importance of the pericope. Hans Wildberger, in fact, goes so far as to declare Ex. 19:3b-8 not deuteronomic or deuteronomistic, not from P, J or E but rather a "Sondertradition . . . welche darum im jetzigen Zusammenhang wie ein Fremdkörper wirkt."[4]

The paraenetic character of these verses is obvious. Analysis of the Sinai pericope, Ex. 19-24, has established that this section composed an initial paraenetic element of a four-fold covenant agreement.[5] Within this section itself, moreover, a similar *four-fold*

---

[1] Cf. M. Noth, *Das System der zwölf Stämme Israels*, 1930, pp. 140-151; von Rad, *Gesammelte Studien*, pp. 44-48. Cf. also S. Mowinckel, *Le décalogue*, Paris, 1927, pp. 128ff.; Muilenburg, *op. cit.*, p. 360. Beyerlin, *op. cit.* pp. 79ff.

[2] Von Rad, *op. cit.*, p. 47 assigns vv. 4-6 to J, apparently presuming for 3b-6 a JE combination, cf. p. 35; A. Kuenen, *Historisch-kritische Einleitung in die Bucher des alten Testaments* 1, 1, Leiden, 1861, p. 235 and M. Noth, *Überlieferungsgeschichte des Pentateuch*, Stuttgart, 1948, p. 33, n. 112, also *Das zweite Buch Mose: Exodus (ATD* 5), 2. Aufl., Göttingen, 1961, p. 126 treat vv. 4bff. as later deuteronomistic interpolation. The majority of scholars prefer E: G. Beer, *Exodus (HAT* 1,3), Tübingen, 1939, pp. 96f.; Schrenk, *TWNT*, III, 249 (JE); O. Eissfeldt, *Einleitung in das AT*, 2. Aufl., Tübingen, 1956, p. 239; Sellin-Rost, *Einleitung in das AT*, 9. Aufl., Berlin, 1959, p. 63 (JE); A. Bentzen, *Introduction to the OT*, 4th ed., Copenhagen, 1958, II, 51; Muilenburg, *op. cit.*, pp. 351f.; Beyerlin, *op. cit.*, pp. 15ff., 78; earlier, K. Steuernagel, *Lehrbuch der Einlietung in das Alte Testament*, Tübingen, 1912, *s.l.*; S. R. Driver, *An Introduction to the Literature of the Old Testament*, 9th ed., Edinburgh, 1913, pp. 29f.; W. O. E. Oesterley and T. W. Robinson, *An Introduction to the Books of the Old Testament*, London/New York, 1934, *s.l.*

[3] von Rad, *op. cit.*, p. 23; Noth, *op. cit.*, p. 33.

[4] Wildberger, *op. cit.*, p. 14; cf. Beyerlin, *op. cit.*, p. 13.

[5] von Rad, *op. cit.*, p. 35: (1) Paränese (Ex. 19:4-6) und geschichtliche Darstellung der Sinaivorgänge (Ex. 19f.); (2) Gesetzesvortrag (Dekalog und Bundesbuch); (3) Segensverheissung (Ex. 23:20ff.); (4) Bundesschluss (Ex. 24).

structure (19:3b-6) has been found which, in comparison with other OT and extra-Biblical texts, bears the trademark of typical covenantal formulation: (1) An introductory formula (v. 3b); (2) Recollection of previous history and God's mighty acts (v. 4); (3) Conditions of the covenant (v. 5a); and (4) Promises of the covenant (vv. 5b-6).[1] Accordingly, it has been concluded that our unit represents "a special covenantal Gattung . . . in nuce the *fons* and *origo* of the many covenantal pericopes which appear throughout the Old Testament."[2]

It is in v. 6 that the final two of the three covenant promises are mentioned (v. 5b: "you shall be to me a סְגֻלָּה "): "you shall be to me a מַמְלֶכֶת כֹּהֲנִים and a גּוֹי קָדוֹשׁ." The stylistic arrangement is a *parallelismus membrorum*[3] which brings the *holy character* of Israel to expression and forms the central statement of vv. 3b-6.[4] The parallelism: מַמְלֶכֶת (A), כֹּהֲנִים (B) / גּוֹי (a), קָדוֹשׁ (b). מַמְלָכָה serves here as an *abstractum pro concreto*, designating collectivity or entirety, *the community of the sovereign's* (JHWH's) *subjects*.[5] Its place in covenantal formulation also outside of the Biblical literature is seen in an inscription of a treaty offered by James Pritchard in his compilation of ancient Near Eastern texts.[6] This example is further support for James Muilenburg's observation that מַמְלֶכֶת כֹּהֲנִים is a form derived from the style of Near Eastern royal speech and that

---

[1] Cf. Baltzer, *op. cit.*, Muilenburg, *op. cit.*

[2] Muilenburg, *ibid.*, p. 352. For further parallels in Biblical and profane literature cf. Muilenburg, *ibid.*, p. 353, Baltzer, *passim*. These parallels make it likely that we are dealing here with a covenant formulation and not an "election proclamation" as Wildberger, *op. cit.*, pp. 16ff., would have it.

[3] This is one of the factors together with those of style, terminology and rhythm pointing to the cultic-paraenetic character of this sequence; cf. Beyerlin, *op. cit.*, p. 82; Moran, *op. cit.*, p. 18.

[4] Not סְגֻלָּה in v. 5 (so Wildberger, *op. cit.*, p. 74) but "holy people" in v. 6 seems to receive the emphasis here. Cf. von Rad, *op. cit.*, p. 47; Muilenburg, *op. cit.*, p. 353.

[5] So Bauer, *op. cit.*, p. 283 citing E. König, *Stilistik, Rhetorik, Poetik*, Leipzig, 1900, p. 65.

[6] *Ancient Near Eastern Texts relating to the Old Testament*, ed J. B. Pritchard, 2nd ed., Princeton, 1955, II, 503f. The inscription, originating in Sujin at approximately B. C. 750 is entitled, "A treaty of Barqu'yah, king of Ktk, with Matti'el, the son of 'Attarsamak, king of Arpad.'" After the list of witnesses to the contract follows the condition: "If Mattiel breaks this treaty and . . . his kingdom shall be a kingdom of sand, a kingdom of sand as long as he rules . . . ." For a recent and comprehensive analysis of covenantal and/or treaty formulation in the Near Eastern documents cf. D. J. McCarthy, *Treaty and Covenant*, Rome, 1963. Cf. earlier G. E. Mendenhall, *Law and Covenant in Israel and the Ancient Near East*, Pittsburg, 1955.

the entire literary form in which this tradition is recorded belongs to the fixed proclamatory style of Near East utterances.[1] A more detailed analysis of terminology and structure has been offered in earlier studies and need not occupy us here.[2]

In the interpretation of this verse wide disagreement prevails. This is readily seen in the varying translations submitted. An exhaustive discussion of opinion is beyond our intention here. R. B. Y. Scott has prepared a brief survey[3] and in the main his criticism and conclusions are well taken. For our purposes the following observations touch the essential points.

(1) The term מַמְלָכָה, whether translated "kingdom," "royal sphere," "royal reign" or "kingly office and rule,"[4] implies the fact that the initiator of this covenant, namely God, is proclaiming Himself as king, the supreme ruler capable of creating and confirming a kingdom. In keeping with the atmosphere of treaty and covenant, there is a dynamic element in the word, as Martin Buber has pointed out over against Wilhelm Caspari's more static, institutionalized proposal.[5] Though the emphasis in v. 6 does not lie on the word מַמְלֶכֶת,[6] an acknowledgment of God as king is implicit in the people's acceptance of the covenant.[7] Thus the term "Königsbund" has been coined to describe this pact.[8]

(2) The qualification of מַמְלָכָה through כֹּהֲנִים is best understood in relation to the second parallel member, גּוֹי קָדוֹשׁ. Occurring at the end of the sentence, this latter comma bears the emphasis: you shall

---

[1] Muilenberg, *op. cit.*, pp. 352f.

[2] Beyerlin, *op. cit.*, has recently entered a more detailed discussion of the terminology (esp. מַמְלָכָה) and its origin.

[3] Scott, *op. cit.*, pp. 216f., lists the possibility of at least five interpretations along with their respective supporters. For more recent literature cf. also Moran, *op. cit.*

[4] "Kingdom" is the customary English translation; cf. e.g. Scott, *op. cit.*, *RSV*, *AV* (*KJV*). German scholars have suggested a variety of possibilities: "Königtum": von Rad, *TWNT*, I, 569; "Königreich": Caspari, *op. cit.*, Schrenk, *op. cit.*, von Rad, *Hexateuch*, p. 35, Junker, *op. cit.*, Eissfeldt, *op. cit.*, Wildberger, *op. cit.*, p. 80, Luther's translation and Zürcher Bibel; "Königbereich,": M. Buber, *Königtum Gottes*, 3. Aufl., Heidelberg, 1956, p. 103, cp. Wildberger, *op. cit.*, p. 21; "Königsherrschaft": Noth, *Das Zweite Buch Mose*: *Exodus* (ATD 5), 2. Aufl., Göttingen, 1961, p. 126; "Königsamt und -regiment": Beyerlin, *op. cit.*, p. 85.

[5] Buber, *op. cit.*, p. 206; cp. Caspari, *op. cit.*, pp. 105ff.

[6] So von Rad, *TWNT*, I, 569; Noth, *Exodus*, p. 126.

[7] Cf. Blinzler, *op. cit.*, p. 58; Beyerlin, *op. cit.*, p. 85.

[8] Buber, *op. cit.*, pp. 99ff.; Beyerlin, *op. cit.*, p. 87. Cf. also G. Fohrer, *ZAW* 71 (1959), p. 21.

be a holy nation! According to the parallelism, then, "kingdom of priests" is to be understood as a coordinate expression of the people's sanctity.[1] Implicit in the concept of holiness is the act of separation or *Absonderung*.[2] The positive correlate is selection or possession by God. Both aspects are expressed in v. 5b: "you shall be My own possession (סְגֻלָּה) from among all peoples (מִכָּל־הָעַמִּים)." With these words Israel is identified as the worshippers of JHWH alone, His private property, His holy nation separated from all the other peoples of the earth.

The comma "kingdom of priests" provides a concrete picture of this holiness: "holy as priests are holy." Though there is still disa-

---

[1] Moran, *op. cit.*, taking his cue from Caspari's earlier study (cf. *supra*, p. 50, n. 3) and attempting to strengthen Caspari's conclusions with more recent materials, presents an appealing argument in favor of the position that מַמְלָכָה is not synonomous with גּוֹי, that מַמְלָכָה is to be understood not in the sense of "kingdom" but rather "a royalty of priests" and that "it is the *mamleket kohanim* plus the *gôy qādôš* which form the totality, the personal possession of Yahweh" (p. 17). Seeing in Ex. 19:3-6 "an old independent tradition of the Israelite amphictyony" (p. 19), he finds the unusual reference to a "royalty of priests" occasioned by the role of the priests which in this cultic setting was "especially prominent" (p. 20).

Moran has marshalled much evidence in support of his case and his study deserves close attention. However, certain important questions must be subjected to further scrutiny before his proposal be given precedence over the traditional understanding of mamlakah as "kingdom": (1) Does not the *par. memb.* of Ex. 19:3b-6 which Moran himself has so carefully described (p. 19) allow, if not encourage, that מַמְלֶכֶת כֹּהֲנִים and גּוֹי קָדוֹשׁ be seen as synonomous parallel members? (2) In the determination of the meaning of מַמְלָכָה, the context of the covenantal formulation ought not be overlooked. When a covenant is "cut," is it not usual that the initiator of the covenant proclaims his *kingship* over the second party (or the "ruledness" [= "Kingdom"] of the second party) rather than that the kingship or royalty of the vassel be announced? If JHWH's kingship is nevertheless implied in this reference to a "royalty of priests," as Moran maintains (p. 20), what then is the specific nature of the priests' royalty? This aspect requires further clarification. (3) Is there not too little evidence concerning the nature of the ancient Israelite amphictyonic league and its priesthood to demonstrate that "the role of the priests is especially prominent" (p. 20)? Klaus Koch, *RGG* v, 574, e.g., represents a common pessimism concerning the possibility of a comprehensive reconstruction of the early history of Israel's priesthood. And even according to the meagre information available Noth concludes that in contradistinction to the powerful and influential priesthoods in the environment of the Old Testament, "in ancient Israel priests hardly ever played a substantial historical or even political role" (*Amt und Berufung* [*Bonner Akademische Reden* 19]. Bonn, 1958, p. 10; [reprinted in *Gesammelte Studien zum Alten Testament* (Theologische Bücherei 6), München, 1960, p. 315]).

[2] Cf. R. Asting, *Die Heiligkeit im Urchristentum*, Göttingen, 1930, *passim*; O. Procksch, *TWNT* I, 87ff.

greement as to the original task of the priest (oracle-mediator, sacrificer, Torah interpreter), it is commonly recognized that a priest at all stages of religious consciousness is one who enjoyed a special intimate relationship with his god. The priest in Israel had free access to his God and shared in the accordant benefits of such nearness. He was holy "from among" the others and participated in the holiness of his holy God. The promise that when Israel is faithful she will be a kingdom of priests is a vow that she will then enjoy the very nearness of JHWH and the status of holiness which only a priest shares. Or as Wildberger has formulated: "Israel als mamleket kohanim für Jahwe ist also der Bereich, in dem Jahwe als König herrscht und zwar über ein Volk, dessen Glieder allesamt mit ihm in vertrautem Umgang leben, wie das sonst nur bei Priestern der Fall ist."[1]

(3) Its position within a covenant formula in particular prohibits this statement concerning the holiness of the folk from being conceived of as an already accomplished state of affairs.[2] As the future conditional protasis "if you will obey My voice and keep My covenant" (v. 5a) indicates, the people's holiness was conditioned by their obedience. At the ratification this again comes to expression (Ex. 24:7f.). This conditional status applies equally to the parallel member, "kingdom of priests."

(4) Though it is questionable that we are dealing here with an "election proclamation" as Wildberger maintains, the idea of Divine election is basic to this text and forms an essential correlate to that of holiness.[3] As vv. 5-6 indicate, the two concepts are mutually inclusive. The act of election is the process of separating out from; holiness is the consequence of election. Through the covenant the King elects and initiates into His holy sphere.

(5) The meaning of the appellation "priests" is not developed. Its significance is limited exclusively by גּוֹי קָדוֹשׁ. "Kingdom of

---

[1] Wildberger, *op. cit.*, p. 80, Sim. Scott, *op. cit.*, p. 218. "Priests" is most likely used here with cultic connotations and not simply as an honorific title similar to that conferred upon the king's sons or high officials of the court (*contra* Wildberger, *op. cit.*, pp. 81-83 and Buber, *op. cit.*, pp. 103f., both of whom refer to 2 Sam. 8:18 and 1 Kg. 4:5).

[2] So Junker, *op. cit.*, p. 14.

[3] Cf. Bauer, *op. cit.*, pp. 285f. The absence of the specific election terms (e.g. בָּחַר, קָרָא) is typical of the more ancient sacral amphictyony's formulation. Cf. Gen. 18:19, Am. 3:2; Ex. 15:16, Dt. 32:6; 2 Sam. 7:24 and G. E. Wright, *RGG* II, 612.

priests" is a concrete example for the quality of holiness. Not priestly function but priestly character is weighted here.[1] The active aspect of holiness, namely obedience, can hardly be identified with the specific function of priests. As a matter of fact, discussion of a "priesthood" is already a subtle departure from the text which contains no mention of an abstraction such as "priesthood" but only the *concretum*, "priests."

(6) Basic here is the element of collectivity.[2] Not individuals but a kingdom and a nation are being described; not "priests" or "holy persons" but "holy nation" and, as it were, "priestly kingdom."

(7) Thus in content, as in structure, vv. 5b-6 offer an integrated unit of thought. The three promises of the covenant center in the two correlates of election and holiness which imply both a Divine act of grace and a human act of obedience. The designation "kingdom of priests" is a consequence of both.

(8) The extreme age[3] of this pericope makes it highly improbable

---

[1] The germ for the development of the functional aspect, however, is here and was possibly the point of departure for the formulation of Is. 61:6; cf. Junker, *op. cit.*, p. 14.

[2] So Scott, *op. cit.*, p. 215.

[3] Its great antiquity is to be seen not only in particular formulations such as "people of God" which reflects the terminology of the Amphictyonic cultic league (Noth, *System*; von Rad, *Hexateuch*, pp. 35f.) or the terminologically non-developed motif of election (cf. *supra*, p. 55, n. 3) but in the age of the cultic celebration in which this pericope had its place (cf. von Rad, *ibid.*). Its differences from the similar passages in Dt. (7:6, 14:2, 26:18) not only indicate its independence from Dt. redaction (so von Rad, *Hexateuch*, p. 35, n. 47 *contra* e.g. Noth, *Pentateuch*, p. 33, n. 112) but also an origin previous to the latter (*contra* Procksch, *op. cit.*, p. 109; cf. von Rad, *Hexateuch*, pp. 29f.). Whereas in Ex. 19:3bff. the people are directly addressed, in Dt. 7:6ff. a description of Israel's status is made by a third party; here Moses rather than God is speaking. In Ex. the people are to "keep the covenant"; in Dt. they are to "keep the commandments and ordinances" (vv. 9, 11, 12) and God will keep the covenant (vv. 9, 12). Dt. looks back to the Exodus event (vv. 8, 15, 18). It further explains election (with the *terminus technicus* בָּחַר, v. 6) as the consequence of God's love (vv. 7f.). Most important, in place of the *gôy qadôš* Dt. substitutes עַם קָדוֹשׁ (v. 6), which is best seen as an accommodation to later terminology in which עַם was the "approved" designation of Israel alone and גּוֹי restricted to the heathen. (This theory would be weakened if it could be proved that גּוֹי was required here as the necessary correlative to מַמְלָכָה. This hypothesis has been suggested by A. Cody in his study, "When is the Chosen People Called a Gôy?," *VT* 14/1 (1964), 1-6. It cannot be overlooked, however, as Cody himself recognizes, that "this is the only place in the Old Testament where Israel is said to be a 'holy nation' [gôy qadôš]" [p. 4] instead of a "holy people" [עַם קָדוֹשׁ]. This unique ascription of holiness to Israel as גּוֹי smacks very strongly of very

that any trace of a polemic against the Levitical institution is to be found here.[1] An interpretation which would find in these words an intentional contrast over against a special priesthood and office of mediation[2] is anachronistic and unsupported by the text. Hubert Junker in rejecting this proposal has noted that the contrast is not over against a Levitical priesthood but over against the Gentiles, as is clear in v. 5b "from among all the peoples."[3] Had such a polemic been intended, then a cause must have been at hand, continues Junker. Since no such cause is present, there is no occasion for suspicion of criticism. A verse which in its polemical thrust formed the grass-roots of the idea of a "general priesthood of believers"[4] is simply not to be found!

Insofar as this Exodus pericope derives from a period far earlier than the establishment of the Levitical priesthood, it appears in-

---

ancient vintage.) Furthermore, in Dt. no mention of a מַמְלֶכֶת כֹּהֲנִים is to be found. Together these variations can only indicate that Dt. represented a later, more reflective theological formulation of the unit met in an earlier stage in Ex. 19. In Dt. the parallelistic structure has been destroyed, "kingdom of priests" omitted probably as inconsistent with the now more developed institutional priesthood, and the emphasis upon holiness shifted from covenant and election to a moral holiness *vis à vis* the Law (Wildberger, *op. cit.*, p. 98). Cf. Beyerlin, *op. cit.*, p. 83, n. 1 for further evidence and literature. Recently reference has been made again to the standpoint that the Pentateuch allusions to JHWH's *kingly* status all fall in the period after the Settlement in Canaan. In the period before this, including the Revelation at Sinai, "ist ein göttliches Königtum unbekannt" (W. Schmidt, *Königtum Gottes in Ugarit und Israel* [Diss., Berlin], *BZAW* 80, 1961, p. 69). In his examination of the material dated before the Settlement, however, the author disregards the Sinai tradition entirely. Ex. 19:6a he dismisses, following Noth (cf. *supra*, p. 51, n. 2), as a "Zusatz deuteronomistischen Stils" (*op. cit.*, n. 31). This is certainly a convenient solution. However, this opinion has not found the approval of most scholars. Likewise, the assertion that the kingship of JHWH is a concept which was expressed in Israel only after the entrance into Canaan (so e.g. A. von Gall, βασιλεία τοῦ Θεοῦ, Heidelberg, 1926, p. 41; v. Rad, *TWNT* I, 563-69, esp. 568; further literature in Schmidt, *op. cit.*, pp. 1f., 64ff.) has found vigorous opposition (e.g. Buber, *op. cit.*, pp. xxxvii ff.; 161, n. 1). The entire question of the concept of JHWH's kingship and its origin is still open to serious debate. Even if the comma מַמְלֶכֶת כֹּהֲנִים is to be ascribed to a period after the entrance into Canaan, its precedence to the Levitical institution is in any case beyond dispute. Insofar, an answer either *pro* or *contra* the question raised by Schmidt will have no effect upon the relationship between "kingdom of priests" and the Levitical ministry.

[1] So also Buber, *op. cit.*, p. 104; Bauer, *op. cit.*, p. 285; Wildberger, *op. cit.*, p. 80.

[2] So Beer-Galling, *op. cit.*, p. 97.

[3] Junker, *op. cit.*, pp. 11ff.

[4] Beer-Galling, *ibid.*; cf. Scott, with reservation, *op. cit.*, pp. 216.

advisable to derive the significance of the phrase "kingdom of priests" from a comparison with this later cultic institution. Such comparisons[1] operate with a *generalized concept of priesthood*, and the texts which they adduce usually have little in common with Ex. 19:6. The idea of the holiness of Israel or its priestly mediating role among the nations in a kind of cosmic universal dimension is difficult to locate here. Nor ought it be expected at this stage of Israel's history.

Again, to speak of a certain "spiritualization" of the concept of priesthood, as does Cerfaux[2] is to import categories of a far later period into a context where they are doubtlessly inappropriate. It is to be questioned whether "kingdom of priests" at this date was meant purely as a metaphor.[3] Rather it has been suggested that this designation reflects an earlier period in Israel's history when the *pater familias* and the first-born still shared in the cult (cf. Ex. 24:5), when priests not of the tribe of Levi also functioned (cf. Num. 16:15, Judg. 6:18, 13:19, 17:5), when one could still compare JHWH's people as an entire "kingdom of priests" with the priestly castes of Egypt, when the promise "holy nation" would relate to the proclamation of Num. 16:3, "the whole congregation is holy."[4]

Ex. 19:6 is to be understood in contrast to a priestly institution or in connection with the universalistic *Weltanschauung* of the prophets but in relation to the covenant. This covenant forms both the literary context and the theological setting for the predicate "kingdom of priests." As Ernst Kinder has remarked: "Das 'allgemeine Priestertum' Gesamtisraels ist der Dienst der Gesamtgemeinde Israel (als Subjekt) *auf Grund* des Bundes und *kraft* des Bundes."[5]

(9) In light of its cultic *Sitz im Leben*, the statement eventually recorded in Ex. 19:6 signified basically the holy nation who worshipped JHWH alone and thus belonged exclusively to Him.[6] The

---

[1] Cf. G. A. Danell, "The Idea of God's People in the Bible," *The Root of the Vine*, Essays in Biblical Theology, ed A. Fridrichsen, Westminster, 1953, pp. 23-26; Kinder, *op. cit.*; Torrance, *op. cit.*, esp. pp. 1-22.

[2] Cerfaux, *op. cit.*, p. 8.

[3] So Cerfaux, *ibid.*

[4] E. König, *Geschichte der alttestamentlichen Religion*, 2. Aufl., Gütersloh, 1915, p. 305, cf. also Schrenk, *op. cit.*, p. 249.

[5] Kinder, *op. cit.*, p. 10.

[6] So K. Galling, *Die Erwählungstraditionen Israels* (*BZAW* 48), 1928, p. 27; Scott, *op. cit.*, p. 219; Beyerlin, *op. cit.*, p. 79.

simplicity and yet all-inclusiveness of this thought explains how this pericope can be said to have contained one of the most dominant and central expressions of Israel's theology and faith in the entire Old Testament.[1]

2. *Isaiah* 61:6

וְאַתֶּם כֹּהֲנֵי יְהוָה תִּקָּרֵאוּ מְשָׁרְתֵי אֱלֹהֵינוּ יֵאָמֵר לָכֶם
חֵיל גּוֹיִם תֹּאכֵלוּ וּבִכְבוֹדָם תִּתְיַמָּרוּ

This passage has been cited as the only other OT verse closely resembling Ex. 19:6[2] and has been so treated in other studies tracing the OT roots of 1 P 2:9.[3] While a similar designation of Israel as "priests" coupled with a context recalling the Exodus (Is. 63:7-14) and the revelation at Sinai (64:1-4) might suggest affinity with the earlier pericope, definite textual contact is doubtful. The certainty of affinity has yet to be demonstrated.

The historical setting of this verse is post-exilic. Israel is loosed from the captive bonds of Babylon. It is an era of salvation and restoration (61:2-4), a time of the Lord's favor and judgment (61:2). In this reversal of fortune Israel's shame is exchanged for Divine favor, a double portion, and everlasting joy (61:7). The majestic hand of the Lord once again establishes with Israel an everlasting covenant (61:8), gracing her with salvation and righteousness (61:10f.). This period of redemption moreover brings with it a new relationship of Israel to the *Goiim*, a restoration of her honor and significance before the eyes of the heathen. This is the weight of concern of v. 6.

Verses 5-6 form one of the middle strophes of the oracle contained in 61:1-9.[4] In v. 6 the epithets כֹּהֲנֵי יְהוָה and מְשָׁרְתֵי אֱלֹהֵינוּ are corre-

---

[1] Cf. Muilenburg, *op. cit.*, p. 351 who further cites R. Kraetzschmar, *Die Bundesvorstellung im Alten Testament in ihrer geschichtlichen Entwicklung*, 1896, p. 130 and E. König, *Das alttestamentliche Prophetentum und die moderne Geschichtsforschung*, 1910, pp. 63f.; so also Wildberger, *op. cit.*, p. 5.

[2] Scott, *op. cit.*, p. 213.

[3] Cerfaux, *op. cit.*, p. 9; Blinzler, *op. cit.*, p. 58; Sevenster, *op. cit.*, p. 403.

[4] Cf. B. Duhm, *Das Buch Jesaia* (*HAT* 3/1), Göttingen, 1892, p. 427; K. Marti, *Das Buch Jesaja* (*HCAT* 10), Tübingen, 1900, p. 386; E. König, *Das Buch Jesaja*, Gütersloh, 1926, p. 511; K. Elliger, *Die Einheit des Tritojesaja* (56-66), Stuttgart, 1928, pp. 24f.; J. Muilenburg, *The Book of Isaiah* (*chs.* 40-66) (*The Interpreter's Bible* V), New York, 1956, p. 708, who maintain the integrity of these verses over against B. Stade, *Die Geschichte Israels*,

sponding parts of a *parallelismus membrorum*. Nowhere else in the OT are both terms applied to Israel in toto but they occur regularly, though not exclusively, as predicates for the Levitical priests.[1]

Opinion on the significance of the term "priests" varies. However in the light of its Levitical flavoring we might heed the suggestion of the Jewish scholar I. W. Slotki: "As the priests subsisted upon what the Israelites allocated to them, so the priestly nation will be supported by the other people since it is dedicated to the Divine Service."[2] The *tertium comparationis* is thus the material support which the Levites received from the other eleven tribes of Israel. The priestly character of Israel in this case is primarily that of reception of a "due" from the Gentiles.

The OT passage closest to this thought is not Ex. 19:6 but Dt. 18:1-5. These two texts are similar both in terminology[3] and content.[4] In both passages the point of concern is the preeminence of the priestly ministers of the Lord and the material support which they receive from others as an appointed due. Neither textually nor contentwise does Is. 61:6 show any dependence upon Ex. 19:6. It is much more likely that the author was describing the status of Israel among the *Goiim* in analogy to the status of the Levitical priests among the Israelite tribes as depicted in Dt. 18:1-5.

Not an anti-cultic or anti-Levitical polemic, however, is to be seen here but rather a comparison and an analogy. This is clear in 66:21 where the Levitical institution is definitely affirmed.[5] Spoken against the background of an eschatological hope and couched within the motifs of election and universalism, this statement de-

---

Berlin, 1887-88, II, 86, n. 1 and P. Volz, *Jesaia II* (*KAT IX Jes.* 40-66), Leipzig, 1932, p. 254.

[1] כֹּהֲנֵי יְהוָה: 1 Sam. 14:3, 22:17, 21; 2 Chr. 11:14, 13:9. Cp. Jer. 2:8, 29:26. מְשָׁרְתֵי אֱלֹהֵינוּ: 1 Chr. 16:4; 2 Chr. 23:6; Ezr. 8:17; Ps. 103:21; Jer. 33:21. For "servant" in the noncultic sense cf. 2 Sam. 13:17, 18; 1 Kg. 10:5; 2 Kg. 4:43, 6:15; Esth. 2:2, 6:3, Pr. 29:12. This is also a frequent predicate for Joshua who is called the "servant" or "minister" of Moses: Ex. 24:13, 33:11; Num. 11:28; Jos. 1:1.

[2] I. W. Slotki, *Isaiah*, (*Soncino Books of the Bible*, ed. A. Cohen), London, 1949, p. 299. Cf. Duhm, *op. cit.*, p. 426.

[3] יְהוָה: Dt. 18:1, 2 (*bis*), 5 (*bis*). יְהוָה אֱלֹהֶיךָ: 18:5. לְשָׁרֵת (= מְשָׁרֵת): 18:5 שָׁרֵת = in Dt. the Levitical service (cf. 10:8, 21:5), cp. 17:12, 18:7.

[4] Dt. 18:3: "And this shall be the priests' due from the people . . ." Dt. 18:5: "For the Lord your God has chosen him out of all your tribes, to stand and minister in the name of the Lord, him and his sons for ever."

[5] Sim. W. W. Graf Baudissin, *Die Geschichte des Alttestamentlicher Priesterthums*, Leipzig, 1889, pp. 249f.

scribes Israel's priestly character in its cosmic dimension.

It is in this light that Is. 61:6 approaches the thought of Ex. 19:6. In the Final Age, as formerly at the giving of the covenant, Israel in her entirety shall be called the priests of JHWH. But beyond the older tradition something new is inferred: the broader horizon of the prophet suggests that this priesthood of Israel implies a *mediatorial* function. Israel is to be a "covenant to the people and a light to the *Goiim*" (42:6, 49:8, 59:20, 60:1-3). Through her the Gentiles too shall minister (שָׁרֵת) before JHWH (56:6, 60:7,10). Israel is to have a *mission* to the world: to proclaim the glory of the Lord among the nations (43:21, 66:19). Of those who hear the news and are thence gathered from all the nations God will select some also to be His priests and Levites.

In this sense the comments of those scholars who find a mediatorial motif implied in v. 6 are partly justified.[1] Nevertheless, such a motif is not primary and is only inferable from context. Quite unconvincing, however, is Cerfaux's dismissal of this motif with the comment that here an echo of Ex. 19:6 occurs in which the accent is upon מַמְלָכָה rather than on sacerdotal mission.[2] To the contrary, Paul Volz has observed that it is especially significant of this prophet who was so perceptive of the national character of Israel that in his discussion of salvation he rejects a messianic kingdom in the national sense "und dass er mit keinem Wort vom der Weltherrschaft Israels spricht."[3]

Did Is. 61:6 contain an allusion to Ex. 19:6?. Or indeed was the prophet here "interpreting" the earlier passage?[4] Such a suggestion seems quite tenuous. Though its context contains random similarities to words and phrases of Ex. 19:3bff. (e.g. "covenant" [56:4; 59:21; 61:8]; "crown of beauty" and "royal diadem" [62:3]; "my chosen" [65:9,15,22]; "Your holy people" [62:12], these similarities do not appear in such a unity as to imply reflection and interpretation of the covenant formula in Ex. 19. Textually the sole point of contact is that in both passages the term "priests" is used to describe Israel *in toto*. However, even here the connotation varies. Whereas in Ex. 19:6 this term denoted the *holiness* of Israel, in Is.

---

[1] Cf. Duhm, *op. cit.*, p. 426; Muilenburg, *op. cit.*, p. 712. Cf. also Volz, *op. cit.*, p. xxv ff.

[2] Cerfaux, *op. cit.*, p. 9.

[3] Volz, *op. cit.*, p. xxiii.

[4] So Junker, *op. cit.*, p. 14.

61:6 it described her *position of privilege* among the heathen.[1] Whereas in Ex. 19:6 no comparison with a Levitical caste was made, the later passage was conceived in analogy to the *privilegium Leviticorum* as defined in Dt. 18:1-5. That the prophet was aware of the covenant tradition reflected in Ex. 19:3ff. is quite possible; that he composed 61:6 as an interpretation of the same is a postulation exceeding the textual evidence.

We *summarize* the results thus far. Ex. 19:3b-6 contains one of the central and dominant expressions of the theology and faith of the OT People of God. Couched in covenantal formulation, it has been preserved as part of the Sinai-tradition, owing its origin and transmission to ancient cultic observance. Verse 6 presents the central emphasis of this pericope: when Israel is faithful to the covenant then she shall be a kingdom of priests, that is, a holy nation sharing the holiness of her holy God and enjoying the access to Him which is typical of priests. Israel is to be a kingdom of priests on the basis of the covenant—in virtue of her election and her obedience. In this ancient text is no trace of a polemic against the Levitical priesthood. An emphasis not upon priestly function but rather upon a priestly relationship to JHWH is the concern.

Specific reference to such a "kingdom of priests" is nowhere else to be found in the OT. Later echoes of the covenant formula regularly omit this phrase. The only passage possibly resembling Ex. 19:6 is Is. 61:6. The sole point of contact, however, is the idea that Israel as a whole shall be, or shall be called, "priests." Otherwise, in both terminology and content the prophet shows affinity with Dt. 18:1-5 and the analogy of Levitical privilege. The context possibly implies that Israel's priesthood is to comprise further a mediatorial and missionary function among the *Goiim*—a new aspect of Israel's priestliness consistent with the universalistic view of the prophet. But this can only be inferred. The text itself speaks only to the question of priestly privilege.

If it could be shown that Ex. 19:6 was definitely re-echoed here, then this verse would offer a most unusual combination of a conception of Levitical priesthood with a conception of a universalistic priesthood which in its inclusion of the heathen as priests transcends

---

[1] Marti, *op. cit.*, p. 387: "die privilegierte Stellung der Juden in der Welt." L. Dennefeld, *Les Grands Prophètes* (*La Sainte Bible* VII), Paris, 1952, p. 216: "Les paiens seront désormais les serviteurs des Israelites, qui occuperont dans l'humanité le même rang que les prêtres dans le peuple élu."

the boundary not only of the Levitical lineage but of the House of Israel as well.

B. The LXX Version of Ex. 19:6

ὑμεῖς δὲ ἔσεσθέ μοι βασίλειον ἱεράτευμα καὶ ἔθνος ἅγιον[1]

Transplanted from Palestinian to Alexandrian soil, the Exodus Formula (=EF) received both new lingual dress and new nuance appropriate to a new milieu and a new historical situation. In their translation of this verse the Alexandrians produced the problematical phrasing βασίλειον ἱεράτευμα which can be understood as either two substantives or as an adjective and a substantive; thus either (1) "kingdom" (or "royal residence") and "body of priests" or (2) "royal body of priests."[2]

The word order of the *text* is identical to that of the MT. However, it is uncertain that the *parallelismus membrorum* has been retained. This depends upon the function of βασίλειον. Seen aside from the original MT formulation, this sentence could be taken in its Greek form as a literary chiasmus in which case βασίλειον would then be functioning—similar to ἅγιον—as an adjective. Though this is possible syntactically, the close correspondence of the Greek version to the Hebrew original argues that such a chiasmus was not intended but rather that this term was intended as the Greek equivalent for מַמְלֶכֶת. This would imply that the original form of the *parallelismus membrorum* was not retained.[3] Instead of the first member's being qualified by the second member as the third is qualified by the fourth (as in the MT), the first and second members would be inde-

---

[1] Unless otherwise stated, the textual edition of the LXX followed is that of A. Rahlfs, *Septuaginta, id est Vetus Testamentum Graece iuxta LXX Interpretes*, 5th ed., Stuttgart, 1952.

[2] Reproduction of the particular nuance of the term ἱεράτευμα has somewhat escaped our modern languages and requires almost a phrase and point of analogy. Reasons for the translation chosen are offered in the following discussion.

[3] Even if βασίλειον were taken as adjective the original form of the *par. memb.* would not be reflected. For then the first and second members would have exchanged their original roles and instead of the second member qualifying the first (MT), the first would qualify the second (LXX). (It appears advisable to describe the difference in these terms rather than to see "priestly kingdom" (MT) in contrast to "royal body of priests" (LXX) because the former phrasing is frequently regarded as an inadequate rendition of מַמְלֶכֶת כֹּהֲנִים.)

pendent nouns, "kingdom, body of priests" joined to a third, "(holy) nation."[1] Whether this function of βασίλειον as substantive is supported by general LXX usage remains to be demonstrated.

Since the basic theological significance of this verse has already been discussed, the main task at this point is the determination of the meaning and nuance of terms βασίλειον ἱεράτευμα and the degree to which this phrase reproduced or altered the intention of the original Hebrew text.

We begin with ἱεράτευμα. What is the *specific meaning* of this term?

The word is of late origin[2] and absent in profane Greek literature, found only in the Scriptures and related Jewish or Christian writings.[3] Thus, as far as we can determine, in the period between the composition of the LXX and the NT literature[4] it appears eight times: LXX Ex. 19:6, 23:22;[5] Greek Fragment 67 (relating to Test. Levi 11:6); 2 Mcc. 2:17; Philo, *De Sobr.* 66, *De Abrah.* 56; and 1 P 2:5,9. The rarity of its appearances would suggest that these eight texts might have something in common. As the investigation of this chapter will show, all are reflections of or allusions to Ex. 19:6. The LXX formation apparently played an influential role in subsequent reference to the EF and therefore it is proper that our analysis of the term ἱεράτευμα begins here.

Since this word fails in all profane Greek literature, determination of its precise meaning through a comparison of usage is impossible. Nevertheless, from an analysis of other substantives similarly formed from the—εύω verb and/or the nominal suffix—εύς (-εύξ) we may gain a reasonable impression of its significant characteristics.

Ἱεράτευμα derives ultimately from the ἱερ- root (ἱερός = "holy")[6]

---

[1] Though the parallelistic *form* be discontinued, this does not necessarily imply that the original emphasis upon the element of holiness has been abandoned, however.

[2] So Hort, *op. cit.*, pp. 109f.; Cerfaux, *op. cit.*, p. 12; and H. Frisk, *Griechisches Etymologisches Wörterbuch*, Heidelberg, 1960, I, 712-14 who offers the most recent etymological information on the ἱερ-root.

[3] Cf. *BAG s.v.*

[4] Since our concern is limited to those texts possibly bearing an influence upon 1 P, this is the only period which interests us here.

[5] This instance involves the recurrence of Ex. 19:5 (in slightly altered form) and 19:6a in 23:22, forming, in part, a doublet to 23:23. As Origen already noted (*Origenis Hexaplorum quae supersunt sive veterum graecorum in totum Vetus Testamentum fragmenta*, ed. F. Field, Oxford, 1861-74, I, *sub* Ex. 19:6), these words are absent in the MT and thus are to be regarded as composing an interpolation.

[6] Cf. Frisk, *loc. cit.*

whose abundant occurrences in the adjectival (ἱερός, ἱερατικός), nominal (ἱερεύς, ἱερατεία, ἱερωσύνη), and verbal (ἱερεύω, ἱεράομαι, ἱερατεύω) form are documented by *L-S-J*,[1] E. Mayser,[2] W. Dittenberger,[3] and *M-M*.[4] The terms to which it directly relates are the noun ἱερεύς ("priest") and the verb derived from this noun, ἱερατεύω ("to be a priest or priestess").[5]

The suffix -εύς (-εύξ) denotes a *nomen actoris*, a "doer," one who fulfills a particular function. Accordingly, the denominative -εύω verbs denote the exercise of an activity, an office, or an occupation. These verbs mean "to be what the baseform says," "to occupy oneself with that which the baseform indicates"[6] or "to be something by profession," "to function in a certain capacity."[7] Thus, e.g.: μεσιτεύω "to function as a μεσιτεύς — "to mediate"; βασιλεύω "to function as a βασιλεύς—"to reign"; κυριεύω "to officiate as a κύριος—"to rule." Accordingly, ἱερατεύω means "to function as a ἱερατεύς (= ἱερεύς), "to serve in priestly capacity."

The -ευμα substantives created from -εύω verbs are intimately related to the action of the verb and classify generally as *nomina actionis*. A comparison of such substantives[8] shows a number of groups bearing certain similarities and differences. (1) Some substantives are pure nomina actionis denoting the *executing of the verb*.[9] (2) Akin to this basic designation, other terms denote the *state of the verb*.[10] (3) Some designate the *product of the verb*.[11] Others depict

---

[1] *A Greek-English Lexicon* compiled by H. G. Liddell and R. Scott. A New Edition revised and augmented throughout by H. S. Jones, 9th ed., Oxford, 1940.

[2] E. Mayser, *Grammatik der Griechischen Papyri aus der Ptolemäerzeit*, I-II/3, 2. Aufl., Berlin, 1936.

[3] *Sylloge Inscriptionum Graecarum*, ed. W. Dittenberger, I-IV, 3rd ed., 1915-24.

[4] J. H. Moulton and G. Milligan, *The Vocabulary of the Greek New Testament Illustrated from the Papyri and Other Non-Literary Sources*, London, 1952.

[5] This and the following definitions are given according to L-S-J.

[6] E. Schwyzer, *Griechische Grammatik*, München, I, 732.

[7] F. Blass, *Grammatik des neutestamentlichen Griechisch*, bearbeitet von A. Debrunner, 9. Aufl., Göttingen, 1954, § 108, 5, p. 71.

[8] According to the list of 224 terms compiled by E. Locker in *Rückläufiges Wörterbuch der griechischen Sprache*, ed. P. Kretschmer, Göttingen, 1944, pp. 60-62.

[9] μνείστευμα "courtship, wooing," from μνειστεύομαι "to court, woo"; ἡγεμόνευμα "leading," from ἡγεμονεύς (-ών) "leader," (from verbal noun); δράπευμα "running away," from δραπεύω "to run away."

[10] νόσευμα "sickness," from νοσεύομαι "to be sick"; ἁγίστευμα "sanctuary," from ἁγιστεύω "to be holy"; περίτευμα "superfluity," from περιτεύω "to

also the *instrument of the verb.*[1] Still other substantives can be found designating the *person or thing acted upon.*[2] When used in connection with persons, -ευμα substantives were occasionally employed in a *pejorative* sense.[3]

From the examples noted it can be seen that all substantives maintain a close connection with the verbs from which they have been formed. The active quality is inherent, if not explicit, in all these words. Particularly interesting, therefore, are the occasions where these substantives were used of persons, both positively and pejoratively.

(6) Finally, there is a group of substantives which have retained not only an active quality but also the personal aspect of the original *nomen actionis.* Characteristic of these terms is their *communal* aspect. That is, in these we find incorporated three qualities of the -ευμα substantives: person-relatedness, action, and collectivity. τὸ βούλευμα,[4] τὸ τεχνίτευμα,[5] and τὸ πρέσβευμα[6] are

---

overflow." This denotation cannot be sharply differentiated from the first. A strict categorization is impossible.

[11] ἡμίσευμα "a half," from ἡμισεύω "to halve"; μάντευμα "oracle," from μαντεύομαι "to prophesy" (sim. προφήτευμα); ἀρίστευμα "deed of prowess," from ἀριστεύω "to be the best" (ἀριστεύς = "he who excels in honor").

[1] ὀΐστευμα "an arrow from the bow," from ὀϊστεύω "to shoot arrows"; ὀχέτευμα "duct or passage of the nose," from ὀχετεύω "to conduct water"; cp. also τιθάσ(σ)ευμα "device for taming," from τιθασεύτης "one who tames" (instrument of the verbal noun).

[2] παίδευμα "that which is reared or educated, a pupil," from παιδεύω "to teach"; φύτευμα "that which is planted, a plant," from φυτεύω "to plant"; νύμφευμα (sing) "the person married," from νυμφεύω "to give in marriage, betroth."

[3] δούλευμα, normally a "service," from δουλεύω "to be a slave," pejorative: "slave"; σκυλάκευμα "whelp, cub," from σκυλακεύς "puppy," pejorative: used of a young boy—a "brat."

[4] A βουλεύς is a "counselor" and βούλευμα is the "resolution, purpose," from βουλεύω "to take counsel, to deliberate." However, βούλευμα can also mean the "sitting of a βουλή" ("council, senate" composed of οἱ βουλεῖς). That is, the substantive βούλευμα denotes not simply the activity of one officer or functionary but rather the activity of a group, *the communal functioning of men in a certain capacity*—as senators.

[5] τὸ τεχνίτευμα, "work of art," from τεχνιτεύω "to fabricate," also designates the "theatrical profession." A τεχνίτης is an artist in the theater or music (SIG 399.12—Amphict. Delph. [3rd Cent. B. C.]). The use of τεχνίτευμα in the personal collective sense as a "body of artificers, guild of artisans" occurs in a 3rd Cent. B. C. inscription noted by *M-M* (*sub* ἱεράτευμα [OGI 51.11]). (For abbreviations of the authors and sources cf. *L-S-J*, pp. xvi-xlviii.)

[6] τό πρέσβευμα demonstrates this aspect of collectivity even more clearly. A πρεσβεύς is an "ambassador." The substantive πρέσβευμα means "ambassa-

helpful examples of one type of substantive within this group. All three terms designate a specific *communities of persons functioning in a particular capacity*, as "senators," "artisans," and "ambassadors." Significant for all three terms is the fact that the -ευμα substantives do not relate to single isolated individuals but rather designate a *community*. To an original personal element the suffix -(ευ)μα has lent the idea of collectivity while at the same time stressing the aspect of activity; thus: "the communal functioning of persons with a common charge."

A second representative type of substantive similarly personal and collective in character appears to have assumed this character rather than to have inherited it from the original *nomen actionis*. In these terms the verbal aspect is especially prominent, as, for example, in τὸ πολίτευμα[1] and τὸ στράτευμα.[2] In contrast to the former type these latter terms designate not a community of persons in a particular profession (such as senator, artisan, or ambassador) but rather a community of people in more general terms, a political mass, a fighting mass. An original -εύς *nomen* is not at hand and that which the members of the community have in common is determined therefore not by the noun but by the verb: "a body of people being citizens," "a body of people fighting."

Nevertheless, such fine distinctions are admittedly tenuous. For even the word τὸ βούλευμα, the "sitting of a council" and not simply "body of senators," demonstrates the proximity of both groups.

Generally speaking, then, these terms indicate the personal aspect which the substantives preserved or received, the completely active character of such substantives, and their corporative aspect which

---

dors" (in the plural, ie. two or more ambassadors [E. Supp. 173; cf. Rh 936]) or, collectively, the "embassy" (Plutarch, *Timaeus* 9).

[1] τὸ πολίτευμα basically means the "business of government," the "act of administration," from πολιτεύω "to be a citizen"; most frequently in the middle voice: "to take part in the government," "to hold public office," to administer." ὁ πολιτευτής designates the "statesman." *L-S-J*, however, list τὸ πολίτευμα as the *concretum* in contrast to ἡ πολιτεία "civil polity," "form of government," so that πολίτευμα takes on the meaning "the citizens themselves" (Aeschines 2.172), or a "corporate body of citizens" (OGI 299.60 [Smyrna, 3rd Cent. B. C.]; OGI 592; PTeb 32.17 [2nd Cent. B. C.]; SIG 633.59 [Milet, 2nd Cent. B. C.]), or an "association" (of women: BCH 15.182.205).

[2] τὸ στράτευμα "expedition," "campaign," from στρατεύω "to advance with an army or fleet," also falls under this category. For it was from the verb and the verbal substantive, and not from an original -εύς noun (cp. στρατιώτης = "soldier") that the communal meaning developed: "the group of those carrying out the campaign," "the army."

is related more to the persons in the former group and more to the action in the latter.

These examples, dating from as early as the second and third centuries before the birth of Christ, that is, about the time of the composition of the LXX, offer convincing evidence for the supposition that ἱεράτευμα is also to be understood in this personal, active and corporate sense.

τὸ ἱεράτευμα thus denotes "the community of those functioning as priests," "a body of priests."[1] According to the substantives listed above, ἱεράτευμα relates more to the first group because it derives from the *nomen actoris*, ἱερεύς (ἱερατεύς). This suggests the meaning "a body with a priestly charge" rather than the more general "a priestly community." As. F. J. A. Hort has emphasized, ἱεράτευμα designates "not simply the sacredness or even the performance of sacred rites, but the function of an official priesthood."[2]

An adequate translation must maintain this triple connotation of person-relatedness, action, and community. For this reason the English "priesthood" and the German "Priestertum" are to be rejected as inappropriate.[3] Such translations are too abstract, too static, too weak in expressing the communal factor. They relate more to the Greek noun ἡ ἱερατεία "the priesthood," the more abstract substantive of the ἱερατεύ-root/stem.

A comparison of the substantives ἱεράτευμα and ἱερατεία, as well as similar terms ending in the -ευμα and -εία suffixes, indicates beyond doubt that whereas both suffixes depict *nomina actionis*, -ευμα contains the more concrete personal connotation (i.e. where personal activity is at all involved) and -εία the more abstract "categorized" sense.[4]

---

[1] So *L-S-J*, *M-M*, *s.v.*

[2] Hort, *op. cit.*, p. 109. However, Hort stresses the aspect of function to the exclusion of person and community.

[3] The Latin "*sacerdotium*" likewise fails to do justice.

[4] For example, whereas ἀρίστευμα denotes the "deed done by a valiant one," ἀριστεία indicates the abstract state of "prowess," "excellence." While πολιτεία can mean "body of citizens" (Aristole, *Politica* 1292ª 34), its far more customary meaning is "citizenship" as a general category (the first definition given by *L-S-J*; cf. Herodotus 9.34) or "government" (cf. *L-S-J*, *s.v.*). Or στράτευμα often designates the "body of soldiers" themselves, the military body, whereas στρατεία, "expedition," "campaign," denotes only the action of the verb and tends to exclude any reference to persons. *L-S-J*, *s.v.*, note that according to the available evidence στρατεία never means "army" but always "campaign."

The translation "Priesterschaft" is regularly accepted by the majority of modern German commentators in preference to Luther's "Priestertum." In the English realm many variations have been offered. The translation "body of priests" has been selected here for lack of a more appropriate collective designation. Perhaps the more awkward phrase "body of functioning priests" would justify itself by accounting more adequately for the active ingredient.

The origin of this term is difficult to determine with certainty. Its first occurrence in the LXX and the late appearance of -ευμα substantives in the Koine point to a late derivation. As for geographical area its appearance in the LXX and 2 Mcc. 2:17[1] and double occurrances in the writings of Philo suggest Alexandria, within the reign and reach of the Ptolomies.

Cerfaux finds this *terminus sui generis* to be a peculiar LXX construction and his explanation leads to the question of its *theological significance*. Cerfaux,[2] followed also by Blinzler,[3] points to the relationship between the Diaspora Jews as a ἱεράτευμα and as a πολίτευμα, thereby arriving at a congenial explanation of the theological relevance of this term. τὸ πολίτευμα was the designation for a community of citizens of the same people or nation living on foreign soil, as e.g. the Jewish populace of Alexandria. This existence fostered assimilation and, as N. A. Dahl has noted, the concept of the *polis* also determined the social thinking of Hellenistic Judaism: "Jude sein, heisst also, nach der jüdischen Verfassung leben. . . ."[4] The term ἱεράτευμα, then, brought the religious dimension of this Diaspora-folk to expression. The Jews did not wish to see themselves simply as a foreign colony of aliens in a Hellenistic city but as a priestly community charged with the worship of the true god. With the construction ἱεράτευμα the LXX translators were adapting the EF to the situation of the Jews in the Egyptian Dispersion and were pointing to the thought that the Jews, as a grand organization of priests amid a Hellenistic world, had a divinely endowed religious mission to fulfill.

This explanation favorably coincides with the philological factors

---

[1] Regarding Alexandria as the place of composition of 2 Mcc. 1:10-2:18 cf. *infra*, pp. 90–96.

[2] Cerfaux, *op. cit.*, pp. 11-13.

[3] Blinzler, *op. cit.*, p. 59.

[4] Dahl, *op. cit.*, p. 97. Cf. LXX Esth. 8:12, 2 Mcc. 6:11, 11:25; 3 Mcc. 3:4; 4 Mcc. 2:8, 23, 4:23, 5:16.

discussed above while also accounting for its sole occurrence in a Jewish/Christian tradition and its manufacture at the hand of the theologians of the LXX. One will be careful to distinguish, however, between πολίτευμα and ἱεράτευμα. ἱεράτευμα is not merely a πολίτευμα seen from a theological point of view. It is not simply a "religious" body of citizens—as little as πρέσβευμα implies a body of citizens seen as ambassadors, or τεχνίτευμα, the citizenry as a guild of artists. Therefore Cerfaux's statement that ἱεράτευμα expresses "le charactere religieux de ce πολίτευμα"[1] can be accepted only with reservation.

What role did βασίλειον play in this new formulation? Is it a substantival equivalent for מַמְלָכָה or has the original noun been converted to an adjective?

In *profane Greek* the *adjective* βασίλειος, -ον means "royal," "belonging to the king or prince of the land."[2] It is found among the tragedians, and, as Selwyn notes, seems to connote "a more intimate and personal relationship than βασιλικός . . . almost equivalent to τοῦ βασιλέως.[3]

The *substantive* τὸ βασίλειον is used as "kingdom" in the sense of the area circumscribed by the king's reign[4] though its more prevalent usage, especially since the Ptolemaic era, is as a designation of a concrete possession of the king:[5] "king's house, royal residence, palace,"[6] "royal throne,"[7] "king's crown, diadem,"[8] "royal city, capital,"[9] "royal treasury."[10]

In the *Septuagint* βασίλειος, -ον appears twenty-nine times. *H-R*

---

[1] Cerfaux, *op. cit.*, p. 13.

[2] *L-S-J s.v.*: F. Passow, *Handwörterbuch der Griechischen Sprache*, 5. Aufl., Leipzig, 1831, I, *s.v.*

[3] Selwyn, *op. cit.*, pp. 165f. Cf. the example offered by Schwyzer, *op. cit.*, II, 177: "Αρεως πάγος, βασιλέως στοά for "Αρειος πάγος, στοὰ βασίλειος.

[4] CIG 1.5127 b 2: Ptolemy III calls certain regions near his kingdom τὰ ἔγγιστα τοῦ βασιλείου μου.

[5] Schwyzer, *op. cit.*, I, 470: "-ιον, -εῖον bezeichnen besonders Kollektivität, Werkzeug, Ort . . ."; so also Mayser, *op. cit.*, I, 3, pp. 12ff., who lists the following examples: σιτοποιεῖον, "cornmill"; γραμματεῖον, "writing instrument"; ἱερεῖον, "animal for sacrifice"; βασίλειον, "king's crown."

[6] Xenophon, *Cyr.* 2. 43. Cf. *L-S-J* s.v., Passow, *op. cit.*, s.v. who also includes "royal tent." *L-S-J* notes that this meaning is more common in the plural, cf. Herodotus 1. 30, 178.

[7] Cf. Mayser, *loc. cit.*, p. 14.

[8] Rosetta Stone 45 (196a); cf. Mayser, *ibid.*, and II, 1, p. 3.

[9] Polybius 3.15.3; Diodorus Siculus 19.18; Strato I.2.25.

[10] Herodotus 2.149.

list twenty-three occurrences as substantive and six as adjective (among which they include the two verses, Ex. 19:6 and 23:22). It is doubtful, however, that this classification is final.

As *substantive* it translates eight various Hebrew constructions for four main categories:[1]

(1) "kingdom" - more static, referring to the object ruled[2]

(2) "rule, reign, leadership, supremacy" - more active in connotation[3]

(3) "palace"[4]

(4) "crown, diadem."[5]

Significant is its use as "kingdom." Though βασιλεία is the usual LXX rendering of the Hebrew מַמְלָכָה (approx. eighty-five occurrences), βασίλειον (sing. and pl.) was employed on three occasions (seen aside from Ex. 19:6, 23:22): 3 Km. 5:1, 14:8, 4 Km. 15:19.[6]

According to *H-R*, βασίλειος, -ον occurs as *adjective*, aside from Ex. 19:6, 23:22, four times: Dt. 3:10 (Vaticanus), Sap. 18:15, 3 Mcc. 3:28 (Alexandrinus), 4 Mcc. 3:8. The text of Dt. 3:10 (Vaticanus) is most likely the product of a scribal error, however.[7] The reading of 3 Mcc. 3:28 (Alexandrinus), furthermore, is to be rejected in favor of the better attested βασιλικοῦ. According to the best witnesses, βασίλειον probably occurred originally only twice as

---

[1] These categories are only general. Uncertainty in precise meaning, especially in the first two groups, makes exact categorization impossible.

[2] Translating מַמְלָכָה: 3 Km. 5:1 (Alex.) (=MT 1 Kg 5:1): τοῖς βασιλείοις (3 Km. 2:46b [Vat.]: ταῖς βασιλείαις); 3 Km. 14:8; 4 Km. 15:19 (Alex.): τὸ βασίλειον (Lucian: τὴν βασιλείαν). Translating וּמַלְכוּתָא: Dan: 7:22: τὸ βασίλειον. Cf. also Sap. 5:14. Perhaps Sap. 1:14 and 2 Mcc. 2:17 are to be included here, though they might also fit under the next designation, "rule, reign." When meaning "kingdom," βασίλειον occurs in both sing. and pl.

[3] E.g. 3 Km. 14:8 (Alex.); 1 Chr. 28:4; 1 Esd. 4:40, 43 (possibly "throne"?); Sap. 1:14 (cf. above note). Occurrence only in the singular.

[4] Esth. 1:9, 2:13; Pr. 18:19; Nah. 2:7; Ep. Jer. 58; Dan. 5:1, 6:9; Sap. 5:16. Except for Pr. 18:19 occurrence only in plural.

[5] 2 Km. 1:10; 2 Chr. 23:11. Occurrence only in the singular.

[6] In two further passages, Ps. Sol. 17:4, 6, βασίλειον is used interchangeably with βασιλεία. Both verses are involved in an allusion to 2 Km. 7:12 ff. where τὴν βασιλείαν was originally used for the MT אֶת־מַמְלַכְתּוֹ. This would seem to suggest along with the passage just mentioned that a sharp differentiation between terms was not consistently made.

[7] Dt. 3:10 (MT) reads עָרֵי מַמְלֶכֶת עוֹג as do the other Greek MSS: πόλεις βασιλείας τοῦ Ωγ "the cities of the kingdom of Og." Though the Vaticanus has βασιλείαι, the more original form thus appears to be βασιλείας, the gen. sing. of ἡ βασιλεία. Either a scribe miswrote ι instead of ς, or he was purposely altering the form from a feminine genitive singular to a feminine nominative plural.

adjective and twenty-four times as substantive,[1] Ex. 19:6 and 23:22 excluded.

Factors supporting the *adjectival* function of βασίλειον in Ex. 19:6 would include several points. First, according to normal syntax there is nothing suggesting that the term is anything but an ordinary adjective modifying "body of priests." The word order βασίλειον ἱεράτευμα καὶ ἔθνος ἅγιον would be the product of customary chiastic structure: adjective - noun / noun - adjective. Secondly, there is an absence of parallel examples of the co-substantival occurrence of βασίλειον in both the LXX and profane Greek literature. Third, in this period of history the alliance of certain groups such as the artists' guild of Dionysos with a Hellenistic ruler and their identification with his cult was not an uncommon thing. Such alliances might suggest the analogy of the thought of Ex. 19:6: "a priesthood in the service of the king."[2] βασίλειον would then be expressing a consecration to the "Roi par excellence, Souverain, Roi des rois."[3] This subjection to the King *par excellence* would also imply the royal honor and distinction transferred to the participants in such an alliance: "a body of priests adorned with honor."[4]

The factors favoring the *substantival* function of βασίλειον present a solid counter-position. First, the word order of Ex. 19:6 is in all points identical to that of the MT. Against the supposition of a chiastic arrangement necessitated by those presuming βασίλειον to be an adjective, it can be argued that the LXX has remained faithful to the original text whose nominal form "kingdom" would suggest a nominal function of βασίλειον.

Secondly, the proportion of its occurrences in the LXX as substantive in comparison with those as adjective (24 substantives - 2 adjectives!) argues very strongly for its substantival function here also. The point that instances of its co-substantival occurrence are lacking carries little weight, for this is a use determined by occasion

---

[1] In two of these cases, 2 Km. 5:1 (2:46b) and 4 Km. 15:19, βασίλειον is opposed by variant readings. In the former, at least, the reading of the Alexandrinus is more faithful to the MT; cp. 2 Km. 2:46b and 46k. With certainty we can speak of twenty-two original substantival occurrences. If the two verses from Ps. Sol. are to be added, then the total number, aside from Ex. 19:6, 23:22 and the two texts just mentioned, amounts to twenty-four again.

[2] So Cerfaux, *op. cit.*, pp. 13ff.; Blinzler, *op. cit.* p. 59.

[3] Cerfaux, *ibid.*, p. 14.

[4] So *Str-B* III, 789; K. L. Schmidt, *TWNT* I, 593; Blinzler, *ibid.*, who lists this implication of "Ehre" and "Würde" as a possibility.

and intent rather than by semantic or syntactical rule. On the other hand, the almost exclusive use of βασίλειον as substantive in the LXX would suggest a regularity of practice affecting also Ex. 19:6 and 23:22, unless there were conclusive evidence semantically or syntactically to the contrary.

Finally, the constancy of the Versions as well as the entire chain of allusions to Ex. 19:6 in treating the first member of this verse as noun cannot be overlooked. Aside from Jub. 33:20 where the EF underwent radical alteration in which both first and second members became adjectives,[1] all other Versions of Ex. 19:6 and all references to the EF present the first member as a *noun*. If βασίλειον were intended here as adjective, the LXX would be the one exception among all the Versions. Compelling grounds for such an exception, however, are not present. Furthermore, other documents also identified with the Alexandrian locale, the festal letter of 2 Mcc. and two writings of Philo, also regarded βασίλειον as substantive and took steps to insure this reading.[2]

In summa, the weight of evidence appears to favor the latter alternative, whereby βασίλειον in Ex. 19:6 and 23:22 would best be taken as meaning either "*kingdom*" in the sense of the people under the rule of God the King (as intended in the MT) or "*royal residence*" in the sense of the people in whom God has made His dwelling-place (as stated in Philo, *De Sobr.* 66).[3]

Finally, what can be said about the nuance and novelty of the LXX rendering? Israel is presented as a kingdom (or royal residence) and priestly community charged with a priestly task. In this choice of words her historical situation played no mean role. This community of Israel in Alexandria was not the resident of the Promised Land flowing with milk and honey but a people *in diaspora*. Here in Egypt she again took on the role of Abraham, the pilgrim and sojourner. Furthermore, in this era of post-exilic Judaism a trend toward absolutism characterized Israel as a religious community.

---

[1] Cf. *infra*, pp. 80ff.

[2] Gk. Frag. 67, likewise reflective of the LXX wording, also treats the first member of Ex. 19:6 as a noun; cf. *infra*, pp. 85–90.

[3] A recent study by S. Aalen, "'Reign' and 'House' in the Kingdom of God in the Gospels," *NTS* 8 (1962), 215-40, treats the meaning of the cognate βασιλεία and points out a trend beginning in pre-Christian Judaism in which βασιλεία designates less the sense "kingly reign" and more the *local* aspect, "reign, community, house of God." Might βασίλειον have participated in this same trend?

She was on her way to becoming a society defined by the precepts of the Law.[1] The Torah was developing into the sole norm for Israel's ethic and her single fountain of life. The concept of covenant was evaporating in the fire of legal observance. With the priesthood restricted to the house of Aaron, the thought of a non-Levite performing priestly functions could be only a reminiscence or a hope.

Not so the priestly service of Israel *in toto*, however. As the holy People of God, Israel was thought to have a priestly obligation toward her environment; namely that of remaining holy and faithful to the one true God. Her constant task was the maintenance of her sanctity and exclusiveness in contrast to the holy cults and holy regimes of a holiness-intoxicated yet pagan environment.

For this *milieu* the phrasing βασίλειον ἱεράτευμα καὶ ἔθνος ἅγιον was chosen. In relation to the MT, the basic expressions of God's kingship, Israel's priestliness, and the emphasis upon holiness remains. However, a new formulation brought with it a new nuance and a new direction of vision. Whereas in the MT the first two terms were syntactically dependent through the *status constructus* of מַמְלֶכֶת, in the LXX two independent terms were given which were then joined to a third comma, "holy nation." The original *parallelismus membrorum* was relinquished, so that the first comma is no longer strictly qualified in meaning by the second. Further, whereas in the MT the corporative element of the first comma was expressed in the term מַמְלֶכֶת, in the LXX both terms convey this collective aspect. In ἱεράτευμα was offered a term which incorporated not only the personal element "of priests," but also the functional and corporative aspect. Not ἱερατεία or ἱερωσύνη, the customary nouns for "priesthood," but rather ἱεράτευμα was chosen: a "body of active priests." Here is revealed an arbitrariness and a creativity born of a particular spirit and intention.[2]

If Cerfaux's suggestion is to be accepted, and there are no compelling reasons to the contrary, then this intention involved for Israel a sense of witness and mission to her environment, a priestly charge implied in her election and executed in the maintenance of

[1] Cf. M. Noth, *Die Gesetze im Pentateuch, Schriften der Königsberger Gelehrten Gesellschaft*. Geisteswissenschaftliche Klasse. 17. Jahrg. (1940), Heft 2, Halle (Saale), pp. 49-86 [reprinted in *Gesammelte Studien zum Alten Testament* (*Theologische Bücherei* 6), 2. Aufl., München, 1960, pp. 81-136].

[2] Cf. R. Hanhart, "Fragen um die Entstehung der LXX," *VT* 12 (April 1962), 139-63, who stresses that this creativity was born in the confrontation between Greek-speaking Jewry and the revelation of the God of Israel.

her sanctity. According to the formulation of the text, this was to be a witness of Diaspora Israel as total community and a testimony ultimately to the fact that she was the kingdom of the King or the royal residence in which He alone dwelled. In contrast to the MT, not only is there introduced the possibility of Israel's being viewed as the residence of God, but here a concern is shown for the *positive* relationship of Israel to her environment. Election and possession by God is presented not simply as a selection by and an orientation to God, but also as involving a priestly service to mankind. Insofar, this thought is not unrelated to the eschatological hope of Deutero-Isaiah.

If LXX Ex. 23:22 is not to be viewed simply as an erroneous duplication of 19:5-6, then this interesting recurrence of the EF shows that it had become a special concern of the translators.[1] Furthermore, it supplies the first example for the separation of this text from its context and its treatment as an independent element.

As following observations will show, in regard to textual form, terminology, and theological intent, LXX Ex. 19:6 is a passage which proves determinative for subsequent references to the Exodus Formula.

We *summarize*. The LXX text of Ex. 19:6, though maintaining the word order and basic sense of the original MT, has been seen to offer a version adapted to its particular *milieu*. A comparison of ἱεράτευμα with other related substantives has shown that ἱεράτευμα incorporates the three aspects of activity, person-relatedness, and collectivity. This three-fold character must be visible in a translation of this term if its meaning is to be properly represented. Thus the rendering has been proposed: "body of (functioning) priests." The origin of this term is late and, until evidence can be produced to the contrary, may be regarded as a creation of the authors of the LXX. βασίλειον, according to general LXX usage, the faithfulness of the LXX to the word order of the original MT, and the consistent treatment of the first member of the EF as a substantive among the Versions, is best taken as substantive rather than adjective. Thus it might be rendered either "kingdom" or "royal residence." The intention behind this LXX formulation seems to have been a missionary consciousness and the concern for witness to the *Umwelt*. With these words Diaspora Israel is presented as a priestly corporation charged with

---

[1] So Blinzler, *op. cit.*, p. 59.

the task of the maintenance of holiness; not mediation of man to God but witness to Him Whose Kingdom or Whose dwelling place they are, Whose holy will they mediate to the world. Subsequent occurrences of ἱεράτευμα in writings falling within the period spanning the LXX and the NT suggest that this version of Ex. 19:6 might have had a determinative influence upon later allusions to the Exodus Formula.

C. The Targumic Versions of Ex. 19:6

Further versions of the Pentateuch, the Aramaic *Targumim*, display similarity with the rendition of the LXX. In all cases the original מַמְלֶכֶת כֹּהֲנִים has been rendered through two substantives: "kings (and) priests and a holy nation."

The official Targum to the Pentateuch, Targum Onkelos,[1] reads:[2] ואתון תהון קדמי מלכין כהנין ועם קדיש.[3]

Targum Jerushalmi I, otherwise known as T. Pseudo-Jonathan,[4] has embellished the Exodus text with the midrashic comment: "And you shall be before me kings wearing the crown and officiating priests and a holy nation" (מלכין קטרי כלילא וכהנין משמשיי).

Targum Jerushalmi II, or the Palestinean Targum, reads similar to T. Onkelos: ואתון תהוון לשמי מלכין וכהנין ואומה קדישה.[5]

In addition to these three *Targumim*, a recent discovery has

---

[1] According to tradition this was the translation of the proselyte Onkelos in the first half of the second Christian century; cf. b. Megilla 3a. In reality, "Onkelos" = the Babylonian version of "Aquila," the proselyte disciple of Rabbi Akiba. Bentzen, *op. cit.*, I, 69, notes that T. Onkelos "rests on a long tradition of translation, dating back to pre-Christian times." For a closer discussion of date and place of composition cf. Paul Kahle, *The Cairo Geniza*, 2nd ed., Oxford, 1959, pp. 191ff., who suggests Babylonia in the 2nd cent. A. D. Cf. also Kahle, "Das palästinische Pentateuchtargum und das zur Zeit Jesu gesprochene Aramäisch" *ZNW* 49 (1958), 100-16. *Contra* Kahle, cf. E. Y. Kutscher, "The Language of the Genesis Apocryphon: A Preliminary Study," *Scripta Hierosolymitana* 4 (1958), 1–33, esp. 9ff.

[2] According to A. Sperber's edition, *The Bible in Aramaic*, Vol. I. *The Pentateuch according to Targum Onkelos*, Leiden, 1959.

[3] MS. No. 282 of the Sassoon Library, London, reads ממלכין in place of מלכין.

[4] A less accurate translation than T. Onkelos, T. Jerushalmi I contains much midrashic material, some of which, however, dates from at least "the beginning of the second pre-Christian century" (Kahle, *Cairo Geniza*, p. 203).

[5] MS. Heb. e 43 fol. 61a of the Bodleian Library, Oxford; cf. Catalogue 2610, No. 16. The MS. containing this portion of Exodus (19:1-20:23) was published by P. Kahle in *Massoreten des Westens*, Stuttgart, 1930, II, 49-60; cf. in particular p. 56.

produced an Aramaic version of exceptional importance, Codex Neofiti I.[1] In this document we possess a "totius Pentateuchi Targum hierosolymitanum seu palestinense" considered to be the "antiquissima versionis aramaicae Pentateuchi redactio."[2] Folio 150 recto, lines 2-3, containing Ex. 19:6, read: ואתם תהיו לי ואתון תהוון לשמי מלכין וכהנין ואומה קדישה.

Thus this earliest Targum in existence provides definite proof for the reading "kings and priests" already before the birth of Christ and together with T. Onkelos and T. Jer. I points to a firm and ancient Jewish tradition of translation.[3]

In addition, the following observations might be made: (1) all four *Targumim* read "priests" similar to the MT, dissimilar to the LXX "body of priests." (2) All four read "kings," varying from the MT and the LXX which contain the collective "kingdom" or possibly "royal house" (LXX). (3) The *st. abs.* "kings" resembles the LXX's alteration from *st. const.* to *st. abs.* (4) The earliest of the four, Cod. Neofiti I, contains a conjunctive *waw*, reading as do T. Jer. I and II, "kings *and* priests." (5) The original MT וגוי has been replaced with ועם or its Aramaic equivalent ואומה.[4]

The variations are not difficult to explain. The personal "kings" was substituted for the collective "kingdom" and thereby accommodated to the personal "priests." The added *waw* conjunctive paralleled the second *waw*, "*and* holy nation," and afforded a more fluent verse. T. Onkelos shows that the *waw*, however, was not a constant feature. The trend reflected in the Deuteronomic composition where עם was substituted for גוי probably accounts for similar substitution among the *Targumim*.

---

[1] For the first publication discussing discovery and significance of Codex Neofiti 1 cf. A. Diez Macho, *Estudios Biblicos* XVI, Madrid (1956), 446f. Cf. further, P. Boccaccio, *Biblica* 38 (1956), 237-39; P. Winter, "Eine vollständige Handschrift des Paläst. Targums aufgefunden" *ZNW* 48 (1957), p. 192; Kahle, "Palästin. Pentateuchtargum"; *Cairo Geniza*, pp. 201ff.

Until this find, the existence of other *Targumim* to the Pentateuch (*Targumim* Jer. II and III) was known only in fragmentary form; cf. Kahle, *Masso-reten des Westens*, II, pp. 1-65; *Schweich Lectures*, 1941, pp. 120ff.; *Cairo Geniza*, pp. 202f. I am most grateful to Dr. Wolfgang Gerber of the *Institutum Judaicum Delitzschianum* in Münster/Westfalen for making available to me his microfilm copy of Codex Neofiti I.

[2] Boccaccio, *op. cit.*, p. 237. Regarding its antiquity cf. further A. Diez Macho, "The recently discovered Palestinian Targum: Its Antiquity and Relationship with the other Targums," *Congress Volume Oxford 1959* (*Supplements to Vetus Testamentum*, VII), Leiden, 1960, pp. 222–45.

[3] Cf. Charles, *AP*, II, 38.

[4] Cp. the Samaritan Pentateuch whose text is identical to that of the MT.

The alteration from "kingdom" to "kings" is noteworthy in that whereas in the MT and LXX "kingdom" implied the kingship of *God*, the *Targumim* transfer this kingship from God to *Israel*. Rather than being the domain of God the King, Israelites themselves are called "kings." Whether this change is to be traced beyond stylistic accomodation to underlying theological motives is difficult to determine. Was a tripartite division of the folk implied, i.e. a folk composed of kings, priests, and a remaining holy nation? The parallelism of the MT has been destroyed and hence "holy nation" is no longer an equivalent of "kings" or "priests." T. Jer. I seems to suggest such a division. There is only a single crown to be worn by the kings and the priests are described as "officiating priests." This would imply that at least the author of the latter Targum attempted to coordinate this text with the situation subsequent to the Establishment as more in keeping with his present situation. It is uncertain, however, if this can be said for the other *Targumim*.

From the various Versions of Ex. 19:6[1] we turn to *citations* of or *allusions* to this passage in the late Judaic and early Christian era.

D. Jubilees 16:18, 33:20

This book known also as the *Little Genesis* composes a haggadic-halachic midrash on Genesis 1 through Exodus 12[2] and contains two

---

[1] Among the other Old Testament Versions we note the following renditions of Ex. 19:6. According to F. Field's edition of the Hexapla, *Origenis Hexaplorum* I, *ad loc.* and A. E. Brooke—N. McLean's edition, *The Old Testament in Greek: According to the text of the Codex Vaticanus Supplemented from other Uncial MSS*, Cambridge, 1909, I, Part II, *ad loc.*, the three Greek translations of Aquila, Symmachus and Theodotion read as follows:

Aquila: "kingdom of priests" (βασιλεία ἱερέων)
Symmachus and Theodotion: "kingdom, priests" (βασιλεί[α] ἱερεῖς).
However, cf. G, Schrenk, *TWNT* III, 249: βασιλέι[α] ἱερῶν

Further:
Syrohexapla: "kingdom, priests"
Peshitta: "kingdom and priests"
Sahidic and Armenian: "kingdom and priesthood"
Bohairic: "holy kingdom"
Old Latin: "most holy kingdom" (*regnum sacratissimum*)
Vulgate: "priestly kingdom" (*regnum sacerdotale*).

[2] The majority of scholars locate its date about the turn of the first century B. C. Cf. Charles, *AP* II, pp. 1, 6; Eissfeldt, *op. cit.*, p. 751, who rejects the conjectures of Zeitlin (5th Cent. B. C., cf. *JQR* 30 (1939), pp. 1-31), and Albright ("early third cent., possibly even to the late fourth cent.," *From the Stone Age to Christianity*, 2nd ed., New York, 1957, p. 347); Bentzen, *op. cit.*,

allusions to Ex. 19:6. The first of these occurs in ch. 16, verse 18:

> For he should become the portion of the Most High and all his seed had fallen into the possession of God, that it should be unto the Lord a people for (His) possession above all nations and that it should become a kingdom and priests and a holy nation.[1]

The *context* of this verse treats the appearance of the angels to Abraham at Hebron and the renewed promise of a son (16:1-4). Verses 5-9 recount the destruction of Sodom, Gomorrah, and Zeboim and Lot's deliverance. Verses 10-19 discuss Abraham's stay at Beersheba and the birth and circumcision of Isaac whose seed was to be the portion of God. Angels relate the events and decrees pertaining to Abraham, "that he should not die until he should beget six sons more, and should see (them) before he died (vv. 15f.), and (that) all the seed of his sons should be Gentiles and be reckoned with the Gentiles; but from the sons of Isaac one should become a holy seed and should not be reckoned among the Gentiles" (v. 17). Thereupon follows v. 18 supporting this thought concerning holiness and selection from among the Gentiles with the statement from Ex. 19:6.

The Ethiopic text of the allusion to Ex. 19:6 varies from both the MT and the Latin version (*regnum sacerdotale*). Nevertheless, as R. H. Charles has shown, it may be regarded as representing the original Hebrew composition of Jubilees.[2]

II, 237; Sellin-Rost, *op. cit.*, p. 184; L. Rost, *RGG* III, 960f.; F. C. Grant, *Ancient Judaism and the New Testament*, New York, 1959, p. 86.

[1] Translation according to R. H. Charles, *The Book of Jubilees or the Little Genesis*, Translated from the Editor's Ethiopic Text, London, 1902, pp. 115f.; cf. also Charles, *AP* II, 38. The only complete extant text is an Ethiopic version (cf. Charles, *The Ethiopic Version of the Hebrew Book of Jubilees*, Oxford, 1895). A third of the text exists in a Latin translation which together with the Ethiopic rests upon a Greek translation of the Hebrew original. Fragments of a Hebrew text have been discovered at Qumran Cave I.

[2] Behind the Ethiopic "a kingdom and priests" Charles, *Jubilees*, p. 116, note to 16:18, sees βασιλεία καὶ ἱερεῖς. This exact wording is also found in Apoc. 5:10 (cf. 1:6) and the Syriac version. In these texts, together with the T. Onkelos and T. Jerushalmi I, he finds "an ancient Jewish way of treating this phrase." He concludes "that the Ethiopic text represents the Hebrew original and that the Latin 'regnum sacerdotale' is borrowed by the Latin translator of Jubilees from the Vulgate." Though the Ethiopic varies from the MT, Charles' proposal that the Latin offers a superior and more faithful rendition is unacceptable. Whereas in the Latin version of Jub. and in the Vulgate "kingdom" is emphasized and "priests" reduced to the adjective "priestly," in the MT not מַמְלָכָה but rather כֹּהֲנִים receives the stress.

Concerning the mode of allusion to and significance given the Ex. passage we might make the following observations:

(1) The actual reference to the Exodus pericope involves the words "that it should be unto the Lord a people for (His) possession above all nations and that it should become a kingdom and priests and a holy nation" (Ex. 19:5b, 6a; 5c: "for all the earth is mine" is omitted).

(2) The two verses preceding this reference, vv. 16f., relate to Gen. 17:19 (=v. 16), 17:20 (=16:17a), 17:21 (=16:17b), 21:12 (=16:16), and 21:13 (=16:17a). The combination of allusions involves various promises of the Abraham-Isaac-Jacob covenant interpreted in midrashic fashion. To this cento of passages the verses from Ex. 19:5b and 6a were added and applied specifically to the lineage of Abraham as promises of the Abrahamic covenant.

(3) Thus, though a covenant is under discussion, it is not the covenant of Sinai as in Ex. 19:3ff. but the bond made with Abraham.[1]

(4) Those to whom these predicates are ascribed compose Israel *in toto*; specifically, the descendents of Jacob.[2]

(5) The purpose of this citation appears to be the expression of Israel's elected and selected character.[3] Kingdom, priests, and holy nation play no role as individual epithets. Rather it is the ancient proclamation of Israel's election and holiness incorporated in the covenant pericope of Ex. 19:5f. which relates this passage to this particular context.

Finally, concerning the textual tradition of Ex. 19:6, the variations from the MT ("kingdom" = *st. abs.*, addition of a copula "kingdom *and* priests") resemble those of both the LXX and/or the *Targumim*. Thus this text provides additional evidence for the early treatment of "kingdom" and "priests" as two separate nouns.

The second reference to the Ex. passages appears in ch. 33:20:

> And there is no greater sin than the fornication which they commit on earth; for Israel is a holy nation unto the Lord its God, and a nation of inheritance and a priestly and royal

---

[1] Cf. Gen. 21:13, 18; cp. 12:2f., 15:1ff., 17:3ff., 18:18, 22:17f., 26:3f., 28:13f., 32:12, 35:11, 46:3.

[2] Cf. Gen. 28:3f., 13; 17:19ff.

[3] Cf. Jub. 19:18: "For I know that the Lord will choose him (Jacob) to be a people for possession unto Himself, above all peoples that are upon the face of the earth" (Charles, *Jubilees*, p. 127).

nation for (His own) possession; and there shall no such uncleanness appear in the midst of the holy nation.[1]

This verse offers an interesting variation of the Exodus Formula and introduces it in a new context, that of legal purity.

The immediate *context* treats the question of sexual impurity and incest. Ch. 33:1-9 discuss Reuben's illegitimate relationship with his father's concubine, Bilhah.[2] Verses 10-20 concern the laws pertaining to incest. Verse 10 mentions the "heavenly tablets" forbidding incest as the commission of an uncleanness. Verse 11 continues: "And there shall be nothing unclean before our God in the nation which He has chosen for Himself as a possession." Verses 13ff. relate God's command to Moses that he should write down this law for all Israel . . . "and tell them these words of the covenant" (v. 19). Thereupon follows v. 20, an allusion to the EF as substantiation for the fact that Israel is a *holy* nation. Verses 21ff. commence a new section.

The *text form* deviates radically from all other renditions of the EF considered thus far. In v. 20 the order of Ex. 19:5-6 has been inverted: "for (His own) possession" (=Ex. 19:5b) follows "a priestly and royal nation" (=19:6a). The intervening words of Ex. 19:5bc "among all peoples, for the earth is mine" have been omitted. Most important, the nouns for "kingdom" and "priests" have been converted and reduced to adjectives. In addition, their order of appearance has been inverted: "priestly and royal" in contrast to מַמְלֶכֶת כֹּהֲנִים. "Nation" appears as the primary noun and holiness as its primary characteristic. Together with "holy," "royal" and "priestly" modify nation in this sense.

Further, we note that (1) as in 16:18 the EF has been combined with other OT allusions. The preceding clause of Jub. 33:20ab reflects Lev. 20:24, 26. The emphasis upon holiness made here in Jubilees betrays affinity with the Levitical Holiness Code, Lev. 17-26.

(2) The introduction, "*For* Israel is a . . . priestly and royal nation . . ." indicates that the author is citing this text for substantiation and support, just as in 16:18. This introductory "for" is

[1] Charles, *Jubilees*, p. 199. In his note on 33:20 he offers the Greek and Latin texts: λαὸς ἱερατικὸς καὶ βασιλικὸς καὶ περιούσιος (or οὐσίας); *populus sacerdotalis et regalis et +sanctificationis+* (++ corrupt). "Royal nation" (MS a) = literally, "nation of a kingdom"; cp. Mss c d.

[2] The midrash is expanding upon Gen. 35:22.

absent in the original Exodus text but occurs later in covenantal formulae given in Dt. 7:6 and 14:2. Thus the *promise* which the EF presents is recalled by later generations as a *factual description* of Israel's nature.

(3) Mention of the "covenant" in v. 19 suggests that the author was not unconcerned for the original covenant context of the EF or unaware of the original wording, even though his own alterations might give that impression.

(4) The purpose of allusion to the EF was to underline and substantiate the holy character of Israel, the primary thought of this section. Though intimation is made of Israel's election in the thought of her belonging to God, it is not primarily the correlation between election and holiness which accounts for the emphasis upon holiness (as in Ex. 19:5f.) but the thought of uncleanness and legal impurity: "for Israel is a holy nation . . . there shall no such uncleanness appear in the midst of the holy nation." The entire context betrays affinity with the Levitical Holiness Code, Lev. 17-26.[1]

(5) The EF, as in 16:18, has been applied to Israel *in toto*.

(6) As in 16:18, the terms "priestly and royal nation" are of no individual significance. Rather, this phrase serves as a parallel to "nation of inheritance" and "holy nation," serving exclusively the theme of purity.

The EF has been paraphrased here in a manner unique among all the references which we shall meet. Because of the liberty which the author has taken with his reformulation of the original text, it is difficult to determine with certainty the textual tradition which he was following. His separation of the two adjectives "priestly" and "royal" and his inclusion of the conjunction suggest, nevertheless, the same tradition as that followed in 16:18.

The factors observed in both Jub. 16:18 and 33:20 would strongly urge a reconsideration of the conclusions of both Cerfaux and Blinzler.

Cerfaux, noting the apocalyptic character of Jubilees and its "idealization" of history, Law, and cult, would account for reference to the EF against this background.[2] He sees citation of the EF

[1] Cf. the particular laws regarding incest: ch. 18, 20:11; also Dt. 22:30, 27:20. Cf. the general exhortation to holiness: Lev. 19:1f., 20:22ff.; also Dt. 26:16-19, 28:9.

[2] Cerfaux, *op. cit.*, pp. 20f.

motivated by an idealization of worship and the worshipping community. According to Cerfaux, Jubilees develops a picture of a celestial cult and a celestial priesthood through which Israel enjoys communion with God and the angels. In this perspective, he maintains, the priesthood was extended to all Israelites.[1]

Such an explanation, however, fails to comprehend the particular use of the EF in the two passages discussed. Neither in Jub. 16:18 nor in 33:20 is there any immediate concern for the celestial cult. Jub. 16:18 refers not to a celestial priesthood of Israel but to the elected and selected character of the sons of Jacob. Israel is not called a kingdom, priests, and a holy nation in view of a future heavenly communion with the angelic hosts but on the basis of her election. Likewise in 33:20 the point of contact is not an idealized portrayal of Israel's priestly or royal character but the legal demand of holiness. As a royal, priestly, and holy nation belonging to God, Israel is to have no part in fornication and uncleanness.[2]

Cerfaux has interpreted these verses only according to the general context of the entire book without taking sufficient note of the immediate context, the combinations of various passages in which the EF was involved, and the specific import or thrust of each particular pericope. In point of fact, the EF has not been alluded to in order to develop a conception of a "celestial priesthood" but to support the themes of election and holiness.[3] Nor is there any evidence for Cerfaux's proposal[4] that here in Jub. 16:18 and 33:20 the element of priesthood rather than that of kingdom or royalty received primary stress.

Blinzler sees this reference to the EP in connection with the Law and the hope of Israel's future position of domination among the nations: "Priester sind sie durch den Besitz und die Befolgung des Gesetzes, Könige dagegen nur *in spe*, durch die Aussicht auf eine künftige Herrscherstellung unter den Völkern."[5] Though the centrality of the Law in the conception of Jubilees is certainly fundamental, again it must be asked if such an explanation does not fail to reflect the specific content of each of these specific contexts. Though in 33:20 the EF is cited in a context dealing with

---

[1] *Ibid.*
[2] Sim. Sevenster, *op. cit.*, pp. 404f.
[3] Sevenster, *ibid.*, also calls into question Cerfaux's explanation.
[4] *Ibid.*
[5] *Op. cit.*, p. 59.

the legal purity, the point which the EF underlines is not a concept of priestliness but the element of holiness. True, the expression of Ex. 19:5f. has been conformed to a conception of the Law. However, it is not an image of Israel's priestliness which has been revised but rather one of her holiness, a holiness no longer correlative primarily to her election but to her ethical purity.

Where is the evidence for Blinzler's statement that "kingdom" or "royal" pertain to Israel's future position of domination? This certainly was *not* the point being made.

As a matter of fact, it is clear that in both 16:18 and 33:20 the individual terms "kingdom" ("royal") and "priests" ("priestly") receive *no emphasis as individual terms*. In both instances these terms could be omitted with absolutely no loss to the sense of each respective verse. This indicates that no weight was given these terms *in se*. It was not an image of priesthood or royalty that was developed here; rather, the point concerned Israel's election, her separation and exclusiveness, and her holiness—thoughts expressed in other sections as well.[1]

We *summarize*. Jub. 16:18 introduces Ex. 19:5-6, merged with other OT passages describing the Abraham-Isaac-Jacob covenantal promises, as support for the thought of Israel's divine election, exclusiveness, and holiness. A connection was apparently made between the promises of the Sinaitic covenant and those of the Abrahamic pact. The epithets of the EF are applied to Israel *in toto*. The textual formulation with its independent nouns "kingdom" and "priests" and its copula shows affinity to the LXX, Targumim, and other Versions. Jub. 33:20 offers a severely altered version of the EF. Occurring again in a covenant (Mosaic) context, the paraphrase, merged with other OT allusions, served to provide the divine basis for the imperative of legal purity and the forbiddance of fornication. Again the epithets from the EF are ascribed to Israel in her entirety. The alteration of the nouns to adjectives ("priestly and royal") and their inversion as well as the inversion of vv. 5 and 6 present a treatment unique in the entire chain of allusions to the EF. The significance of the EF within each passage is determined by its immediate context rather than by the general scope of the entire book. No emphasis has been put upon the terms "kingdom" ("royal") or "priests" ("priestly") *in se*; no concept of Israel's

[1] Cf. esp. Jub. 2:19-21, 19:31.

priesthood or her royalty has been developed here. Rather, the Exodus Formula as a whole has been adduced as evidence of God's covenant with and His promises to Israel and thereby has been intended to support the themes of Israel's exclusiveness, holiness, and possession by God.

E. A Greek Fragment relating to Test. Levi 11:4-6

αὐτὸς καὶ τὸ σπέρμα αὐτοῦ ἔσονται ἀρχὴ βασιλέων ἱεράτευμα τῷ Ἰσραήλ[1]

This passage is surrounded by a host of uncertainties which include not only the dating of the Testaments of the Twelve Patriarchs and their relation to late Judaic, early Christian literature in general,[2] but also the dating of this Greek Fragment in particular and its proposed dependence upon a Hebrew source serving as the

[1] Text according to the edition of R. H. Charles, *The Greek Versions of the Testaments of the Twelve Patriarchs*, Edited from nine MSS together with the Variants of the Armenian and Slavonic Versions and some Hebrew Fragments, Oxford, 1908, Appendix III, p. 253.

[2] There is no common agreement regarding the date of origin of the Test. 12 Patr. Determination of date is made difficult by the fact that the Testaments in their present form show numerous traces of Christian formulation and interpolation. Opinion varies between those who take the Testaments as originally Jewish documents later abundantly interpolated by Christian redactors and those who see them as the direct product of (a) Christian author(s) making use of pre-Christian sources. While the latter view is not without avid supporters (cf. the analysis of M. de Jonge in his Leiden dissertation, *The Testaments of the Twelve Patriarchs*, Assen, 1953; also J. T. Milik, *RB* 62 (1955), 297f., 398-406 and *Ten Years of Discovery in the Wilderness of Judea* (SBT 26), London, 1959, pp. 34f.; J. Danielou, *Theologie*, pp. 17ff. and *The Dead Sea Scrolls and Primitive Christianity*, Baltimore, 1958, pp. 114-118), the majority of scholars favor the former view suggesting a date ca. B. C. 100: Charles, *Testaments*, pp. ix, xlii f., *AP* I, 282; Bentzen, *op. cit.*, II, 249; Grant, *op. cit.*, p. 86; Eissfeldt, *op. cit.*, 785f. place both Jubilees and the Test. 12 Patr. in the area of the Qumran literature; Sellin-Rost figure with Christian additions but favor a dating after A. D. 70. *Contra* de Jonge cf. F.-M. Braun, *RB* 67 (1960), 516-49 who with A. S. van der Woude, *Die Messianische Vorstellung der Gemeinde von Qumran*, Assen, 1957, also assigns the Testaments to the world of Qumran; cf. also A. Dupont-Sommer, *Les écrits esséniens découverts près de la Mer Morte*, Paris, 1959, p. 318, and M. Philonenko, *Les interpolations chrétiennes des Testaments des Douze Patriarches et les Manuscrits de Qumrân* (*Cahiers de la Revue d'Histoire et de Philosophie Religieuses* no. 35) Paris, 1960. For de Jonge's critique of van der Woude and Philonenko cf. "Christian Influence in the Testaments of the Twelve Patriarchs," *Nov Test* 4 (1960), 182-235; cf. further, "Once more: Christian Influence in the Testaments of the Twelve Patriarchs," *NovTest* 5 (1962), 311-319, for de Jonge's response to F.-M. Braun.

common source of both the Testaments and the Book of Jubilees.[1] Its significance for our purposes lies in the words βασιλέων ἱεράτευμα which offer a phrasing not identical with but similar to the LXX version of Ex. 19:6.

The Greek Fragment containing this verse was found by R. H. Charles in a tenth century MS of the Testaments of the Twelve Patriarchs.[2] It was interpolated in the midst of Test. Levi 18:2 and shows close correspondence with two other Aramaic fragments relating to this Testament.[3] On the basis of a comparison of this correspondence and the close similarity of these texts with sections from the Test. Levi and Jubilees, Charles has found that they are not translations of each other but rather independent versions of a common original. This source, however, according to Charles, was not the Test. 12 Patr. but an older underlying Hebrew original of the latter "which formed a common source both of the Testaments and of the Book of Jubilees."[4]

In our connection, this theory, if correct,[5] would then suggest that Gk. Frag. 67 represents a more faithful version of the original source underlying the Test. Levi than does the common reading of the MSS. α, β, and A in the parallel to the Gk. Frag., Test. Levi 11-4-6. This says nothing, however, about the age of composition of this

---

[1] Cf. Charles, *Testaments*, pp. liii-lvii.

[2] *Ibid.*, p. liii.

[3] A Cambridge Fragment, discovered by H. L. Pass in the Geniza collection of the Cambridge University library and identified by him as a part of the Test. 12 Patr. and an Oxford Fragment, found by A. Cowley among the Geniza fragments in the Bodleian Library. Both texts are printed together with the Greek Fragment in Charles, *Testaments*, Appendix III, pp. 245-56.

[4] *Testaments*, p. lvi.

[5] Certain fragments of the Aramaic pre-stage of Test. Levi have been uncovered at Qumran, cf. DJD I, 87ff., plate 17 (1Q 21); Milik, *RB* 62 (1955), 398-406 (4Q Levi, 4Q Levi^{b}); P. Grelot, *RB* 63 (1956), 391-406. Likewise, a Hebrew fragment of Test. Naphtali has been identified (cf. Milik, *Ten Years*, p. 34). The fragments from Cave IV, moreover, coincide with two of the three Greek Fragments contained in the Mt. Athos MS which also incorporates the Greek Fragment under discussion. Though these Aramaic texts substantiate the theory of the existence of a stage of the Test. Levi previous to its present form, so far only an Aramaic stage and not a Hebrew text has been uncovered. On the other hand, they do not *a priori* deny the possible existence of such a Hebrew text. Before rejecting Harris' hypothesis of a Hebrew *Urtext* we would do well to wait for more conclusive evidence. For our purpose it matters little whether the text underlying our Greek Fragment was written in Hebrew or Aramaic for the words which concern us, as we shall see, were independent of and added to the translation of the original version.

fragment. For while it must have been composed before the original source became extinct, there is little evidence for determining whether this extinction occurred soon after the composition of the proposed Hebrew recensions, after those of the Greek versions α and β, or even later.

The internal evidence, however, can possibly shed some light on the question.

The context of the passage under consideration concerns Levi's description of his marriage to Melcha and the birth of their sons, Gersom, Kohath, and Merari, and their daughter, Jochebed (11:1-8).

The main verse in question is Gk. Frag. 67 and Test. Levi 11:6. The readings differ in the explanation of the name Kohath (Kaath). Test. Levi 11:6 (MSS. α, β, and A) reads: Διὰ τοῦτο ἐκάλεσα τὸ ὄνομα αὐτοῦ Καάθ, ὅ εστιν ἀρχὴ μεγαλείου καὶ συμβιβασμός; Gk. Frag. 66b-67: καὶ ἐκάλεσα τὸ ὄνομα αὐτοῦ Καάθ (66b); καὶ ὅτε ἐγεννήθη ἑώρακα ὅτι ἐπ' αὐτῷ ἔσται ἡ συναγωγὴ παντὸς τοῦ λαοῦ, καὶ ὅτι αὐτὸς ἔσται ἡ ἀρχιεροσύνη ἡ μεγάλη, αὐτὸς καὶ τὸ σπέρμα αὐτοῦ ἔσονται ἀρχὴ βασιλέων ἱεράτευμα τῷ 'Ισραηλ (67).

Charles has bracketed Test. Levi 6b as a gloss because it cannot be given as an explanation of the name. He suggests that this gloss may be "a corrupt survival of the text which may be more truly handed down in the Gr. Frag." (v. 67bc).[1] It is questionable, however, if all of v. 67bc is to be regarded as representative of the original text. The correspondence between the Gk. Frag. and v. 6b, namely, appears to involve only v. 67ab and not 67c, formulated according to the phrasing of v. 65.[2] Its relation is solely to v. 67b and not to the name Kaath, of which it can hardly be offering an explanation. The parallel of v. 67ab in the Cambridge Aramaic Fragment, but total absence of parallel words to v. 67c, apart from the last two words "(for all) Israel," coincides with these observations and leads to the conclusion that the majority of v. 67c constitutes a younger textual interpolation. According to the Aramaic, the earlier text may thus be constructed: v. 67a as it reads, followed by 67b καὶ ὅτι αὐτὸς ἔσται ἡ ἀρχιεροσύνη ἡ μεγάλη τῷ

[1] *Ibid.*, p. 50, n. 22. συμβιβασμός from συμβιβάζειν "to bring together, unite," however, is not totally unrelated to קהל, כנשת (Aramaic Fragment), συναγωγή. It appears as an attempt to offer a corresponding Greek term, as though συναγωγή were not enough.

[2] Cp. αὐτὸς ἔσται ἡ ἀρχιεροσύνη (67b) and αὐτὸς . . . ἔσονται ἀρχὴ βασιλέων ἱεράτευμα; cp. 67c with 64b: ὅτι ἐκβεβλημένος ἔσται αὐτὸς καὶ τὸ σπέρμα αὐτοῦ ἀπὸ τῆς ἀρχῆς ἱεροσύνης ἔσται.

'Ισραηλ. The interpolation would then include αὐτὸς καὶ τὸ σπέρμα αὐτοῦ ἔσονται ἀρχὴ βασιλέων ἱεράτευμα.

The comma βασιλέων ἱεράτευμα suggests acquaintance with and adaptation of the LXX version of Ex. 19:6. It was integrated with a phrasing taken from v. 64b and this combination was then interjected into v. 67 as a parallel to v. 67b, describing Kaath and his descendents: "he and his seed shall be the chief (or "beginning") of kings, a priesthood to Israel."

ἱεράτευμα, then, was used to designate not the elect People of God but rather the Levitical priesthood. It is unlikely that this gloss was the product of a Christian author who would never have used this term describing the Church of the NT to designate the Jewish priesthood. Therefore, we may assume that it was a gloss by a Jewish hand intent upon ascribing to Kaath and the lineage of Levi an age-old predicate of honor. The date of the interpolation remains undeterminable. More speaks in favor of its pre-Christian origin than of its inclusion at a later Christian period.[1]

In any event, the interpolation received no acknowledgment in other MSS of the Test. Levi and, as far as can be seen, assumed no significance in a conception of the Jewish institutional priesthood. The use of Ex. 19:6 here is unique in the entire group of allusions to the EF.

Mention of this Greek Fragment which is parallel to Test. Levi 11:4-6 has been made here following our treatment of the Book of Jubilees, despite the uncertainty of its date, because recent discoveries have shown that sources of both documents enjoyed a common place in the thought world of the literature found at *Chirbet Qumran*.

This fact is significant for our study insofar as it raises the question of the importance or place which the EF and its expression of the priestly character of Israel possibly was ascribed in this Qumran literature. Certainly reference to this passage would hardly be unexpected within this *milieu* where the concept of priesthood assumed such a significant role. Indeed, the fact that the community at Qumran held the priesthood in high esteem and so organized itself and prescribed for its novices and initiants a pattern of life according to priestly, levitical regulations has led to the widespread

[1] These conclusions are tentative and are offered more in the form of a hypothesis than as an assertion. In view of the evidence, however, they seem to present the most reasonable explanation of the material.

opinion that the community considered itself to be a priestly organization.[1]

Noteworthy in this *milieu*, therefore, is the conspicuous absence of any explicit references to the Exodus Formula. Research, of course, is still in progress so that this statement can only pertain to the present stage of discovery and textual reconstruction. The fragments of a Greek version of Exodus found in Cave VII[2] allow at least the possibility of its eventual appearance in the form of a Bible Version.

In the form of a citation or allusion, however, there has yet to be found any certain reference to Ex. 19:6. Conjectures involving the EF in the textual reconstruction of certain passages, for instance, for lack of verification must remain interesting suggestions.[3] Nor can the fragment, 1Q 21 (1Q Levi), be considered a parallel to Gk. Frag. 67 or, much less, to Jub. 16:18, 1 P 2:5,9, Apoc. 1:6, 5:10 and the underlying Ex. 19:6 as Barthélemy-Milik have allowed.[4] Careful analysis has shown rather the correctness of their primary suggestion that 1Q 21 relates to Test. Levi 8:11f., i.e. 8:14.[5]

Hence, according to the present stage of research, it appears safe

---

[1] For further discussion of the priestly character of the Qumranic community cf. *infra.*, pp. 209–13.

[2] Cf. R. De Vaux, *RB* (1956), p. 572 (7Q LXX Ex.); DJD III, 142f.

[3] Cf. the reconstruction proposal of the 1QH XIV, 44ff. in T. H. Gaster, *The Scriptures of the Dead Sea Sect*, London, 1957, p. 185: "(Through them hast Thou kept Thy covenant) and confirmed Thy pledge, to render us unto Thee (a kingdom of priests and) an holy (nation) for all generations of time and for all the (ages to come)."

[4] DJD I, 88, plate XVII, The line in question reads:
בין מלכות כהונתא רבא מן מלכות.

[5] Cf. Grelot, *op. cit.*, pp. 395f. Grelot shows that the three degrees of the Levitical caste are listed and two royalties mentioned, the sacerdotal royalty and the military royalty. He further maintains that a revision in the text of Charles' edition on the basis of the reading of 1Q Levi would yield a sensible progression of thought: a division into three lots shall be made (Test. Levi VIII 12-13); the first lot shall be great; the second lot shall be the priesthood; the third shall compose the chiefs, judges, and scribes (v. 17); and he shall give you two royalties, the royalty of priesthood and the royalty of the sword (the former involves the presentation of sacrifices to God and the consumption of the choice produce of the land, i.e. the priestly lot; the latter, engagement in war, combat, massacre, etc. Braun, *op. cit.*, pp. 534ff., has seconded Grelot's proposal regarding the "royaute du sacerdoce" (מלכות כהונתא) and the "royaute de l'epee" (מלכות חרבא) and has shown the correspondence between 1Q Levi and the Bodleian Aramaic Fragment, as has done Milik, *RB* 62 (1955), 398-406.

to say that the EF played no significant role in the conception of the sacerdotal character of the sectaries at Qumran.[1] Its appearance in two texts whose sources were known to this community cannot be ascribed to influence of the conception of priesthood prevalent at Qumran.

In *summary*, the allusion to the EF in Gk. Frag. 67c appears to have composed a gloss added to a Greek version of an earlier work serving as source of the Test. Levi. This gloss was added by a later Greek scribe, presumably by a Jew of the pre-Christian era. The formulation was an adoption of LXX Ex. 19:6 and ascribed as an honorific epithet to the second son of Levi, Kaath, and his descendents. As a designation for the Levitical priesthood instead of for Israel *in toto*, this use varies from the original and customary sense of the EF. However, no influence upon this allusion or upon those in Jubilees is traceable to the sacerdotal interests of the Qumran sectaries.

F. 2 Maccabees 2:17

ὁ δὲ θεὸς ὁ σώσας τὸν πάντα λαὸν αὐτοῦ καὶ ἀποδοὺς τὴν κληρονομίαν πᾶσιν καὶ τὸ βασίλειον καὶ τὸ ἱεράτευμα καὶ τὸν ἁγιασμόν[2]

This passage demonstrates not only the influence which the Alexandrian formulation of Ex. 19:6 had upon subsequent references to the EF but also a further development in the allusion to and application of this text.

The second book of the Maccabees is, in the main, a Greek composition of an Alexandrian Jew intent upon fostering "reverence for the temple in Jerusalem and also strictness in the observance of the Maccabean festivals as a bond of union between the Jews of Palestine and Egypt."[3] It is purportedly an anonymous ἐπιτομή or "digest" (2:26,28) of an earlier Maccabean history composed by the Hellenistic Jew, Jason of Cyrene, which condenses Jason's five books into one. The epitomator's apparent purpose was to magnify the two festivals of Channuka and Nicanor's Day as the ceremonial glories which recall the heroism of Judas Maccabeus.

---

[1] For the implications of this fact for Flusser's theory of the correspondence between 1 P 2:4-6 and IQS VIII, 4-11 cf. *infra*, pp. 209–13.

[2] Text according to A. Rahlfs, *Septuaginta*, 5th ed., 1952.

[3] Moffatt, in Charles, *AP* I, 129. Cf. also M. Abel, *Les Livres des Maccabees*, 12th ed., Paris, 1949, pp. 285ff.; Eissfeldt, *op. cit.*, pp. 25ff.; Bentzen, *op. cit.*, II, 222; Sellin-Rost, *op. cit.*, p. 166; Schunck, *RGG* IV, 621f.

Since the present form of this book is not the product of a single author, at least two or more dates of origin must be reckoned with. Prefixed to the epitome (2:19ff.) are two letters. The first (1:1-9) is addressed "to the Jewish brothers in Egypt" from "the Jewish brothers in Jerusalem and the land of Judea" (1:1). The second missive (1:10-2:18), containing the verse under consideration, 2:17, is sent from "those who are in Jerusalem and Judea and the senate and Judas" to "Aristobulus, the teacher of King Ptolomy, who is of the stock of the anointed priests, and to the Jews in Egypt" (1:10).

With great likelihood these epistles were not part of the original composition of the epitomator but were added by a later hand.[1] For the latter "letter" a date in the second half of the first century B.C. is generally accepted.[2] The similarity of form which both these missives show to other non-genuine "letters" (e.g. Dan. 3:31-4:34, Ep. Jer., Syr. Ap. Bar. 77-87, Esth. 9:20-32) might suggest that we are dealing here not with genuine letters but with "epistles," "Kunstbriefe." Perhaps according to the similar form and intention of Esth. 9:20-32 (encouragement to celebrate the feast of Purim), 2 Mcc. 1:1-9, 10-2:18 are to be considered as two "Festbriefe."[3]

If these two "letters" are Greek translations of Hebrew originals, this would mean that 2:17 is Palestinian thought though reclothed

---

[1] In contrast to the epitome, the literary form of both "letters" presupposes a Hebrew original; cf. Abel, *op. cit.*, pp. 285, 302; Eissfeldt, *op. cit.*, p. 720.

[2] So Eissfeldt, *ibid.*; Bentzen, *ibid.*, notes the *terminus a quo* as subsequent to 1 Mcc. which the epitomator has used; so also Moffatt, *ibid.*, Schunck *ibid.*, and *Die Quellen des I. und II. Makkabäerbuches*, Halle, 1954, p. 101, sets the date of the epitome before B. C. 60 and the addition of both "letters" *circa* the birth of Jesus. However, Sellin-Rost, *ibid.*: "Kurz vor 70 nach Christus." E. Bickermann, "Ein jüdischer Festbrief vom Jahre 124 v. Chr. (2 Makk. 1,1-9)" *ZNW* 32 (1933), 233f., has dealt extensively with the question of date and has arrived at the year B. C. 60. His reasons: (1) The formula of salutation, χαίρειν καὶ ὑγιαίνειν, has been found to have been used only 100 years after Judas' death, i.e., ca. B. C. 60. (2) Judas' assumed High Priesthood (Josephus *Ant.* 12, 414, 434) was not yet mentioned; nor was the Jewish version of the death of Antiochus IV (1:13) discussed. In any case Bickermann's dating is preferable to Abel's, *op. cit.*, p. 310: "contemporaine de Simon ou même du fils de Jean Hyrcan qui le premier prit le titre de roi (104-103)."

[3] So Eissfeldt, *op. cit.*, p. 26. Bickermann, *op. cit.*, pp. 233f., and Abel, *op. cit.*, pp. 299-302, regard particularly the latter epistle as a genuine "festival letter" typical of the Jerusalemite practice of encouraging the brethren to celebrate a feast and providing the proper date of celebration—orally through messengers. For the "letter" *Gattung* cf. P. Wendland, *Die urchristlichen Literaturformen* (*HNT* 1/3), Tübingen, 1912, pp. 340ff.

in Greek-Alexandrian dress. In either case both the epitome and the prefixed letters received their final Greek shape and form in Alexandria.[1]

In the second epistle (1:10-2:18) there re-echoes the encouragement of the first "to keep the days of the feast of Tabernacles in the month of Chislev" (1:9): "We are now about to celebrate the purification of the temple on the 25th day of the month of Chislev. We consider it our duty to inform you that you too keep the feast of Tabernacles" (1:18). Following an excursus which attempts to trace historically the origin of the feast and the Purification to Nehemiah (1:18b-2:15), the theme of the Purification is resumed in 2:16: "Thus, as we are about to celebrate the Purification (τὸν καθαρισμόν) we write to you. It is good for you to observe these days." 2:17f. continue: "It is God who has saved all His people and has returned to all of them the heritage and the βασίλειον and the ἱεράτευμα and the holiness, just as He promised through the Law. For we hope in God that He will speedily have mercy upon us and will gather us together from under heaven into the holy place; for He has delivered us from great misfortunes and has purified 'the place.'"

Ch. 2:19-32 begins a new section containing the preface to the epitome, and introduction to the story of Judas Maccabaeus and his brothers, the wars, and the great rededication of the temple.

2:17 is undoubtably a reflection of LXX Ex. 19:6.[2] This is the only text at this time containing the word ἱεράτευμα and accordingly the only place where βασίλειον and ἱεράτευμα occur in combination. ὁ ἁγιασμός represents a substantization of the adjective ἅγιος in the LXX comma ἔθνος ἅγιον.[3]

The later passage, however, shows important variations. The parallelism of the original MT text is no longer evident. Instead three definite substantives have been created. This alteration is undoubtably traceable to the LXX where βασίλειον was already intended as substantive, thus destroying the original parallelism between "kingdom of priests" and "holy nation" and paving the way for later substantizations of the same nature. This substan-

---

[1] So all commentators mentioned above.

[2] So Cerfaux, *op. cit.*, p. 18; Abel, *op. cit.*, p. 309; Dabin, *op. cit.*, p. 30; Blinzler, *op. cit.*, p. 59.

[3] So Abel, *ibid.*, who sees the change required by ἀποδούς (v. 17b): "Dieu à donné à Israël des moyens de sanctification de façon à en faire une nation sainte." Sim. Schrenk, *op. cit.*, p. 250.

tization was accomplished through (1) the addition of the definite article: τὸ βασίλειον, τὸ ἱεράτευμα, τὸν ἁγιασμόν thus clarifying the ambiguity of the LXX rendering; (2) the creation of the substantive "holiness" from the Ex. passage "holy nation"; (3) the inclusion of the copula functioning in the same corrective manner as the article, combining all three terms as independent substantives.

Furthermore, the *context* into which these terms have been introduced is dissimilar from that of Ex. 19:6. This allusion to Ex. 19:6 is not made in a covenant context, nor have these words been quoted together with their original context.[1] Rather the terms have been isolated and applied to Israel as *Ehrenprädikate*, "predicates of honor." In this sense they were accordingly combined with another characteristic of Israel, "the inheritance" (v. 17b), which perhaps derived from a separate tradition.[2]

The situation occasioning this allusion to Ex. 19:6 and its reformulation was the present celebration of the feast of Purification.[3] The historical event being recalled was the purification of the Jerusalem temple on the 25th of Chislev through Judas Maccabeus exactly three years after its desecration at the hand of Antiochus Epiphanes. According to 2:17, in this event occurred the restoration of honor to the community of Israel as a saving act of God. God had been faithful to His promise (v. 18), and the sanctification of the temple (τὸν καθαρισμόν, v. 16) was a sign that He was upholding His people as His inheritance, His kingdom, His body of priests, and His holiness.

---

[1] Nevertheless the phrase καθὼς ἐπηγγείλατο διὰ τοῦ νόμου (2:18a) indicates that though no mention of "covenant" has explicitly been made, the author was apparently aware that the words to which he was alluding were originally intended as a Divine promise.

[2] ἡ κληρονομία has occurred already in 2:5 which relates not only to Dt. 32:47-50, 34:1-4 but also to an earlier passage in the Song of salvation at the Reed Sea, Ex. 15:17. Allusions to this Song are also evident in the prayer, 1:24-29. It is not unlikely that these are traces of a separate Ex. 15 tradition. In 2:17 then we would have a combination of two early elements of tradition both reflecting the redemption of the λαὸς τοῦ θεοῦ. The idea of election and holiness is brought out clearly in 1:25 and the close correspondence in terminology and content between 1:25-29 and 2:17 suggest that 2:17 was meant to contain the answer to the prayer of 1:25ff. The mutual relationship of both to Ex. 15 as well as to each other deserves closer analysis.

[3] The expression in 1:9 is possibly misleading. Though mention is made of the celebration of "the days of the Camping Out" (the feast of Tabernacles), the feast apparently implied was the feast of Purification which was celebrated in similar manner to the feast of Tabernacles, as explained in 2 Mcc. 10:5-9 (i.e. eight days).

It has been proposed that these three substantives re-echoing Ex. 19:6 are to be taken as concrete signs of political independence and cultic restoration: the sceptre, the legitimate institutional priesthood, and the temple purification.[1] On the one hand, such an explanation is sympathetic to the historical situation: Maccabean supremacy had rekindled the spark of messianic hope; Israel's star had risen once again; independence, a legitimate priesthood, and a purified temple were the trophies of a divine victory.

On the other hand, however, such an explanation which so localizes the expression of Ex. 19:6 overlooks two vital factors. First, this letter was composed after the demise of John Hyrcanus, that is, after the radical breach between the Pharisaic party and the Hasmoneans (ca. B. C. 103ff.). The sharp criticism which the Pharisees exercised against hierarchy and priesthood after this break make it very unlikely that this passage from the pen of a Pharisee (in its final form at least) would be extolling the virtues of the very institutions which the Pharisees themselves were criticizing. These terms, however, if seen as applied not to the institutions within Israel but to Israel *in toto* as God's people would be much more consonant with the latter development of events as well as with Pharisaic thinking as a whole.

Secondly, such an explanation ignores the emphasis which the author has laid upon τὸν πάντα λαὸν αὐτοῦ and πᾶσιν (2:17a) referring explicitly twice to the totality of Israel. It appears that the predicates of Ex. 19:6 have been introduced because there, as in 2 Mcc. 2:17, the entire people of God was the object of concern. The *entire people* has been the object of God's salvation according to F. M. Abel.[2] The verse makes references to the worship and preeminence of the entire Jewish people and not to institutions within that nation: "separe des paiens et destine a maintenir le culte de Jahveh (ἱεράτευμα, fonction sacerdotale), le peuple juif devait par le fait même jouir d'une preeminence sur autres nations (βασίλειον)."[3]

---

[1] So Cerfaux, *op. cit.*, pp. 18f.: βασίλειον = the sceptre and regained independence, ἱεράτευμα = the legitimate institutional priesthood, ἁγιασμός = the temple purification; sim. Blinzler, *op. cit.*, p. 59, and Sevenster, *op. cit.*, p. 404. However, according to Schrenk, *op. cit.*, p. 205, no translation other than "Königsdiadem," "Königswürde" is possible; similarly, ἱεράτευμα = "Priesterwürde."

[2] Abel, *op. cit.*, p. 309: "Le Dieu qui a sauvé *tout* (italics Abel) le peuple est celui de l'exode (14:30). La terre promise est envisagée ici comme l'héritage donné en vertu des promesses à Israël et partagé entre les tribus."

[3] *Ibid.*

Not to be forgotten in this respect is the occasion for this letter, the feast of the temple purification. Cerfaux and Blinzler find τόν ἁγιασμόν referring to this event. Yet the deed of purification is designated in 2 Mcc. 2:16(18) not as ὁ ἁγιασμός but as ὁ καθαρισμός (ἐκαθάρισεν)! Reference to the "holiness" theme of Ex. 19:6 might well have been occasioned by the event and celebration of the Purification but it was not identified with it. Similar identification of βασίλειον with "sceptre" and ἱεράτευμα with "legitimate priesthood" thus likewise would be most doubtful. Attempts to localize or limit the implications drawn from Ex. 19:6 to institutions fail to appreciate the fact that each predicate applies to Israel *in toto* and not representatives thereof. The optimism expressed here is not so much a messianism bound to the sceptre and the mitre as it is a confidence founded in the faithfulness of God to His covenant promise. The reign of Israel and a royal messianism is simply not expressed in this passage, the assertions of Cerfaux notwithstanding. And the alternative which he poses between the interpretations of a Palestinian messianism (emphasizing "kingdom") and an Alexandrian "spiritualization" (of "priests") finds little support in this text.[1]

We *summarize*. 2 Mcc. 2:17 occurs in the second of two letters (1:10-2:18) prefixed to the body of 2 Mcc., an epitome of an earlier word, a digest intent upon recalling the heroic deeds of the Maccabeans and magnifying the celebration of the purification of the temple. Originally a festival letter composed in Hebrew (Aramaic) by the Jews in Palestine addressed to their brothers in Egypt, the missive obtained a Greek form not earlier than B. C. 60 and was added to the epitome together with the first letter (1:1-9) by an Alexandrian redactor probably about the time of the birth of Jesus. Reference to the "kingdom" ("royal house"), "body of priests" and "holiness" is made in connection with this feast of the Purification. The allusion derives from LXX Ex. 19:6 and is contained in a context bearing marked similarities to the priestly prayer of 1:24b-29 which in turn shows correspondence to the song at the Reed Sea, Ex. 15:1b-18. These predicates adapted from Ex. 19:6 are applied to Israel *in toto* similar to the method of application in the original text. The author shows awareness of the covenant context from

---

[1] In addition to all other arguments against such an antithesis, the mere fact that this passage and this letter received their final form in Alexandria makes such a postulation unlikely. Cf. also *infra*, pp. 120ff.

which he drew his phrase by referring to the "promise contained in the Law." Alteration of the original text resulted in the creation of ὁ ἁγιασμός and the coordination of the three substantives through the addition of articles and copulae. The EF was adduced as a sign of the restoration of Israel's honor as the People of God and the terms served as *notae essentiae* λαοῦ τοῦ θεοῦ. Over against an interpretation which would see in these terms expressions for the Hasmonean sceptre, the legitimate priesthood, and the temple purification, 2 Mcc. 2:17 presents an optimism grounded not in the advent of a political messiah but in the faithfulness of God to His promise that Israel (and not her institutions) shall be His βασίλειον, His ἱεράτευμα, and His ἔθνος ἅγιον.

G. Philo: De Sobrietate 66, De Abrahamo 56

Two texts of the Jewish philosopher of religion and apologist, Philo Judaeus of Alexandria (ca. A. D. 39/40), show contact with both the LXX rendition of Ex. 19:6 and the textual trend reflected in the foregoing passage, 2 Mcc. 2:17: *De Sobrietate* 66 and *De Abrahamo* 56. These texts assume large significance through the fact that they are not only further links in a particular chain of textual formation but also formulations contemporary with the writings of the Apostolic Church.

1. *De Sobrietate* 66

> οὗτος τῶν δώδεκα κατάρχει φυλῶν, ἅς οἱ χρησμοὶ βασίλειον καὶ ἱεράτευμα θεοῦ φασιν εἶναι κατὰ τὴν πρὸς τὸν πρῶτον Σὴμ εὐλογίαν, οὗ τοῖς οἴκοις ἦν εὐχὴ τὸν θεὸν [ἐν]οικῆσαι· βασίλειον γὰρ ὁ βασιλέως δήπουθεν οἶκος, ἱερὸς ὄντως καὶ μόνος ἄσυλος.[1]

The *context* of this first passage contains Philo's commentary upon Gen. 9:27, Noah's blessing to his sons, Japheth and Shem: "God enlarge Japheth and may He dwell in the tents ("houses") of Shem."[2] God, as ruler of the world, naturally does not live (κατοι-

---

[1] This and the following texts are cited according to the edition of L. Cohn and P. Wendland, *Philonis Alexandrini opera quae supersunt*, I-VI, Berlin, 1896-1915. *De Sobr.* 66 = *C-W* II, 228. Cp. *Loeb Classical Library, Philo*—with a translation by F. H. Colson and G. H. Whitaker in 11 volumes, London, 1949-54; *De Sobr.* 66 = *LCL* III (Colson-Whitaker), 478f.

[2] *De Sobr.* 59 (*C-W* II, 227): πλατύνει ὁ θεὸς τῷ Ἰαφεθ καὶ κατοικησάτω ἐν τοῖς οἴκοις τοῦ Σημ.

κεῖν) in a house in a spatial sense, states Philo.[1] But he encourages that prayer be made to Him that He raise this tiny house, reason (τοῦτο οικοδόμημα, τὸν νοῦν), from earth to heaven.[2] Reference is then made to Shem and his lineage is traced; he is the root of moral excellence laid in the earth.[3] Wise Abraham is the ensuing tree bearing fruit; Isaac is the tree's fruit; and from the seed of this fruit spring the virtues of the industrious life in which Jacob exercised himself to mastery.

Philo identifies Jacob, then, as the father of the twelve tribes of whom the oracles (οἱ χρησμοί) say that "they are God's royal residence and body of priests" (§ 66a).[4] This appelation, Philo continues, is consistent with the relationship between the twelve tribes and their forefather, Shem. For according to the blessing given to him, God shall dwell in his houses (§ 66b); "for surely by βασίλειον is meant the 'king's house' which is holy and alone inviolable" (§ 66c).

This interpretation of the term βασίλειον is highly instructive. Concerning the *text* we may make the following observations:

(1) The wording βασίλειον καὶ ἱεράτευμα θεοῦ is a reflection of Ex. 19:6 in its LXX version, whereby no explicit mention has been made of ἔθνος ἅγιον.

(2) In contrast to the LXX a καί has been added, similar to 2 Mcc. 2:17 and the *waw* of the *Targumim*, and the genitive θεοῦ.

(3) βασίλειον has been understood by Philo as a substantive and explained as the "king's house, dwelling," "royal residence." As § 66c shows, Philo has drawn the correspondence between βασίλειον θεοῦ and ὁ βασιλέως οἶκος. Inasmuch as God is King, the "royal residence of God" is identical to the "house of the King."

(4) The term ἱεράτευμα received no commentary. As is clear from the context, reference was made to the EF not for the sake of ἱεράτευμα but because of βασίλειον.

(5) It is the term βασίλειον, namely, which Philo uses to establish the connection between the designation of the descendents of Shem and the promise given their forefather. The EF has been cited to

[1] *De Sobr.* 63 (*C-W*, *ibid.*).
[2] *De Sobr.* 64 (*C-W*, *ibid.*).
[3] *De Sobr.* 65 (C-W, *ibid.*).
[4] Cf. *Die Werke Philos von Alexandria in Deutscher Übersetzung*, hrsg. von L. Cohn, Breslau, 1909, V, 97: "Königsresidenz und Priestertum Gottes." Sim. Schrenk, *op. cit.*, p. 250. Colson-Whitaker, *op. cit.*, p. 479: "palace and priesthood of God." Blinzler, *op. cit.*, p. 59: "Königspalast."

substantiate the fact that the blessing originally given to Shem, namely that God would dwell in his houses, has been realized among Shem's descendents who have been called "God's kingly dwelling place and body of priests."

(6) Thus this ascription for Israel *in toto* has been interpreted as meaning that God is dwelling among His favored people. The original motif of election in the EF is not evident, though § 66c (ἱερὸς ὄντως καὶ μόνος ἄσυλος) indicates that the element of holiness was still essential for Philo. Behind § 66c then we might see the influence of the other comma of the EF, ἔθνος ἅγιον, which comes to explicit expression in the second reference to the EF, De Abrah. 56.

2. *De Abrahamo* 56

> . . . τὴν δὲ περίσεμνον τριάδα καὶ περιμάχητον ἑνὸς εἴδους ἐπιλεγομένου βασίλειον καὶ ἱεράτευνα καὶ ἔθνος ἅγιον οἱ χρησμοὶ καλοῦσι.[1]

This passage shows similarity to the former in both text and context.

The *context* again involves the theme of moral virtue and reference is made again to the patriarchs Abraham, Isaac, and Jacob. In § 47[2] Philo names Noah, Enoch, and Enos as the triad of men exemplifying degrees of perfection and the quest after virtue. Abraham, Isaac, and Jacob likewise formed a triad. They all belonged to one house, they all loved God and were bound to His name; they all were of one family (ἑνὸς γένους) (§ 48-50). These men were prime examples of virtue. Abraham exemplifies virtue which has been learned; Isaac, natural virtue which has been inherited by birth; and Jacob, virtue gained through exercise and practice (§ 52-55).

In § 56 Philo compares the "fatherhood" of Adam and Noah to that of Abraham, Isaac, and Jacob and thereby introduces the EF: "While Adam represented the first man, the earth-born, as father of all that were born up to the Flood, and Noah who with his house alone survived that great destruction because of his justice and excellent character (may be considered) in other ways as the father of a new race (καινοῦ γένους ἀνθρώπων) which would spring up fresh, the oracles speak of this august and significant triad as the parent

---

1 *C-W IV*, 13; *LCL VI*, 33.
2 *C-W* IV, 13. Cp. *LCL* VI (Colson), 32f.

of one species called a 'royal residence and body of priests and holy nation.'"

The following section (§ 57) contains an explanation of the high position of Israel through an analysis of the name "Israel" in the Hebrew tongue: "He who sees God." A discourse on the analogy of sight and wisdom then follows. The EF receives no commentary or further mention.

Concerning the *text* and the use of the EF we note the following points:

(1) The phrasing is a definite reflection of Ex. 19:6 in its LXX version, whereby the second member of the verse, "and a holy nation," is also included in contrast to *De Sobr.* 66 where it was only possibly implied in § 66c.

(2) Again a καί is present, joining βασίλειον and ἱεράτευμα.

(3) The coordination of βασίλειον, ἱεράτευμα and ἔθνος ἅγιον which this conjunction effects demonstrates that βασίλειον was again taken as substantive not as adjective.

(4) The EF was mentioned but received no further explication as in *De Sobr.* 66. It was cited as containing predicates for Israel; specifically, for the children of the Abraham-Isaac-Jacob lineage. The purpose of this reference was through these worthy and honorific epithets to underline the nobility and significance of the forebears of this holy nation: Abraham, Isaac, and Jacob.

The similarities between *De Sobr.* 66 and *De Abrah.* 56 shed a light upon Philo's use and interpretation of the EF which would put some former theories into question.

(1) Both references to the EF are introduced as evidence of the *Biblical* witness (οἱ χρησμοί).

(2) Both allusions occur within larger contexts treating the subject of virtue as exemplified by the triad Abraham, Isaac, and Jacob.

(3) In both cases the predicates from the EF were cited as honorific epithets belonging to Israel; specifically, to the descendants of Abraham, Isaac, and Jacob. Obvious in both these latter observations is the connection which Philo intended to make between the Abraham-Isaac-Jacob lineage and the folk to which was ascribed the EF predicates.

(4) Both passages resemble closely the terminology of the LXX. In their inclusion of the copula καί they show even greater affinity to another Alexandrian text, 2 Mcc. 2:17.

(5) This affinity is further strengthened in the fact that βασίλειον in both *De Sobr.* 66 and *De Abrah.* 56 has been taken as a ***substantive*** and ought to be translated with consistency: "royal residence," "King's residence," "King's palace" or the like.

Unexplainable are the inconsistent translations of both the German and English versions! Whereas M. Adler (Cohn edition) renders βασίλειον at *De Sobr.* 66 "Königsresidenz,"[1] at *De Abrah.* 56 J. Cohn (Cohn edition) translates "Königreich."[2] At least in both cases the substantival function of βασίλειον has been recognized. Unfortunately, in Colson's translation (Loeb Classical Library) not even this fact received its due. At *De Sobr.* 66 he has translated "the palace"[3] but then at *De Abrah.* 56 treats βασίλειον as an adjective and renders it "royal."[4] Does not the consistency of Philo's terminology demand an accordant consistency in translation? Is there any evidence to suggest that for Philo the EF and βασίλειον changed its meaning so that in *De Sobr.* 66 it meant "royal residence" and in *De Abrah.* 56, "kingdom"? Hardly! Even more puzzling is Colson's assumption that in the former instance βασίλειον meant "palace" but in the latter, "royal." The copula καί separating βασίλειον and ἱεράτευμα alone is enough to defeat this theory. In a note to *De Sobr.* 66 Colson arbitrarily assumes that in the LXX version to which Philo was referring βασίλειον "no doubt means 'royal'"; "Philo's interpretation," he continues, "is, however, grammatically possible."[5] In lieu of this opinion it is not difficult to understand how Colson could feel justified in rendering βασίλειον "correctly" as "royal" in *De Abrah.* 56!

Another misconception is entertained when it is held that both passages are determined and colored by a conception of "spiritualization" whereby ἱεράτευμα is applied to the Jewish people and the pious soul. Cerfaux who lets this thought dominate his commentary on the use of the EF in Philo speaks of Israel's "sacerdotal office" as "consisting in the maintenance of the purity of body and spirit according to the precepts of the Law, to know the true God, having been instructed through the same Law and to offer to Him in the name of all humanity prayers, sacrifices, and the celebration of the

---

[1] Cf. *supra*, p. 97, n. 4. Transl. M. Adler.
[2] Cohn, *op. cit.*, I, 108. Transl. J. Cohn.
[3] Cf. *supra*, p. 97, n. 4.
[4] *LCL VI*, 33.
[5] *Ibid.*, III, 478.

feasts."[1] As evidence for this statement, however, he refers not to our two texts but to the cultic discussions in *Spec. leg.* II, § 163-167. Such a procedure is dubious. Though Philo does indeed make numerous references to the priestly character of Israel,[2] such references have absolutely no bearing upon our two texts. Not only is the terminology different,[3] but also the texts and contexts have nothing in common. No thought on the priesthood of Israel is being developed in either of our texts. And when Philo does treat such a theme, it never appears, as Sevenster has pointed out,[4] in connection with the term ἱεράτευμα from Ex. 19:6.

In *summary*, the EF has been mentioned twice by Philo in a version similar to that of the LXX, with the addition of a καί between βασίλειον and ἱεράτευμα, moreover, similar to the copula of the *Targumim* and 2 Mcc. 2:17. In both instances the EF was introduced as evidence of the Biblical witness. In both cases the subjects bearing these honorific predicates have been identified as the descendants of Abraham, Isaac, and Jacob. The purpose of allusion to the EF was not to develop or explicate a theory of the priesthood of Israel. No "spiritual" interpretation is evident here. Rather, in the first instance the EF was used to substantiate the fact that God had fulfilled the blessing given by Noah to Shem—that God might dwell in his houses. The term βασίλειον in particular supplied the proof of this fulfillment, so that this term received further explication demonstrating its substantival function and its meaning "royal residence, king's house." In the second instance the worthy predicates of the EF were cited to underline the excellence and distinction of the ancestors of the nation to which they were ascribed, Abraham, Isaac, and Jacob.

---

[1] Cerfaux, *op. cit.*, pp. 16f.

[2] Cf. *De Gigant.* 61; *Quod Deus sit immut.* 134f.; *De Plant.* 63ff.; *De Ebriet.* 126, 128; *De Congressu Eruditionis Grat.* 106; *De Vita Mos.* II, 224; *De Spec. Leg.* I, 243; II, 145f., 162ff.; *De Virtutibus* (*De Nobilit.*) 185.

[3] A good example is Philo's discussion of the priestly character of Israel as expressed in the Passover festival. On the Pasch, he explains, "the victims are not brought to the altar by the laity (οἱ ἰδιῶται) and sacrificed by the priests, but as commanded in the Law, the whole nation acts as priests, each individual bringing what he offers on his own behalf and dealing with his own hands. Now, while all the rest of the people were joyful and cheerful, each feeling that he had the honor of priesthood (ἱερωσύνης), there were others passing the time in tears and sorrow" (*De Vita Moses* II, 224 = *C-W* IV, 252). Likewise, *De Spec. Leg.* II, 145f. (= *C-W* V, 120) states in connection with the Pasch: "But on this occasion the whole nation performs the sacred rites and acts as priest with pure hands (ἁγναῖς χερσὶν ἱερουργεῖ καὶ ἱερᾶται)."

[4] Sevenster, *op. cit.*, p. 405.

H. The Rabbinic Literature

The final sources of Jewish allusion to the EF are contained in the literature of the Rabbinic School and the Early Synagogue.[1] This body of writing is conspicuously reticent in its reference to this covenant formula which earlier played such a significant role in Israel's expression of her faith and understanding of herself. References, where they occasionally do appear, shed little new light on the theological significance of this passage. Furthermore, all the passages which are mentioned originate, in their written form at least, in the period subsequent to the composition of 1 P. Neither they nor their oral sources seem to have had any influence upon the formulation or interpretation of the EF in 1 P.

The *Mishnah* contains no citation of Ex. 19:6. Likewise, in the collection of Tannaitic tradition closely allied to the Mishnah, the *Tosefta*, there are no references to the EF.

In the *Talmud* it has received occasional citation in the Gemara. In the Babylonian Talmud, for instance, mention is made in Shabbat 86b, 87a, and Zebachim 19a. Shabb. 86b discusses the day on which the Ten Commandments were given and the dating of the New Moon.[2] This is also the theme in Shabb. 87a.[3] In both cases Ex. 19:6 is not being interpreted or used to support a theme on the royalty or priesthood of Israel but rather has been employed in a "locating," "chapter and verse" capacity; that is, it locates, as would a verse number many centuries later. It serves to designate a particular section of Exodus; namely, the introductory covenant formula, Ex. 19:3ff.

Zeb. 19a concerns a conversation about the proper wearing of vestments and the statement from Ez. 44:18: "They shall not gird

[1] The historical writings of the soldier-historian Flavius Josephus, a Palestinian contemporary of Philo, contain no reference to the EF. As Cerfaux has pointed out (*op. cit.*, p. 17), Josephus, in his polemic *Contra Apion* (2.22.188) expressly rejects the thought of a priesthood exercised by the whole people of Israel. The function of priesthood is restricted to the Levitical institution where priests are the intermediaries between God and the people.

[2] "Rabbi Jose holds that the New Moon was fixed on the first day of the week (Sunday) and on that day he (Moses) said nothing to them on account of their exhaustion from the journey. On Monday he said to them: 'and you shall be to me a kingdom of priests.'"

[3] Here it is told that other Rabbis hold that the New Moon was fixed on Monday and that on *Tuesday* he said to them "you shall be to me a kingdom of priests."

themselves with anything that causes sweat" (Zeb. 18b). Ex. 19:6 has been cited to demonstrate that Israelites, since they have been called a "kingdom of priests and a holy nation," are to wear their clothes as do the priests.[1]

A few appearances are found in the halakic and haggadic Scriptural interpretation of the *Midrashim*.

According to one Midrash on Exodus, the Mekilta of Rabbi Simeon ben Jochai (ca. A. D. 150),[2] Ex. 19:6 relates to Israel's reception and her execution of the words of the Torah"; 'and you shall be to me': selected for me, busy with the Torah, busy with my commandments."[3]

The Midrash on "kingdom of priests and a holy nation" concerns the nature of Israel in the coming Messianic Age. Since there is some disagreement as to its interpretation, we render the following translation of the text:[4]

> "Kingdom": I shall not make king over you someone from among the nations of the world (R. Ishmael adds: rather only 'from among you'). And likewise it says [Cant. 6:9]: 'My dove, my perfect one, is the only one' etc. R. Eliezer [ca. A. D. 180], the son of R. Jose the Galilean [ca. A. D. 150], says: From what source do you say that each individual Israelite will then [in the Messianic Age] have sons [as many as the number of those] as departed from Egypt? Because it says [Ps. 45:16a]: 'Instead of

---

[1] Rabbi Ashi (A. D. 427) is quoted as saying: "Hanna ben Nathana (ca. A. D. 350) told me, 'I was once standing before King Izgedar a Persian king; my girdle lay high up, whereupon he pulled it down, observing to me, "It is written, 'a kingdom of priests and a holy nation.'" H. Freedmann, *The Babylonian Talmud*, Seder Kodashim, Zebahim 19a, ed. Soncino, London, 1948, p. 94, n. 9, explains: "Hence you must wear your girdle like priests, and not so high."

[2] This Baraita collection is actually that of R. Akiba (d.A.D. 135). It has been attributed to Akiba's student, Simeon b. Jochai, because it begins with a saying of the latter. Cf. J. Winter and A. Wünsche, *Ein Tannaitischer Midrasch zu Exodus*, Leipzig, 1909, p. ix; H. L. Strack, *Introduction to the Talmud and Midrash*, New York/Philadelphia, 1959 (1931), pp. 206-08.

[3] *Mechilta de-Rabbi Simon b. Jochai*, ed. D. Hoffmann, Frankfurt/Main, 1905, p. 95; *Mekhilta D. Rabbi Sim'on b. Jochai*, Fragmenta in Geniza Cairensi Reperta, ed. J. N. Epstein and E. Z. Melamed, Jerusalem, 1955, p. 139.

[4] According to *Mechilta d' Rabbi Ismael*, ed. H. S. Horovitz and I. A. Rabin, Frankfurt/Main, 1931, pp. 208f. Cf. further, *Sefer Mekilta of Rabbi Ishmael to the Book of Exodus*, ed. M. Friedmann, Vienna, 1870 (reprinted in New York, 1948). For translations (English) cf. *Mekilta de Rabbi Ishmael*, ed. and transl. J. Z. Lauterbach (*The Schiff Library of Jewish Classics*), Philadelphia, 1949, II, 205-06; (German) cf. Winter-Wünsche, *op. cit.*, pp. 196f.; *Str-B* III, 789.

> your fathers shall be your sons.' If 'sons,' it could be thought that they would be liable to suffering and affliction. Therefore it says [Ps. 45:16b]: 'You will make them princes in all the earth.' If 'princes,' it could be thought 'merchants.' Therefore it says [Ex. 19:6]: 'kingdom' [ממלכת]. If 'king' [מלך], then it could be thought that he will go about and coerce.[1] Therefore it says: 'priests.' It could be thought 'priests who travel about.' Therefore it says 'a kingdom of priests.' If priests, then it could be thought 'possessing leisure' as it says [2 Sam. 8:18]: 'and David's sons were priests.'[2] Therefore it says 'and a holy nation.' Thus they [the Sages] have said: 'All Israelites were worthy of eating the holy foods [בקדשים] before they had made the Golden Calf. However, after they had made the Calf, they [the holy foods] were taken away from them and given to the priests, as it says [Jer. 50:17]: 'Israel is a scattered sheep . . .' "Holy": Holy and sanctified, separated from the nations of the world and their abominations.

Concerning the meaning given the terms "kingdom" and "priests" and the use of this comma made by R. Eliezer three thoughts have been given expression.

(1) Regarding the term מַמְלָכָה it is stated that God will only set Israelites upon Israel's throne.

(2) Concerning the term "priests" the Sages reflected upon the former priesthood of Israel *in toto* and its subsequential loss resulting from her idolatry. They apparently reckoned the term כֹּהֲנִים not merely as an appositive to "holy nation" but as a description of Israel's function previous to her idolatry. A functional priesthood of Israel *in toto* was assumed. Subsequent to her worship of the Golden Calf, however, this priestly privilege was removed from the entirety of Israel and restricted to the house of Levi.[3] Considered methodologically, the priestly activity of the Levites has been retrojected and seen as the prerogative of Israel *in toto* before her idolatry. Aetiologically, an attempt has been made to explain the eventual delimitation of priesthood to the progeny of Levi. A similar explanation of delimitation can be seen in the Midrash on Ps.

---

[1] So *Mek. R. Ishmael* (*Horovitz-Rabin, op. cit.*, p. 209). *Mek. R. Sim. b. Jochai* (*Epstein-Melamed, op. cit.*, p. 139) reads: "If kings (מלכים), then it could be thought 'war' (מלחמה)." The reading "king" or "kings" is interesting not only as an instance of difference between the texts of Rabbis Ishmael and Simeon b. Jochai, but also as an indication that ממלכת was taken in both cases in the personal sense of the *Targumim* (מלכין).

[2] Cf. also Yalkut Ps. 45:17 for this explanation of "priests."

[3] Cf. L. Ginsberg, *The Legends of the Jews*, Philadelphia, 1913ff., III, 85ff.

132:13[1] and in a comment of Rabbi Acha contained in the Aggadat Bereshit.[2]

(3) According to the words of Rabbi Eliezer ben Jose, "kingdom of priests" illustrates the peaceful and dignified character of Israel in the Messianic Age. The phrase has been employed to qualify a foregoing term, eventually to help illustrate the statement that each individual Israelite will have as many sons as the number of those who partook in the Exodus. This statement is first substantiated by Ps. 45:16a. The term "sons" in Ps. 45:16a could imply suffering, therefore "sons" is qualified by "princes" (Ps. 45:16b). "Princes" could imply "business merchants," however, so "princes" is qualified by "kingdom" (Ex. 19:6). "King(s)" which could suggest conquest and force is explained as qualified by "priests." And vice versa: "priests," which could imply people of very limited means wandering about in search of the priestly due, is qualified by "kingdom," a royal status. Whereas "priests" might then suggest "idleness" or "leisure," it is seen as qualified by "holy nation," i.e. people busy with the task of holiness.

The point underlined by Ex. 19:6 in this analogy is Israel's dignified benificence, her peaceful status[3] and her engagement in the task of holiness in the Messianic Age. Thus Blinzler's allusion

---

[1] "Three things were given conditionally (by the Lord), the Land of Israel, the Temple and the Throne of the house of David . . . Until Jerusalem was chosen, any place in the land of Israel was thought suitable for the sacrifice of burnt-offerings. But after Jerusalem was chosen, the sacrifices elsewhere in the Land of Israel ceased to be suitable (as in Dt. 12:13f.) . . . Until the eternal habitation was chosen, the whole of Jerusalem was suitable for the divine presence. But after . . . , the rest of Jerusalem ceased to be suitable (as in Ps. 132:13-14) . . . Until Aaron was chosen, the rest of the children of Israel were thought fit for the priesthood. But after . . . , the rest of the children of Israel were no longer thought fit (as in Num. 18:19; 25:12-13) . . . Until David was chosen, all the children of Israel were thought fit for kingship. After David was chosen, the rest of the children of Israel were no longer fit (as in 2 Chr. 13:5)" (translation according to W. G. Braude, *Midrash on the Psalms, Midrash Tehellim*, New Haven, 1959, II, 137-39).

[2] Aggad. Beresh. 79: "R. Acha (ca. A. D. 320) has said, 'Why are the names of the tribes written on the stones (of the high priest's breastplate)?' Because at Sinai they were all called priests, as it says: 'And you shall be to me a kingdom of priests,' said God. It is impossible that they all present (the sacrifice) at the altar; therefore all their names were to be written on the heart of the high priest. Then when the high priest enters in order to sacrifice before me, it is as if each of them were a high priest before me, clothed in the priestly vestments.'" Cf. *Str-B* III, 390.

[3] Sim. Schrenk, *op. cit.*, p. 250.

to "Jewish world-rule"[1] lacks foundation. In this passage "kingdom" receives no more emphasis than any of the other qualifications. It in no way implies a political messianic hope of Jewish world domination. Rather it is explained first as referring to the fact that only Israelites shall occupy the throne of Israel. Secondly, in the explanation of Rabbi Eliezer b. Jose, it is said to point to the fact that Israel, as priests in the Coming Age, shall possess the dignity proper to royalty. Since מַמְלָכָה is qualified by כֹּהֲנִים, as R. Eliezer points out, it is explicitly prohibited from being misunderstood as implying domination!

Among other references to Ex. 19:6, the Midrash on Ex. 12:43 shows how Ex. 19:6a,b was used to demonstrate the hermeneutical rule of the general and the particular.

Finally, a Midrash on Ps. 10 might be mentioned in which Ex. 19:6 has been cited in connection with Lev. 19:2.[2] This passage is interesting in that the EF is used to underline the theme of holiness. This use might recall the content and context of Jub. 33:20.

We *summarize.* References to the EF in the Rabbinic literature are relatively rare. These few citations were employed in a variety of ways. Thus the passage served to locate the date of the New Moon (Gemara of Shabb. 86a, 87), to provide an analogy for the proper wearing of vestments (Zeb. 19a), or to afford an example of a hermeneutical rule (Mek. Ex. 12:43). Where Ex. 19:6 was the direct subject of a Midrash (Mek. Ex. 19:6), מַמְלָכָה was explained as signifying that the throne of Israel would be occupied only by Israelites, or, further, to assure the royal, i.e. dignified and self-supported, character of Israel in the Messianic Age. כֹּהֲנִים is explained as qualifying מַמְלָכָה, prohibiting any implication of domination. Further, it is said to be qualified by "holy nation," implying an engagement in the task of holiness. It was also interpreted as inferring the priestly prerogative and function of Israel *in toto* before the idolatry of the Golden Calf, after which occasion this prerogative was limited to the lineage of Levi. In a Midrash on Ps. 10:1, Ex. 19:6 was related to Lev. 19:2 and the thought of Israel's holi-

[1] Blinzler, *op. cit.*, p. 60.

[2] The Midrash to Ps. 10:1 notes that to the children of Israel was said, "You shall be holy" (Lev. 19:2). "By this command the Holy One, blessed be He, meant: Since you were hallowed for my purpose even before I created the earth, therefore ye are to be holy, as I am holy: Ye shall be unto me a kingdom of priests and a holy nation" (translation according to Braude, *op. cit.*, I, 150).

ness. Though occasionally the old theme of holiness does appear in connection with Ex. 19:6 in this Rabbinic literature, the correlate is not the original element of election but that of ethical obedience and faithfulness to the Torah. All these Rabbinic references in their earliest written form, of course, are post-Apostolic. Though there is the possibility that the written tradition can be traced back to a far earlier oral stage, in the case of the EF the evidence seems to suggest that even if an earlier oral tradition could be ascertained it exerted no direct influence[1] upon the New Testament's formulation or interpretation of Ex. 19:6.

I. Apocalypse 1:6, 5:10, 20:6

Within the NT literature at least two documents contain reference to the EF, 1 Peter and the Apocalypse of St. John. Though writing in far different styles and addressing dissimilar situations, the authors of both compositions have shown an awareness and appreciation of the historical and theological significance of this formula. Alongside the references of Philo these verses in the Apoc. offer the closest chronological point of contact with 1 P while also demonstrating a further manner of Christian interpretation. Particularly important for our purposes is what the use of the EF here indicates concerning its relatedness or unrelatedness to the interpretation of 1 P.

Initial reference to the EF occurs in the Christological hymn, in ch. 1, verses 5-6. This hymn appears again in somewhat altered form in ch. 5:9f.[2]

> ('Ἰησοῦ Χριστοῦ) ὁ μάρτυς ὁ πιστός, ὁ πρωτότοκος τῶν νεκρῶν καὶ ὁ ἄρχων τῶν βασιλέων τῆς γῆς. Τῷ ἀγαπῶντι ἡμᾶς καὶ λύσαντι ἡμᾶς ἐκ τῶν ἁμαρτιῶν ἡμῶν ἐν τῷ αἵματι αὐτοῦ, καὶ ἐποίησεν ἡμᾶς βασιλείαν, ἱερεῖς τῷ θεῷ καὶ πατρὶ αὐτοῦ . . .

The *context* in which this hymn appears for the first time is composed of a literary salutation (v. 4a) and blessing (v. 4b), a prophetic word concerning the coming of the Lord (v. 7), and a direct

[1] Although, however, the relation preserved in the Rabbinic tradition between priestliness and holiness certainly is consistant with the emphasis in other texts quoting the EF.

[2] Frequently ch. 20:6 is mentioned as being related to 1:5f. and 5:9f. In this verse, however, there is no mention of the hymn common to both previous passages and allusion to Ex. 19:6 is rather vague (cf. *infra*, pp. 114-117). Cerfaux, *op. cit.*, p. 29, Sevenster, *op. cit.*, p. 401, suggest also 22:3-5; however, it is difficult to find any specific reflection of Ex. 19:6 here. Not every reference to priestly service or to royal rule is necessarily an allusion to Ex. 19:6.

word from God Himself (v. 8), which together with the hymn form the unit vv. 4-8, the prologue to the book. Ernst Lohmeyer has called attention to the hymn's Hebraic conclusion and posited that the unity of this section may be accounted for by the liturgical custom and style of Jewish and early Christian worship services.[1]

Three strophes compose the *hymn*. This triad is evident in the three predicates ascribed to Jesus Christ (v. 5a) and by the three brief verbal clauses: "to Him Who loves us, and freed us from our sins by His blood, and made us a kingdom, priests to His God and Father" (vv. 5b-6a). Ex. 19:6 has been alluded to in such a way that it provides the substance of the last of these verbal clauses describing the salvatory work of Jesus Christ.

The Hebraic character of these verses has also been cited by R. H. Charles who has noted the "pure Hebraism" of the construction τῷ ἀγαπῶντι . . . καὶ ἐποίησεν "in which the participle of the first line is resolved into a finite verb in the second."[2] This would be a factor pointing to relatively early composition.

Commentators are agreed that allusion has been made here to Ex. 19:6; however, opinions regarding the original reading of 1:6 and the Version or Versions from which it ultimately derives are quite diverse. Whereas Wilhelm Bousset and Alfred Loisy describe this verse simply as a poor translation of מַמְלֶכֶת כֹּהֲנִים,[3] other scholars postulate that the author was following a textual tradition differing from that of the MT. This question we shall take up at the end of this chapter. With Nestle, the preferred textual reading is βασιλείαν, ἱερεῖς over against the younger variants βασίλειον[4] (apparently an attempt at correlation with 1 P 2:9b), βασιλεῖς καὶ[5] (an attempt to accommodate with ἱερεῖς),[6] βασιλείαν καὶ[7] (a *lectio facilior* provided through καί), and ἱεράτευμα[8] (also a likely correlation with 1 P 2:5,

[1] E. Lohmeyer, *Die Offenbarung des Johannes* (*HNT* 16), 2. Aufl., 1953, pp. 9-13, p. 9.

[2] R. H. Charles, *A Critical and Exegetical Commentary on the Revelation of St. John* (*ICC* 18/1-2), 1920, I, 15. So also A. Loisy, *L'Apocalypse de Jean*, Paris, 1923, p. 71; Lohmeyer, *ibid.*, p. 11.

[3] W. Bousset, *Die Offenbarung Johannis* (*KEK* 16), 6. Aufl., 1906, p. 188; Loisy, *ibid.*

[4] Maj. 046, Min 69, al. For an extensive listing of witnesses cf. H. C. Hoskier, *Concerning the Text of the Apocalypse*, London, 1929, II, 34f.

[5] Porfirianus, Min. 1, al.; cf. same reading by same Witnesses at 5:10.

[6] *Contra* Lohmeyer, *op. cit.*, p. 11, who allows the "glatter" βασιλεῖς as possibly the original reading!

[7] Min. 99, Vulg. cod, Tertullian *Exhort. cast.* 7.

[8] Min. 42, 69, al.

9). Significant in the preferred reading as well as in the variants is that the first two members of the EF are presented, in contrast to the MT and similar to the LXX, as independent nouns.[1] The younger variants are characterized by their efforts to improve upon this independence and provide for a smoother text, in part attempting to relate the text to 1 P 2:9 and its basis, LXX Ex. 19:6.

What might be said concerning the purpose and use of the EF here? First, the omission of the second comma, "holy nation" suggests that the factor of holiness assumed no significance for the author. With the original *parallelismus membrorum* already destroyed, there was no necessity then for its inclusion in the text. The structure and nature of the hymn in which the EF has been incorporated indicate, rather, that though these two predicates have been ascribed to the believing community, it is not the community but Jesus Christ Who is the primary concern in vv. 5-6. His making "us a kingdom, priests before God and His Father" has been coordinated with His "loving us and redeeming us." That is, application of the EF is presented explicitly as a product of the saving activity of Jesus Christ. "Kingdom" and "priests" are not simply honorific titles attributed God's people to express her worthy character (cf. *De Sobr.* 66, *De Abrah.* 56); nor are these terms used to illustrate the themes of election or holiness (cf. Ex. 19:6, Jub. 16:18, 33:20) but are cited as familiar *notae* of Jesus Christ's redeeming work (cp. the redemption motif of 2 Mcc. 2:17).

The absence of any attempt to explain this allusion would suggest that the significance of the EF was sufficiently known, thus making further comment unnecessary. It has often been suggested that the terms "kingdom" and "priests" have been occasioned by and derived from similar predicates for Jesus as "king" and "priest."[2] Though there is no explicit statement to this effect, perhaps the phrase ὁ ἄρχων τῶν βασιλέων τῆς γῆς (v. 5),[3] the thought of incorporation in v. 9: "I, John, your brother, who share with you *in Jesus* the tribulation and the *kingdom* (βασιλείᾳ) and the patient endurance,"

[1] M. Kiddle - M. K. Ross, *The Revelation of St. John* (*Moffatt Commentary*) London, 1940, p. 5, have ignored this independence in their translation: "He has made us a realm of priests for his God and Father."

[2] For a recent treatment cf. Best, *op. cit.*, pp. 292ff., earlier T. Zahn, *Die Offenbarung des Johannes* (*ZKNT* 18), Leipzig, 1924, I, 174f. Cf. also Congar, *Lay People*, p. 67 and *passim*.

[3] Cp. the striking resemblance with Gk. Frag. 67. A closer examination of this similarity, however, would extend beyond the purview of our study.

and the image of the priestly attired figure of "one like a son of man" (v. 13) offer implications of this connection. However, the only point bearing any weight for the hymn—which is to be envisioned also apart from its context—is the phrase of v. 5. In any event, the important fact is that the EF has not been used to develop any concept of the royalty or priesthood of the believing community but rather to describe one facet of the saving work of Jesus Christ. Insofar, these terms hardly represent a "language of compensation" applied consolingly to oppressed and humble Christians![1] Indeed, according to the structure of 1:6, they describe an indispensable step in the process of salvation.

That this hymn with its incorporation of the EF enjoyed a firm place in the liturgy[2] and thought of the circle of churches for which the Apocalypse was intended is demonstrated by its second occurrence in ch. 5:9-10. Here the hymn, in somewhat longer and revised form, is identified as the "New Song" (v. 9): "and they sang a new song saying

> ἄξιος εἶ λαβεῖν τὸ βιβλίον καὶ ἀνοῖξαι τὰς σφραγῖδας αὐτοῦ, ὅτι ἐσφάγης καὶ ἠγόρασας τῷ θεῷ ἐν τῷ αἵματί σου ἐκ πάσης φυλῆς καὶ γλώσσης καὶ λαοῦ καὶ ἔθνους, καὶ ἐποίησας αὐτοὺς τῷ θεῷ ἡμῶν βασιλείαν καὶ ἱερεῖς, καὶ βασιλεύουσιν ἐπὶ τῆς γῆς.

The *context* incorporating this liturgical unit is a vision of the Lamb at the throne in heaven surrounded by four living creatures and twenty-four elders (5:1-4). The Lamb has taken the scroll with the seven seals and is about to open it (vv. 6f.). The central thought of this section is that only the Lamb is worthy of opening the seals.[3] In proclamation of this fact, the four creatures and the twenty-four elders sing a "new song" to Him Who is *worthy* to take the scroll and open its seals (vv. 9f.). As in 1:5f. the burden of this hymn is a

---

[1] *Contra* C. F. D. Moule, "Sanctuary and Sacrifice in the Church of the New Testament," *JTS* n.s. 1/1 (April 1950), p. 36.

[2] The numerous points of contact between Apoc. 1:5f. and the Christological hymn reflected in Col. 1:13-20 suggest their mutual use of a common liturgical source. Cf. M. Dibelius, *An die Kolosser, Epheser and Philemon* (*HNT* 12), 3. neubearbeitete Aufl. von H. Greeven, Tübingen, 1953, pp. 10ff.; E. Lohmeyer, *Die Briefe an die Kolosser und an Philemon* (*KEK* 9/2), 9. Aufl., 1953, pp. 40-68; E. Käsemann, "Eine Urchristliche Taufliturgie," *Festschrift für Rudolf Bultmann*, Stuttgart, 1949, pp. 133-48 [reprinted in *Exegetische Versuche* I, 34-51].

[3] Lohmeyer, *Offenbarung*, p. 53: "Um den Begriff von ἄξιος dreht sich die ganze Vision."

Christological statement regarding the sovereignty and honor of Him Who effected ransom and salvation.

Seven strophes compose the song, according to Lohmeyer.[1] It opens with an ascription of praise ("Worthy are You . . . seals") which is followed by three verbal statements explaining this worth: "because (1) You were slain and (2) by Your blood ransomed for God men from every tribe and tongue and people and nation, and (3) made them before our God a kingdom and priests, and they are kings upon the earth."

The differences from 1:5f. are explained in part by the fact that 5:9f. depicts the hymn as being sung in heaven to the Lamb by the celestial choir of creatures and elders. Here the hymn is addressed to the Lamb in the second person.[2] Accordingly, "by *Your* blood" appears instead of "by *His* blood" (1:5); "*you* made" instead of "*He* made" (1:6); and "*them*" instead of "*us*" (1:6). Beside the addition of "our (God)" (5:10), 5:10 also has a different word order than 1:6: the dative τῷ θεῷ does not follow "kingdom and priests" as in 1:6 but precedes it and καὶ πατρὶ αὐτοῦ is omitted.

The wording of the allusion to the EF is best taken along with Nestle as βασιλείαν καὶ ἱερεῖς. Aside from the addition of the copula,[3] the phrasing is identical to that of 1:6. As in 1:6, the younger variants attempt to accommodate and improve.[4]

Particularly noteworthy in a comparison of 1:6 and 5:10 is the interpretative clause added in the latter verse: "and they are kings on earth."[5] Rather than intended proleptically,[6] this verb seems

---

[1] *Ibid.*, p. 56. The scheme is thus aabbbaa.

[2] Lohmeyer, *ibid.*, p. 57, has noticed that the hymns of the elders, with the exception of 4:8 and 7:12, occur regularly in the second person singular.

[3] The copula provides a smoother formulation; its presence however, is not questioned in the Witnesses.

[4] Koine, Porfirianus, Min. 1, pl. read "kings," as preferred also by von Soden. Here an accommodation has been made to "priests." Cp. the Ethiopic: "And of them You place in the Kingdom of God priests and kings." Sinaiticus reads "a kingdom and a priesthood," accommodating the second member to the first; cp. the Sahidic: "You made us a kingdom for our God and priest." The Syriac palimpsest offers "a kingdom and priests and kings"; cf. Ethiopic. Cf. further, Hoskier, *op. cit.*, II, pp. 156f.

[5] Significant textual attestation for both βασιλεύουσιν and βασιλεύσουσιν makes a determination of the original reading difficult; for the compilation of Witnesses cf. Hoskier, *ibid.* Since, however, the Witnesses favoring the future show tendencies toward correction, perhaps the Alexandrinus and accompanying MSS deserve the benefit of the doubt.

Furthermore, the sense of this passage would also argue for the present tense. The three preceding aorists indicate a present reality. If Christ (the

to have been used to describe the believers' present condition.[1] Whereas 1:5-6 might represent a liturgical source which the author of the Apocalypse incorporated into his work, insofar revealing little concerning the author's evaluation of the EF, this clause added to the hymn and following the EF in 5:10 indicates that the *significance of the EF* for him lay in the term "kingdom" and *the royal status of the believing community*. The term "priests," as is seen, received no comment. Further, addition of the phrase "from every tribe and tongue and people and nation" represents a familiar universalistic motif[2] which the author has annexed to the EF and included in the hymn. These additions indicate that though the thrust of the hymn remains essentially Christological, the author was also intent upon stating something about the breadth and status of the Lamb's followers.

This status, however, must be seen within its proper boundaries. An explanation of the terms of the EF as they are employed in the Christ hymn in 1:5f. and 5:9f. which fails to explore the remainder of the references to the EF which have been treated thus far fails proportionately to comprehend the significance which these terms bear. Little can be gained, for instance, by seeking the sources of 1:6 or 5:10 in a Melchizedek tradition,[3] or in "the dream of a nation of 'prince-priests.'"[4] As inappropriate as it is to interpret the first member of the EF in the general terms of "royal freedom" and "a right to rule,"[5] so equally out of place are comments concerning the second member which speculate about the relationship between ordained priest and layman or the layman's limited sharing in

---

Lamb) *has made* the believers a kingdom, then they are already enjoying this status; it is not something yet to be attained in the future. Cf. e.g., 1:9 where "kingdom" is also treated as present reality—in connection with the thought of 1:6. The future tense might have been influenced and encouraged by 20:6. In any case, in comparison with the present the future is a *lectio facilior*. It is easier to imagine a scribe altering the present to a future (in the awareness that believers are not yet ruling the earth) than to conceive of his substituting a present for a future. Preference for the present has also been shown by Westcott-Hort; Bousset, *op. cit.*, p. 261; Charles, *op. cit.*, p. 148; and Lohmeyer, *op. cit.*, p. 57.

[6] So Charles, *ibid.*

[1] So Lohmeyer, *ibid.*

[2] Cf. 7:9, 10:11, 11:9, 13:7, 14:6, 17:15.

[3] Cf. P. Ketter, *Die Apokalypse* (*Herders Bibelkommentar* 16/2), 3. Aufl., Freiburg, 1953, p. 38.

[4] Kiddle-Ross, *op. cit.*, pp. 8f.; Best, *op. cit.*, p. 280.

[5] A. Schlatter, *Die Briefe und die Offenbarung des Johannes*, 1950, pp. 136f.

priestly dignity.[1] Here we have two extremes typical of "protestant" exegesis in the former case and Roman Catholic exegesis in the latter. However, both the ideas of freedom and privilege, hierarchy and sacrifice are theological reflections which have nothing in common with our texts.

Nor is Charles' conclusion, representative of many commentaries, devoid of a slight misstatement. "Our text, then," he says, "means that Christ has made us a kingdom, each member of which is a priest unto God."[2] Actually, not a single word of the hymn in either 1:5f. or 5:9f. concerns individuals or has been sung by individuals *qua* individuals. Rather, reference is only made to "us" and "them"; those who have been made the objects of Christ's redeeming activity are mentioned only in the plural. Admittedly, the term ἱερατευμα was not used. If we are to assume that this word was intentionally avoided, then it may be held that for the original composer of this hymn the idea of collectivity was not of central importance. It may be, however, that his formulation of the EF is simply dependent upon a phrasing represented also in the Versions of Symmachus and Theodotion. Nothing can be proved upon the assumption that the composer "avoided" a particular formulation. In any event, nevertheless, "priests" in the plural and not "priest" is the text. And despite the clause "and they are kings upon the earth" added in 5:10, the hymn speaks of the believers' having been made "*a kingdom.*" This collective term allows no thought of individuality. As throughout the entire chain of allusions to the EF, *these predicates have been ascribed not to individuals but to the people of God in toto.*

Awareness of the interpretation which this EF had received previous to its allusion in the hymn of Apoc. 1:5f. and 5:9f. affords a likely clue as to its use here. Throughout the entire chain of allusions these terms have been used to describe not the honor or significance of particular individuals but rather the essence of a people, a nation,

[1] Cf. Ketter, *op. cit.*, pp. 38f., 98: "Auch der Laie hat bis zu einem bestimmten Grad Anteil an der priesterlichen Würde. Durch die Erlösung steht auch ihm der Zutritt zu Gott offen. Jeder Christ ist durch die Taufe und Firmung berufen, anbetend vor Gott zu stehen, ein Segenspender für die andern zu sein und sie zu Gott zu führen" (pp. 38f.); p. 98: "Zuch die Laien nehmen Anteil am hierarchischen Apostolat der Kirche . . . Jedem gibt der Taufcharakter die Fähigkeit, in Christus und durch Christus dem Vater Opfer darzubringen, ohne dass dadurch dem Weihepriestertum etwas von seiner besonderen Würde und Aufgabe entzogen würde."

[2] Charles, *op. cit.*, p. 16 (regarding 1:6).

which is the private possession of God and the object of His saving activity. There is no indication that this hymn departs from either of these basic thoughts. Here privileges are not being doled out to single persons or to "den einzelnen Gläubigen,"[1] a thought which has led to the most fanciful and anachronistic theories of democratization. Rather the condition of the entire believing community is being described. The *novel* feature of this Christian employment of the EF is not a fragmentation or individualization of this ancient statement concerning the people of God but rather the connection which is drawn between these predicates and the work of Jesus Christ, the Lamb of God. This is a development upon the second factor implicit in the use of the EF, a factor typical for 1 P also and thus for all the New Testament references to Ex. 19:6. It is namely through and on account of Jesus Christ, His suffering and death, resurrection and exaltation, that the believing community has become a kingdom and priests. The saving activity of God has been effected through Jesus Christ and those who confess Him as Lord He has made partakers in this salvation and insofar "a kingdom and priests."

Reference to a future existence as "priests of God and of Christ" and similarity with the final clause of 5:10 hint that perhaps also 20:6 was alluding to the EF:

> μακάριος καὶ ἅγιος ὁ ἔχων μέρος ἐν τῇ ἀναστάσει τῇ πρώτῃ· ἐπὶ τούτων ὁ δεύτερος θάνατος οὐκ ἔχει ἐξουσίαν, ἀλλ' ἔσονται ἱερεῖς τοῦ θεοῦ καὶ τοῦ Χριστοῦ, καὶ βασιλεύσουσιν μετ' αὐτοῦ τὰ χίλια ἔτη.

The differences from 1:6 and 5:10, nevertheless, raise serious doubt as to whether an allusion to Ex. 19:6 was actually intended. 1:6 and 5:10 indicate that the EF was known to the author as part of a Christological hymn. The context here bears no connection with the former hymn, but is rather a prophetic paraenesis on martyrdom presented in the form of a celestical vision.[2] Further, the sole suggestion of relatedness with the EF is the term ἱερεῖς. The first member of the EF does not appear but can, at best, be implied in the clause "and they shall reign with Him a thousand years." Third, in this section on martyrdom and resurrection not Jesus Christ or the Lamb but the martyrs are the center of attention. Fourth, whereas in 1:6 and 5:10 "kingdom" and "priests"

[1] Lohmeyer, *op. cit.*, p. 11.
[2] Cf. Lohmeyer, *op. cit.*, pp. 161ff.

describe the *present* condition of the redeemed, according to 20:6 these are qualities to be realized only in the *future* (cf. the future tense of the verbs). Fifth, in contrast to 1:6 and 5:10—and for that matter all previous references to the EF[1]—not Israel *in toto* or the entire community but only a segment thereof, the martyrs, is promised these predicates.

These considerations are complicated by the fact that the precise wording of the original text is in question. 20:5a, for instance, has been omitted by certain witnesses.[2] Lohmeyer has also noted that the strophic arrangement of vv. 4-6 diverges from that of the verses preceding and following.[3] Further, the MSS vary concerning the tense of the verb in the final clause of v. 6, reading both present[4] and future.[5] With Nestle the future is probably to be preferred, though this reading introduces a certain conflict with v. 4 (καὶ ἐβασίλευσαν [aor.] μετὰ τοῦ Χριστοῦ χίλια ἔτη) which v. 6 apparently parallelled.[6] In this case, ἐβασίλευσαν may be taken as a proleptic aorist from which the author then shifted into the tense of the "prophetic future"[7] which is continued through v. 8. The textual problems raise questions beyond the scope of our study and need not detain us any further. These difficulties indicate that disagreement on the textual structure was early and that a redactor was possibly at work here.

In seeking the meaning of this verse, Charles attempted to reconcile 20:6 with 1:6.

> "All the faithful are already kings and priests to God (1:6). On the other hand, when the messianic kingdom is established, the glorified martyrs will in a special sense be kings and priests; for in that kingdom the priesthood and kingship of the glorified martyrs will come into actual manifestation relative to the

---

[1] With the exception of Gk. Frag. 67.

[2] Sinaiticus, a large number of other MSS, and the Syriac; cf. Hoskier, *op. cit.*, p. 556.

[3] Lohmeyer, *loc. cit.*

[4] Alexandrinus.

[5] Sinaiticus, Laudianus and a number of Min.; cf. Hoskier, *loc. cit.*

[6] Alexandrinus, Min. 1, and other MSS were possibly aware of this parallelism and hence omitted τὰ (χίλια ἔτη) in an attempt to coincide this reading with χίλια ἔτη of v. 4. This attempt at correspondence might also explain Alexandrinus' reading of the present βασιλεύουσιν (= ἐβασίλευσαν, v. 4) in v. 6. For the future "they shall reign" cf. also 22:6; cp. also the MSS favoring this reading in 5:10.

[7] Cf. Lohmeyer, *op. cit.*, p. 162.

heathen nations who will then be evangelized by them (20:6); ... the priestly office of the blessed in the millennial kingdom have to do with the nations who are to be evangelized during this period (14:6-7, 15:4)"[1]

The passage to which Charles points in support of this suggestion (14:6-7, 15:4), however, substantiate no such connection between the "priests" of the EF and the Christ hymn and the thought of evangelization. Therefore, Loisy justifiably rejected this hypothesis as inconsistent with the intent of the book as a whole: "Evangélisation et sacerdoce sont deux, et nulle part notre livre n'insinue qu'une oeuvre d'évangélisation proprement dite doive s'effectuer par les élus du regne de mille ans."[2]

Rather, we must ask if 20:6 contains any reference to Ex. 19:6 at all. The single point of contact is ἱερεῖς. Not even the verb βασιλεύσουσιν can be assumed to reflect the first member of the EF; rather, it has more likely been suggested by the verb ἐβασίλευσαν of v. 4. When the correspondence of Apoc. 20:6 with the LXX version of Is. 61:6 is considered (ἱερεῖς κυρίον κληθήσεσθε λειτουργοὶ θεοῦ), there is even greater reason to believe that 20:6 recalls not Ex. 19:6 but this prophetic expression of eschatological hope. Not only the terminology (ἱερεῖς τοῦ κυρίου / ἱερεῖς τοῦ θεοῦ καὶ τοῦ χριστοῦ) but also the futuric aspect ("shall be called" / "shall be, shall reign") is similar.[3] Finally, a point making the reference here to Is. 61:6 more than likely is the citation of a verse from this same complex of Isaiah in Apoc. 21:2, Is. 61:10.

The purpose of this reference to Is. 61:6 was to supply substance to the prophetic paraenesis. The glorified martyrs are lauded for their courageous faith, and by implication, are established as an example for the suffering Church by the double clause promising them in the resurrection a priesthood and a reign with Christ in the Millennium. The fact that this priesthood and kingship were not promised to the Israel of God, the Church *in toto*, but exclusively to the martyrs, the fact that these attributes were not considered

---

[1] Charles, *op. cit.*, I, 16f.; II, 186.

[2] Loisy, *op. cit.*, pp. 354f.

[3] The promises of the Covenant Formula, while originally also expressed in the future tense, were regarded by the Church as fulfilled through the saving work of Christ. As 1:6 and 5:10 show, the predicates of the EF were regarded as present reality for them that believe. Thought of a future realization of this condition would be a direct contradition of that which was sung in 1:5f. and 5:9f.

a present possession but a future hope, and the fact that these predicates were limited to the Millennium together indicate the uniqueness of the thought developed here and its variance from the significance of the EF as employed in the Apoc. Not in 1:5f. or 5:9f. but here the apocalyptic vision of the author comes to direct expression.[1]

1:5f., 5:9f. and 20:6 represent the author's use of not the same but rather different sources and themes. Whereas the EF contained in the Christ hymn describes a realized result of Christ's redeeming task, Is. 61:6 in Apoc. 20:6 constitutes a portion of the apocalyptic vision of the Millennium. It is difficult to see how Cerfaux could maintain that in the Apocalypse the three streams of pre-Christian interpretation which he proposes (Palestinian Rabbinic messianism with its emphasis upon royalty, spiritualization of Alexandria and its emphasis upon priesthood, apocalypticism of Jubilees and its celestial priesthood) were unified.[2] In the first place, the very existence of these three proposed streams is highly doubtful. In the second, Cerfaux has identified Apoc. 20:6 with 1:6 and 5:10 without stopping to ask if such a relation did in fact exist. 20:6 does speak of a celestial priesthood and reign but 1:6 and 5:10 do not. Traces of a "spiritualized" interpretation are completely absent. The only nuance, among those which Cerfaux has named, which can be demonstrated is the first, the accent upon kingship found in 5:10. This, moreover, is the sole piece of evidence throughout the entire group of allusions to the EF for Cerfaux's proposed stream of Palestinian messianic accent upon the first member of the EF and the theme of royalty! As we already noted, this final phrase of 5:10, absent in the original hymn, represents the hand of the author using this thought of the hymn to assure his addressees of the reality of this existence as kingdom and priests.[3]

---

[1] It is possible, if not likely, that 22:3-5 relate to 20:6, presenting the final vision and the final state after the interlude of 20:4ff.; cf. the final clause of 22:5 "and they shall reign forever and ever" and λατρεύσουσιν αὐτῷ (22:3); cp. Is. 61:6: λειτουργοὶ θεοῦ. This would preclude rather than include any affinity of 22:3-5 then to Ex. 19:6.

[2] Cerfaux, *op. cit.*, p. 29.

[3] Schrenk, *op. cit.*, p. 265, holds that "der Anteil der Glaubenden an der königlichen Herrschaft aus dieser basileia gefolgert wird." Perhaps 5:10bgn to be best understood in this sense as not suggesting an independent reisi of the believers but rather participation in the βασιλεία of God.

Summarizing, we have noted that in the Apocalypse the EF was presented as an element of a Christ hymn reflected in 1:5f. and 5:9f. Integrated in each case with two preceding clauses, it was used to denote one of the fruits of the redemptive activity of Jesus Christ. Applied, as in other allusions to the EF, to a total community, the Israel of God, the novel feature of this NT allusion in comparison with its predecessors is the connection drawn between the EF and Jesus Christ. Application of Ex. 19:6 to the believing community was seen as a product of the passion and exaltation of Jesus Christ. The text resembles that of Symmachus and Theodotion, following the MT more closely than the LXX. Nevertheless, the first two members of the EF appear as independent nouns. In 5:10 they are even separated by a copula. This latter context presents a more elaborate form of the hymn, including a phrase denoting the universalistic aspect of Christ's redemption (5:9) and a clause stressing the present realization of the "kingdom" of the EF upon earth (5:10). 20:6, occurring within a celestial vision of the Millennium and referring to the future priesthood and kingship of the martyrs with Christ in this thousand year period, relates not to Ex. 19:6 and the Christ hymn but to Is. 61:6. This was not a description of a present reality but a forecast of a future condition. Its purpose was to compose part of a prophetic paraenesis designed to encourage the *Ecclesia militans* in the face of persecution. In contrast to this picture of priesthood and kingship in 20:6, 1:5f. and 5:9f. develop no idea of a celestial cult or a future political or heavenly reign but rather express the concrete and present product of Christ's saving work.

Though in these verses we have "das einzig Wort des NT, in dem das persönlich gefasste Priesterbild auf die Christenheit übertragen wird,"[1] this personal aspect does not imply an individualistic interpretation. There is no concentration here upon the singular individual "priest" but upon "us" as the total believing community (1:6) and upon the great number "from every tribe and tongue and people and nation" (5:9). The word "kingdom" preserves a collective significance. Believers are a "kingdom and priests" and even "kings upon earth"; but they are so only as a group, only in the plural, only as Church. From this statement the author of the

---

[1] Schrenk, *ibid.*

Apocalypse made no deductions concerning the rights or privileges of the individual believer. Questionable, therefore, are the discourses on Christian liberty, ecclesiastical structure, or ministry and service which are offered so often in connection with these verses. It is the Church as one single corporate entity and not individual believers to which this hymnic expression of the salvation wrought through Christ applies.

In this connection it may be held that the predicates of kingship and priesthood ascribed to the Church coincide with the same predicates ascribed to Jesus Christ. The Apocalypse does hint that the faithful were seen as participants in the priesthood and kingship of Christ. But again it must be emphasized that no such explicit statement to this effect has been made by the author. This can only be inferred. The essential fact here is that the primary function of the EF is to make a Christological-soteriological statement rather than to describe the Church or, far less, her ministry and/or her ranks of privilege.

It is this essential fact which is the bond between Apoc. 1:6, 5:10, and 1 P 2:9: application of the predicates of the EF to the believing community is a consequence of the death and resurrection of Jesus Christ. In their respective uses and interpretations of the EF, the texts of Ex. 19:6 which they follow, and their over-all literary conceptions, however, each author goes his separate way; no direct dependence of either upon the other is detectable.[1] In view of the integration of Ex. 19:6 in a more or less fixed Christological hymn and in view of the clearer explication of this Christ/EF relationship in the Apocalypse, we may assume that this hymn represents a stage of interpretation of and development upon the EF later than that of 1 P 2:9. Insofar, though these passages in the Apocalypse indicate the firm position which the EF was given in early Christian liturgical expression, they exerted no direct influence upon the formulation of 1 P.

The NT literature as a whole reflects the situation found in its OT counterpart: the explicit role played by the EF is a strikingly minor one. Cerfaux has commented that "the silence of St. Paul is significant."[2] The opinion that Ex. 19:6 together with Dan. 7:22 was "of utmost significance for the conception of the reign of God

[1] Cf. Sevenster, *op. cit.*, p. 407.
[2] Cerfaux, *op. cit.*, p. 32.

as it appears in the teaching of Jesus and in the NT generally"[1] is an overstatement lacking evidence. That the significance of the EF relates to the very core of the Christian evangel is evident in both Apoc. 1:5f. and 5:9f. Explicit reference to this formula, however, is traceable only to these two texts of the Apocalypse and the passage to which we now turn, 1 P 2:4-10.[2]

Summary and Conclusions

References or allusions to Ex. 19:6 in the Jewish and Apostolic literature evince variations as well as similarities in both the textual formation and the theological interpretation of this ancient Hebrew tradition. Nevertheless, despite all differences these texts display a number of basic affinities which derive from the fundamental significance of this passage throughout Israel's history and its mode of transmission. It is precisely these affinities, therefore, which may be assumed to have exercised a determinative influence upon the formulation and interpretation of 1 P 2:5 and 9.

From our observations concerning the *textual formation* and transmission of the EF *two main text modes* have become evident. On the one hand, we have met a reading in which the first and second members of the EF are *mutually dependent*. Such a formation occurs with marked infrequency, being represented only, in the original MT and the Version of Aquila (βασιλεία ἱερέων), the Bohairic ("holy kingdom"), the Old Latin (*regnum sacratissimum*) and the Vulgate (*regnum sacerdotale*).[3] On the other hand, the alternative text form in which the first and second members occur as *two independent nouns* is represented in variation by the entire remainder of references to or versions of Ex. 19:6. The length and breadth of this formation is one of the factors arguing for the substantival function of βασίλειον in the ambiguous text of the LXX, βασίλειον ἱεράτευμα. If these factors substantiating βασίλειον as substantive may be re-

---

[1] Richardson, *op. cit.*, p. 86. He arrives at this conclusion possibly because he has identified the EF with "covenant terminology" in general.

[2] For post-Apostolic references to the EF—by this time via its interpretation in either 1 P 2:9 or Apoc. 1:6, 5:10—cf. Cerfaux, *op. cit.*, pp. 32ff.; B. Lohse, *RGG* V, 578ff.

[3] Representative of this text form but only distantly related are the Latin Version (*regnum sacerdotale*) of Jub. 16:18, the Vulgate's translation (*regale sacerdotium*) of 1 P 2:9, and the Syriac ("priestly kingdom") and Ethiopic ("holy kingdom") Versions of Apoc. 1:6.

garded as sufficiently convincing, then we may conclude that this second text form of the EF began with the LXX and included the *Targumim* (מלכין וכהנין, Codex Neofiti, T. Jerus. I, II; מלכין כהנין, T. Onk.) and other Versions such as Symmachus and Theodotion (cf. the Syrohexapla) (βασιλεία ἱερεῖς), the Peshitta ("kingdom and priests"), Sahidic and Armenian ("kingdom and priesthood") as well as all the references treated in this chapter: Jub. 16:18 ("kingdom and priests"),[1] Gk. Frag. 67 (ἀρχὴ βασιλέων ἱεράτευμα), 2 Mcc. 2:7 (τὸ βασίλειον καὶ τὸ ἱεράτευμα), *De Sobr.* 66 and *De Abrah.* 56 (βασίλειον καὶ ἱεράτευμα), Apoc. 1:6 (βασιλείαν ἱερεῖς) and 5:10 (βασιλείαν καὶ ἱερεῖς).

In explanation of certain variations within this second stream of text form, "mistranslation"[2] or "misquotation" have occasionally been suggested. Ernest Best, in fact, discussing 2 Mcc. 2:17, goes so far as to deduce from this supposed misquotation of the text that "little importance was attached to the idea of a general priesthood"![3] Yet if this assumption were true, it would be difficult to account for any reference to the EF whatsoever! In addition to Best's misjudgment of the significance of the allusion to Ex. 19:6 in 2 Mcc. 2:17, his inference of a casual attitude toward the text is far too superficial an explanation of this variation, let alone of others.

Further attempts to account for these variations involve the postulation of one or more text forms differing from both the MT and the LXX, which then served as a basis for later allusions to the EF. These theories however, are riddled with inconsistencies and raise just as many problems as they intend to solve. In view of this second text form in which the first two members of the EF are separate and independent, there has been postulated, for instance, a Hebrew text which contained not the *status constructus* מַמְלֶכֶת of the MT but rather a *status absolutus*: מַמְלָכָה כֹּהֲנִים. This text is held to have been reflected in Ethiopic Jub. 16.18, Apoc. 1:6, 5:10, Symmachus and Theodotion, and the *Targumim*.[4] Charles, while

[1] Jub. 33:20, though rendering both members as adjectives ("a priestly and royal and chosen nation"), also represents this separation or independence.

[2] Charles, *Jubilees*, p. 116 and *AP* II, 38, in his note on Jub. 16:18 describes LXX Ex. 19:6 as an incorrect translation of the MT eventually adopted also by 1 P. Bousset, *op. cit.*, p. 188 and Loisy, *op. cit.*, p. 71 suggest that Apoc. 1:6 is likewise a poor translation of the MT.

[3] Best, *op. cit.*, p. 277.

[4] Cf. Hort, *op. cit.*, pp. 124ff; Cerfaux, *op. cit.*, p. 6; Dabin, *op. cit.*, p. 30; Lohmeyer, *op. cit.*, p. 11.

agreeing that Apoc. 1:6 and 5:10 probably rested upon such a Hebrew text,[1] posited the existence of a further pre-Christian Greek version, a later "revised form of the LXX which was subsequently revised and incorporated by Theodotion in his version" and which also influenced the formation of the Apocalypse passages.[2] That is, Charles imagines the existence of not only one but two texts, a Hebrew and a Greek, and maintains that Apoc. 1:6, 5:10 were influenced by both. However, the postulation of a second text when not even the existence of the first has been proved leads to only greater confusion rather than to clarification of the matter. Furthermore, in regard to the proposed Hebrew text, it appears inconsistent when another supporter, Lohmeyer, declares that Apoc. 1:6 depends upon a text reading "*kingdom*, priests" and then speculates that the original reading of Apoc. 1:6 was "*kings*, priests"![3] Certainly a reading of "kings, priests" (cf. also the *Targumim*) would hardly suggest dependence upon an earlier text which read "kingdom, priests."

Similar objections might be directed against Schrenk's proposal of a text different from the LXX, upon which not only Apoc. 1:6 and 5:10 but also 2 Mcc. 2:17 and *De Sobr.* 66, *De Abrah.* 56 were dependent.[4] Representing this tradition, he maintains, are also the *Targumim*, the Peshitta and the Syrohexapla. Again, it must be asked what similarity is to be found between the *Targumim* (which he previously describes as representing a Synagogue tradition where all Israelites are regarded as kings)[5] and these other Versions aside from the fact of the independence of "kings" and "priests." Moreover, in suggesting that 2 Mcc. 2:17 and the two texts of Philo belong to a textual tradition other than that of the LXX, Schrenk overlooks the definite terminological affinities between these passages and the LXX, βασίλειον and ἱεράτευμα, both of which are absent in all of the other texts of his proposed tradition.[6] Secondly,

---

[1] *Revelation* I, 16. He likewise draws the connection between these passages, the Syriac, and Eth. Jub. 16:18 and the *Targumim* (cf. *supra*, p. 121, n. 2).

[2] Charles, *op. cit.*, lxvi, lxxx.

[3] Lohmeyer, *loc. cit.*

[4] Schrenk, *op. cit.*, pp. 249f.

[5] *Ibid.*, p. 249.

[6] Cf. Blinzler, *op. cit.*, p. 61, *contra* Schrenk's suggestion: "Aber die beiden Ausdrücke (βασίλειον καὶ ἱεράτευμα), besonders der zweite, sind doch von einer so einmaligen Seltsamkeit, dass die Annahme, sie seien hier nicht aus der LXX geflossen, als abwegig erscheinen muss."

he disregards the *local relationship* of these four Alexandrian texts. Of all the passages reflecting the EF, it is precisely these Alexandrian texts which show the *closest affinity to the LXX*![1]

In the final analysis, these hypotheses not only lack conclusive evidence for the actual existence of the proposed Hebrew or Greek texts; they even fail to account for the disparities of the passages taken to demonstrate the existence of such a text or textual tradition. The only fact demonstrated with certainty by the evidence is that there was a trend, a tradition of text transmission in which the first two members of the EF were treated as independent nouns. An explanation of this fact does not require the supposition of the existence of further Hebrew or Greek text forms. Rather, this fact as well as the variations within this textual tradition are adequately explained when the LXX is taken as the basic text influencing and determining the text form of latter references to Ex. 19:6.[2] This ambiguous phrasing βασίλειον ἱεράτευμα can be taken as a combination of an adjective and a noun or as two separate nouns. Gk. Frag. 67, 2 Mcc. 2:17, *De Sobr.* 66, *De Abrah.* 56 offer evidence that the LXX text was frequently understood in the latter sense. Furthermore, 2 Mcc. 2:17 (addition of article and separating copula) and the texts of Philo (addition of copula) demonstrate the steps taken to insure this independence of βασίλειον and ἱεράτευμα and avoid unclarity. This LXX formation likewise influenced the text forms of other Versions which, though not reproducing its exact wording, maintained the separation between the first and second members. Whereas the *Targumim* accommodated "kings" to "priests," Symmachus and Theodotion rendered "kingdom, priests," a phrasing also represented in Apoc. 1:6, 5:10, the Peshitta, and Jub. 16:18. This is a formation in which, according to Blinzler,[3] the

[1] A far more reasonable conjecture would be that originally a καί stood in the LXX text (βασίλειον καὶ ἱεράτευμα) and was later omitted by a scribe inadvertantly or intentionally. This original reading would then have been the one represented in three Alexandrian texts closest to the LXX, 2 Mcc. 2:17 and *De Sobr.* 66, *De Abrah.* 56. Furthermore, a similar stituation corresponding to this procedure is to be found among the Targumim where the earlier Codex Neofiti contains a copula ("kings *and* priests," cf. also T. Jerus, I, II) whereas the later T. Onkelos omits it ("kings, priests"). Nevertheless, this conjecture could not be proved conclusively and the reading of 1 P. 2:9 suggests that the text of the LXX which we now possess most likely represents the original one. The readings of the Alexandrian texts, moreover, can be accounted for adequately through another explanation.

[2] Sim. Blinzler, *ibid.*

[3] *Ibid.*, pp. 61f.

equivocal βασίλειον was replaced by the unambiguous βασιλεία and the new construction ἱεράτευμα, by the simple *concretum* ἱερεῖς. In some cases a separating copula has also been added. Other texts also display the attempt which was made to correspond these two terms as either two concrete terms (*Targumim*, various MSS of Apoc. 1:6, 5:10) or as two abstract terms (Sahidic and Armenian Versions, other MSS of Apoc. 1:6, 5:10[1]).

These conclusions generally agree with those of Blinzler who has found this second text form and its variations "innerhalb der von der LXX ausgehenden Entwicklungslinie."[2] Yet he holds that the LXX text form itself belonged to the first form represented by the MT, and that it is to be regarded as a combination of adjective and noun: "königliche Priesterschaft."[3] If this were the case, then the entire tradition incorporating this second text form would have to be regarded as originating in an error, i.e. in a misconception of the "true" function of βασίλειον. Is such an assumption necessary? Our investigation of the LXX has shown that the evidence for βασίλειον to be taken as substantive is just as compelling, if not more so, than that suggesting its adjectival function. In view of this fact it seems unnecessary, if not unwarranted, to presume that an entire textual tradition rests upon an error of judgment. The more likely alternative rather is to take a hint from those sources which were nearer the LXX than we and to conclude that their phrasings are also strong evidence for the fact that this tradition not only had its origin in the text of the LXX but also *correctly* represents the intention of the same.

The textual variations in the transmission of and reference to Ex. 19:6 are by no means unrelated to the *interpretations* which this text received. In more than one case the former is a medium of the latter. Despite all variations and particular nuances a fundamental significance of the expression of Ex. 19:6 can be found underlying and relating all references to this verse: *God's true people, Israel, is His elect, holy, and private community.* The purposes which its citation or allusion served and the further interpretation which it received varied from instance to instance. But its basic implication of Israel's election and holiness, though occasionally only implicit,

---

[1] For examples of both concrete and abstract terms cf. *supra*, p. 108 n. 5 and n. 7, respectively.

[2] Blinzler, *op. cit.*, p. 62.

[3] *Ibid.*, p. 61.

remain constant. And in later references these two factors are integrated essentially with the activity of Divine redemption.

The keynote for this significance was given in the original setting of the statement, the Covenant Formula preserved in the text of Exodus 19 and transmitted orally in the cult of the worshipping Hebrew community. As a "holy nation" Israel was a "kingdom of priests" elected by and subordinated to JHWH her king, made holy and commanded to be holy according to her possession by Him. In the *milieu* of the Alexandrian Diaspora the authors of the Septuagint laid particular stress upon Israel's communal character and her mission to the environment. They chose a unique formulation which conveyed Israel's corporateness and the positive aspect of witness implied in her election and holiness. The *Targumim* made a personal application and insofar shifted the kingship from JHWH to Israel, describing her concretely as a nation of "kings (and) priests."[1] In the Book of Jubilees the EF was employed to illustrate the ancient promise of God and the fact that Israel is His elected and private possession (16:18) as well to stress the holiness of God's people and substantiate an exhortation to moral purity. Philo cited this verse similarly as demonstration of the fact that God, by dwelling among His people which form His "royal residence," has fulfilled the patriarchal blessing of Noah upon his sons Shem and Japheth (*De Sobr.* 66). Again, in *De Abrah.* 56 the honorific predicates for Israel contained in the EF are cited to illustrate the dignity and excellence of the ancestors of this noble race: Abraham, Isaac, and Jacob. 2 Mcc. 2:17 mentioned the predicates of the EF as the hallmarks of a nation which had once again experienced the saving activity of her God. By redeeming His people, God had been faithful to His covenant promise and once again restored the worthy status of Israel. This implication of salvation is re-echoed in new and ultimate circumstances in the Christian employment of the EF. According to the Christ hymn cited in Apoc. 1:5f. and 5:9f., it is Jesus Christ Who has made those who believe in Him a "kingdom (and) priests" and in this act of salvation has given the EF its ultimate significance.

In all instances it is Israel or the true People of God to whom

---

[1] It is uncertain, however, if this transference is reflective of theological intention rather than merely of terminological accomodation. Rabbinic references, especially the Mekilta Ex. 19:6, would deny rather than support any theory of the kingship of all Israelites in connection with Ex. 19:6.

these predicates of election and holiness have been ascribed. The sole exception is Gk. Frag. 67 where these predicates were used to celebrate the superiority of Kaath, Levi's son, and the Levitical lineage. However, this appears to be a gloss whose irregularity of interpretation is accompanied by textual problems raising questions of authenticity and genuineness. In all other cases it is the entire community which is being described, 2 Mcc. 2:17 included.[1] In this connection the absence of any mention of the EF among the literature found at Qumran and the absence of any relation with the sacerdotal system of these sectaries is not to be overlooked. On the other hand, nowhere has the EF been employed or intended as a polemical statement against the Levitical institution.

In the constant identification with Israel and her character as the elect and holy nation of God a historical perspective becomes evident. The versions of an allusions to the EF not only are adapted to particular *milieux* and contemporary situations but reflect simultaneously a cherishing of Israel's past and her point of origin as the nation of God. True, not all references make this concern explicit. In *De Abrah.* 56, for instance, as in Apoc. 1:6, and 5:10, we seem to meet mere honorific predicates for the *Gottesvolk*. Behind the very reference to these terms, nevertheless, lies the *awareness and concern for a historical continuum* manifested explicitly in passages such as Jub. 16:18 and 33:20, *De Sobr.* 66, and 2 Mcc. 2:17. It is the continuation of Israel as the elect and holy people of God, her abiding relationship with God, and her continued preservation through Him which are important here.

Attempts such as those of Cerfaux and Blinzler to categorize these passages as indicative of varying trends of interpretation or emphasis fail to comprehend their basic intention. Both scholars have not established the significance of the EF as a single thought unit but have distinguished between "kingdom" and "priests" and from there have developed the separate concepts of "royalty" and "priesthood." Cerfaux would find three distinct patterns of interpretation: (1) an emphasis upon the first member of the EF and the idea of royalty typical of Palestinian Messianism (2 Mcc. 2:17, *Targumim*, cf. also Is. 61:6); (2) an Alexandrian "spiritualization" which ignored the first member and concentrated upon the idea of priesthood (LXX, Philo's writings); (3) and apocalyptic "ideali-

[1] *Contra* Blinzler, *op. cit.*, p. 60.

zation" celebrating the celestial priesthood of Israel (Jub., Apoc.).[1] Blinzler makes no such general categorization but refers to a line of development in which both the first and second members received varying degrees of emphasis, and varying interpretation.[2] The first member, he holds, at first received no emphasis; later, it supposedly received equal stress with the second member (Jub., 2 Mcc., Philo); and eventually in Rabbinic Literature, exclusive emphasis. Originally pointing to the kingship of God, it later became a "Würdeprädikat" for Israel herself, religiously colored (LXX), and applied to the present situation (2 Mcc.) or the future Messianic Age (Jub., Rbb. Lit.). The second member, Blinzler maintains, served originally as a metaphor applied to Israel *in toto* but later was understood literally and employed in connection with the cult. This supposedly led to unclarity of interpretation (Philo, Jub., LXX), reduction of the title to a designation of the institutional priesthood (2 Mcc.), transference of the statement to the future (Is. 61:6), or relative unconcern for the expression (Rbb. Lit.).

Individual differences of opinion concerning the interpretation of particular texts have been noted above and need not be repeated. Important here is the question of methodology and the overall view of the material. The weakness in the analyses of both Blinzler and Cerfaux is their assumption that particular stress was laid upon either one or the other of these members of the EF. As the evidence shows, this formula was not cited in support of a theory of a present or future royalty, an earthly or heavenly priesthood. True, the variations of text and exegesis indicate that the EF was adapted to a specific historical situation and/or a specific theological point. Yet it was not an idea of kingship or priesthood which this verse supported but the elected and holy status of Israel as the special people of God. Though the general theme of the document in which the EF appears must be kept in mind, to allow this theme or a process of interpretation of its author (e.g. Jub., Apoc., and Philo's texts, respectively) to so determine the meaning of the EF as Cerfaux has done prohibits any attempt to secure the underlying significance of the EF *in se* and ignores the meaning which this verse might have assumed in a larger tradition of transmission and interpretation. The geographical distinctions which Cerfaux pro-

[1] Cerfaux, *op. cit.*, pp. 6-21, esp. p. 21.
[2] Blinzler, *loc. cit.*

poses are doubtful not only in content (cf. e.g. 2 Mcc. 2:17—certainly Alexandrian and not Palestinian!) but also in proposed interpretation (what, for instance, is "spiritualistic" about the texts or connotations of the LXX or *De Sobr.* 66, *De Abrah.* 56?)

The evidence suggests rather that the EF was not fragmented into separate concepts but was cited as a unit of thought. References to the EF fit not so much into various categories or specific trends of exegesis but belong to a historical continuum involving the Chosen People of God and orient regularly to a fundamental statement concerning the election and holiness of the nation belonging to the covenanting and saving God.

As we shall see in the following chapter, both the textual tradition and the theological interpretation of the EF played a significant role in the formulation employed in 1 P 2:4-10.

CHAPTER THREE

THE UNITY OF VERSES 6–10

In the preceding chapter we have seen the significance which the EF assumed in the period of history between the Hebrew OT and the NT Church. This survey appeared desirous in view of the important, if not central, position which Ex. 19:6 seems to have been given in our pericope. The next step of our study now concerns a closer examination of the significance which this passage assumed in the pericope 1 P 2:4-10. This involves two basic considerations: (1) the *form* in which the EF and the other OT passages were known to Peter and/or the *formal arrangement* which they were given and (2) the *interpretation* which was made of this cited material. In this chapter we shall concentrate on the first of these considerations and in Chapter IV we shall deal with the second.

As to the question of *form*, there are three main possibilities concerning the present shape of vv. 6-10.

(1) Our previous analysis of the structure of vv. 4-10 has shown that vv. 6-10 contain two subsections, vv. 6-8 and vv. 9-10. The former subsection has been identified as a λίθος complex; the latter, a body of epithets describing the People of God. This obvious difference between vv. 6-8 and 9-10 has led to the suggestion that vv. 9f., in contrast to vv. 6-8 centering in the *Stichwort* λίθος, presented a second complex united by the term λαός (ἔθνος).[1] According to this theory, either Peter was responsible for the composition of this "λαός complex" or this group of OT passages, analogous to the λίθος complex, represents a compilation effected already in a pre-Petrine state. In any event, Peter would have been responsible for the combination of both λίθος and λαός complexes.

(2) The presence of elements from both vv. 6-8 and 9f. in other NT documents has led to an even more inclusive proposal. Is it not possible that Ex. 19:6, together with the other OT passages in vv. 9f., was combined with Is. 28:16, Ps. 118(117):22, and Is. 8:14 already previous to the construction of 1 P? Does not the peculiar nature of vv. 6-10 (composed almost exclusively of OT texts) suggest one large source from which the author drew?

[1] So Cerfaux, *op. cit.*, pp. 22f.; cf. also Michel, *op. cit.*, pp. 216f.

(3) A third possibility is that Ex. 19:6 was not arranged within a "λαός complex" or contained within a larger body of material organized previous to 1 P but was cited individually to support a specific intention and purpose of the author. In this case, Peter would have been making direct reference to the LXX version of Ex. 19:6. Furthermore, the collation of OT passages in vv. 9f., as well as their combination with those in vv. 6-8, then would be attributable to him alone.

In evaluating these various possibilities it will be profitable to commence with the hypotheses positing a longer pattern involving vv. 6-10. Broadly speaking, there are two postulations: (1) vv. 6-10 contain OT passages drawn from a "Testimonia" collection; (2) these verses represent an adaptation of an early Christian hymn.

A. A "Testimonia" Source?

The theory of a collection of "*Testimonia*" or "*excerpta*" to explain the composite quotations made in the NT was current already in the preceding century.[1] It was given its fullest articulation by J. Rendel Harris in his two volume work, *Testimonies*.[2] In the *Testimonia* collection edited by Cyprian in the third Christian century[3] as well as in other patristic collections[4] Harris found examples of a use of OT Testimonies which he felt could be retraced to the NT period.[5] For his argumentation the group of NT λίθος texts were used as an important piece of evidence. He attributed to these "stone" sayings a significant position in his proposed Testimony Book, tracing their use from Cyprian to Peter and Paul.[6] Certain passages of Justin Martyr[7] are mentioned also. However, it is the so-called Epistle of Barnabas, ch. 6, which Harris considered

[1] Cf. esp. E. Hatch, *Essays in Biblical Greek*, Oxford, 1889, pp. 203-214; H. Vollmer, *Die alttestamentlichen Citate bei Paulus*, Freiburg, 1897, pp. 38-48.

[2] J. Rendel Harris, *Testimonies*, I-II, Cambridge, 1916, 1920.

[3] *Testimonia ad Quirinum*, in *CSEL* 1, 35-184; *MPL* 4, 679-780.

[4] Melito (cf. Eusebius, *Ecclesiastical History* IV, 26); Tertullian, *Adversus Judaeos*; Gregory of Nyssa, *Collectanea Sacra* (authorship uncertain); Bar Salibi, *Against the Jews*.

[5] *Ibid.*, pp. 2ff.

[6] Harris, *ibid.*, I, 18f., pointed to Cyprian, *Testimonia* II, 16 "Quod idem et lapis dictus sit" and II, 17 "Quod deinde idem lapis mons fieret et impleret totam terram" where Is. 28:16 and Ps. 118(117):22 are cited. (Significantly, Is. 8:14 is absent and is also omitted in a later reference to these "stone" sayings by Gregory of Nyssa).

[7] *Dialogue*, chs. 34, 70, 76, 86, 100.

the "connecting link between Cyprian and Peter and Paul."[1] All the "stone" or "rock" *Testimonia* had their origin, according to Harris, in a saying of Jesus. "It was Jesus . . . who set the Stone rolling."[2] From the general anti-Jewish polemical character of the later patristic Testimonies and from the same polemical traits of the "stone" sayings in particular, Harris concluded that the *Testimonia* source supposedly used by NT writers including Peter and Paul was a compilation of Messianic proof-texts intended for the purposes of anti-Jewish polemic.

This thesis has found varying degrees of favor among scholars, ranging from wholehearted support to cautious allusion.[3] Among the studies devoted particularly to the Testimony hypothesis and the use of the OT in the NT, Harris has found relatively little support. D. Plooy in his *Studies in the Testimony Book*[4] did not proceed beyond Harris' hypothesis but offered more supporting material. N. J. Hommes, three years later, however, in his *Het*

---

[1] *Ibid.*, I, 31; cf. further I, 28ff.; II, 12, 18, 96, 106 for Harris' discussion of "stone" texts.

[2] *Ibid.*, II, 96.

[3] In addition to P. Prigent, *Les Testimonia dans le Christianisme primitif. L'Épître de Barnabé I-XVI et ses Sources* (*Études Bibliques*), Paris, 1961, 16-28, Ellis, *op. cit.*, pp. 98-107, offers a concise discussion of the "Testimony Book" hypothesis and a representation of the opinions of scholarship pro and con. In addition to those whom Ellis has mentioned as favoring such a thesis we might add H. Windisch, *Der Barnabasbrief* (*HNT* Ergänzungsband III) Tübingen, 1920, pp. 313f., 332f., 409f.; also *Die Katholischen Briefe*, 2. Aufl. 1930, p. 60 (cp. Windisch-Preisker, *op. cit.*, p. 158); G. Stählin, *Skandalon*,, Untersuchung zur Geschichte eines biblischen Begriffs (*FBChrTh* 2/24), Gütersloh, 1930, p. 193; M. Dibelius, *ThR* 3/4 (1931), p. 227, who treated the Testimony theory with caution; L. Cerfaux, "Vestiges d'un florilège dans 1 Cor. 1:18-3:24," *RHE* 27 (1931), 521ff., who suggested the existence of a florilegium containing combined OT quotations used by the NT authors; also "Un chapitre du Livre des Testimonia," *EphLov* 14 (1937), 69-74; *RSPhTh* (1939), 23ff.; and *La Théologie de l'Église suivant S. Paul* (*Unam Sanctam* 10), Paris, 1942, pp. 73ff.; Holzmeister, *op. cit.*, pp. 112, 241; T. W. Manson, "The O. T. in the Teaching of Jesus," *BJRL* 34 (1951/52), 312-32. J. Dupont, "L'Utilisation apologétique de l'A. T. pour la prédication et l'apologétique chrétienne," *EphLov* 26 (1953), 289-327; Michel, *op. cit.*, p. 200; J. Daniélou, *Théologie* pp. 102-04; P. Prigent, *ThZ* 15 (1959), 419-30; Congar, *Temple*, p. 135, n. 4; Schelkle, *op. cit.*, p. 62. A. F. J. Klijn, "Die Wörter 'Stein' und 'Felsen' in der syrischen Übersetzung des Neuen Testaments," *ZNW* 50 (1959), 99-105, assumes that it is the influence of early Christian "Stein-Testimonia" which accounts for the unusual rendition "stone" instead of the expected "rock" in the Syrian translation of the NT.

[4] *Verhandlingen der Koniglijke Adademie van Wetenschappen te Amsterdam*, Afdeling Letterkunde, Nieuwe reeks 32, No. 2. Amsterdam, 1932.

Testimoniaboek[1] at the hand of a thorough examination of the NT and patristic evidence completely rejected the position of Harris and Plooy as untenable. Disputing primarily the methodological legitimacy of "transporting a third century situation into the time of Peter and Paul"[2] and pointing out the variations of quotation and combination of OT texts which hardly indicates a constant "Testimony Book,"[3] he himself argued for the use of "Stichwortgroepeeringen" ("catchword combinations") and thematic arrangements as the best explanation of the merged quotations in the NT.[4]

Likewise, in a more recent treatment of the use of the OT in the NT, the three volume work *Oudtestamentische Citaten in het Nieuwe Testament,*[5] C. Smits finds this and similar theories of a "Testimony Book" or *Florilegium* collection wanting. Discussing the OT passages pertinent to 1 P 2:6-10 (and Rom. 9:25ff.) he finds a source which is "een christelijke combinatie . . . in de oudste catechese gevormd."[6]

C. H. Dodd, exploring the "substructure of NT theology," has also raised valid objections to the postulation of a "Testimony Book."[7] He maintains that Harris' theory "outruns the evidence which is not sufficient to prove so formidable a literary enterprise at so early a date."[8] His threefold objection sums up the main arguments brought against this hypothesis.[9] First, the late emergence of this work in the third century under the editorship of Cyprian hardly coincides with its supposed apostolic (Matthean) authorship, prevalent use, and early origin. Secondly, verses which show the characteristics implying a Testimony source are relatively few and insufficient to prove a general theory. Thirdly, passages

---

[1] *Het Testimonaboek*, Studien over O. T. Citaten in het N. T. en bij de Patres, met Chritische Beschouwingen over de Theorieen van J. Rendel Harris en D. Plooy (Dissertation: Amsterdam), 1935.

[2] *Ibid.*, p. 87.

[3] *Ibid.*, p. 90.

[4] *Ibid.*, pp. 304-20, 365ff.

[5] In the series *Collectanea Franciscana Neerlandica*, 8/I-III, 's Hertogenbosch, 1952-57.

[6] "A Christian combination . . . formed in the oldest catechesis" (*op. cit.*, II, 355, n. 5); cf. also II, 369; I, 73-75; III, 491.

[7] Dodd, *op. cit.*, pp. 24-27. Against Dodd's own proposal that certain large sections of the OT were treated by the NT authors as whole contexts from which particular verses were quoted, cf. A. C. Sundberg, "On Testimonies," *NovTest* 3 (1959), 268-81.

[8] *Ibid.*, p. 26.

[9] *Ibid.*, pp. 26f.

linked together by the *Stichwort* "stone" compose the only such *Stichwort* grouping of any particular weight.

In the last decades, the discoveries of form criticism, particularly concerning the liturgical and catechetical nature of much of the NT material mentioned by Harris, an appreciation of the influence of Rabbinic methodology, and a more comprehensive view of the use of the OT in the NT all have contributed in the depreciation of a "Testimony Book" theory and an excessive emphasis upon anti-Jewish polemic.[1]

In this light we will be cautious in weighing the significance of the so-called "*Testimonia*" discovered at Qumran (4Q Testimonia,[2] 4Q Florilegium[3]). Though these texts afford examples of early written collations of significant OT passages, they are too fragmentary to supply proof of extended collections, much less a book. Nor as yet has the relation of these fragments to the NT been sufficiently established.[4]

B. A Christian Hymn?

Selwyn[5] did not categorically reject the possible existence of such "Testimony" manuals but considered a "proof-passage" methodology a poor implement to the Christian proclamation in areas of Asia Minor. He, in turn, offered a totally different evaluation of the material in 1 P 2:6-10. In his opinion these verses represented an *early Christian Hymn*.[6]

Reference to the alleged hymnic character of 1 P 2 is not recent. Already thirty years ago Hans Windisch described 1 P 2:1-10 as "ein Hymnus auf die heilige Bestimmung der Christenheit" containing four strophes, vv. 1-3, 4-5, 6-8, 9f.[7]

Selwyn, too, agreed to the presence here of hymnic material but

---

[1] Cf. Ellis, *op. cit.*, pp. 102ff. for literature.

[2] Published by J. M. Allegro, *JBL* 75 (1956), pp. 182-87.

[3] *Ibid.*, pp. 176f. and *JBL* 77 (1958), pp. 351-54.

[4] Cf. F. F. Bruce, "Qumran and Early Christianity," *NTS* 2 (1955/56), 179f.; J. A. Fitzmyer, "4Q Testimonia and the New Testament," *TS* 18 (1957), 513-37; Dupont-Sommer, *op. cit.*, 328-33; P. Prigent, "Quelques testimonia messianiques," *ThZ* 15 (1959), 419-30. For a more optimistic evaluation of the information which the Qumran *Testimonia* might supply the *Testimonia* theory cf. Prigent, *Testimonia*, pp. 26f.

[5] Selwyn, *op. cit.*, p. 273.

[6] *Ibid.*, pp. 268-81.

[7] Windisch. *op. cit.*, 2. Aufl. 1930, p. 58.

found it necessary to revise Windisch's hypothesis. First, the text shows that vv. 1-10 are not themselves a hymn but rather include a hymnic source. "For there is nothing hymnodic in structure in verses 4, 5."[1] Nor do the available examples of Jewish and Christian hymnody contain "such prosaic and matter-of-fact insertions as διότι περιέχει ἐν γραφῇ."[2]

These objections and the following observations also demonstrate the unlikelihood of Preisker's renewed attempt in the third edition of Windisch's commentary to treat 1 P 2:1-10 as a "dreistrophiges Festlied (ὕμνος)," vv. 1-3, 4-5, 9-10, which was the rendition "eines einzelnen Pneumatikers."[3]

Formal and terminologal aspects of vv. 6-10 according to Selwyn, seem to betray an underlying source. He found this suspicion corroborated by the following points.[4] (1) The similarities among the NT documents are often traceable to a common hymnic source. (2) Such early Christian hymns often served as instruments of instruction, as is indicated in Col. 3:16. (3) According to available examples of Jewish and Christian hymnody, these hymns were quite often mosaics of earlier texts.[5] The rhythmic structure of these verses betrays the presence of a hymn. (4) Certain terminology and phrasing show the poetic quality germane to a hymn.[6] (5) The similarity with the differences from Rom. 9:25 are best explained

---

[1] Selwyn, *op. cit.*, p. 276, n. 2.

[2] *Ibid.*

[3] Windisch-Preisker, *op. cit.*, p. 158. Preisker has, of course, recognized the non-hymnic character of vv. 6-8 and therefore has modified Windisch's four strophe hymn to three, holding vv. 6-8 to be a later interpolation introduced with the formula of 2:6a, possibly deriving from a "*Testimonien-sammlung*" (*ibid.*). However, Selwyn was perfectly justified in rejecting vv. 1-3 as belonging to a proposed hymn. The imperatives of vv. 1f. are certainly out of place in a hymn. Furthermore, how would a later interpolation then explain the earlier presence of ψ 117:22 and Is. 28:16 in v. 4? Should vv. 6-8 then be considered as a simple gloss added for support or proof? To whom could such redaction be ascribed? But these objections to an "Einschub" are elementary in comparison to the main argument against an interpolation, namely, the intimate parallelism which has been observed between vv. 4-5a and 6-8. Preisker's suggestion completely overlooks the correspondence between these verses as well as the connection between the midrash in v. 8b, for instance (λόγος), and 1:23, 2:2. The postulation that this is the rendition of a single Spirit-filled enthusiast ignores the integrity of these first ten verses with the entire foregoing section.

[4] *Ibid.*, pp. 273-81.

[5] Cf. ψ 14:3a-c; Ps. Sol.; the Canticles in Lk. 1 and 2.

[6] Cf. 2:9: ἐξαγγέλλειν and ἀρετή and the phrase "Who called us out of darkness into His marvelous light."

by the assumption that Paul quoted directly from the Hosean source whereas the author of 1 P, farther removed from the symbolical picture of the two children, cited a hymn containing this motif. (6) The structural parallelism in 2:10 reflects the parallelism common to hymns. (7) Verses 4-5 appear to anticipate and interpret vv. 6-7 and 9f. respectively.

On the basis of these points, Selwyn cautiously posited an underlying hymn composed of two strophes, vv. 6b-8c and 9-10. The first strophe, containing two distichs and a tristich, was faithfully reproduced in vv. 6-8 with the exception that, according to Selwyn, a καί was added at the beginning of v. 8a by Peter and that he also transposed ἀπιστοῦσι(ν) δὲ from its original place in the hymn (before λίθος προσκόμματος) to v. 7a. Selwyn also suggested that the hymn originally read ἀπιστοῦσι without the final ν; likewise προσκόπτουσι instead of προσκόπτουσιν where Peter in v. 8b had again added a final ν.[1] This hymn, according to Selwyn, was introduced with the words περιέχει ἐν γραφῇ which also makes allusion to its existence in written form.[2]

Can Selwyn's arresting attempt at the construction of an underlying hymn be reckoned as successful? Does the evidence support the likelihood of Peter's adaptation and incorporation of a written hymnic source in ch. 2:6-10? Observations of form and content yield only a negative answer.

First, it might be asked upon what justifiable basis Selwyn allowed himself so much liberty in the transposition of word order. Textual alteration defended simply through factors of rhythm is methodologically questionable. This is all the more true since, as Selwyn himself acknowledged, "of the rule of rhythm governing Greek versions of Psalms or hymns we know next to nothing."[3]

As to *form*, early Christian and Jewish hymnody has shown us that stichs regularly began with relative pronoun clauses (cf. Phil. 2:6-10, Col. 1:15-20, 1 Tim. 3:16; also Eph. 1:3-14).[4] In fact, we need not go beyond 1 P itself in order to observe this (e.g. 1:3-9, 1:19-21, 2:21-25, 3:18-22).[5] The alluded texts also reveal the

---

[1] Obviously Selwyn's accentuation, *ibid.*, p. 281, προσκοπτοῦσι, must be reckoned as a typographical error. Cp. προσκόπτουσι, p. 277.

[2] *Ibid.*, p. 163.

[3] *Ibid.*, p. 276.

[4] For a brief discussion of NT hymnody and its characteristics cf. G. Bornkamm, *RGG* II, 1003.

[5] Cf. R. Bultmann, "Bekenntnis- und Liedfragmente im ersten Petrus-

customary use of participial phrases and clauses. In 1 P 2:6-10, to the contrary, few such elements are to be found. Verse 10 offers the closest parallel. Otherwise the pronouns and participles belong either to the original OT verses quoted or to the midrash which certainly bears no hymnic resemblances.[1]

We might also note the "un-parallelism" between a strophe containing two distichs and a tristich and a second composed of two tristichs and a distich.

Another weakness in this hypothesis is Selwyn's suggestion that Paul, in Rom. 9:33, was making use of the common (hymnic) source[2] but that in the same continuity of thought verses earlier in 9:25f. he was quoting directly from the Hosean text.[3] Is it likely that Paul in one instance would have excerpted from the hymn but in the other, disregarded the hymn and quoted the original OT text directly? Furthermore, in comparison with 1 P 2:6-10, the order of reference in Rom. 9 is inverted; first in Rom. 9:25f. the Hosean reference (=1 P 2:10) is introduced, then the λίθος complex (=1 P 2:6-8) follows in Rom. 9:33. Would the use of a fixed hymnic pattern coincide with such liberal alteration of text? Paul's procedure in 9:33 and the alteration once again encountered (omission of Ps. 118(117):22, transposition of Is. 28:16 and Is. 8:14) can encourage only a negative answer.

Also *content-wise* all hymnic quality is lacking. Each proposed strophe contains a different subject. Verses 6-8 treat the stone, i.e. Jesus; v. 9-10 *address* the hearers/readers and describe the *Gottesvolk*. Selwyn presumed that the first strophe "represents words placed in the mouth of God."[4] For the second strophe he appears to have favored the original presence of second person plural forms (ὑμεῖς, ἐξαγγείλητε, ὑμᾶς [but he writes ἡμᾶς in the pattern!]).[5] This would be the case, he maintained, if the two strophes stood together. "Otherwise, the first person plural more probably stood in

---

brief," *CN* 11 (1947), 1-14; Schleier, *op. cit.*, pp. 37ff. ad Eph. 1:3ff.; M-E. Boismard, *Quatre Hymnes Baptismales dans la Première Épître de Pierre*, Paris, 1961.

[1] Selwyn, *ibid.*, recognized that the midrashic character of v. 7a clashes with the supposed hymnic pattern and accordingly isolated it from the hymn. Yet what accounts for his inconsistent retention of the midrashic fragment, v. 7bα?

[2] *Ibid.*, p. 277.

[3] *Ibid.*, p. 280.

[4] *Ibid.*, p. 281.

[5] *Ibid.*

the hymn."[1] This still does not account for the inner relationship between these two "strophes." Moreover, we might add that early hymns have shown that the first person is more likely to be the original form in a hymn rather than the second. The latter frequently occurred as a gloss or adaptation of the author using the hymn for didactic purposes. If we applied this observation here, then in this proposed hymn we would best presume original first person plural forms. However, then according to Selwyn's conclusion we must regard vv. 6-8 and 9-10 as two distinct strophes transmitted separately. In such a case no integral hymn is left at all. In regard to the thematic unity of these strophes Selwyn has offered no explanation.

Further, the complete absence of other examples or traces of this hymn is significant. Though parallels to individual texts and to the λίθος complex are ascertainable, no other example of the combination of OT passages contained in vv. 6-10 is to be found in either Jewish or Christian sources. The closest parallel is in Rom. 9 but the divergences between this text and 1 P clearly indicate the looseness and flexibility of the common material employed as well as the originality and interpretative freedom assumed by both Paul and Peter. Nor is the section Rom. 11:30-32 complete enough to offer a real parallel to 1 P 2:6-10.[2]

Finally, διότι περιέχει ἐν γραφῇ (v. 6a) does not allude to a hymn[3] but to the same passages introduced so variously by Mk. 12:10 (οὐδὲ τὴν γραφὴν ταύτην ἀνέγνωτε), Mt. 21:42 (οὐδέποτε ἀνέγνωτε ἐν ταῖς γραφαῖς), and Lk. 20:17 (τί οὖν ἐστιν τὸ γεγραμμένον τοῦτο).[4] The impersonal rendering "For it stands written"[5] is possible but not more probable than "for it stands in *Scripture*," a use of γραφή which Test. Zeb. 9:5 illustrates.[6] The repeated use of γραφή(αί) or a verbal cognate in the formulae introducing Ps. 118(117):22 (f.), Is. 28:16,[7] and the combination of Is. 28:16 and 8:14[8] in their other NT oc-

[1] *Ibid.*

[2] *Contra* Selwyn, *op. cit.*, p. 281.

[3] *Contra* Selwyn, *ibid.*, p. 163.

[4] Cf. Schrenk, *TWNT* I, 742-73.

[5] Beare, *op. cit.*, p. 92; cf. p. 98.

[6] According to Schrenk, *TWNT*, I, 754, the introductory formula employed in Test. Zeb. 9:5 (Ἔγνων γὰρ ἐγὼ ἐν γραφῇ τῶν πατέρων μου) is a reference to the entire OT.

[7] Cf. Rom. 10:11: λέγει γὰρ ἡ γραφή.

[8] Cf. Rom. 9:33: καθὼς γέγραπται, a stock Pauline phrase for reference to the OT (cf. Rom. 1:17, 2:24, 3:10ff., 4:17, etc.).

currences and its constant designation of the OT leaves little doubt that its occurrence in 1 P 2:6a is to be similarly understood. The variation of v. 6a from the usual use of γραφή with its article coincides with the variations within the Synoptics. Apparently the introductory formula was as little fixed as the λίθος verse or complex which it introduced. Therefore we may agree with Smits[1] in rejecting Selwyn's theory concerning v. 6a as unfounded.

Other weaknesses of the Selwyn theory could be cited, such as the proposed authorship of this hymn by Silvanus.[2] But we need go no further. The factors already listed suffice in demonstrating the inadequacies of the postulation of a hymnic source.

Both theories taking 1 P 2:6-10 to reflect the use of an integral pre-Petrine pattern prove inadequate. Both *Testimonia* and hymn hypotheses overextend the evidence. They fail to account sufficiently for the present form of the text and fail to provide an adequate explanation for this text's content and its relation to its context.

C. A "λαός Complex"?

What may be said concerning the suggestion of two independent complexes, the latter of which (vv. 9f.) united its composites through the *Stichwort* λαός? Is it likely that the term λαός afforded the link binding these passages or that they, analogous to the members of the λίθος complex, already belonged to some pre-Petrine tradition?

On the one hand, in contrast to the λίθος complex in vv. 6-8, these OT passages in vv. 9f. all relate in identifying a new object: the people of God. They share a common purpose and a common sense. The recurrent term λαός is also common to both verses, being contained once in v. 9 (= Is. 43:21a) and twice in v. 10 (= Hos. 1:9, 2:3, 25). Nevertheless, according to the available evidence, the theory that λαός served as coordinating *Stichwort* in vv. 9f. is as improbable as the conjecture that vv. 9f. reflect the existence of a pre-Petrine λαός complex.

The *Stichwort* theory is unable to explain the presence of Ex. 19:6 in v. 9b where the term λαός is absent. It might be argued that the word is implicit from 19:5 (ἔσεσθέ μοι λαὸς περιούσιος). Yet if λαός

---

[1] Smits, *op. cit.*, II, 354.
[2] Selwyn, *op. cit.*, p. 277.

had served as *Stichwort* it would be unexplainable why explicit reference to Ex. 19:5 was then omitted here. ἔθνος certainly cannot be taken as equivalent to λαός. For since the composition of the LXX λαός more and more was regarded as a *terminus technicus* for Israel, signifying both her ethnic and her religious/theological character,[1] whereas ἔθνος (ἔθνοι) served to designate the Gentiles, the *Goiim*.[2] In the NT both words describe the community of believers but this would be no support for the proposed *Stichwort* function of λαός in vv. 9f. Our investigation of the EF references, furthermore, has shown that there was no essential relationship between λαός and the first two members of Ex. 19:6.[3] Likewise, the NT shows that the EF was not attracted to or subsumed under a λαός complex.[4] This conclusion is further substantiated by the occurrences of λαός in the writings of the Apostolic Fathers (cf. e.g. I Cl. 64:1 and Barn. 14:6, sections so close to the thought of 1 P 2:9f. that if the EF had belonged to a λαός complex it would be difficult to account for its absence in each instance).[5] Finally, Rom. 9:24ff., the other NT passage making direct reference to the Hosean merged quotation

[1] Cf. the comprehensive study of λαός made by H. Strathmann and R. Meyer, *TWNT* IV, 29-58. Strathmann also notes the exceptions to this trend.

[2] This distinction was carried through in the NT era; cf. Act. 11:1, 14:5, 21:21; Rom. 3:9, 9:24. Act. 26:17 and Rom. 15:10 make this differentiation especially clear.

[3] Either the term does not appear at all (cf. *De Sobr.* 66, *De Abrah.* 56, Apoc. 1:6) or when it does occur—in either text or context—it designates Israel in the *ethnic* sense (cf. Gk. Frag. 67, 2 Mcc. 2:17). In Apoc. 5:9 both λαός and ἔθνος are added to the Christ hymn in a phrase illustrating the universality of the salvation event but no connection with the EF in particular is evident. The sole instances where λαός and EF are coordinated in a theological sense are Jub. 16:18 and 33:20. The latter passage where the first two members of Ex. 19:6 are subordinated to λαός as adjectives is a text form *sui generis*.

[4] In addition to the inverse proportion of NT occurrences of λαός in comparison with the EF in the NT (cp. the similar situation in the LXX), appearances of λαός within merged OT passages demonstrate that though the tenor of these complexes often was conducive to the use of the EF, no such citation of the EF was made. Cf. e.g. 2 Cor. 6:16-18, Tit. 2:14, and Apoc. 21:3.

[5] 1 Cl. 64:1: (θεός) ὁ ἐκλεξάμενος τὸν κύριον Ἰησοῦν Χριστὸν καὶ ἡμᾶς δι' αὐτοῦ εἰς λαὸν περιούσιον; cp. 59:1; Barn. 14:6: (ὁ πατὴρ) λυτρωσάμενον ἡμᾶς ἐκ τοῦ σκότους ἑτοιμάσαι ἑαυτῷ λαὸν ἅγιον. On the whole, despite a certain similarity with 1 P, both passages agree more with Tit. 2:14 and the Dt. formulation upon which this passage is based (Barn. 14:3f. = Dt. 9:12-17; 14:5f. = Dt. 7:6-8). Bultmann, *TNT*, I, 98, without further explanation or proof, traces Barn. 14:6 and 1 P 2:9 to Dt. 7:6 and Tit. 2:14, 1 Cl. 64:1 to Ex. 19:5.

found in 1 P 2:10, graphically indicates the improbability of the existence of any λαός complex. Should the EF and Is. 43:20f. have been collated with the Hosean merger in a single complex, it would be inconceivable that Paul had omitted these passages which would have been so pertinent to his point. Rather his introductory formula (9:25a) shows that the only complex which he knew was the one involving the merger of Hosean texts.

Therefore, since there is no evidence for the existence of a λαός complex containing the OT passages Is. 43:20f., Ex. 19:6, or the merged quotation of Hosean verses apart from 1 P 2:9f. and since a λαός *Stichwort* theory cannot account for the presence of Ex. 19:6 in 1 P 2:9, it may be concluded that *1 P 2:9f. represent a combination of OT passages made by the author of 1 P himself.*

Of the three possibilities concerning the *form* in which Ex. 19:6 and the other OT passages in vv. 6-10 were taken over by Peter, only the third is made likely by the evidence. Accordingly, vv. 6-10 were not dependent upon a "*Testimonia*" source, nor were they a quotation or an adaptation of a Christian hymn, nor did they compose two complexes united by the *Stichworte* λίθος (vv. 6-8) and λαός (vv. 9-10) respectively. Rather, only one distinct complex is evident: a λίθος complex drawn from common Christian tradition (vv. 6-8). To this complex Peter annexed a second group of OT predicates describing the chosen people of God. It was not a pre-Petrine pattern or literary source which dictated the form of the entire section, vv. 6-10; rather its formal arrangement was determined by the author himself.

The presence of Ex. 19:6 and the Hosean merger, as well as elements of the λίθος complex, in other NT documents demonstrates that the novelty of vv. 6-10 does not lie in the quotation of unusual OT passages. Rather this fact points to a common Christian attitude toward certain OT statements. At the outset it can be said that the reference to these passages in 1 P is similar to other NT documents in so far that this reference reveals an awareness of the historical continuity with God's nation of old and a certainty of the eschatological realization of this entity in the believing community of the New Age.[1] Behind this general attitude, nevertheless, lies a more particular concern. This is suggested in the specific combination of the OT passages effected by Peter, a combination which is unique

[1] Cf. Strathmann, *op. cit.*, p. 54.

within the NT. The first clue to the motive prompting this collation of passages and the specific formal arrangement of vv. 6-10 is found in the factor uniting the OT references of vv. 9f.

D. An Election Theme

The analysis of Chapter I dealing with vv. 9f. has shown that not a word but rather a *theme* is the one characteristic common to these OT passages; namely, the theme of *election*. The content of these OT citations involve predicates for the Chosen People of God. Further NT parallels to vv. 9f., though employing the OT material in a manner different from 1 P, also reveal traces of the election theme connected with these passages.[1] Moreover, attention has been called to the deliberate arrangement of v. 9 whereby γένος ἐκλεκτόν introduces this entire group of epithets. This leads to the conclusion that rather than the proposed *Stichwort* λαός, it was the theme of election which served as the magnet drawing together these terms in vv. 9f. In the EF this theme of Israel's election received its classic expression. Accordingly, as explication of this theme, it was cited in v. 9. And, as v. 5b-d demonstrates, it was Ex. 19:6 upon which Peter commented as the *prima pars pro toto*.

A closer look at the structure of vv. 6-10 not only corroborates the centrality of the election motif for vv. 9-10 but suggests that it was according to this theme that Peter effected the unity of vv. 6-10 as a whole.

Despite the obvious disparity between the original Christological and descriptive character of the λαός complex on the one hand and the ecclesiological and addressive nature of vv. 9f. and their predicates on the other, there is a bond which supersedes this variance and creates a unity. The key word of this bond is the adjective ἐκλεκτός.

It is this term, namely, which serves as *initial modifier* both within vv. 6-8 and vv. 9f. Both λίθος in v. 6b (= Is. 28:16) and γένος in v. 9a (= Is. 43:20) are modified by ἐκλεκτός and in neither case is this fortuitous. Each comma betrays the designing hand of

[1] Cf. the reference to the Hosean merger in Rom. 9:24ff. where certain terminology points to an underlying election motif: esp. ἐκάλεσεν (v. 24), καλέσω (v. 25), κληθήσονται (v. 26). Likewise, Rom. 11:28ff., whose relation to 9:25-33 Selwyn has noted (*op. cit.*, p. 281), betrays elements of an election motif; ἡ κλῆσις τοῦ θεοῦ (v. 29); συνέκλεισεν (v. 32); κατά δὲ τὴν ἐκλογὴν (v. 28) = ἡ κατ' ἐκλογὴν πρόθεσις τοῦ θεοῦ (9:11) which introduces the whole section of chs. 9-11.

the author. In the citation of Is. 28:16 the reading of the LXX has undergone change. Among other variations,[1] the original πολυτελῆ has been omitted, thereby establishing ἐκλεκτόν as the first modifier of λίθον in this λίθος complex.[2] Likewise, in v. 9a where ἐκλεκτός appears as the first adjective among the modifiers of vv. 9f., the comma γένος ἐκλεκτόν deliberately was given a prominent position by the author.

This arrangement in v. 9 is noteworthy. The position of the first two OT references cited here is far from normal. Ex. 19:6 does not simply follow Is. 43:20f., nor vice versa; rather, *the Isaiah passage has been interpolated into the Exodus verse*. This fact is overlooked by almost all the commentators. Usually it is agreed that allusion has been made to these two OT verses, but invariably Ex. 19:6 is said to have been interpolated into Is. 43:20f. (v. 9a, cd).[3] This conclusion is possible only when the introductory words ὑμεῖς δέ are overlooked. A comparison with the LXX shows that these words belong to the original formulation of Ex. 19:6: ὑμεῖς δὲ ἔσεσθέ μοι βασίλειον ἱεράτευμα καὶ ἔθνος ἅγιον. Hence the reference to Ex. 19:6 begins not with βασίλειον ἱεράτευμα but already with ὑμεῖς δέ.[4] This means that the EF was not interpolated into the Isaiah citation but, vice versa, a portion of Is. 43:20f. was interjected into the Exodus verse.

---

[2] For the LXX text of Is. 28:16 cf. *supra*, p. 23, n. 1.

[1] The textual witness for v. 6 is not uniform. Disagreement concerns the word order: in particular, the position of ἐκλεκτόν. Sinaiticus, Alexandrinus, Koine, most other Greek witnesses, the entire Latin tradition, and the Thomas revision of the Syriac read ἀκρογωνιαῖον ἐκλεκτὸν ἔντιμον, as preferred by Tischendorf. Vaticanus, Ephraem the Syrian, Min. 69, a few other MSS, and the Peshitta render the LXX word order, as accepted also by Nestle. Though suspicion of correction might lie at hand, whereby the former witnesses would then represent the earlier reading, Nestle's choice is corroborated by the sense of Peter's arrangement in v. 4. Here it is obvious that ἐκλεκτόν was for Peter the primary adjective among the three modifiers of λίθος in v. 6 (or among the four in Is. 28:16). ἀκρογωνιαῖον as well as πολυτελῆ and εἰς τὰ θεμέλια have all been omitted as irrelevant to the point. It is more likely that the original position of ἐκλεκτόν in v. 6 was that given by the Nestle text than that Peter purposely altered the normal word order of the LXX and modified λίθος initially with ἀκρογωνιαῖον. Such a change would hardly coincide with this concern as reflected in v. 4. The alternate reading may then be seen as an attempt to correspond v. 6 (ἀκρογωνιαῖον ἐκλεκτὸν ἔντιμον) with v. 4 (ἐκλεκτὸν ἔντιμον). Cp. Barn. 6:2 which follows even more closely the phrasing and word order of the LXX.

[3] Cf. recently, Beare, *op. cit.*, p. 102.

[4] Selwyn, *op. cit.*, p. 279, saw this but failed to draw any consequences.

What accounts for this unusual arrangement? The answer already lies at hand: in vv. 9f. the theme of the Elected People of God was central. To emphasize this fact *formally* the author so arranged his citations that the comma γένος ἐκλεκτόν, "chosen race," signaled the significance of the predicates to follow.

This observation has important consequences. First. contrary to the majority of opinion, ὑμεῖς δέ are not original words of Peter introducing the epithets to follow but belong to the EF which he cites. This implies, secondly, that vv. 9f. need not necessarily be seen as a contrast to the statement of v. 8, as is also assumed by most scholars. It is, for instance, commonly held that ὑμεῖς δέ introduced a contrast to vv. 7-8, i.e. contrasting believers (vv. 9f.) with the unbelievers (vv. 7-8).[1]

Verse 8, however, belongs to its own complex, which in itself offers no logical contrast to v. 9. One might hold that the interjected midrash of vv. 6-8 created such a possibility of contrast. Yet we have seen that this midrash frames in vv. 6-8 while at the same time creating a balance of positive (believers, v. 7a) and negative (unbelievers, v. 7b, 8b) statements.[2] Verses 9-10, therefore, could only correspond to vv. 6-8 as a whole. Such contrast could not have been according to the theme "unbelievers/believers" (vv. 6-8/9-10) because vv. 6-8 discuss not only unbelievers but believers as well.

If ὑμεῖς δὲ γένος ἐκλεκτόν and the rest of vv. 9f. did not present an alternative to the unbelievers and disobedient of vv. 7-8, then the reasonable point of correspondence appears to be the λίθον ἐκλεκτόν of v. 6b: Jesus as the elect Stone (v. 6b). Thus it was to draw attention to this correspondence that the adjective was given its initial and prominent position in v. 6b and v. 9a. This has accentuated the parallelism:[3] Jesus is the λίθος ἐκλεκτός, the believing community is the γένος ἐκλεκτόν.[4]

---

[1] E.g. Knopf, *op. cit.*, p. 95; Schlatter, *Petrus*, p. 98; Blinzler, *op. cit.*, p. 58; Windisch-Preisker, *op. cit.*, p. 61.

[2] Cf. *supra*, pp. 36–38.

[3] This parallelistic structure was noted over half a century ago by H. von Soden, *Briefe des Petrus* (*HCNT* 3/12), 3. Aufl., Freiburg i. Br., 1899, p. 143 who found Is. 43:20f. attracted "durch den Anklang an λίθον ἐκλεκτὸν wodurch auch das οἶκος = γένος ein ἐκλεκτόν wird." The reference to Is. 43:20f., however, cannot be regarded with v. Soden as a mere formal attraction. More recently Smits, *op. cit.*, p. 45 has also seen this parallelism.

[4] δέ is not exclusively a *conjunctio adversativa*. In 1 P 3:8, 4:7, 5:10 it functions as a resumptive or transitional particle. In v. 9a the author used it not in its original adversative sense in Ex. 19:6 but as effecting a relation

This type of correspondence and interchange of predicates between Jesus and the Church[1] is an interpretative procedure long noticed by scholars who described this as a "transference of attributes."[2] Not only is this transference of attributes a common NT device but it plays no mean role in the thought of 1 P.[3]

On the other hand, the limits of this correspondence must also be noted and maintained. Not all attributes in vv. 9f. relate to attributes of Jesus Christ. βασίλειον, ἱεράτευμα, λαὸς εἰς περιποίησιν are by no means derived from predicates for Jesus. In these terms there is no parallelism between Jesus-attributes and community-attributes. The concept of election and the adjective ἐκλεκτός is the sole medium of correspondence. Predicates for the Church in vv. 9-10 are not derived from Jesus-predicates (as e.g., λίθοι ζῶντες; cp. ἡ τιμή) but from attributes of the Old Covenant Israel. The possibility of application of course derives from the salvation event and the work of Jesus Christ. Yet these predicates themselves were never applied to Jesus and then transferred to the community of the faithful. This was not done, if for no other reason, because all the terms in vv. 9f. are corporative and, as such, *designations never of a person*[4] *but of a community.*

This fact deserves special mention in connection with βασίλειον ἱεράτευμα. Neither of these terms has anything to do with Jesus-attributes. There is not the faintest hint in the entire epistle that βασίλειον is an attribute which has been transferred to the Church

between two similar objects (from v. 6b and v. 9). Cf. also Mt. 1:2-16, 2 P 1:5-8; further, Mt. 5:31, 6:16; Rom. 14:1; 1 Cor. 7:1, 8:1, 12:1, 15:1, 16:1 where similar objects are brought into relationship through δέ (*BAG s.v.*).

[1] ἐκλεκτός is a designation for *Jesus* (Lk. 23:35, Jn. 1:34 [Sinaiticus - original hand; Old Latin a, b, e, ff²; and Syriac - the palimpsest and Curetonian edition], cp. Lk. 9:35) and for the *believers* (Mt. 24:22ff., Rom. 8:33, Col. 3:12, Apoc. 17:14, and *passim*).

[2] Dodd, *op. cit.*, p. 106. He traces many such attributes (e.g. "vine/branches" [Jn. 15:2, 5], "son/sons" [Apoc. 2:7, 12:5, 19:5], "seed of David" [Act. 2:30, 13:33-37, 15:16f.]) which, similar to Is. 28:16 and Is. 43:20, derive from OT expressions, to the "twofold—individual and corporate—connotation" of these images (pp. 102ff.). For the roots of the transference of ἐκλεκτός we might think of ψ 88:4, 20; Is. 42:1, 45:4 and *passim*; cf. also Enoch 38:4, 39:4ff., 41:2, 53:6, 62:1.

[3] Cf. the instances in our pericope: λίθον ζῶντα (v. 4.) λίθοι ζῶντες (v. 5a); ἔντιμον (v. 4b, 6b)/ ἡ τιμή (v. 7a); (cp. τίθημι, v. 6b/ἐτέθησαν, v. 8c). Further, ἀμώμου, ἀσπίλου (1:19)/ ἅγιοι (1:15); ἀφθάρτου . . . λόγου (1:23)/ κληρονομίαν ἄφθαρτον (1:4); πάσχων / πάσχοντες (2:20f., 23; 3:17, 18 [Vaticanus, Koine, and a greater number of other MSS], 4:1f., 12).

[4] Seen aside from the symbolic naming of Hosea's son (Hos. 2:3, 25).

in accordance with Jesus' kingship or that ἱεράτευμα has been transferred in correspondence to a priesthood of Jesus. The medium of correspondence is the factor of election and no other. The predicates in vv. 9f. are peculiar to the community of God alone. They relate to Jesus inasmuch as they explicate the elected character of those who believe in the Elect Stone of God.

In conclusion, that which accounts for the structure and content of vv. 6-10 as a whole is not a hypothetical pre-Petrine pattern or source. A review of the points of contact between 1 P 2:6-10 and other New Testament passages containing similar or even parallel statements demonstrates beyond question that much of the material in this section of 1 P belonged to a strata of the common oral catechetical and possibly liturgical tradition of the primitive community. However, there is nothing to indicate conclusively that such tradition had assumed any set or specific pattern. Rather, the arrangement which this material received in 1 P 2 may be best seen as determined by the unifying theme of election. In support of this theme a Christological complex containing a statement concerning Jesus as the Elect Stone (vv. 6-8) was combined with a group of OT passages describing the believing community as the Elect People of God (vv. 9-10). Whereas neither a "*Testimonia*" theory, a hymn hypothesis, nor the postulation of a formal *Stichwort* arrangement can adequately explain the construction of these verses, the election theme accounts for both form and content. With this formal arrangementof the adapted material *the author emphasized the Divine saving event as an event of election.* In both the subsections vv. 6-8 and 9-10 ἐκλεκτός commata introduce the material and thereby effect a parallelism between the Elect Stone and the Elect Race. Insofar, the application of titles for the Chosen People of God is founded in the relationship of this community to the Chosen One of God. Or, in other words, "der λίθος ἐκλεκτός schafft und trägt das γένος ἐκλεκτόν."[1]

In that this theme affords vv. 6-10 a unity of thought, vv. 4-5 correspond to these verses as a unit and it is here in the interpretation of vv. 4-5 that the theme of election receives its fullest explication.

---

[1] Schrenk, *TWNT* IV, 195.

CHAPTER FOUR

VERSES 4–5 AND THE ELECTION AND HOLINESS OF THE BODY OF THE FAITHFUL

A. The Election Motif in Verses 4-5

Verses 6-10 form a unit explicating an election theme. This material, though disparate in original form and concern (vv. 6-8 representing a Christological λίθος complex and vv. 9f., originally separate OT expressions pertaining to the People of God) was so formally coordinated as to present the parallelism: Christ, the elect Stone/ the faithful community, the elect race.

Such an arrangement apparently was chosen in order to coincide vv. 6-10 with vv. 4-5. According to the observations made in Chapter I, the structure of vv. 4-10 indicates that vv. 4-5 took over, reformulated, and interpreted the material contained in vv. 6-10. Hence, vv. 4-5 and 6-10 related to each other in such a way that vv. 4-5 anticipated and concentrated the material which was to follow in vv. 6-10. Reciprocally, vv. 6-10, especially through the arrangement of its incorporated material, supported the emphasis and illustrated the content of vv. 4-5.

Verses 4 and 5 account for both the form and content of the pattern of coordination achieved in vv. 6-10, for the prominence given the motif of election and for the depicture of the relationship between Jesus and His believers.

That the motif of election occupied the foreground of vv. 4-5 is seen (1) in the emphasis given the phrase in v. 4b: παρά δὲ θεῷ ἐκλεκτὸν ἔντιμον. The totality of v. 4b represents Peter's interpretation of the λίθος complex which he then cites in vv. 6-8. He has abbreviated, inverted, and reformulated in order to stress a particular point: the One Whom the believers are approaching is the Chosen and Precious Stone of God. Of the entire λίθος complex, it is the phrase from Is. 28:16 (=v. 6b) which the author gives first rank, a phrase concerning the *electedness* of the Messiah.

(2) Verse 5 describes how the believing community corresponds

to the Lord described in v. 4. In v. 5. also the motif of election is paramount. As v. 4 stresses the one element of the λίθος complex pertaining to the electedness of the Stone, so v. 5 selects from among the OT passages contained later in vv. 9-10 the election passage *par excellence*, Ex. 19:6, as the basis of its interpretation. Thereby the Chosen People is made to correspond with Jesus the Chosen Stone, just as the "living stones" relate to the "living Stone." This parallels and is supported by the arrangement of vv. 6-10: vv. 6-8 (=v. 4), the λίθος ἐκλεκτός / vv. 9-10 (=v. 5), the γένος ἐκλεκτόν.

According to the opening verses of this epistle where Peter addresses his audience as the "exiles of the Dispersion . . . chosen according to the plan of God the Father through the sanctifying activity of the Spirit . . ." (1:1f.), the factor of election might well be seen as permeating and determining of the thought of 1 P as a whole. Schrenk, for instance, speaks of 1:1f. as a "beherrschender Obertitel" and calls attention to the fact that "1 Petrus ist das einzige Schreiben des NT, in dem ἐκλεκτός von Anfang an thematische Bedeutung erhält."[1] That is, the reality of the believers' electedness and accordant holiness provided the major pre-requisite and basis for the paraenesis which followed. This reality then received direct treatment in 2:4-10. Blinzler has touched the heart of the matter when he states that vv. 4-10 were meant to show "was die Leser an ihrer Erwählung haben."[2]

Insofar, this thematic relation between our pericope and the epistle's introduction underlines the central position which vv. 4-10 assumed in the explication of the Divine indicative underlying all the exhortation of this writing. Inasmuch as the key to the significance of this section lies in its first two verses, we have added reason for seeking here the interpretation given the election theme. Having established the sense of these verses, we may then ascertain in a final section how this pericope relates to its context and the general development of thought.

The emphasis given the exaltation-election motif in v. 4 has already been mentioned and the function of this verse as a transition from the preceding context to the pericope which it introduces will be discussed at greater length below. For the present we shall concentrate upon v. 5.

---

[1] Schrenk, *op. cit.*, *TWNT* IV, 195.

[2] Blinzler, *op. cit.*, p. 51; sim. earlier, T. Spörri, *Der Gemeindegedanke im ersten Petrusbrief*, Gütersloh, 1925, p. 26.

B. The Structure and Content of Verse 5

1. *Syntactical Considerations*

To begin with, we recall that v. 5 has a double orientation. On the one hand, it continues the thought of v. 4. On the other, it incorporates formulation adapted from the OT passages which appear in their more original form in v. 9. The fact that these OT passages are different from and *in se* have little in common with those which v. 4 embodies must be kept in mind. For as we shall see, this might well have accounted for some of the problems involved in the connection of v. 5 to v. 4.

The opening words of the verse offer no difficulty. καὶ αὐτοὶ ὡς λίθος ζῶντες obviously relate not to v. 9 but to v. 4b, corresponding to λίθον ζῶντα. The next word, οἰκοδομεῖσθε, appears to be a verb based upon and developing the λίθος analogy—in the sense of stones being built together. But how does the next phrase, οἶκος πνευματικός, fit in? Problematical is its syntactical relation to what precedes. As a nominative, οἶκος cannot be the object of the verb οἰκοδομεῖσθε —in the sense "you build up a house." Is it an appositive to the subject of the verb: "you too are being built up—a Spiritual house"? Or is it to be considered the predicate of an elliptic clause: "(you are) a Spiritual house"?

Its connection with the following is just as uncertain. Could it stand in apposition to ἱεράτευμα ἅγιον? If so, how is the intervening preposition εἰς to be explained? ἱεράτευμα is the first word whose relation to v. 9 and Ex. 19:6 is obvious. What about ἅγιον? Is it an adjective supplied by the author or does the comma ἱεράτευμα ἅγιον represent an abbreviation of the entire phrase βασίλειον ἱεράτευμα, ἔθνος ἅγιον? Might a further parallel to the verbal clause in v. 9d, "that you proclaim the mighty deeds of Him Who called you out of darkness into His marvelous light," be seen in v. 5d: "to offer through Jesus Christ Spiritual sacrifices acceptable to God"?

The list of problems could be extended. We could note, for example, the disparity between the images "house" (inanimate) and "body of priests" (animate) which, nevertheless, are two adjoining predicates both applied to an animate body of believers. However, the difficulties already mentioned suffice to demonstrate the reason that v. 5 is considered unanimously by commentators as a *crux interpretum*.

2. Οἶκος πνευματικός

Of the main questions raised by v. 5 we consider first the meaning of οἶκος πνευματικός. Though the term is not foreign to the image of stones and building, it is clear from the analysis of the λίθος complex in Chapter I that it did not belong to the proper content of such a complex. Nor does it correspond to any particular term in v. 4. On the other hand, it also has no *literal* affinity with any word among the passages cited in v. 9. Is it a term which the author has added according to the λίθος-"building" analogy? If so, what accounts for the uncertainty of its syntactical relation to the foregoing? Or is there a term among the OT references cited in v. 9 to which it does relate? The evidence, in fact, favors this latter alternative and indicates that οἶκος πνευματικός represents the author's interpretation of βασίλειον and is so formulated as to create a transition from the λίθος-"building" image to the term ἱεράτευμα and its connected thought.

To corroborate this fact let us begin with a few basic considerations concerning the wording of Ex. 19:6 used in v. 9b.

a. βασίλειον and οἶκος πνευματικός

The text form concurs exactly with the LXX version (except for the omission of the initial words ἔσεσθέ μοι and the καί between ἱεράτευμα and ἔθνος). In the LXX βασίλειον most likely functioned as a substantive and this use was reflected in three later texts dependent upon the LXX formulation, 2 Mcc. 2:17, *De Sobr.* 66, and *De Abrah.* 56. These latter two texts are important insofar as they indicate a textual form and an interpretation current in the first Christian century and hence contemporary to the composition of 1 P.

Usually the relevance of these facts for the clarification of βασίλειον in 1 P 2:9b is either ignored or denied.[1] Urbanus Holzmeister[2] and Selwyn[3] provide two exceptions. Selwyn favors βασίλειον as

---

[1] Cerfaux, *op. cit.*, pp. 24f., e.g., acknowledges the wording of the LXX, 2 Mcc., and the Philo passages but decides that they had no influence upon the use of βασίλειον in 1 P; cf. Blinzler, *op. cit.*, p. 62.

[2] Holzmeister, *op. cit.*, p. 248.

[3] Selwyn, *op. cit.*, pp. 165-67. Recently A. M. Stibbs, *The First Epistle General of Peter* (*The Tyndale New Testament Commentaries*), Grand Rapids, 1959, pp. 103f., has allowed that βασίλειον, on the basis of its substantival function and meaning ("palace" or "king's court") in its only other NT occurrence (Lk.

substantive for the following reasons: (1) The texts of 2 Mcc. and Philo testify to the current exegesis of Ex. 19:6. (2) The word order: "if βασίλειον were an adjective, it would most naturally follow ἱεράτευμα as ἐκλεκτόν follows γένος and ἅγιον follows ἔθνος." (3) βασίλειον is interpreted with another substantive in v. 5b, οἶκος πνευματικός.

To these may be added the observation of Holzmeister that (4) not only the Armenian and Coptic Versions but likewise the Peshitta and Old Latin render Ex. 19:6 with two substantives. When the double substantives in Apoc. 1:6, 5:10 and the *Targumim* are also taken into account, an ancient as well as a wide-spread textual tradition meets the eye. This regularity occurs not only in Greek texts or those directly related to the LXX but in Aramaic Jewish sources as well. Certainly this is not the ultimate determinative factor for the function of βασίλειον in 1 P 2:9. However, any occurrence of the first member of the EF in other than substantival form would prove inconsistent with the major portion of texts treating Ex. 19:6 and at least require a justifying explanation.

The late American co-editor of the English edition of Walter Bauer's *Wörterbuch zum Neuen Testament*, William Arndt, attempted a refutation of Selwyn's position.[1] His arguments, however, fail to convince. Questionable is his reasoning that since in 2 Mcc. 2:17 the two nouns are separated by a καί this reading cannot be equated with the LXX and 1 P. 2 Mcc. 2:17 as well as the Philo passages stand together in an Alexandrian tradition immediately dependent

7:25), might possibly be taken in this sense here, "as describing the Christian community as a 'king's house' or 'royal residence.'" As "even more probable (particularly in light of the distinctive biblical meaning of the Hebrew and Greek words commonly translated 'kingdom,' and in the light of statements such as Zc. 6:13 and Rev. 5:10)" he suggests, however, "that Christians are here described as sharing with Christ in kingship or sovereignty as well as in priesthood" (p. 104). This explanation of βασίλειον, particularly popular among commentators of the early decades of this century, though it recognizes the substantival form, fails to appreciate the sense of the term in its context. Nowhere in 1 P has any expression been given to the idea of Christian kingship or co-reigning with Jesus Christ. Nor is such an emphasis upon the first member of the first comma of the EF to be found in any of the references or citations of this formula. Furthermore, this interpretation disregards the correspondence between v. 9 and v. 5 and attributes to βασίλειον a meaning incoherent with οἶκος πνευματικός of v. 5. Finally, an examination of the variations between 1 P 2:5 and 9 and Apoc. 5:10 has shown the unlikelihood of any influence upon 1 P 2 by the Apoc. references to the EF. Against the position that Christians—according to 1 P—are pictured as "sharing with Christ in kingship or sovereignty as well as in priesthood" cf. *infra*, pp. 169–74.

[1] "A Royal Priesthood," *CTM* 19/4 (1948), 241-49.

upon the LXX. It is more likely that their additions of a καί separating the first and second members of the EF and/or a definite article were measures taken to clarify the LXX rather than to revise it. Insofar as 1 P 2:9 reproduces the LXX text form and thus also joins this Alexandrian tradition, the relevance of 2 Mcc. and the Philo passages for v. 9 is beyond doubt.

Over against Selwyn's observation concerning word order Arndt suggested that Peter was influenced by the "rhythm of Ex. 19:6," a rhythm which would be interrupted suddenly by the appearance of two nouns. Yet though the parallelism of MT Ex. 19:6 allows the description "rhythmic," the LXX text upon which 1 P depended had already abandoned this parallelism and hence the original rhythmic pattern.

Cerfaux and Blinzler both regard βασίλειον as an adjective, but have spoken of the rhythm of 1 P 2:9 rather than of Ex. 19:6. However, the evidence of pattern and style upon which they base their decision is just as inconclusive. Cerfaux argued that the rhythm of v. 9 and the pattern of the commata (substantive combined with adjective: γένος ἐκλεκτόν, ἔθνος ἅγιον) signal βασίλειον as adjective.[1] Blinzler agreed, finding that then the sentence would read smoother, rhythmically and stylistically.[2]

Admittedly, γένος ἐκλεκτόν and ἔθνος ἅγιον offer the scheme *noun/adjective*. The fourth comma, nevertheless, contains *two nouns*: λαὸς εἰς περιποίησιν. If Peter had been concerned with rhythm and style, he could have chosen the more common phrase λαὸς περιούσιος. The prepositional phrase badly fits a supposedly stylistic structure. Furthermore, βασίλειον as modifier of ἱεράτευμα would have been an exception to the pattern of a noun followed by adjective—again a stylistic inconsistency. This also would have been an exception to the general rule that an adjective follows its referent unless preceded by a definite article, in which case it may then stand before its referent (e.g. τὸ βασίλειον ἱεράτευμα).[3]

Style and rhythm thus fail to account for the differing arrangement of βασίλειον ἱεράτευμα. Rather, we may conclude that the author was citing the Exodus text as he knew it from the LXX. Remaining consistent with the greater portion of the post-LXX textual tradition, he rendered βασίλειον as a substantive. His con-

[1] Cerfaux, *op. cit.* p. 24.
[2] Blinzler, *op. cit.* p. 62.
[3] Cf. *Bl-D* §270, p. 169.

cern was didactic and his arrangement of texts was thematic rather than poetic or rhythmic.

Final corroboration for the substantival function of βασίλειον is the correspondence between this term and the phrase of v. 5c: οἶκος πνευματικός. This correspondence, in turn, sheds new light on the meaning of οἶκος πνευματικός and the interpretation of Ex. 19:6 in v. 5.

The most important external indication of the correspondence is a text which we have examined above, *De Sobr.* 66.[1] As was seen, in this passage the βασίλειον of Ex. 19:6 was explicitly interpreted as the "king's house or dwelling place." Ex. 19:6 was alluded to in order to demonstrate that Noah's blessing of Shem had been fulfilled by God: God was dwelling in the houses of Shem, for the Scriptures had named his descendents "God's royal residence and body of priests." Philo thus regarded βασίλειον as a synonym for οἶκος: inasmuch as God is the King, ὁ βασιλέως δήπουθεν οἶκος is a direct parallel to βασίλειον καὶ ἱεράτευμα θεοῦ. The similarity between this treatment of βασίλειον and that in 1 P 2:5 is so striking and singular that the most likely conclusion is that Peter was not only acquainted with a traditional EF text form in general but found an interpretation of Philo in particular as useful for his discourse in 2:4-10. Influence of this text upon 1 P 2:5 and 9 accounts for both the correspondence of v. 5 and v. 9 and the syntactical unclarity concerning the combination of images in v. 5b-c.

Credit for this observation of 1 P's affinity with *De Sobr.* 66 goes originally to Blinzler, who in many respects is responsible for new insights into this pericope.[2] His deductions in this case, however, are not far-reaching enough. He saw only the influence of *De Sobr.* 66 upon v. 5 without considering the same influence upon v. 9. Hence the logical inference that βασίλειον in v. 9b was understood by Peter as a substantive was not drawn. Blinzler's decision for βασίλειον as adjective is actually inconsistent with his own observation! Noting that v. 5 might suggest that βασίλειον was a substantive, he favors the term as adjective, maintaining that the substantive as meaning "temple" would be quite foreign to Gentile-Christian readers.[3]

---

[1] Cf. *supra*, pp. 96–98.

[2] Blinzler, *op. cit.*, pp. 55, 59.

[3] *Ibid.*, p. 62.

Is, however, the assumption that βασίλειον signified "temple" justifiable? Blinzler arrives at this designation on the basis of the deduction from *De Sobr.* 66 that βασίλειον = "king's palace," king = God, therefore βασίλειον = "temple."[1] Such a deduction goes too far. According to the context of *De Sobr.* 66, not a "temple" but only a "royal residence" is mentioned. The identification which appears so natural, "house of God = temple," was not carried out by Philo. To the contrary, the οἶκοι of the previous section were identified not with cultic sanctuaries but with *people*, Shem's descendants.[2] "House" or its equivalents means a "dwelling place" and is treated here metaphorically; an objective-spatial denotation is expressly denied.[3] When Israel has been termed the βασίλειον . . . θεοῦ, this signifies that she is the dwelling place of the Divine King.[4] There is no inference that she is a "temple." Such a meaning was so uncommon for βασίλειον that if the word were meant in this sense, an appropriate explanation would be required. And such an explanation or interpretation by Philo is not at hand.

Therefore Blinzler's assumption concerning the meaning of βασίλειον and his preference for the adjective in v. 9 are unfounded. Rather, βασίλειον is best taken as a substantive paralleled by and interpreted through the substantive οἶκος (πνευματικός).

οἶκος πνευματικός, therefore, is Peter's explanation of βασίλειον as an attribute for the Christian body of the faithful. That this body is a "house of the Divine King" means that it is a "Spiritual house," "a house in which the Divine Spirit resides."

πνευματικός does not mean "spiritual" in the metaphorical sense of "immaterial,"[5] "non-external,"[6] "geistig" or "geistlich,"[7] or "heavenly."[8] Rather, πνευματικός is meant in the non-metaphorical, real sense of "Spiritual," "caused by or filled with the Holy Spirit."[9]

---

[1] *Ibid.*, p. 59.

[2] Cf. § 64 also where the human νοῦς is called an οἰκόδημα.

[3] Cf. § 63.

[4] Cp. *Exsecr.* 123, *C-W* V, 364, where διάνοια is named a βασίλειον of God; that is, not a "temple" but a "dwelling place of God."

[5] Bigg, *op. cit.*, *ad loc.*

[6] Beare, *op. cit.*, pp. 96f.

[7] Windisch-Preisker, *op. cit.*, pp. 59f. Earlier, von Soden, Gunkel.

[8] Knopf, *op. cit.*, p. 90: "überirdisches, göttliches, himmlisches Bauwerk"; Holzmeister, *op. cit.*, p. 242: "non terrena sed divina, societas supernaturalis."

[9] *BAG s.v.* Cf. Spörri, *op. cit.*, pp. 29f.; earlier, Schlatter, *Briefe*, p. 28, also B. Weiss, Kühl, Wohlenberg; E. Niebecker, *Das Priestertum der Gläubigen*, Paderborn, 1936, p. 90; R. N. Flew, *Jesus and His Church*, A Study of the

πνευματικός occurs twenty-seven times in the NT. "In none of the twenty-five cases (twice in 1 P)," points out Engelbert Niebecker, "does it have the meaning 'symbolisch,' 'uneigentlich,' 'nicht wirklich,' 'nur bildlich.' "[1] Rather, this term designates primarily "that which belongs to the sphere of the Holy Spirit."[2] "πνεῦμα is the miraculous divine power that stands in absolute contrast to all that is human";[2] "Spiritual" describes something which comes to man from beyond, which comes to him as a gift.[3] This gift is the Divine approach to man embodied ultimately in the presence of the Spirit.

This is precisely the implication of πνεῦμα in 1 P (1:2, 11, 12; 4:14).[4] The πνεῦμα is the Spirit of God (4:14), of Christ (1:11), the "Holy Spirit" (1:12), Who enables the proclamation of the Evangel (1:12) and effects election and holiness (1:2). Therefore the gifts received by the hearers/readers are described as χαρίσματα, bestowals "of the varied grace of God" (ποικίλης χάριτος θεοῦ, 4:10). In summary, "the Spirit is the creative principle in the Ecclesia" and insofar οἶκος πνευματικός designates "a house created, filled, and dominated by God's Holy Spirit," "das Werk und Eigentum des Geistes Gottes."[5]

Excursus 2

πνευματικός *and the Method of "Spiritualization"*

The word "spiritual" as a translation for πνευματικός is ambiguous. This is true of its equivalents in other languages as well (e.g. "geistig, geistlich," "spirituel"). A plurality of meanings is possible; "enthusiastic" in contrast to "rational"; "divine" versus "human";

Idea of the Ecclesia in the New Testament, 2nd ed., London, 1943, pp. 159f.; Dabin, *op. cit.*, pp. 188ff.; Blinzler, *op. cit.*, p. 54; Schlier, *op. cit.*, p. 44, n. 3; Congar, *Temple*, p. 179 and *passim*; Schelkle, *op. cit.*, p. 59.

[1] *Loc. cit.*

[2] Schlier, *op. cit.*, p. 44: "Die Worte auf -ικος bezeichnen im allgemeinen das, was zu dem Begriff, von dem sie abgeleitet sind, gehört, was seine Art trägt, was seines Wesens ist." Cf. *Bl-D* 113, 2, p. 75. E. Schweizer, *TWNT* VI, 435, n. 706, to the contrary, includes 1 P 2:5 with Barn. 16:10, Did. 10:3, and 1 Cor. 10:3 and doubts whether these elements are "Träger des Pneuma." However, do these texts belong to the same category?

[3] Cf. R. Bultmann, *TNT* I, 153ff. τὰ πνευματικά = "Spiritual gifts" (1 Cor. 12:1, 14:1); cp. (τὰ) χαρίσματα (Rom. 12:6; 1 Cor. 12:4).

[4] 1 P 3:18 and 4:6 relate to each other, appearing as varying formulation of the same (hymnic) source; both contrast σάρξ / πνεῦμα. 1 P 3:4 is its sole occurrence in a strictly profane sense: "disposition."

[5] Vielhauer, *op. cit.*, p. 148, cited approvingly also by Blinzler, *op. cit.*, p. 54.

"metaphysical" in contrast to "physical"; "immaterial" in contrast to "material"; or "figurative, metaphorical," in contrast to "literal." In theological language all these meanings have been implied at one time or other.

Responsible for much of the inclination to render πνευματικός as "immaterial" or "metaphorical" is an exegetical method described as "spiritualization," "Spiritualisierung," "Vergeistigung."[1] Implied is a method of interpretation which traces beyond the NT to earlier Rabbinic, late Judaic, Hellenistic, and OT exegesis. Subsequent to the destruction of Jerusalem in B. C. 587/86 and the elimination of the temple and its cult, certain concepts and aspects of Israel's life and worship, particularly cultic concepts, received new interpretation and meaning *apropos* a new situation. With the absence of the temple and its priesthood, the former mode of worship was no longer possible. Yet a departure from the sacrosanct prescriptions of the Fathers was just as impossible. As a result, former entities such as temple, priesthood, and sacrifice were interpreted metaphorically and applied to the "temple" of the human body, the "priestliness" of individual nobility and wisdom and the "sacrifice" of personal piety and ethical accomplishment.

The most comprehensive analysis of this type of interpretation has been made by Hans Wenschkewitz in his study, *Die Spiritualisierung der Kultusbegriffe Tempel, Priester, und Opfer im Neuen Testament.*[2] "Spiritualisierung" he has described as a method in which "die Frömmigkeitsformen geistiger Art die Ausdrucksformen der kultischen Frömmigkeit für sich in Anspruch nehmen, sie in Sinnzusammenhänge ihrer Gestalt einfügen und dadurch umdeuten."[3] Treating the three entities temple, priest, and sacrifice, Wenschkewitz traced the period from the late prophets to the era of the Talmud and showed how this method was employed in Jewish and Greek literature as well as in the NT. The acme of a "reflective (i.e. "rationalized and justified") spiritualization" is to be found in Rabbinic Judaism where a concern for the Law in study and obedience is the equivalent replacing temple, priest, and sacrifice.[4] Thus the formulation of the so-called "Aequivalenz- oder Substitutionstheorie."[5] The later prophets, Psalms, Apocrypha and Pseudepigrapha, Stoics, Philo, and the NT, on the other hand, "spiritualized" in a more "naive" fashion.[6] Accordingly, the NT presents a Christianity which used cultic terminology in an expli-

---

[1] Cf. Bultmann, *TNT* I, 115ff.

[2] Printed in *Angelos* 4 (1932), Leipzig. For a treatment of this subject in connection with the Pauline coprus cf. M. Fraeyman "La spiritualisation de l'idee du temple dans les épîtres pauliniennes" *EphLov* 33 (1947), 378-412.

[4] *Ibid.*, p. 8.

[5] *Ibid.*, pp. 24ff.

[3] *Ibid.*, pp. 30ff.

[6] *Ibid.*, p. 9.

cation of the kerygma but saw itself as a "religion without temple, priests, and sacrifice, . . . freed from the cultic institutions."[1]

For our purpose the main question involves the bearing this method of exegesis had upon 1 P 2.[2] Discussing 1 P 2:5, Wenschkewitz finds here "eine Häufung von Kultusbegriffen bei der gleichzeitigen Spiritualisierung des Tempel-, Priester-, und Opferbegriffes."[3] οἶκος apparently is *a priori* assumed to denote "temple." As we shall soon see, however, such an assumption is questionable. Furthermore, what would πνευματικός mean in this connection? Is it to be taken as a *terminus technicus* proper to this method of interpretation, thereby meaning something like "metaphorical" or "unreal"? This meaning, notes Niebecker, is favored by those scholars opposing the reality of the common priesthood.[4] For them "spiritual house" and "spiritual sacrifices" mean "figuratively speaking, a house," "figuratively speaking, sacrifices." Cerfaux held that Peter carried a Philonic, Alexandrian mode of "spiritualization" to its ultimate consequence and suggested that πνευματικός signifies something "immaterial" or "interior" in contradistinction to the external, material cult of the ancient institution.[5] However, this is by no means demonstrable—not only in view of the non-"spiritualistic" mode of interpretation throughout 1 P but also in respect to the non-"spiritualistic" manner in which the EF is treated by Philo as well. For Wenschkewitz, πνευματικός does not necessarily denote something as "immaterial" or "unreal." To the contrary, on one occasion he explains that it points to the "Divine Spirit dwelling within the Christian."[6]

In the light of frequent identifications of πνευματικός with this method of "spiritualistic" interpretation, one might regret that this latter observation of Wenschkewitz' did not receive greater clarification in his study. As the NT shows, the meanings of πνευματικός and this exegetical method must be sharply distinguished; for this adjective designates not a process of metaphorization or abstraction but something *de facto reale*, something belonging to the Holy Spirit of God.[7]

b. οἶκος: House(hold)

A further question concerns the precise meaning of οἶκος. Accor-

---

[1] *Ibid.*, p. 105.

[2] *Ibid.*, pp. 160-62.

[3] *Ibid.*, p. 161.

[4] Niebecker, *op. cit.*, p. 90.

[5] Cerfaux, *op. cit.*, pp. 25ff.: "Le temple est spirituel, c'est l'Eglise formée de pierres vivantes (Spirituellement vivantes), les fidéles. Les sacrifices sont spirituels, ce sont les sacrifices du culte intérieur . . . Le 'corps sacerdotal' sera lui aussi spirituel par opposition au sacerdoce 'matérial' de l'ancienne institution."

[6] Wenschkewitz, *op. cit.*, p. 126.

[7] Cf. Congar, *Temple*, p. 153.

ding to NT usage it could denote a "house" (in the sense of "edifice"), or "house (of God)", "temple" (cultic sense). A survey of the complex οἶκος, οἰκοδομέω, οἰκοδομή yields no definite conclusions concerning the meaning of οἶκος in 1 P 2:5.[1] Though this term is frequently taken to signify "temple", the context of 1 P and the tradition of interpretation which the author was following indicate that οἶκος meant not "temple" in a cultic connotation but "house" or "household".

Excursus 3

οἶκος: *a Temple?*

Neither οἶκος nor οἶκος πνευματικός is a technical designation in the NT for "temple."[2] Nevertheless, such a meaning is frequently favored at 1 P 2:5 for one or more of the following reasons: (1) the Apostolic and post-Apostolic material suggesting a common conception of the Church as the new eschatological temple of God;[3] its assumed affinity to (2) the λίθος complex and the Messianic connotations of the temple foundation-stone or copestone,[4] (3) the

---

[1] For comprehensive discussions of the material cf. the studies of Vielhauer and Congar already cited; further, O. Michel, *TWNT* V, 122-61; *BAG s.v.*

[2] τὸ ἱερόν occurs most frequently and designates generally the temple together with the temple grounds (e.g. Mt. 4:5, 24:1; Jn. 5:14). ὁ ναός indicates the temple proper (e.g. Mt. 23:16, Jn. 2:19; more frequently in the epistles: 1 Cor. 3:16f., 6:19, Eph. 2:21). ὁ οἶκος appears often in the LXX as translation of the Hebrew בַּיִת (e.g. 3 Km. 7:31). In the NT, the only instances where it means "temple" are citations of the LXX; cf. Mt. 21:13, Mk. 11:37, Lk. 19:46 (all three passages are citing Is. 53:7). Otherwise it is qualified by an additional phrase. Cf. Mt. 12:4, Mk. 2:26, Lk. 6:4 (τὸν οἶκον τοῦ θεοῦ); Jn. 2:16b (τὸν οἶκον τοῦ πατρός μου). Lk. 11:51 provides an exception; its parallel, Mt. 23:35, shows that Lk. accepted οἶκος as a synonym for ναός (as the "Holy of Holies"). But this was most likely an attempt by Lk. to coincide with the text of 2 Chr. 24:21 (οἴκου κυρίου).

[3] E.g. 1 Cor. 3:16f.; 2 Cor. 6:16f.; Eph. 2:19-22; 1 Tim. 3:15; Heb. 3:1-6, 8:1f.; 10:21f.; Apoc. 21; 2 Cl. 9:3; Barn. 16:10; Ign. *Mag.* 7:2; P. Hermas Sim. 9.13.9, 9.14.1. These passages are assumed to be related to others speaking of the individual Christian as a temple; e.g. 1 Cor. 6:19, 2 Cor. 5:1ff. Such expressions are seen consistent with and possibly derived from Jesus' identification of Himself with the Jerusalem temple (Mk. 11:17 and pll.; Mk. 14:58 and pll.). Selwyn discusses most of these passages and decides that οἶκος πνευματικός is best rendered as "God's true temple" (*op. cit.*, p. 291; pp. 286-91). Cf. also O. Cullmann, *Early Christian Worship* (*SBT* 10), London, 1953, p. 73; Windisch-Preisker, *op. cit.*, p. 60; *BAG sub* οἶκος; Schlier, *op. cit.*, pp. 141-45. Congar, *Temple*, pp. 117ff., 177 and *passim*. According to Congar, *ibid.*, p. 218, in the Gospels Jesus is the temple and in the epistles, the temple is the community of the faithful; in 1 P and Apoc. appear combinations of both. Cf. also Schelkle, *op. cit.*, pp. 60-63.

[4] Cf. e.g. Wenschkewitz, *op. cit.*, p. 162; Dabin, *op. cit.*, pp. 187f.; Jeremias, *WNT* IV 278.

Qumran conception of the community as the incorporation of the eschatological temple;[1] (4) the phrase εἰς ἱεράτευμα ἅγιον following οἶκος in 1 P 2:5, which is said to give οἶκος a cultic connotation.[2] On the whole, the authorities favoring the meaning "temple" hold that v. 5 and the entire pericope were intended as an anti-Jewish polemic enunciating the finality and supercession of an institutional cultus.[3]

This temple theory is not shared by all. Philipp Vielhauer, whose dissertation treats this οἰκ- complex, recognized a common Christian interpretation of the community as temple but holds that the emphasis in 1 P 2:5 is not upon the Church's temple character but upon her growth.[4] "From the 'stones' of the OT citations the author of 1 P constructed a house."[5] It is probable that the collective designation "temple," "house of God" arose from the thought of the eschatological temple popular in apocalyptic Judaism but in 1 P 2:5 not "temple" but rather "house" is meant in its original and proper sense.[6] Thus, according to Vielhauer, this Christian tradition of the house/temple analogy was not so rigid as to dictate one constant meaning in every one of its occurrences.

Blinzler has emphasized further that neither οἶκος nor οἶκος πνευματικός is a *terminus technicus* for "temple" and that the image cannot be understood primarily as anti-cultic in the sense "you are the true Temple."[7]

Moreover, the particular use of οἶκος in 1 P indicates not the connotation "temple" but still a further meaning: "household." οἶκος is this sense occurs often in the NT,[8] and is so used in 1 P 4:17 where τοῦ οἴκου τοῦ θεοῦ obviously denotes not a temple but the Christian congregation in the communal sense. Likewise in 4:10 members of the community are described as "good *house-stewards* of God's varied grace." This domestic motif appropriately follows an extended *Haustafel* (2:14-3:9) and insofar suggests that not a

[1] Cf. e.g. Flusser, *op. cit.*, p. 234. Betz, *Felsenmann*, pp. 49-77, points out the differences as well as the similarities between the Jewish and the Christian formulations.

[2] So Blinzler, *op. cit.*, pp. 54f., who maintains that this and none of the other reasons is the sole indication that οἶκος is not just "house" but "temple."

[3] Representative is the study of C. F. D. Moule, "Sanctuary and Sacrifice in the Church of the New Testament," *JTS* 1/1 (1950), 29-41.

[4] Vielhauer, *op. cit.*, pp. 60-62, 145-50.

[5] *Ibid.*, p. 147.

[6] *Ibid.*, pp. 146f.

[7] Blinzler, *op. cit.*, p. 54. Against the meaning "temple" cf. also Schlatter, *Briefe*, pp. 28f,: not a new "temple" but a new community!

[8] This communal sense was not only prevalent at Qumran but traces its roots to OT expressions such as "house of Israel," "house of Jacob," "house of David" which found their place in the NT (cf. Mt. 10:6, 15:24, Act. 2:36, 7:32; Lk. 1:33, Act. 7:46; Lk. 1:27, 69, 2:4, respectively). οἶκος was used frequently in the sense of "*familia*," "household" (cf. Act. 10:2, 11:14, 16:15, 31, 18:8; 1 Cor. 1:16; 1 Tim. 3:4, 15, 5:4).

cultic but a domestic motif was represented by the term οἶκος in 1 P. That οἶκος is to be understood exclusively as "household" in 2:5 is doubtful. As Selwyn has pointed out, the verb οἰκοδομεῖσθε requires the architectonic sense of "house."[1] No doubt we do best to follow Beare[2] and find both implications present: "house" which fits the building image in 2:5 and "household" which accords with the domestic motif in 2:13ff.

In summary, (1) When Christians are described as the "temple of God" in the NT οἶκος is never used. (2) Aside from 1 P 2:4ff. it never occurs in connection with the λίθος complex. Eph. 2:21 contains the nearest connection and here the term is not οἶκος but οἰκοδομή. Therefore the meaning "temple" cannot be derived from any supposed relation of οἶκος with the λίθος complex. (3) οἶκος is no specific designation for "temple." Such a meaning would have to be encouraged by the context of v. 5. (4) This context, however, points not to "temple" but to an analogy of building and growth and the influence of the EF tradition unrelated to the idea of temple. Hence, it cannot be agreed that ἱεράτευμα suggests a cultic connotation for οἶκος. (5) As Beare has noted,[3] Peter might have been acquainted with a "temple" tradition but the fact that he used οἶκος instead of the usual term of this tradition, ναός, discourages any ideas of an emphasis upon the cultic aspect or a polemic against the Jewish institution.

When all pre-judgments concerning the "polemical" character of vv. 4-10 or their "sacerdotal" tone are put aside, Petrine as well as NT usage in general encourages no other meaning than "house (hold)."

This meaning coincides with βασίλειον which implies not specifically a temple but a royal house. The application of both terms is to the house, i.e. community of the faithful. Thus the royal house of the Eschaton, the elected βασίλειον of the Messianic Age, is the house created and sustained by the Divine Spirit, The house of the Divine King is in reality the house of the Divine Spirit.

3. ἱεράτευμα *and Verse* 5c-d

a. Syntax and Construction of Thought

This first point of correspondence with the EF leads directly to a second and explicit reference to the same: ἱεράτευμα. As οἶκος πνευματικός, so ἱεράτευμα and its following phrase[4] have a double orientation, relating both to the development of thought in vv. 4-5 as

[1] Selwyn, *op. cit.*, pp. 159f.
[2] Beare, *op. cit.*, p. 96.
[3] *Ibid.*
[4] The epexegetical infinitive ἀνενέγκαι connects intimately with ἱεράτευμα

well as to the OT passages incorporated in v. 9. ἱεράτευμα anticipates the second predicate of the EF in v. 9b, ἅγιον relates to the comma ἔθνος ἅγιον, and the infinitival phrase of v. 5d parallels the verbal clause of v. 9d.

The syntactical relationship of εἰς ἱεράτευμα ἅγιον in v. 5, however, is not so clear. It can hardly depend upon the verb οἰκοδομεῖσθε which is never constructed with εἰς. Nor is there any sense to the thought "you are being built together into a holy body of priests." One can speak of the building of a house but never of a body of priests. "To build" and "body of priests" are "totally disparate concepts."[1] εἰς has been omitted by some MSS, apparently to facilitate a smoother reading in which οἶκος πνευματικός and ἱεράτευμα ἅγιον would be appositives.[2] Since the preferred reading according to the better MSS includes εἰς ,however, εἰς is best taken as subordinating ἱεράτευμα ἅγιον to οἶκος πνευματικός and indicating *purpose*.[3] Thus: "a Spiritual house to be a holy body of priests . . ."[4]

The epexegetical infinitive ἀνενέγκαι continues this thought, introducting a description of the purpose and function of this body of priests: "to offer Spiritual sacrifices acceptable to God through

---

by defining the purpose and function of the body of priests so that v. 5c-d is best taken as a logical whole.

[1] Blinzler, *op. cit.*, p. 54, n. 14 quoting E. Kühl, *Handbuch über den* 1. *Brief des Petrus*, 5. Aufl., Göttingen, 1887, p. 133.

[2] The preposition is omitted by undistinguished representatives of the Koine text type, Mosquensis, Angelicus, and Porfirianus rescriptus, by Minuscule 33, the majority of the remaining witnesses, the Vulgate, the Thomas Revision of the Syriac, and the Church Father Clement of Alexandria. This omission is also favored by editors Weiss, Merk, and Tischendorf, the latter of whom accordingly places a comma between πνευματικὸς and ἱεράτευμα, treating the respective phrases as appositives. Nestle's choice is supported by the weightier group of Witnesses, Vaticanus, Alexandrinus, and Ephraemi rescriptus; so also Blinzler, *op. cit.*, p. 54 *contra* Dabin, *op. cit.*, p. 188. This εἰς is not comparable to the obvious LXXism in v. 7 (ἐγενήθη εἰς κεφαλὴν γωνίας = Ps. 118:22: הָיְתָה לְרֹאשׁ פִּנָּה) *contra* Cerfaux, *op. cit.*, p. 25. Apart from his citations Peter is guilty of no LXXisms. The omission creates a *lectio facilior* and a better coordination of the two images. Such a reading, together with the influence of v. 9 (so Beare, *op. cit.*, p. 96), probably accounts for its absence in latter MSS. εἰς constructions are characteristic of 1 P (39 occurrences), appearing, apart from 2:5, approximately 17 times to indicate purpose or goal. This was its most likely function here. For the contemporary and widespread use of εἰς as indicating "goal, purpose, intention, and qualification" cf. Mayser, *op. cit.*, II, 2, 409.

[3] So Blinzler, *ibid.*

[4] A similar εἰς construction indicating purpose within the pericope is v. 9c: λαὸς εἰς περιπόιησιν.

Jesus Christ." Formally, "*Spiritual* sacrifices" correspond to "*Spiritual* house." And διὰ Ἰησοῦ χριστοῦ belongs to ἀνενέγκαι[1] rather than to εὐπροσδέκτους.[2] This latter term, in turn, relates to τῷ θεῷ[3] and expresses the consequence of the fact that these sacrifices are "Spirit-infused": because they are Spiritual they are acceptable to God. The stressed position which διὰ Ἰησοῦ χριστοῦ is given at the end of v. 5 indicates the import which this phrase contained for v. 5 and v. 4 as well.

Content-wise, both v. 5b and 5c, οἶκος πνευματικός and ἱεράτευμα ἅγιον, circumscribe the same communal entity: the community of believers. ἱεράτευμα, of course, occurs with the same meaning as in Ex. 19:6 and v. 9b, not "priestly office" but "body of priests."[4] Both are also determined by the Divine Spirit. The holy body of priests which offers "Spiritual sacrifices" reveals a characteristic proper to the "Spirit-dominated house." Coinciding with the EF and v. 9b, οἶκος πνευματικός and ἱεράτευμα ἅγιον are two sides of the same coin.

In the progression of thought of v. 5, however, these two terms for the body of the faithful have been found to present a problem. At first glance they appear to represent an abrupt change of metaphor.[5] First, in continuity with the "stone" image (vv. 4b-5a), the believers are denoted as an architectonic entity, a house; then, as

---

[1] So Schlatter, *Petrus*, p. 95; Vielhauer, *op. cit.*, p. 149; Blinzler, *op. cit.*, p. 51; Beare, *op. cit.*, p. 97. Blinzler calls attention to the fact that a διά designation in the NT never occurs in connection with εὐπρόσδεκτος or its synonyms, but rather with the verb of offering (cf. Heb. 13:15). The separation of component parts of a sentence is not unusual for Peter; cf. 3:21. 1 P 1:3, 5, 21, 3:21, and 4:11 clearly indicate that διά designates not a mediatorial but a *causal* function of Jesus Christ. On the basis of their relationship to Jesus Christ and what He has wrought believers can hope, can believe, are washed, can praise God. Cf. also Rom. 1:8, 7:25; Col. 3:17, and Blinzler, *ibid.*, pp. 56f.

[2] So Hort, *op. cit.*, p. 114; Bigg, *op. cit.*, p. 129; Knopf, *op. cit.*, p. 91; Holzmeister, *op. cit.*, p. 242; Selwyn, *op. cit.*, pp. 162f.

[3] So Beare, *ibid.* τῷ θεῷ does not belong to the verb as Blinzler, *ibid.*, holds ("to offer to God") but to the adjective ("acceptable to God"). Other NT occurrences of εὐπρόσδεκτος or its synonyms show the consistent connection made between the adjective "acceptable," "pleasing," etc., and God; cf. Rom. 15:31 (adj. with dative) and Phil. 4:18, 1 Tim. 2:3, Rom. 12:1 and Heb. 13:16. Cp. the similarity with θεῷ ἐκλεκτὸν ἔντιμον (v. 4b). Blinzler is inconsistent. Though he rejects the instrumental use of διὰ Ἰησοῦ χριστοῦ and the idea of mediation (*ibid.*, pp. 56f.), he uses this very image to defend the proposed connection between τῷ θεῷ and the verb (*ibid.*, p. 51).

[4] So also Blinzler, *ibid.*, p. 55.

[5] So most commentators on this verse.

an active living entity, a functioning body of priests. Yet when two important facts are kept in mind, the likeliness of a confusion of metaphor disappears: the double connotation of οἶκος ("household" as well as "house") and the parallelism between v. 5 and the EF (v. 9).

A confusion of metaphor is mentioned usually by those scholars taking οἶκος to mean "temple." If οἶκος did mean "temple," then a confusion would indeed be present; for then the believers would be described as both a temple and the priests functioning within the temple. But as has been demonstrated above, οἶκος does not mean "temple" here.[1] Rather, the term implies both "house" and the more personal "household" and insofar coincides appropriately with the personal and communal "body of priests." In this case Peter is not guilty of an abrupt mixture of imagery but rather must be credited with an apt choice of words.[2]

Such appropriateness may be doubly appreciated when the transitional function of οἶκος πνευματικός is clearly seen. The phrase serves, namely, to join the succeeding elements (v. 5cd) with the foregoing (v. 5a) in a combination which, though stiff syntactically, maintains a reasonable *logical continuity*.

The factor offering the author the greatest problem in vv. 4-5 is the disparity of the two groups of material (the λίθος complex and the cento of OT passages pertaining to the elect people of God) which he here comments upon. The motif under which he subsumes and unites this material is that of election. Hereby v. 4 describes Jesus as the elect and precious "stone" and v. 5, the believing community as the elect and holy people. Reference to the community commences in v. 5a: καὶ αὐτοὶ ὡς λίθοι ζῶντες. These words continue the λίθος analogy of v. 4b, affording formal as well as logical continuity. The verb οἰκοδομεῖσθε[3] proceeds a step further in the analogy,

---

[1] Blinzler's proposal that ἱεράτευμα suggests for οἶκος the meaning "temple" is unfounded. ἱεράτευμα among all the allusions to Ex. 19:6 (excepting Gk. Frag. 67) never was associated with the temple or the institutional priesthood. On the contrary, it is a term proper only to Israel *in toto* and free of all Levitical connections. ἱεράτευμα in v. 5 as little encourages the meaning "temple" for οἶκος as it does this meaning for the correspondent term in the EF, βασίλειον. Instead of clarifying, Blinzler's proposal would only confuse the issue; for then we would have to asume that Peter was *purposely* creating a confused metaphor!

[2] Cf. Beare, *op. cit.*, p. 96.

[3] The reading ἐποικοδομεῖσθε (Sinaiticus, Alexandrinus [first corrector], Ephraemi rescriptus, Minuscule 36, Old Latin MSS b, d, o, Vulgate, and the

suggesting λίθοι as building material and introducing the thought of construction, "you also as living stones are being built up."[1]

This is as far as the "stone" analogy reaches. Verse 5b-d describes the believers under the aspect of the EF and Is. 43:21, the material contained in v. 9. But through his interpretation of βασίλειον Peter arrived at a formulation which was germane to both components and provided a neat transition. οἶκος, namely, complements the thought of v. 5a as well as fits precisely as an explanation of βασίλειον. Thus "Spiritual house(hold)" forms a bridge between the two images of the community as "living stones" and "body of priests."

This transition was not accomplished without a certain lack of syntactical cohesion, however. The two explanations[2] usually offered for the function of οἶκος πνευματικός treat this phrase as either

Church Father Cyprian) is most probably secondary, apparently occasioned through assimilation to Eph. 2:20—so the majority of commentators.

[1] As noted above (cf. p. 16, n. 1), the context favors its function as 2nd person plural present indicative middle/passive rather than as 2nd person plural present imperative middle/passive. This sense is also supported by further occurrences of the verb in NT and LXX. In the LXX οἰκοδομεῖσθαι never occurs as an imperative in either middle or passive. For the passive cf. Is. 54:12, 14, 58:12; Jer. 12:16. Often the passive is used as "reverential periphrasis" for the activity of God; cf. Ps. 89(88):3; Is. 54:12, 14. This is especially clear in Is. 44:28 (LXX) where Οἰκοδομηθήσῃ and θεμελιώσω (subject is κύριος, v. 24) are correlate members of a *par. memb.*; cf. also Jer. 38(31):4, 12:16. In the Psalms it is God Who is considered the One Who builds Jerusalem, her walls, and her house (temple); cf. Ps. 51(50):18, 78(77):69; 102(101):16, 127(126):1, 147(146):2. For God as builder cf. also Amos 9:11; Jer. 38(31):28, 40:7, 49(42):10; Jdth. 16:14; Sap. 9:8; for Rabbinic usage cf. *Str-B* I, 732. In the LXX the reflexive middle ("to build oneself up") never appears. In the NT all occurrences of οἰκοδομεῖν which are not active are passive, never middle. Apart from 1 P 2:5 there are four such instances: Lk. 4:29, 6:48; 1 Cor. 8:10, 14:17. The cognate ἐποικοδομεῖσθε is also passive; cf. Eph. 2:20, Col. 2:7. 1 Thess. 5:11 shows that when the imperative force was intended the imperative active was used (οἰκοδομεῖτε), not the indicative middle. Jude 20 indicates that when the sense of "building up each other" was intended in the reflexive sense, not the middle but rather the active with a reflexive pronoun was used (ἐποικοδομοῦντες ἑαυτούς); cf. also 1 Cor. 14:4. Later writings also maintain this passive sense; cf. Barn. 16:10, Ign. Eph. 9:1.

Thus the evidence strongly indicates the indicative passive use of the verb in 1 P 2:5, best taken as a "reverential periphrasis" for Divine authorship. Ultimately God is the One Who builds; "man does not build his own life, rather everything which he possesses is something which he has received" (R. Bultmann, "Paulus" *RGG*, 2. Aufl., Tübingen, 1930, IV, 1037). In this sense cf. 1 Cor. 3:6f., Heb. 3:4. In the adjective πνευματικός and πνευματικάς this Divine authorship of the Spirit becomes explicit (so Blinzler, *op. cit.*, p. 54).

[2] Cf. Windisch-Preisker, *op. cit.*, p. 60.

predicate nominative[1] or appositive.[2] However, when v. 5ab is understood in the sense "you too as living stones are being built up, (you are) a Spiritual house(hold) . . . ," there is little difference between an appositive or a predicate nominative function. If an ellipsis is presumed, then οἶκος is a predicate nominative: "you are a Spiritual house." Without an ellipsis, οἶκος is an appositive to the subject "you" in v. 5a. In either case οἶκος belongs not to the preceding verb but to the following phrase εἰς ἱεράτευμα ἅγιον. Syntactically there is a caesura between οἰκοδομεῖσθε and οἶκος—a trace of the fact that in v. 5a a combination of two different entities has been effected. The price paid for this combination and a structure parallel to that of v. 4 was the lack of complete syntactical coherence, a lack often overlooked or concealed by a smoothly flowing translation.[3] An attempt to explain this verse would do well not to obliterate the fact that was not a member of the λίθος complex or building analogy, at least not at the time of the composition of 1 P,[4] but belonged to the predicate ἱεράτευμα and the EF whose interpretation it was introducing.

With this construction a certain ascendency in the thought of *community* and *growth* is established. First the believers are, in common, "living stones"; then they are "being built up" (together); finally together they form a "Spiritual house(hold)" and "body of priests."

At the same time the formal parallelism to v. 4 is maintained as well as the parallelism of vv. 4 and 5 to vv. 6-8 and 9-10. As the thought in v. 4 proceeds from the "living Stone" to the "elected and precious Stone," so in v. 5 the "living stones" are then described as the "elect and holy community." On the other hand, the progression from the λίθος image to the predicates of the elected people correspond precisely with the arrangement of the material in vv. 6-8 and 9f.

From the observations made on vv. 4-5 thus far it has become

---

[1] Blinzler, *op. cit.*, p. 51.

[2] Holzmeister, *op. cit.*, p. 242.

[3] Beare's translation (*op. cit.*, p. 92), for instance, fails to reflect the disjunction present in the Greek text: "you yourselves also, as living stones, are built up as a spiritual house." This rendering implies that a ὡς stands before οἶκος in the Greek text. Such a translation says more than the original text and thereby fails to bring the problem of syntax to attention. It also implies that οἶκος belongs to the verb though in fact it does not.

[4] A close parallel to 1 P 2:5, Eph. 2:21, shows in its phrasing αὔξει εἰς ναὸν ἅγιον how syntactical and logical clarity subsequently was achieved by making οἶκος (replaced by ναός) the *object* of the verb of growth.

apparent that these two verses, and in effect vv. 4-10, revolve about two objects: Jesus and the believing community. It is an election theme under which statements concerning both were subsumed. Jesus is the elect Stone of God; the community is the elect People of God, the house of His Spirit,[1] the covenantal body of priests. This election motif portrays both as objects of the exalting activity of God. Underlying this correspondence between the living and elect Stone and the living stones, the elect community, is a second factor, namely the act of believing, that is, the peoples' permanent commitment to and firm confession of Jesus Christ as their Lord, the relationship through which Divine election was effected. These people are members of the elect community only because each one believes in Jesus, the elect of God. Expressions of the relationship to Jesus Christ ("coming to Him,"[2] v. 4a; "through Jesus Christ,"

---

[1] οἶκος refers to and includes only the believers, not the believers and Jesus Christ. The subject of v. 5 is exclusively the *community* in contrast to v. 4b where *Jesus* is the point of concern. The text contains no statement that the believers are being built together with Christ (so Beare, *op. cit.*, p. 96; sim. Dabin, *op. cit.*, p. 188) or that they constitute a house built upon Christ the foundation-stone (so Blinzler, *op. cit.*, pp. 51, 54, 56). οἶκος, as ἱεράτευμα, ultimately owes its presence here to the EF; if ἱεράτευμα refers only to the Christians and not to Christ, as Blinzler shows (*op. cit.*, p. 56), then the same must be assumed for οἶκος (*contra* Blinzler, *ibid.*). If Christ was implied to have a place in the Spiritual edifice (Blinzler, *ibid.*, p. 51), then the appropriate verb would have been συνοικοδομεῖσθε as in Eph. 2:22 rather than the textual οἰκοδομεῖσθε. The picture in Eph. 2 represents a more reflected and developed presentation than in 1 P 2: "you are . . . built upon the foundation of the apostles and prophets, Christ Jesus Himself being the chief cornerstone, in Whom the structure is joined together and grows into a holy temple in the Lord; in Whom you also are being built together for a dwelling place of God in the Spirit" (Eph. 2:19-22). Choice of the compound verb ἐποικοδομεῖσθε, inclusion of "cornerstone," explicit adaptation of ναός (instead of οἶκος) to the temple analogy, and the presence of ἐν πνεύματι instead of πνευματικός all demonstrate the elaborateness and precision of the Ephesian formulation in comparison with 1 P 2. The author of Ephesians obviously was using the same material as Peter, if not expanding upon 1 P itself. At any rate the treatment in Eph. 2:19ff. is younger than that of 1 P 2:5 (*contra* C. L. Mitton, "The Relationship between 1 Peter and Ephesians," *JTS* 1/1 [1950], pp. 67-73) and it would seem advisable to avoid interpreting 1 P in the light of Eph. 2.

[2] The verb cannot be ingressive; the believers are not making their first decision to "come to faith" (*contra* J. Schneider, *TWNT* II, 682). This is obvious from 1:3, 14, 18, 22, 23 where the verbs describing the faith of the hearers/readers are all aorists or perfects. Even more so, the preceding verse states an accomplished fact: "you tasted that the Lord is good" (2:3). This verb is an adaptation of ψ 33:6 and the modification of the original aorist imperative προσέλθατε into a present participle makes a proposed imperative

v. 5d)[1] form the beginning and close to vv. 4-5. They frame in these verses and give the statement on election its basis.

The thread of thought might be so paraphrased: This is He (i.e. the κύριος, v. 3) in Whom you believe; He is the resurrected Stone rejected by the unbelievers but elect and precious in the sight of God. Therefore because you believe in Him Who is the living Stone, you too are living stones which are being built up. Through Him, the Elect of God, you too are an elect People, a Spirit-filled house (hold), whose task is as a body of priests to offer through Him Spiritual sacrifices acceptable to God. In Him you believe and through Him you have become what you are.

What now remains to be determined is the significance which "holy body of priests" and "to offer Spiritual sacrifices" assumed in this line of thought. What factors determine their meaning here and their place within the immediate and then also the remote context of 1 P? The answer to this question forms the *crux* to the understanding of this final segment of v. 5.

b. ἱεράτευμα: Active Body of Priests

First, in respect to ἱεράτευμα we recall the triple personal-corporative-active character of the term. The word derives from the text about to be cited in v. 9, LXX Ex. 19:6. Such a triple aspect has been seen to have been a characteristic of this unusual LXX construction. It designates a community of persons functioning as priests; hence the translation "body of priests." Verse 5 has already yielded evidence of a definite relationship to an LXX tradition (specifically to Philo's texts) and insofar corroborates the fact that

---

mood or inceptive sense most unlikely. Nor is the verb to be understood exclusively cultically as in Heb. 4:16, 7:25, or 10:1 (*contra* Schneider, *ibid.*) but rather as an expression for "to believe" with cultic overtones, i.e. belief in the sense of "approach to the Deity" (cf. Heb. 12:18, 22, esp. Heb. 10:22). The various meanings of this verb in the NT are not equivocal; cf. also 1 Tim. 6:3 where it means "to agree with." Each occurrence must be explained according to its particular context. This applies also to 1 P 2:4, as Beare has noted (*op. cit.*, p. 54), where the verb relates both to v. 3 and vv. 4f. According to Blinzler (*op. cit.*, p. 51), the sense "an Christus glauben" is evident from v. 6 where ὁ πιστεύων ἐπ' αὐτῷ parallels v. 4. The present tense expresses continuation and perseverence in this relationship to Jesus.

[1] This final phrase of v. 5 though relating immediately to the verb "to offer," applies to the entire verse insofar as Christians are "built up," a "Spirit-filled house," and a "holy body of priests" alone through (i.e. "because of") Jesus Christ. Again, in contrast to Eph. 2:19ff. the statement is not "with" or "upon" but "*through* Jesus Christ"!

ἱεράτευμα in both formulation and meaning depends closely upon its LXX source.[1]

Some interpreters feel compelled to choose between a corporative or a functional denotation. Hort and Beare, for example, favor the latter sense: "the function of an official priesthood,"[2] "the exercise of priestly functions."[3] Verse 9 should have warned them, nevertheless, that ἱεράτευμα simultaneously designates a *corporative* entity: "*body* of priests" along with "race," "nation," and "people." In v. 9 the *personal* aspect is also obvious, for the term depicts not a function but people, the addressees: ὑμεῖς δὲ . . . ἱεράτευμα;[4] yet not so as individual persons but as a collective entity, a community. Beare, who strangely disregards this significance for v. 5, states most aptly at v. 9 that the Church, with a profound social and political self-consciousness supplemented by a powerful historical element, derived the sense "that she was not merely an association of like-minded persons co-operating with one another for specific purposes, but an enduring social organism, having a corporate life and a corporative significance not wholly expressed in her institutional forms and her moral and spiritual principles, but grounded in a continuum of historical experience and development."[5] This corporate significance is just as much a property of ἱεράτευμα in v. 5 where it is bound to οἶκος πνευματικός and delineates the same community as does the "Spirit-filled house."

The infinitive ἀνενέγκαι and v. 5d point out the third feature of ἱεράτευμα as a *nomen actionis*: *a community of persons charged with a priestly task*. The words which then follow describe this task as the "offering of Spiritual sacrifices."

'Αναφέρω literally means "to bring or take up."[6] In the LXX this verb was bound with the object of sacrifice and hence became a *terminus technicus* in the cultic nomenclature: "to bring up (to the altar) a sacrifice," "to offer" (cf. Lev. 14:20, 16:25, 17:5f.; 1 Esdr. 5:49; Is. 57:6; 2 Mcc. 1:18, 2:9).[7] When hymns and praise were

---

[1] Cf. Schrenk, *op. cit.*, p. 250.

[2] Hort, *op. cit.*, pp. 109f.

[3] Beare, *op. cit.*, p. 96.

[4] Blinzler, *op. cit.*, p. 55: "'Priesterschaft, Priesterkorporation,' nicht 'Priesteramt'; denn in 9 ist das Wort Bezeichnung für etwas, was die Christen *sind* (ὑμεῖς δὲ sc. ἐστέ)." For the NT term for "priestly function" cf. Lk. 1:9, cp. 1:8: ἱερατεία.

[5] Beare, *loc. cit.*, p. 101.

[6] Cf. Mt. 17:1, Mk. 9:2, *BAG s.v.*

[7] The LXX authors used this verb to translate a larger number of Hebrew

considered to be objects of sacrifice after the destruction of the temple, these too became objects of the verb.[1] In the NT the verb occurs in both a non-cultic[2] and a cultic[3] sense. It can also mean "to take up" in the sense of "to remove."[4] Often Heb. 13:15 is compared to v. 5d; however, we would be careful not to automatically equate πνευματικὰς θυσίας with θυσίαν αἰνέσεως (Heb. 13:15). *A priori*, 1 P 2:5 as little implies a "sacrifice of praise" as does Heb. 13:15, "sacrifices governed by the Spirit."

With its cultic overtones the phrase "to offer Spiritual sacrifice" thus was appropriate in depicting the functional character of ἱεράτευμα. N. B.: it was not the thought of offering Spiritual sacrifices which occasioned and give birth to the term ἱεράτευμα but vice versa. As we have seen above, v. 5 anticipates and interprets the OT passages about to be cited in v. 9. That is, these passages provide the subject matter for v. 5 Ἱεράτευμα, as part of the EF cited in v. 9 and explained in v. 5, was not mentioned in order to substantiate or explicate a conception of sacrifice but to denote the believing community as the elect People of God. The Church is not a "body of priests" because she offers sacrifice,[5] but she offers sacrifice because she is a "body of priests." According to vv. 5 and 9, the Church's nature prescribes her function and not vice versa. True, priesthood and sacrifice are correlates;[6] just this fact is demonstrated by the coherence of v. 5c and 5d. However, it is the community's priestliness which leads to the thought of sacrifice. Her essence as ἱεράτευμα enables her to offer. Sacrifice is the consequence of her election through Christ and her becoming a "body of priests." The activity of the body of priests is described in the metaphor of the cult as an assimilation to the cultic connotation of "body of *priests*."

---

terms so that it also takes other objects. Cf. Ex. 18:19, 22, 26; Lev. 2:16; Num. 14:33, 2 Km. 1:24; Is. 66:20.

[1] E.g., 2 Chr. 29:31; 2 Mcc. 10:7.

[2] Cf. Mt. 17:1; Mk. 9:2; Lk. 24:51.

[3] Cf. Heb. 7:27, Jac. 2:21.

[4] Cf. Lk. 24:51; Heb. 9:28 = Is. 53:12 (probably the source for 1 P 2:24 also where the verb contains a double connotation).

[5] Though not a small number of scholars make this assumption; cf. e.g., Bigg, *op. cit.*, p. 134; H. Behm, *Der Begriff des allgemeinen Priestertums*, Schwerin in Meckl., 1912, pp. 32f.; Knopf, *op. cit.*, p. 96; H. Asmussen, *Das Priestertum aller Gläubigen*, Stuttgart, 1946, pp. 22f.; Blinzler, *op. cit.*, pp. 55, 57; Manson, *op. cit.*, p. 64.

[6] So Blinzler, *ibid.*, p. 63; Congar, *Lay People*, pp. 144, 148, 159.

She cannot be a priestly body *insofar as* she offers sacrifice, for then her being a body of priests would always be a conditional status—a body of priests only when she offers.[1] This condition would be dependent not upon the elective and saving grace of God but upon human achievement. Verse 9, however, eliminates such a possibility. Here the only condition and cause for the community's election and her priestliness is the mighty deeds of Him Who called her from darkness to light. His mercy (v. 10) alone accounts for her ascription with the epithets proper to the chosen people of God.

In v. 5 ἱεράτευμα implies that this high calling is something to be carried out and put into action. This signifies that the "Spiritual house" is not a sanctuary for loiterers but a community of Spirit-filled offerers. The house(hold) has a purpose (εἰς): to be an active body of priests. And this body has a function: to offer Spirit-motivated sacrifices acceptable to God.

Excursus 4

Variations between 1 P and other NT Statements on Christian Priesthood

Variations between 1 P and other NT statements concerning priesthood involve both terminology and general conception of thought. One important factor is the uniqueness of the term ἱεράτευμα in the NT. The closest parallels to 1 P 2:5, 9 are Apoc. 1:6, 5:10—at least as far as citation of the EF is concerned. Yet despite the fact that these passages along with 1 P 2:5, 9 are the sole instance in the NT where believers are explicitly identified as "priests,"[2] the difference between the form ἱερεῖς (Apoc.) and ἱερά-

[1] *Contra* Blinzler, *ibid.*, p. 55: "Die Christen sind insofern Priester, als sie berufen sind, 'geistliche, wohlgefällige Opfer Gott durch Jesus Christus darzubringen.'"

[2] In contrast to the abundant occurrences of ἱερεύς in the Jewish and Greek literature of this period, its relative scarcity in the NT is noteworthy. Manson, *op. cit.*, p. 44, attributes this to the fact that "at this stage in the history of the Christian community there was no room for a regular priesthood, *as priesthood was understood at that time*" (italics Manson). For apart from references to the Jewish priesthood (Mt. 8:4; Mk. 1:44; Lk. 1:5; Jn. 1:19, etc.) and to heathen priests (Act. 14:13), this term in its contemporary sense had no literal referent in the primitive Christian community where "to be a priest" meant "to be a male member of one of the existing Jewish priestly families" (Manson). Cf. sim. S. von Dunin-Borkowsky, "Die Kirche als priesterliche Gesellschaft," Esser-Mausbach, *Religion, Christentum, Kirche*, II, Kempten, 1921, pp. 56f. *In toto* ἱερεύς in singular and plural occurs 31 times in the NT. Literally, it designates Jewish or heathen priests as in the

τευμα (1 P) reveal a different direction of emphasis. Whereas 1 P cites the version of the EF in which the *corporateness* of the priestly people comes to clearest expression, Apoc., unconcerned about the element of corporateness, chooses a text where the simple ἱερεῖς appears. Whereas the second member of the EF assumes an important place in the exposition and interpretation of 1 P, ἱερεῖς in the Apoc. receives no word of comment and plays no role in the thought to which it is introduced. Whereas in 1 P ἱεράτευμα is brought into no connection with a priestly function or office of Jesus Christ, in the Apoc. ἱερεῖς and the EF are placed into a context which suggests a connection with the kingship and priesthood of Jesus.[1] Certainly the thought is not far removed that the "Ruler of the kings on earth" and the One clothed in priestly garments made His people a "kingdom" and "priests" (1:5f.).[2] Such a theory of participation of the believers in the royalty and priesthood of Jesus Christ is not to be found in 1 P, however.

For similar reasons 1 P is to be differentiated from the basic conception of the Ep. Hebrews.[3] Heb., as the Apoc., develops the thought of a heavenly cultus, presenting the Church in her consummated form as a celestial people of God, a heavenly cultic community.[4] But the author of the Epistle to the Hebrews has construed this idea differently from the writer of the Apoc., though in places they might be seen to have used common material.[5] Here the major antithesis is the celestial versus the earthly, the heavenly cultic congregation in contrast to its OT prototype.[6]

This conception has nothing in common with 1 P which discusses

---

above-mentioned texts; figuratively, it designates Jesus (Heb. 5:5ff., 8:4, 10:21) or the believers (Apoc.). If Rom. 15:16 where Paul describes his ministry as "serving the gospel as a priest" (ἱερουργοῦντα τὸ εὐαγγέλιον) is to be included, then a five-fold application of ἱερεύς and its compounds is to be found in the NT, as observed by Kinder, *op. cit.*, pp. 5f. Among these instances ἱεράτευμα would resemble the Apoc. insofar as it is a predicate for the believers.

[1] According to Apoc. 9:11, 15:3, 17:14, 19:16 Jesus is a king; indeed, the "King of kings and Lord of lords" (19:16, cp. 17:14). In 1:13 the priestly garments in which He appears suggest that He was also thought to be a priest. Chs. 4ff. and the celestial worship, the bride's clothing of priestly linen (19:8), the service of the priest-martyrs within the celestial temple (7:15), the 24 thrones about the Throne (4:3f.), and the formulation "reign(ed) with Christ" (20:4, 6; cf. 22:5) point to the priestly and royal status of those worshipping this King and Priest.

[2] Cf. Cerfaux, *op. cit.*, p. 29.

[3] So also Blinzler, *op. cit.*, pp. 56f.

[4] Cf. M. Dibelius, "Der himmlische Kultus nach dem Hebräerbrif," *ThBl* 21 (1942), 1-11 [reprinted in *Botschaft und Geschichte* II, Tübingen, 1956, pp. 160-76].

[5] E.g. Od. Sol. 33 in Heb. 12:22f., Apoc. 14; cf. E. Käsemann, *Das wandernde Gottesvolk*, 4. Aufl., Göttingen, 1961, pp. 31f.

[6] So Käsemann, *ibid.*, pp. 34f.

not a heavenly community but rather an empiric earthly entity not distinct from but participant in a historical continuity.[1] Furthermore, the realization of the cultic service, according to Heb., takes place not on earth but in heaven.

> "Opfer, Weihe, Eingang und Priesterdienst Jesu Christi im Himmel sind das einzige Kultmysterium, das für Christen noch Geltung hat . . . und es gibt für Christen keinen anderen Kult als die Beteiligung an diesem himmlischen Mysterium,"

noted Martin Dibelius.[2] Thus the attempt of Olaf Moe to find a universal priesthood in Heb.[3] can at best apply only to a heavenly one. In fact, the connotations of the concept "universal priesthood" raise serious questions as to the appropriateness of its application to the picture of the celestial cultic community drawn here.

Ernst Käsemann, at the conclusion of his study on this epistle, has pointed out both the centrality of the concept of the High Priesthood of Christ and its coordination with the motif of the wandering people of God: "alle Ausführungen des Hebr. zwar in der Darstellung des Hohenpriesteramtes Christi gipfeln, ihre tragende und die einzelnen Teile sinnvoll gliedernde Basis aber vom Motiv des wandernden Gottesvolkes her empfangen."[4]

In this point the gulf between the specific treatments of priesthood in Heb. and 1 P is evident. In Heb. the coordination between Christ's priestly activity[5] and the priestly or cultic function of the community[6] indeed allows the conclusion that the believers are pictured as participating and sharing in the priesthood of their Lord.[7] Both the priesthood of Jesus and the idea of the Church's sharing in such priesthood are thoughts foreign to the epistle of 1 P however. Admittedly, Jesus is described in 1 P as the "spotless lamb" through whose blood the believers have been redeemed (1:18f.). Or His atoning work has been pictured in the cultic words of shedding blood (ῥαντισμὸν αἵματος Ἰησοῦ χριστοῦ, 1:2). And possibly 2:24 ("He bore [ἀνένεγκεν] our sins in His body to the tree") is to be reckoned as containing cultic overtones.[8] Yet in no instance

---

[1] Käsemann, *ibid.*, has shown that in Hebrews a maintenance of historica continuity was exactly *not* the point but rather the supersedure of all that was foregoing.

[2] *Botschaft und Geschichte* II, 175.

[3] "Der Gedanke des allgemeinen Priestertums in Hebräerbrief," *ThZ* 5 (1949), 161-69.

[4] Käsemann, *op. cit.*, p. 156.

[5] Heb. 2:17, 3:1, 4:15, 5:1, 6f., 7:11-28, 10:12, 21, 12:24, (mediatorial, cp. 9:15).

[6] Heb. 4:16, 7:19, 10:22, 12:28f., 13:15f.

[7] This idea of participation is made likely by the presence of the term μέτοχοι which occurs in Heb. 3:1, 14; 6:4; 12:8 (cp. 2:14) in the sense "participant."

[8] But cf. Selwyn, *op. cit.*, pp. 94ff., who disputes any reference to sacrifice ere.

does Peter develop from these sparce statements any conception of the priesthood of Christ. Participation in Christ's activity, according to 1 P, is not participation in His priesthood but in His suffering: κοινωνεῖτε τοῖς χριστοῦ παθήμασιν (4:13).

In 1 P Jesus does not appear as a mediator through whom the believers draw near to God but as He through Whom God has drawn near to man (cf. 1:3ff.). He is the holy and spotless lamb "pre-ordained before the foundation of the world" as the object through which God would effect redemption (1:18-20), Whom God raised from the dead in order that faith and hope might be directed primarily not to Jesus but to God (1:21). Through this holy lamb God has made His people holy (1:2, 22). Through this Elect One God has made this people His elect people (1:1, 2:4-6, 9f).

Throughout this epistle the reader cannot avoid the fact that its theological conception is primarily theocentric rather than Christocentric[1]—a factor which again differentiates 1 P and 2:4ff. from other NT developments of thought. Although 1 P is by no means void of Christological statements (cf. 1:18-21, 2:21-25, 3:18-22), even these sections contain theocentric formulation[2] and have been used not to serve an exclusively descriptive Christological end but to support a preceding and succeeding paraenesis—not as example (in the sense of the *imitatio Christi*) but as basis. The suffering, death, and resurrection of Jesus provide the point of departure, the basis, the Christian indicative, for all subsequent imperatives. Though talk of a "subordinationist" viewpoint is not precisely *apropos*, it is noteworthy that all three Christological sections are cited to support the exhortation of subordination to the will of God![3]

This, of course, does not deny the basic position which Peter ascribes Jesus Christ in his idea of the Church,[4] but does indicate that the clue to the meaning of ἱεράτευμα is to be sought neither in a developed conception of Christ's priesthood, His mediatorship,[5]

---

[1] So Selwyn, *ibid.*, p. 76; J. P. Love, "The First Epistle of Peter," *Interpretation* 8/1 (1954), 63-87; Beare, *op. cit.*, p. 33.

[2] Perhaps the most noteworthy are in 3:18-22 insofar as this represents an advanced stage in the development of the conception of a *descensus ad inferos*. Cf. here 3:18a ἵνα ὑμᾶς προσαγάγῃ τῷ θεῷ and the passive construction in v. 18c θανατωθεὶς μὲν σαρκὶ, ζωοποιηθεὶς δὲ πνεύματι; also 3:17b εἰ θέλοι τὸ θέλημα τοῦ θεοῦ, a typical emphasis of Peter upon the will of God (cf. 4:2, 19). Cf. further, 1:20, 21, 5:5c, and 4:11, 5:10.

[3] Cf. E. Krafft, "Christologie und Anthropologie im ersten Petrusbrief," *EvTh* 10 (1950/51), 120-26.

[4] As Selwyn, *op. cit.*, p. 76, following Spörri, *op. cit.*, p. 236, points out.

[5] The phrase διὰ Ἰησοῦ Χριστοῦ, as mentioned above, expresses no mediatorial function of Jesus but rather the fact that He has effected a new relation to God seen as the basis and cause of all worship and glorification of God.

nor in an idea of incorporation into the Body of Christ. Against such a presumption Selwyn has aptly remarked:

> "The mutually inclusive relationship which subsists between Christ and the Church is expressed in the phrase "in Christ," which occurs three times in 1 Peter;[1] but the phrase is not in any way developed or made the basis of an argument, as it is by St. Paul and St. John. It would appear that the thought of Christ as the *sphere* (italics Selwyn) of the Christian life is common ground between the Apostle and his readers: no doctrine of mystical union seems to underlie it or to flow from it."[2]

It is truly difficult to see where the sweeping statements of T. F. Torrance in his study, *The Royal Priesthood*, relate in any way to 1 P 2:5 and 9. "Christian liturgy and priesthood," he maintains, "have their place within baptismal incorporation of the Church into the Body of Christ. The pattern of that liturgy and priesthood derives from the Suffering Servant and is to be enacted in the Body."[3] Though his emphasis upon the corporateness of the Church is indeed a salutary one, the thought that "the ministry of the Church refers primarily to the royal priesthood which pertains to the whole membership of Christ's Body"[4] is not to be found in such terms in 1 P. Peter nowhere develops the idea of the Body of Christ and/or the incorporation of Christians into the same. In 1 P the community is not a body of priests because its "Head" is a priest but because it stands in the historical continuity of the Elect People which through Jesus the Elect One has received new dimensions as a holy "Spirit-filled" entity. Inadmissable is the equation of 1 P 2:4ff. with, or its interpretation in the light of, the σῶμα χριστοῦ conception of Ephesians (4:11ff., cp. Eph. 2:11-22). Seen quite apart from the question of the relationship of 1 P 2:4ff. to ministry and office, these statements involve generalizations which fail to reflect the differing nuances of specific texts and subsume the thought of 1 P 2:4ff. under a concept totally alien to 1 P.

Nor does the term employed by Paul to describe his ministry of the Gospel among the Gentiles, εἰς τὸ εἶναι με λειτουργὸν Χριστοῦ Ἰησοῦ εἰς ἔθνη, ἱερουργοῦντα τὸ εὐαγγέλιον τοῦ θεοῦ (Rom. 15:16) have anything in common with ἱεράτευμα in 1 P. Whereas the latter term derives from Ex. 19:6 and is an appelation for the entire people of Israel, ἱερουργέω derives from the cultic activity and service of the Levitical priest. Whereas Peter depicts the entire believing community as a corporation of priests, Paul is describing his own individual task, conceived here primarily as one of mediation.

---

[1] 1 P 3:16, 5:10, 14.
[2] Selwyn, *op. cit.*, p. 83.
[3] Torrance, *op. cit.*, p. 22.
[4] *Ibid.*, p. 35; cf. p. 33.

In summary, the NT contains no unanimous viewpoint on the subject of a Christian priesthood. Nor can it be said that its authors were especially concerned with the topic. Its role within the primitive Christian kerygma was a limited one, as the limited application of ἱερεύς and/or its cognates to Jesus or the Christian community indicates. The sources and OT conceptions behind such applications vary, as do the applications themselves. The interpretation given ἱεράτευμα in 1 P is not equateable with other NT passages citing the EF or treating the thought of a Christian priesthood. Nor is 1 P 2:4ff. to be identified with or subsumed under a theory of Jesus' priesthood or participation in the same via membership in the Body of Christ. The NT statements vary appreciably and are not reduceable to a common denominator.

These variations lead us back to the context of 1 P. The conclusion attained from an investigation of the EF references is again substantiated: only the context into which this formula has been introduced yields the clue to its particular nuance.

c. πνευματικαὶ θυσίαι and the Holy Life

Peter has described the task of the holy body of priests to be the "offering of Spiritual sacrifices." Within the context of 1 P, what is to be understood under "*Spiritual sacrifices*"?

The term θυσία[1] is used in the NT as a designation for various objects and its specific meaning is frequently dependent upon the particular context in which it appears. Generally speaking, θυσία denotes an animal or cereal sacrifice such as those prescribed by Jewish cultic ritus,[2] or a sacrifice in the transferred sense of a person, object, or deed dedicated to God.[3] H. -D. Wendland distinguishes three types of sacrifice: Christological, sacramental, and ethical. Yet he considers it more correct to speak of the latter two as expressions of Christ's sacrifice in the Church.[4] This, in substance, captures the concern of Philipp Seidensticker who points out that

---

[1] For treatment of the word θυσία or the concept of sacrifice cf. O. Schmitz, *Die Opferaussagen des Neuen Testaments*, Tübingen, 1910; Wenschkewitz, *op. cit.*; Ph. Seidensticker, *Lebendiges Opfer*, Münster, 1954; further, A. Richardson, *An Introduction to the Theology of the New Testament*, London, 1958, pp. 297-301; H.-D. Wendland, *RGG* IV, 1647-51.

[2] E.g. Mt. 19:13 = Hos. 6:6; Mk. 12:33; Lk. 2:24; Act. 7:41f., etc.

[3] E.g. Christ offering Himself (Eph. 5:2, Heb. 9:26); Christians offering their bodies (Rom. 12:1); prayer (Apoc. 8:3f.); praise and thanksgiving (Heb. 13:15); almsgiving (Phil. 4:18); deeds of kindness and brotherly love (Heb. 13:16).

[4] Wendland, *loc. cit.*, col. 1647.

the NT cultic concepts have not been "spiritualized" but rather "Christologized."[1]

1 P stands within this process in which all cultic concepts are orientated to and reinterpreted in the light of the Christ event. Therefore the πνευματικαὶ θυσίαι of v. 5d do not apply to the ritualistic sacrifices of the Old Dispensation but to the products of an offering community which through the Christ event has been called from darkness to light and enlivened by the Spirit of holiness.

Here the connection between πνευματικαὶ θυσίαι and οἶκος πνευματικός becomes obvious. The Divine Spirit Who dwells in the house is the same Spirit Who controls the sacrifices, thereby making them "acceptable to God." It is instructive to note that 1 P 2:5 is the only NT instance where πνευματικός modifies either οἶκος or θυσία. Accordingly, it is the sole NT instance where "Spiritual house" and "Spiritual sacrifices" are so juxtaposed—a certain witness to the designing hand of the author.

Hence, πνευματικαί(άς) can no more mean "immaterial" in contradistinction to "material," "ritualistic" sacrifice than (οἶκος) πνευματικός did in v. 5b.[2] "Spiritual" does not mean "metaphorical" or "unreal" although in both cases it modifies terms which are used in a transferred, metaphorical sense. It does not describe the manner in which a word is used but rather a quality of that word. "Spiritual cult signifies then everything other than unreal or non-actual cult, which, by the way, 'spiritual' might mean in profane religiosity," explains K. H. Schelkle.[3] "For the Spirit as the biblical πνεῦμα is most vivid reality."[4] It is the presence and working of the Divine Spirit that is signaled here.[5] This is not a sample of a "spiritual" exegesis common to the allegorization of Alexandria or late Judaism[6] but an interpretation laying full weight on the eschatological realization of life in the Spirit.[7]

---

[1] Seidensticker, *op. cit.*, pp. 203ff., 325-29.

[2] *Contra* O. Kluge, *Die Idee des Priestertums in Israel-Juda und im Urchristentum*, Leipzig, 1906, p. 57; Schmitz, *op. cit.*, p. 235; Selwyn, *op. cit.*, p. 161; Beare, *op. cit.*, pp. 96f. Cf. *supra* pp. 154-56.

[3] Schelkle, *op. cit.*, p. 59.

[4] *Ibid.*

[5] So Blinzler, *op. cit.*, pp. 55f.

[6] So Cerfaux, *op. cit.*, pp. 25ff.

[7] So Congar, *Lay People*, p. 122; in German translation, *Der Laie*, Stuttgart, 1957, p. 199, n. 36, specifically *contra* Cerfaux. Cf. sim. Seidensticker, *op. cit.*, pp. 218, 325ff.

To suspect these words of expressing an anti-Jewish polemic[1] is to misunderstand the point. Of course the very use of cultic terminology in a transferred sense amidst an appropriation of Israelite honorific predicates might imply such a polemic. Nevertheless, it must be repeated that argument and polemic was not the author's concern. To the contrary, the construction of v. 4 in particular has shown that Peter even avoided terminology scented with an anti-Jewish air. And in v. 5 not a negative polemic but rather a positive emphasis upon Christian responsibility under the influence of the Divine Spirit appears to have been the main interest.

NT usage shows that θυσία as an expression of Christian activity, of dedication to, and worship of, God assumes various forms. Alan Richardson distinguishes, for example, five such forms: (1) the offering of self (e.g. Rom. 12:1); (2) deeds of charity and well-doing (e.g. Heb. 13:16); (3) material pecuniary gifts (e.g. Phil. 4:18); (4) praises, confession, prayer (e.g. Heb. 13:15, Apoc. 8:3f.); (5) the converts gained through missionary efforts (e.g. Rom. 15:16, 1 Cor. 16:15, Col. 1:28, Apoc. 14:4f.).[2] Theoretically, none of these examples would be impossible for the connotation of θυσίαι in 1 P 2:5d. Richardson himself, as the majority of commentators, suggests an affinity between 1 P 2:5 and Rom 12:1.[3] Actually all further distinctions of sacrifice are ultimately expressions of the first—the surrender and dedication of self to God.[4] This is the fundamental and constitutive sacrifice of the Christian involving every sphere of life and under which all specific oblations are subsumed. Hence some commentators feel that a general reference to all of the various possibilities of Christian sacrifice suffice as an explanation of this term.[5]

However, the context of πνευματικαὶ θυσίαι and the associations which the author has made indicate that the phrase assumed here a specific rather than a general connotation. Of primary importance is the adjective πνευματικός and the significance thereby ascribed the activity and influence of the Holy Spirit. The role of the Spirit is reflected both in the double occurrence of the adjective πνευματι-

---

[1] So Bigg, *op. cit.*, p. 129; Schmitz, *op. cit.*, p. 235; Selwyn, *op. cit.*, p. 161; Windisch-Preisker, *op. cit.*, p. 60. Cf. *supra*, p. 175, n. 2.

[2] Richardson, *op. cit.*, pp. 299-301.

[3] *Ibid.*, p. 300.

[4] Cf. A. Schlatter, *Opfer—ein Verzicht?* Hrsg. von R. Frick, Bad Salzuflen, 1958.

[5] So e.g. Blinzler, *op. cit.*, p. 56; Beare, *op. cit.*, p. 97.

κός and in the adjective ἅγιος (ἱεράτευμα ἅγιον). According to the salution 1:1-2, which serves as an *Expositio* of the presentation to follow,[1] the addressees who are chosen according to God the Father's plan are sanctified by the Spirit (ἐκλεκτοῖς . . . ἐν ἁγιασμῷ πνεύματος). Insofar it is not incidental that "body of priests" is modified by the adjective "holy." As Beare points out, "ἅγιον is not to be taken as a commonplace, a 'permanent epithet' with ἱεράτευμα, as if all priesthoods or priestly services were 'holy'; but rather as distinguishing *this* (italics Beare) priesthood from all others as alone having that relation to God which constitutes holiness."[2] It is the activity of the Spirit which accounts for the inner unity of these descriptions of the believing community in v. 5. And because of this sanctifying action of the Spirit the factor of holiness assumes an important position here. The elect people of God is the people whom the Spirit sanctifies on the basis of this people's faith in Jesus as the Christ. Election and holiness are correlates in the Divine economy.[3] This has been one of the conclusions of our examination of Ex. 19:6 and it is just as true in the NT. As Ragnar Asting has formulated, "In ἅγιον liegt dann die Erwählung der Christen ausgedrückt, Gott zu dienen als seine besonderen Diener, ihre Aussonderung von der Welt und ihre Sonderstellung zu Gott wird damit hervorgehoben."[4]

Yet "holy" has more than one aspect. We might speak of a "passive" and an "active" aspect.[5] Whereas the former connotes the act of being elected and selected by God, the latter involves the obedience or behavior forthcoming from an elected and holy community. Since the time of the later Prophets and their cathartic attempts to free Israel from false misconceptions of sacrifice,[6] this active factor was related to the idea of sacrifice and sacrifice, in turn, was considered in terms of ethical and moral behavior. This con-

---

[1] Cf. *supra*, pp. 147ff.

[2] Beare, *op. cit.*, p. 96. According to the parallelism of vv. 5 and 9 it has been suggested that ἱεράτευμα ἅγιον condenses βασίλειον ἱεράτευμα, ἔθνος ἅγιον (Scott, *op. cit.*,p. 214). Since οἶκος πνευματικός reflects βασίλειον, however, and since ἅγιος relates not only to v. 9 but also to 1:2, 14ff., this suggestion is unlikely.

[3] Cf. R. Asting, *Die Heiligkeit im Urchristentum*, Göttingen, 1930, esp. pp. 74, 133ff.; O. Procksch, *TWNT* II, 87-116, esp. 106ff.; F. Horst, *RGG* III, 149; H.-D. Wendland, *RGG* III, 151.

[4] *Ibid.*, p. 245.

[5] So also Asting, *ibid.*, p. 133f. who also mentions a third "apocalyptic" aspect by which the "holy" are those participating in the Messianic kingdom.

[6] Cf. e.g. Hos. 6:6; Amos 5:24f.; Mic. 6:6ff.; Is. 1:16f.; Ps. 40:7-9, 50:8-14, 51:18f., 141:2.

ception of holiness and sacrifice continued through post-exilic Judaism[1] to the NT. The thought at the basis of this active connotation and its coalescence with the terminology for sacrifice is that of obedience to the holy will of the holy God.

This active aspect, in turn, has both a negative and a positive feature. *Negatively* viewed, the *Gottesvolk* has been elected, "selected out from among" the other nations. Implicit is the idea of separation. Accordingly, one responsibility of the elect and holy people is to maintain this line of demarcation. This negative aspect was expressed in the NT in terms of "separating oneself from" or "abstaining from" (cf. ἀπέχεσθαι [Act. 15:29, 1 Th. 5:22, 1 Tim. 4:3];[2] μὴ συσχηματίζεσθε [Rom. 12:1f.]; or ἀποτίθεσθαι [Rom 13:12, Eph. 4:22, 25, Col. 3:8, Jac. 1:21]) and was given an important position in early Christian paraenesis.[3] Significant is the fact that all three verbs were employed in the exhortation of 1 P: ἀπέχεσθαι (2:11), μὴ συσχηματιζομένοι (1:14), ἀποθέμενοι (2:1, cp. 3:21).

On the other hand, the exhortation to "be holy!" conveyed a *positive emphasis* also, with a view of the way of life as a *positive witness to the environment*. This thought also, as well as the negative aspect of holiness, was given concrete expression in 1 P, forming in fact the central injunction of the first paraenetic section of the epistle, 1:14-2:10: "As He Who called (elected) you is holy, you too be holy in every way of life" (1:15). This statement has been seen by scholars to have stood in direct relationship to 2:5.[4] Ἅγιος (ἱεράτευμα ἅγιον), in particular, has been named the "keyword" uniting 2:5 with the preceding pericope,[5] and θυσίαι have been suggested as a sample of the obedience encouraged in 1:14ff.[6]

The importance which this positive accent upon ἅγιος had for the

---

[1] Cf. Siph. Lev. 20:7; Lev. r. 24:6; Mek. Ex. 15:2. Further, *Str-B* I, 413f.; K. G. Kuhn, *TWNT* I, 98f.; Wenschkewitz, *op. cit.* Among writings found at Qumran cf. 1QS V, 20f.; VIII, 20f.; IX, 5; X, 6; CD. VII, 5; XII, 19-22; XX, 6f.; 4Qflor. I, 6f.

[2] Cf. esp. 1 Th. 4:4: Τοῦτο γάρ ἐστιν θέλημα τοῦ θεοῦ ὁ ἁγιασμὸς ὑμῶν, ἀπέχεσθαι ὑμᾶς ἀπὸ τῆς πορνείας.

[3] Cf. esp. Carrington, *op. cit.*, and Selwyn, *op. cit.*, Essay II, pp. 365-466, who both regard this aspect as the negative component of an early Christian Holiness Code.

[4] Cf. Hort, *op. cit.*, p. 110; Schmitz, *op. cit.*, p. 235; Spörri, *op. cit.*, pp. 59, 62 and *passim*; Selwyn, *op. cit.*, p. 161 and *passim*; Wendland, *RGG* IV, 1649.

[5] Bigg, *op. cit.*, pp. 128f.

[6] Among others, Schlatter, *Petrus*, pp. 95f.; *Opfer*, p. 19; Congar, *Lay People*, pp. 126f., 148ff.

meaning of v. 5 and the particular implication of πνευματικαὶ θυσίαι is demonstrated by two words to which ἅγιος closely relates, ἀναστροφή and ἀγαθοποιία. Through ἅγιος both these terms have a determinative influence upon the connotation of θυσίαι. For as terms central to the preceding (1:13ff.) and following (2:11ff.) paraenesis, terms, moreover, which express the main activity of the believing community, they dictate both the larger context and pattern of thought with which this thought of Spiritual sacrifices has been coordinated.

Excursus 5

ἀναστροφή *and* ἀγαθοποιία

'Αναστροφή is a word which, in comparison with other NT documents, appears to have received particular emphasis in 1 P. It occurs seven times in the rest of the NT[1] and almost as many times in 1 P alone (6 times: 1:15, 18; 2:12; 3:1, 2, 16; 3:11). Wilhelm Brandt, who has devoted a special study to this word and its use in 1 P,[2] has established its meaning as "way of life" ("Lebensführung"),[3] securing this rendering by parallels in the LXX,[4] NT,[5] and Antiquity.[6]

Its connection with ἅγιος and its synonyms is found in passages such as 1:15, 17ff. and 3:2. However, the section where its significance can best be judged, according to Brandt, is 2:11-12. These verses pick up the thought both of 1:1 and 1:14 (παρεπιδήμοις and the idea of renunciation resp.) and suggest that the fact that Christians are "pilgrims and sojourners" is the "*causa cur abstinendum sit.*"[7] At the same time they continue the thought of 2:9d by making more explicit what the "proclamation of the great deeds of God" entails. While 2:9f. (and in retrospect, 1:3ff.) show that which distinguishes the Christian community from the world (election, hope, goal of life), v. 12 indicates that these Christians, nevertheless, remain in the world and that their task of proclamation is a responsibility toward the world. Through their ἀναστροθή they destroy the false opinions of the *Umwelt* concerning them—not

---

[1] Gal. 1:13; Eph. 4:22; 1 Tim. 4:12; Heb. 13:17; Jac. 3:13; 2 Pet. 2:7, 3:11.

[2] "Wandel als Zeugnis nach dem 1. Petrusbrief," *Verbum Dei Manet in Aeternum, Festschrift für O. Schmitz,* Witten, 1953, pp. 10-25.

[3] *Ibid.*, pp. 10f.

[4] Tob. 4:14; 2 Mcc. 6:23.

[5] 1 Tim. 4:12; Jac. 3:13.

[6] Pergamon inscription, B. C. 130, cf. A. Deissmann, *Licht vom Osten,* 4. Aufl., Tübingen, 1923, p. 265.

[7] Brandt, *ibid.*, p. 11.

for their own sakes but that these "outsiders" may eventually glorify God.[1] The factor of separation is not external but internal—not an ascetic separation from the world but from worldly (better: "fleshly") lusts.[2] The καλὴ ἀναστροφή (v. 12) is, in effect, a way of life which corresponds to the will of God (cf. 2:15). The criterium of goodness lies in God's will.[3]

This emphasis upon obedience controls the entire paraenetic section 1:13-21 where the hearers/readers are addressed as the τέκνα ὑπακοῆς (1:13). They realize their "childrenship" and their holiness in that they separate themselves from all that is corruptible and stained and place their confidence in Jesus Christ the unblemished Lamb, thereby approximating in their way of life the nature and will of their Father.[4]

As much as this way of life implies renunciation of worldly lusts, so much does it also involve a concern for man in the world. Both concerns are subsumed under obedience to God's will.[5] The admonitions of 2:12, 15, 3:1, 16 are not made for the sake of Christians but for the heathen—that they might glorify God.[6] This thought is nicely summarized in the words of Beare: "Their conduct amid the pagan environment in which they are called to live, as temporary sojourners in an alien land, is to be a silent testimony to their faith, such a manifestation of the beauty of holiness as may open the eyes of the bitterest opponents and turn them at last to God."[7]

Hence a holy way of life forms a complement to the preached, i.e. spoken, word (cf. 1:12, 23, 2:2, 8, 3:1). "The Christians' way of life is a commentary on this word . . . it is the form in which the once rejected word quietly pursues the disobedient, a permanent recollection of this word."[8]

In his brief but instructive study Brandt has shown a thread of thought running through the sections 1:13ff., 2:4ff., 2:11ff.: *admonition to a holy way of life which in faithfulness and obedience to the Father's will may complement the word of proclamation and afford a further witness to the unbelievers*. This theme is significant for our pericope insofar as it shows that 2:4-10 cannot be considered a "doctrinal discourse or excursus" distinct from the main line of thought. Rather its emphasis upon holiness in v. 5 and confrontation with and sharing of the word (vv. 8, 9) (this emphasis oc-

---

[1] *Ibid.*, p. 12.

[2] τῶν σαρκικῶν ἐπιθυμιῶν cp. 1:14. According to the customary NT differentiation between σαρκικός and πνευματικός (cf. Rom. 15:27; 1 Cor. 3:1ff., 9:11) these "fleshly lusts" contrast to the "Spiritual sacrifices" of 2:5d; so Selwyn, *op. cit.*, p. 169.

[3] *Ibid.*

[4] *Ibid.*, p. 15.

[5] *Ibid.*, p. 16.

[6] *Ibid.*, p. 22.

[7] Beare, *op. cit.*, p. 40.

[8] Brandt, *ibid.*, p. 25.

curring significantly at points revealing the hand of the author) shows that this pericope participates in a development of thought extending from 1:13 to 2:11ff. Insofar, we may assume that the connotation of "Spiritual sacrifices" has been determined accordingly.

In respect to ἀγαθοποιία we might say that if ἀναστροφή provided the more general and comprehensive word under which the totality of the Christian's behavior *coram Deo* and *pro hominibus* was subsumed, then ἀγαθοποιία designated one positive aspect in particular: the "doing of good" or "well-doing."

As ἀναστροφή, so ἀγαθοποιία is "one of the keywords of the epistle, occurring more frequently, in one form or another, than in the whole of the rest of the NT[1] put together."[2] The verb ἀγαθοποιεῖν appears in 2:15, 20, 3:6, 17. The adjective ἀγαθοποιός occurs once in 2:14 and the noun ἀγαθοποιία also once in 4:19.

If the adjective ἀγαθός is to be reckoned to this idea of "well-doing," then 2:18, 3:10, 11, 13, 16 (*bis*) and 3:21 also come into consideration. All told, these amount to an impressive series of occurrences of ἀγαθός and its compounds (12 in number) extending from 2:14 through 4:19.

As W. C. van Unnik has observed, "this Epistle is specially concerned with the attitude of the Christians in the world of their day"[3] and thus it is not surprising to find that this stress upon "active well-doing"[4] falls mainly within the section of 1 P defining social and domestic duties. The material used here reflects the traditional formulation of Jewish-Hellenistic *Haustafeln* and social codes.[5] It is not unlikely that Peter's formulations, formations, and compounds to express the idea of well-doing are adaptations of the thetical statement which was quoted in altered form in 3:11, namely ψ 33:15 (ἔκκλινον ἀπὸ κακοῦ καὶ ποίησον ἀγαθόν).[6] Typical of Peter's use of the OT, however, the Psalm is cited freely and altered to meet the circumstances and thrust of the author's message. That is, Peter adapted his citations that they might apply, thereby remaining master of his source, giving it a particular turn.[7] This concern

[1] However, cp. 1 Cl. 2:2, 7; 33:1; 34:2.

[2] Selwyn, *op. cit.*, p. 89; quoted approvingly also by W. C. van Unnik, "The Teaching of Good Works in 1 Peter," *NTS* 1/2 (1954), 92-110, p. 93.

[3] *Ibid.*, p. 93.

[4] Selwyn, *op. cit.*, p. 227.

[5] So most commentators.

[6] This psalm definitely had an over-all influence upon 1 P as we can see from an earlier quotation in 2:3f. (= ψ 33:9, cf. 33:6) and from the significant position which this quotation assumed as a conclusion to the Domestic Code, 2:13-3:9. A remarkable number of similarities in terminology and content have been assembled by Bornemann (*op. cit.*; cf. also Bigg, *op. cit.*). Selwyn (*op. cit.*, p. 190) has shown how incorporation of parts of this psalm into 1 P reveal the hand and purpose of the author. On Ps. 33 cf. further, *infra*, p. 205, n. 5, and p. 206, n. 1.

[7] So van Unnik, *ibid.*, p. 93.

that the text become "real" for his hearers/readers and, accordingly, his tendency to pick up and repeat words[1] make it likely that the compounds of ἀγαθός and the concept of "well-doing" were Peter's expansion upon ψ 33.

The purpose behind the citation of this psalm is Peter's desire to set before those Christians living "between the times" of Christ's death, resurrection, inthronation and His second coming the conditions of God's judgment: abstinence from evil and the doing of good.[2] Well-doing is the will of God (2:15, 3:17), whereby the well-doer is contrasted not only to the social deviant (κακοποιῶν, 2:14) but, more important, to sinners (ἁμαρτάνοντες, 2:20). A well-doer is she who, as submissive Sarah, places her fear and confidence in God alone (3:6 = Pr. 3:25f., 34; cp. 1 P 5:5 and Jac. 4:6).

To be zealots of the good (3:13) and to produce good works (2:12) is not an endeavor peculiar to Christians alone, however. The pagan philosophers, points out van Unnik,[3] encouraged a similar ethic. In fact, the ethic developed in 1 P, despite its use of Jewish sources, is just as close to the "*bürgerliche Ethik*" of the Greeks as it is to that of the Jews.[4] That is to say, 1 P does not portray a special "Christian" ethic but encourages a truly human code of conduct. The Christian *specificum* lies in the will of God and the awareness of what He has done in Jesus Christ. This is an awareness that in Jesus Christ the Eschaton has already begun, that God is reassembling and electing His people and making it holy.

Ἀγαθοποιία, therefore, is the expression of Christian holiness following the Divine call (2:21, 3:9), because God Himself is holy (1:16). It is the positive aspect of the holy life, a doing of good for the benefit of the "outsider" as well as of the fellow-Christian.

Hence it becomes obvious that these two terms for "way of life" and "well-doing" relate closely in the presentation of 1 P. *Both words are used to denote a holy way of life consistent with the holy will of God.* Both explicate the ethical side of Christian holiness. In this sense the ἀναστροφὴ καλή which the Christians are to lead among the heathen composes their καλὰ ἔργα and ἀγαθοποιία which may eventually prompt these unbelievers to praise God (2:12). The relationship of both terms is explicit in 3:16: "keep your conscience clear, so that when you are abused those who revile your *good way of life* in Christ (ὑμῶν τὴν ἀγαθὴν ἐν Χριστῷ ἀναστροφήν) may be put to shame."

---

[1] Cf. Bigg, *op. cit.*, p. 125; Holzmeister, *op. cit.*, p. 97.

[2] Cf. van Unnik, *ibid.*, pp. 98, 105f.

[3] *Ibid.*, p. 107.

[4] *Ibid.*, pp. 109f.; so also W. Grundmann, *TWNT* II, 551-53; M. Dibelius, *Die Pastoralbriefe* (*HNT* 13) 3. Aufl. von H. Conzelmann, Tübingen, 1955, pp. 32f.; H. Preisker, *Das Ethos des Urchristentums*, Gütersloh, 1949, pp. 195ff.

Taken as the two major designations in 1 P for the personal, living explication of Christian holiness, ἀναστοφή and ἀγαθοποιία suggest what "Spiritual sacrifices" in 2:5 entailed. (1) Both terms characterize the content of the Christian task: to lead a holy life free of fleshly pursuits, to do good before all men. (2) Both are grounded in the fact of Christian holiness. (3) This means that both imply obedience toward the holy God. (4) The eventual goal of both, the glorification of God, further implies a pronounced missionary impulse. The concern for doing good is no mere humanitarian endeavor *in se* but has as its purpose the winning of the unbeliever *ad maiorem Dei gloriam.*[1]

Inasmuch as these are the thoughts which span the entire paraenesis of 1 P and explicate the consequences of Christian election and holiness, *in "Spiritual sacrifices" no other idea is implied but the living of a holy life and the persistence in well-doing through the power of the Holy Spirit to the glorification of God.* These are the oblations acceptable to God.[2]

---

[1] This reversal of the earlier Jewish concept of holiness so that it included a missionary concern is illustrated in Peter's instruction to the wives, 3:1f. In this connection, Dahl, *op. cit.*, p. 223, makes a pertinent observation concerning 1 Cor. 7:14 which applies to 1 P 3:1f. as well: "According to Jewish thinking, the Jews 'caught' impurity through bodily contact with the Gentiles. Paul, however, reverses the thought; the Gentile spouse 'becomes holy' through the Christian partner. "Die Heiligkeit des neuen Gottesvolkes braucht also nicht ängstlich gehütet zu werden (cp. 1 Cor. 5:9f.), wenn nur die Gemeinde und der einzelne Christ nach dem Willen Gottes leben (cp. 1 Cor. 5:11), so wirkt die Heiligkeit der Christen vielmehr selbst 'ansteckend.'" Regarding the final goal as the glorification of God cf. Spörri, *op. cit.*, p. 65. Sevenster, *op. cit.*, pp. 405f., in particular, has called attention to this connotation of "Spiritual sacrifices" within the context of 1 P, describing "sacrifices" as a "lofprizing van God, b.v. in liederen en belijdene acclamatie, maar vor vooral aan goede werken van barmhartigheid en broederliefde, kortom dat geheel van een geheiligd Leven, dat in de paranese van deze brief zulkeen bijzonder accent verkrijgt."

[2] This identification of "sacrifices pleasing to God" with the living of a good life and the doing of good has been made by the Auc. Heb. with almost exactly the same words. In Heb. 13:16, 18 occurs the paraenesis: "Do not neglect the doing of good (εὐποιίας) and the activity of sharing, for God is pleased with such sacrifices (τοιαύταις γὰρ θυσίαις εὐαρεστεῖται ὁ θεός). . . . Pray for us, for we are convinced that we have a clear conscience, desiring to lead a good life in all things (ἐν πᾶσιν καλῶς θέλοντες ἀποστρέφεσθαι)." The leading of a good life and the doing of good are the sacrifices with which God is pleased. And thus in the following benediction (vv. 20f.), the author prays that God "equip you with everything *good* so that you may accomplish His *will*, accomplishing among us that which is pleasing in His sight through Jesus Christ."

The factor adding the final corroboration to this solution, moreover, is the final correspondence between vv. 5 and 9 which now comes to light.

For in v. 9d a similar orientation "outward," to the world, is implied in the words "that you might proclaim the mighty deeds of Him Who called you out of darkness into His marvelous light." The remarkable fact is that this is the portion of v. 9 which, as we have noted earlier, coincides with v. 5d in the formal parallelism of these two verses. This formal correspondence is now corroborated by a correspondence of content. For the cultic expression "to offer sacrifices," so formulated to annex to the phrase "holy body of priests," relates essentially to the cultically colored phrase "to proclaim the mighty deeds."[1] Both expressions underline the place of witness and communication in the Christian task, as recent studies have noted.[2]

On the other hand, these phrases may be distinguished in respect to the mode of communication. Ἐξαγγέλλειν is a verbal activity accomplished with mouth and lips.[3] The fact that it was used in the Church as the verb for the reporting of the empty tomb (Mk. 16, *conclusio brevior*) underlines its narrative character. Therefore, it is possible that a connection was implied with *the word* which was to be proclaimed, namely, the λόγος θεοῦ (1:23, 2:8, 3:1; but also 1:24f., 2:2). This is the Divine word through which the believers were born (1:23). It was the word which was "evangelized" to them (1:25) and this Evangel composed the life, sufferings, death, resurrection—the glory of Christ (1:11f.).

Complementary to this verbal witness and related as to both origin and purpose is the offering of sacrifice, i.e. the leading of a holy way of life. 1 P 3:1f. shows both the similarity and the distinction of these tasks: "Likewise you wives, be submissive to your husbands, so that some, though they do not obey the word (ἀπειθοῦσιν τῷ λόγῳ) may be won without a word by the behavior of their

---

Furthermore, it ought to be noted that εὐάρεστος and its cognates occur together with θυσία almost exclusively in paraenetic sections of the NT and with sufficient frequency to suggest that these terms provided some of the basic NT paraenetic terminology. Cf. Rom. 12:1, 2; 14:18; 2 Cor. 5:9; Eph. 5:10f.; Phil. 4:18; Col. 3:20; Heb. 13:16, 21.

[1] For an OT text illustrating the correspondence of these two expressions cf. Ps. 107(106):21f.

[2] Cf. Brandt, *op. cit.*, pp. 9-12; van Unnik, *op. cit.*, esp. p. 108; earlier, Selwyn, *op. cit.*, p. 295.

[3] Cf. ψ 70:15, 118:13.

wives (διὰ τῆς τῶν γυναικῶν ἀναστροφῆς ἄνευ λόγου κερδηθήσονται)." Witness in word and in deed are not alternatives but compose a double task in which the latter complements and corroborates the former.[1]

In each case, the proclaiming of God's mighty deeds and the sacrificing of the holy life, the witness is not primarily inner-directed but outer-directed. In the words of Johannes Schneider, "the ecclesia of the New Covenant is the chosen race, the holy community of people, the people selected for possession, whose task is service to the world."[2] Christian holiness according to 1 P expresses itself not merely in prayer or almsgiving but, as van Unnik has emphasized, "in the right behavior toward the neighbor, be he Christian or not." Though these other activities indeed form a vital part of the Christian way of life, they fail to exhaust the implications of "Spiritual sacrifices" which pertain primarily to witness to the outsider. Not to be minimized, of course, is the priestly community's obligation of holiness *coram Deo*. However, the entire context of 1:13-2:11ff. indicates that the *bass continuo* underlying the entire ethic of 1 P is that obedience to the holy will of God is manifested through a positive witness to all men.[3]

4. *Verse 5 and Theories concerning Priesthood, Sacrifice, and Ministry*

The statement "a holy body of priests to offer Spiritual sacrifices" thus designates the believing community as the elect, holy, and priestly people of God, whose task is the communication of the word of His mighty acts and the leading of a holy life as a witness to men and as Spirit-empowered oblations acceptable to God.

This emphasis upon the community's election and the explication of her holiness through the holy life is ignored or lost when this passage is taken as referring *only* to the Christian cult, or more specifically, to a priestly sacrifice of the Eucharist. Also questionable is the connection often drawn with the thought of Christian suffering or Christian ministry and Church order.

a. ἱεράτευμα and Mediation

The motif of witness, for instance, reflects the thinking behind

[1] Cf. Brandt, cited, *supra*, p. 180, n. 8.
[2] *RGG* II, 614. Cp. R. Prenter, *RGG* V, 581.
[3] Cf. Spörri, *op. cit.*, p. 40.

the original LXX formulation of Ex. 19:6. As the Old Dispersion, so the New Diaspora of "pilgrims and sojourners" (1:1, 2:11) bears the priestly responsibility of *witness* and *mediation.* And yet to speak of "mediation" is tenuous. For such mediation is not a two-way activity in the specific sense: from God through mediating community to man, from man through mediating community to God. It has been proposed, for example, that witness (v. 9) and sacrifice (v. 5) are given as the double task of the priesthood whereby through witness the word is mediated to the world and through cultus (identified with "Spiritual sacrifices") the world is brought to God.[1] However, this far exceeds the statement of 1 P 2:5 and 9. The sacrifices apply not to cultic activity in the narrow sense but to acts of obedience. They comprise a witness to mankind. This witnessing in both conduct and preaching can be described as "mediatorial" insofar as God's word is brought to man. However, these passages do not imply that the community acts as a mediator between the non-believer and God. The Church may, according to 1 P, prompt the unbelievers to believe but she does not mediate that belief to God. The sacrifices pertain only to the acts affecting the unbelievers; they do not describe the ensuing faith of the Gentiles as, e.g., in Phil. 2:17. The theory that the Christian community as ἱεράτευμα "represents the nations of mankind in the same way as the Levitical priesthood represented Israel"[2] finds no foundation in 1 P. The equation of ἱεράτευμα with the Levitical priesthood is impossible from the standpoint of 1 P as well as the entire EF tradition. Nor has any such idea of representation been developed in 1 P.[3]

b. A Cultic Setting and the Eucharistic Oblation

To speak of the offerings of a holy life and well-doing as "worship" can imply only a *"Gottesdienst"* in the comprehensive sense of "service dedicated to God." To interpret "Spiritual sacrifices" as referring to the Eucharistic oblation is to restrict this sense of *Gottesdienst* to only one aspect of its total reality as well as to propose a meaning completely unsupported by the text.[4] Alone the plural

---

[1] K. H. Schelkle, *Jüngerschaft und Apostelamt,* Freiburg, 1957, pp. 105ff.
[2] Selwyn, *op. cit.*, pp. 291ff.
[3] *Contra* Selwyn, cf. also Best, *op. cit.*, pp. 297f. Cf. further, *infra*, pp. 208–13.
[4] *Contra* O. Casel, "Die λογικὴ θυσία der antiken Mystik in christlich-liturgischer Umdeutung," *JLW* 4 (1924), 37-47; Niebecker, *op. cit.*, pp. 88f.;

form "sacrifices" indicates, as Blinzler has pointed out, that "other forms of sacrifice are in mind."[1] In fact, "nowhere in the New Testament," cautions Congar, "is there any express reference to the worship and priesthood of the faithful in the Eucharist or even in the sacraments . . . or in the Church's public worship."[2] The first explicit combination of the thought of the Eucharist and the priesthood of the faithful was made by Justin Martyr (*Dialogue* 41:7, 116:3, 117:1). The connection of these two entities represents, as far as is determinable, a post-Apostolic synthesis.

That 1 P contains cultic terminology is incontestable. How much of this "liturgical jargon" reflects a supposed Eucharistic celebration is very much open to question, however. The inference that the cultic intimations of 1 P 2:1-10 almost *require* the presence of the Eucharist[3] lacks conclusive evidence. It is methodologically questionable to retroject the traditional identifications of later centuries when "milk" (2:2), "tasting the goodness of the Lord" (2:3), "drawing near" (2:4), "Spiritual house," "sacrifices" (2:5) were incorporated into Eucharistic liturgies and rites, into the era of 1 P. As long as doubt and uncertainty exist concerning the liturgical forms underlying this epistle, arguments for the meaning of ἱεράτευμα and πνευματικαὶ θυσίαι cannot be based upon a hypothetical Eucharistic context.

Another approach in this direction would suggest that the Spiritual sacrifices did not themselves refer to the Eucharist but to the deeds of the Christian life. However, the background and *Sitz im Leben* which prompted the idea of sacrifices is claimed to have been the "worshipping community gathered for the celebration of the Eucharist . . . in particular, perhaps, for the baptismal Eucharist."[4] The same criticism applies here as that above: the evidence for such a proposition is found solely in sources of a date later than 1 P.

The thought that all acts of the Christian life "are hallowed and

---

Seidensticker, *op. cit.*, pp. 265f.; Richardson, *op. cit.*, p. 302, among others. Cf. B. Botte, "L'Antiquité Chrétienne," *La Participation Active des Fidèles au Culte* (*Cours et Conférences des Semaines Liturgiques* XI), Louvain, 1933, pp. 27f.

[1] Congar, *op. cit.*, p. 63, n. 28.

[2] *Lay People*, p. 126; although in n. 26 he allows an implicit reference in Heb. 13:10 and 13:19-22.

[3] E. Lohmeyer, "Vom urchristlichen Abendmahl," *ThR* 9 (1937), 168-228, 273-312, esp. p. 296.

[4] Selwyn, *op. cit.*, p. 297.

gathered up in the Eucharist"[1] is indeed a theological statement true to the tradition and teaching of the Church. Moreover, the scholars who see in this sacrament a re-presentation of *the sacrifice* κατ' ἐξοχήν[2] certainly are expressing a fundamental element of Christian sacramental theology. However, there is nothing in the text of 1 P to suggest that its author shared this point of view or intended to express it.[3]

This criticism applies equally to the postulation that the "royal or general priesthood" to which 1 P 2:5, 9 supposedly refers had its origin "at and through the Lord's Supper."[4] However the other texts offered as evidence for this theory might be evaluated, it is certain that the term ἱεράτευμα and vv. 5, 9 have not been related to or inferred to have evolved from a titulation of the Apostles made by Jesus at the Last Supper.

Therefore, we may agree with those scholars rejecting the theory of a connection between 1 P 2:5, 9 and a celebration of the Eucharist as untenable.[5] The offering of sacrifices, which is intended to describe the significance of ἱεράτευμα, is not confined to or even epitomized in a single cultic event but comprehends the totality of Christian obedience and witness. In this sense it approaches the intention of Rom. 12:1.

c. ἱεράτευμα and Suffering

If "Spiritual sacrifices" refer to the totality of Christian activity,

---

[1] *Ibid.*, p. 296.

[2] E.g. P. Ketter, "Das allgemeine Priestertum der Gläubigen nach dem 1· Pbrf," *TThZ* 56 (1947), 43-51, esp. pp. 47f.

[3] Though Dabin, *op. cit.*, p. 192, rejects a Eucharistic interpretation of v. 5, the basis upon which he does so is hardly tenable: "Saint Pierre, en précisant que les hosties offertes par le sacerdoce saint sont pneumatiques, aurait par la même, etabli une nette distrinction entre le laïcat, que n'aurait à présenter que des victimes spirituelles et le presbytérat qui, seul, est habilité pour l'offrande de la victime matérielle du sacrifice eucharistique." This type of rationalization might be taken as typical of that school intent upon polemic against the "déplorables prétentions de la conception protestante du sacerdoce universal des fidéles" (Dabin, *ibid*).

[4] Torrance, *op. cit.*, p. 65, n. 1, referring specifically to Lk. 22:30; p. 85. For this theory cf. further Congar, *Lay People*, pp. 156, 165ff.; Prenter, *op. cit.*, p. 581; Richardson, *op. cit.*, pp. 315f.

[5] In addition to Blinzler, *op. cit.*, p. 63, n. 28, cf. e.g. Knopf, *op. cit.*, p. 90; Windisch-Preisker, *op. cit.*, p. 59; J. W. C. Wand, "The Lessons of First Peter," *Interpretation* 9 (1955), 387-99. Botte, *op. cit.*, p. 28: "Dire qu'elle constitue une sorte d'ordination en vue de l'offrande eucharistique, c'est aller bien au delà des textes, sinon en fausser le sens."

then the question might be raised concerning the relation between these offerings and the fact of suffering, or between priesthood and suffering.

Though this relationship seems somewhat abstruse on the basis of 2:4-10, in view of certain recent connections made between the concepts of priesthood and suffering, it nevertheless deserves brief consideration. T. F. Torrance in his study, *Royal Priesthood*, has drawn out this relationship at great length.[1] His approach to the question of priesthood in the NT, as we have seen above,[2] is determined by the basic presupposition that NT statements regarding the priesthood or priestly acts are essentially harmonious. Hence, by excerpting ideas on priesthood and sacrifice from various NT documents he has arrived at a composite picture of the corporate Christian priesthood as determined by the conception of the Suffering Servant. This conclusion is reached via the conception of the Church's incorporation into the Body of Christ and into His threefold office of Prophet, Priest, and King. Her ministry, which is the expression of her priesthood,[3] derives from the ministry of Christ the Suffering Servant and is therefore a "suffering-servant-ministry." The essence of Torrance's position can be seen in the following statement.

> The conception of the Suffering Servant is the great characteristic of the Church's ministry, and it is that which above all determines the nature of the priesthood of the Church. That applies to the Church's threefold participation in Christ's Prophetic, Priestly, and Kingly Ministry, for the Church is engaged in all these as servant bearing the Cross like the man of Cyrene (Matt. 27:32). It is indeed in terms of the suffering-servant-ministry that we are to see the basic unity in the Church's prophetic, priestly, and kingly functions.[4]

Concerning such a conception and its relevance for 1 P we recall earlier observations pointing to the fact that such a harmonious image of priesthood as Torrance pictures is not to be found among the disparate statements of the NT.[5] 1 P in particular can hardly be said to develop the theme of priesthood or explicate the EF according to the theory of incorporation into the Body of Christ.

---

[1] Torrance, *op. cit.*, esp. pp. 61, 82, 84 (1 P 2:12ff. cited), 87.
[2] Cf. *supra*, pp. 173f.
[3] *Ibid.*, pp. 35ff.
[4] *Ibid.*, p. 87.
[5] Cf. *supra*, pp. 169ff., esp. 173f.

Nor is it possible to find in 1 P a distinction of "prophetic, priestly, and kingly" functions of the Church. Furthermore, where is ἱεράτευμα related to suffering in 1 P?

Eduard Schweizer, who also has seen the Church's priesthood under the sign of suffering,[1] found this relation of priesthood and suffering in 1 P by identifying, as has Torrance, priesthood and ministry—a ministry not of reconciliation but "of praise and preaching."[2] This ministry, he maintained, is essentially service which "is seen to be so central in its suffering."[3] The texts to which Schweizer referred include 1:6, 2:21-23, 3:14, 4:4, 2:19, and 5:9. Now the abundance of such references to suffering and persecution mark a central factor in the occasion and purpose of this epistle. To demonstrate that this problem of suffering does not relate essentially to ἱεράτευμα, however, we concentrate upon one pertinent set of facts in particular.

Suffering, according to 1 P, appears to belong to the calling and destiny of the Christian (cf. 2:21, 5:10). Furthermore, suffering is presented here as a central characteristic of Jesus Christ's activity (cf. 2:21-24, 3:18, 4:1). In this respect the Christians have been compared with Christ and He has been used as an example to Whom the suffering Christian is to turn (2:20-21, 3:17-18, 4:1). As sufferers, the Christians share (κοινωνεῖτε) in the sufferings of Christ (4:13); they even suffer because they are Χριστιανοί (4:15f.). The suffering of both Christ and Christian, however, is bound essentially with the fact of suffering *innocently* or suffering *though doing good* (2:20-23, 3:13-17, 3:18, 4:14ff.). When we recall that the doing of good is obedience to the will of God (2:14f., 3:17, 4:2, 19; cp. 2:20, 3:5), then we are able to see how these various strands were woven together.

At first glance, 2:21 and 5:10 seem to suggest that Christians are called or elected to suffer.[4] Insofar, one might deduce that the terms which primarily express the election of the Church, 2:5 and 2:9-10, also imply the thought of election to suffering. If so, then the essence of the elected body of priests would be their suffering character and the sacrifices which they offer would be their tribulations, perhaps

---

[1] Schweizer, *op. cit.*, ch. 9a-b, pp. 110-12; ch. 23a-e, pp. 188-93.

[2] *Ibid.*, 9b, p. 112.

[3] *Ibid.*, p. 111.

[4] Cf. H. Braun, *Das Leiden Christi* (*Theologische Existenz Heute* Nr. 69), München, 1940, p. 44: "Gott hat uns zum Leiden gerufen."

even martyrdom, which they endure. In reality, however, the idea of suffering was developed by Peter along other lines.

Primary to his outline of thought is the *basis* of the series of injunctions contained in 1 P, namely *the will of God*. The leading of a holy way of life and well-doing is the action of the believer which corresponds to this will of God. These are the sacrifices offered by the elect people. Yet the doing of good does not guarantee freedom from abuse, rejection, or even persecution. In fact, the former is likely to encourage the latter. The suffering which then occurs when a Christian has done good and is disdained is *innocent suffering*. To strengthen and encourage the believers who are thus suffering, in order that they continue in well-doing despite all, the author alludes to the similar suffering of Christ. He too suffered—in fact, though He had not committed fault (2:21). He was guileless (2:22), not reviling, not threatening (2:23). He died, a just man (3:18). Since Christ suffered in the flesh, those who believe in Him can also cease from sin, fulfill the will of God (4:1f.) and rejoice in suffering for righteousness' sake, assured that thereby they are sharing in His sufferings and glorifying the Divine Name (4:12-19).

Thus the Church has not been elected to suffer but to be obediently holy and to do good. The will of the electing God is not that Christians suffer but that they do good (4:19). In a world alien to the will of God it is likely, if not inevitable, that this obedience will incur abuse and suffering, even as it did in the case of Jesus Christ. During such suffering which God *might* allow (N.B. the circumstantial εἰ in 1:6, 20 together with the optative in 3:14 εἰ καὶ πάσχοιτε and 3:17 εἰ θέλοι τὸ θέλημα θεοῦ) Christians can continue in well-doing, knowing that the Spirit of God rests upon them (4:14) and that theirs is the glory in Christ (4:14, 5:10).

Therefore suffering is not depicted as an essential property of the ἱεράτευμα ἅγιον.[1] Intermediating between the reality of a "Spiritual house to be a holy body of priests" and the act of suffering is the action of obedience and well-doing. Ἱεράτευμα and suffering are not related in principle. Nor is there any trace of such a thought in the

[1] Selwyn, *op. cit.*, p. 293, avers that ἱεράτευμα is to be understood in the light of Christ's mediatorial and redemptive sacrifice of suffering. Yet no such connection is apparent in 1P. Though 2:21-24 and 2:25 depict both these aspects of Christ's work, they do not apply to 2:4-10 where the characteristic of Jesus Christ which is emphasized in contrast to His rejection by mankind is His election by God. It is this latter image to which ἱεράτευμα corresponds.

EF tradition. In respect to the priestly body's fulfillment of *Gottesdienst* in the form of sacrifice, suffering is reckoned as consequential to these offerings but not identified with them. As little as these sacrifices were confined to the single oblation of the Eucharist, so little were they extended to include the accidental and potential consequences of obedience—suffering. To infer anything further than this is to say more than the author of 1 P himself has done.

d. ἱεράτευμα, Ministry, and Church Order

Since this latter theory operates with the identification of priesthood and ministry, a few words should be said concerning the relation of *ἱεράτευμα and the ministry of the Church* in 1 P. The problem is, however, that the author has made no explicit statement concerning this relationship. In fact, it might be suggested that the proposal of such an identification exceeds the evidence and raises a question totally alien to the concern of the author.

In view of the missionary and witness connotations of 2:5, 9 one might speak of a "ministry" of the total community to the world. Proclamation, preaching, is the implication of v. 9. Insofar, one might think of a "ministering of the word of God to mankind." However, by the term "ministry" is implied customarily not so much an "outer-directed" witness toward the world but rather an "inner-directed" ministry within the body of the faithful. Accordingly, the subject of ministry is handled in connection with Church order, authority, and office. Should it be agreed that "the New Testament knows no distinction between ministry and office,"[1] then it must be acknowledged that ministry in this sense and ἱεράτευμα have been given no essential connection in 1 P. For how ἱεράτευμα as implying a ministry to the world relates to this particular ministry within the οἶκος θεοῦ Peter has left a moot question.

There are primarily two sections of 1 P which touch upon ministrations or office within the Church, 4:7-11 and 5:1-5. An extended investigation is unnecessary; it suffices to call attention to a few pertinent facts.

(1) If 4:7-11 can be said to describe the *ministry of gifts* within the community, 5:1-5 treats then the *ordering of responsibility and authority* within the same.

---

[1] Schweizer, *op. cit.*, 25a, p. 206.

(a) 4:7-11 touches on the relation of members of the community to one another,[1] re-echoing the thought of 1:22. The addressees are told in view of the nearness of the consummation to keep a cool head and be alert in prayer (v. 7); above all, to continue unceasingly in mutual love (v. 8, cp. 1:22) and to be hospitable to one another without regret (v. 9). Each has a spiritual gift (χάρισμα) by which he is to serve (διακονεῖν) his fellow member. Thus all are good ("Godpleasing," cf. 2:12) house-stewards[2] of the varied χάρις of God (v. 10).[3]

The χαρίσματα are differentiated into two categories: "speaking" (λαλεῖν) and "serving" (διακονεῖν) (v. 11). The point is underlined that both activities arise from and are nourished by the words and the strength which God supplies.[4] The final purpose of all these deeds is "that in all things God might be glorified through Jesus Christ" (v. 11).

(b) The injunction to the πρεσβύτεροι and the νεώτεροι is based upon the theme of *humility* (5:5).[5] The presbyters or leaders of the community[6] are to shepherd God's flock not with constraint or for gain but willingly (5:2),[7] not lording over the flock but setting it an example—a deed which will be rewarded at the manifestation of the Arch-Shepherd (v. 4). The "younger"[8] are to subject themselves to

---

[1] As indicated by the recurring reciprocal pronouns: (4:8, 10) and ἀλλήλους (4:9).

[2] Is this solely a formal designation for "manager" or specially chosen as fitting Peter's conception of the community as "house of God" (cf. 2:5, 4:17 and the Domestic Code, 2:13ff.)?

[3] Whereby χάρισμα is depicted as a gift of God (θεός) rather than of the Spirit (πνεῦμα).

[4] Both activities are hallmarks of the charismatic ministry and occur frequently in the NT. In fact, certain contexts containing reference to these actions are so similar that the existence of an early Christian code has been posited (cf. Selwyn, *op. cit.*, pp. 415-19). According to Selwyn, it is likely that this code containing a teaching on Church order and unity (reflected in both 1 P 4:7-11 and 5:2-5) based on the precepts of humility and brotherly love "was part of the catechetical teaching from the beginning" (*ibid.*, p. 419).

[5] On the relation of ministry, office and humility cf. Schweizer, *op. cit.*, 21e, pp. 177f.; Selwyn, *ibid.*

[6] πρέσβυς = both "elder" in age and therefore acknowledged as "leader" according to the Jewish system of organizational polity.

[7] ἐπισκοποῦντες in 5:2a is omitted by the weightier Witnesses. However, Beare's note, *op. cit.*, p. 176, deserves consideration.

[8] Most likely those differentiated from the "elders"; namely, the rest of the congregation. For v. 5 appears to address both in the sense of the entire congregation. Beare, *op. cit.*, p. 175, rejects "younger men" as meaning office-

the elder (v. 5a). Finally, all are to practice humility toward each other because this is the deed which God rewards (v. 5b).

(2) From these verses we may conclude that there are various χαρίσματα in the community which can be comprehended at least under the aspects of "speaking" and "serving." Likewise, there is an order in the congregation which is distinguishable as "elder" or "shepherd" and the "younger" or "flock."

(3) Both the exercise of χαρίσματα and the order of responsibility and authority bear no relation to the community as ἱεράτευμα. None of these tasks is essentially "priestly." Nor is there evidence of any attempt on the part of the author to ascribe them new "priestly" quality. True, it is the members of the ἱεράτευμα who are ministering as well as shepherding. Nevertheless, these activities are not *the* essential expressions of the community seen as a body of priests. For in this sense the body of priests also loves, believes, fears God, honors the emperor, is submissive and undergoes suffering, etc. Therefore, it is difficult to agree with Rudolf Bultmann's statement that "the Church's nature as a 'holy priesthood' realizes itself in a Church life ruled by brotherly love: each is to serve the whole with his special gift (4:10f.). The 'elders' receive a special exhortation in this direction (5:1-4), and so do the 'younger men' (5:5)."[1] That the Church *qua* redeemed community fulfills this task is beyond doubt. But there is nothing in 1 P to suggest that she does so *qua* ἱεράτευμα.

(4) Even viewed quantitatively these expressions stand on different levels. As we have seen, the significance of the term ἱεράτευμα is its collective, corporate character; the believers are depicted hereby as one entity, as community. It is impossible to speak here of sundry priests. Not individuality but corporateness is the hallmark of ἱεράτευμα and the pericope 2:4-10. Contrariwise, 4:7-11 presupposes individuality. *Each* (ἑκαστός) believer is to love the other; *each* is to be hospitable to his fellows; *each* has a χάρισμα and the χαρίσματα are *varied. One* might speak; *another* might serve. As the χαρίσματα are diverse, so are the stations within the Church (5:1-5). *Some* are elders and tend the flock; *others* are younger men and submit to authority. *As body of priests, all have the same nature and the same function; as individuals ministering χαρίσματα, their functions are*

bearers. Schweizer, *op. cit.*, 24g, p. 199, n. 745, allows the possibility after having denied it and quoting Beare (9b, p. 111)!

[1] Bultmann, *TNT* II, 183.

diverse. Corporateness and individuality are, of course, both properties of the Church—but from different aspects. If these aspects were equated, they would lose their essential character.[1] The sum of all ministering individuals is no more a body of priests than is the sum of all working carpenters a house. In this case the whole is not equal to the sum total of all its parts.[2]

(5) The ministry explicated in 4:7-11 and 5:1-5 is an *inner-directed service*, concerning the believers in their relation to one another. The task of the ἱεράτευμα, on the other hand, is an *outer-directed mission* pertaining to the witness of the Church toward all that is non-Church.[3] The inner-directed ministry is comprehended under the aspect of brotherly love and humility; ἱεράτευμα, under that of election and holiness. The former is a consequence of the latter and not identifiable with it.[4]

---

[1] Schweizer, *op. cit.*, 9b, p. 112, also differentiates sharply between the individualistic thrust of 1 P 5:1-5 and the collective character expressed in 2:5 and 9: "But the honorific title of king and priest is given, not to individuals such as these, but to the Church as a whole, whose priesthood is not a ministry of reconciliation, but of praise and preaching (2:9)." By identifying ministry with suffering, however, (*ibid.*, p. 111), and suffering with priesthood (*ibid.*, 23d, p. 191), he fails to carry through this necessary distinction.

[2] Manson, *op. cit.*, p. 69, speaking more generally on the subject of the relationship between the Church's priesthood and her ministry, does not call attention to the corporateness of ἱεράτευμα in particular in contrast to the individuality of the ministrations in 4:7ff., but does emphasize the distinction between priesthood and ministry: "This divinely appointed ministry in the Church seems clearly enough to be something less than the total numbers of the members . . . while all believers are priests, all believers are not ministers."

[3] Cf. Richardson, *op. cit.*, who distinguishes between "The Apostolic and Priestly Ministry" (Ch. 13) and "Ministries Within the Church" (Ch. 14). Cf. esp. p. 302: "the Church is the appointed priest-nation to the 'Gentile' world, i.e. to all that is not-Church."

[4] The identification which Käsemann, *Amt und Gemeinde*, p. 123, would make rests upon no more than a superficial analogy: "Als Haushalter der vielfältigen Gottesgnade, also als Charismatiker, die einander nach dem Mass ihrer Gabe zu dienen haben, sind alle Christen die lebendigen Steine des Gottesbaues und Repräsentanten dessen, der zunächst lebendiger Stein ist. Als geistliches Priestertum bringen sie das gottwohlgefällige Opfer, welches in der Erbauung der Gemeinde besteht." The sacrifices of 2:5 do not involve inner-community *Erbauung*—the Spirit is the author of this process—but a mission to the world, as Käsemann himself has noted in respect to v. 9d: "im konkreten gegenüber zur Welt." Käsemann has overlooked the correspondence between v. 5 and v. 9, not seeing that both relate to the outer-directed witness to the environment. By identifying the "Spiritual sacrifices" of v. 5 with the ministry described in 4:7ff. he has equated two tasks which

Though these concepts are by no means mutually exclusive, they are also not equateable. The term ἱεράτευμα and the discourses on ministry in 4:7-11 and 5:1-5 stem from two different sources, are used by the author to describe two different aspects of the Church's nature and function, and are oriented in two different directions.[1]

We *summarize.* Verses 4-5 reveal that the material contained in vv. 6-8 and 9-10 was gathered together, condensed, reformulated, and interpreted in these two introductory verses under the theme of *election.* Verse 4, anticipating the λίθος complex of vv. 6-8, describes Jesus Christ as the Elect and Precious Stone of God. Verse 5, anticipating the OT passages in v. 9 and paralleling the thought of v. 4, explicates the significance of the electedness and holiness of the believing community.

Οἶκος πνευματικός interprets βασίλειον of the EF appearing in v. 9b and denotes the Christian community as *Spirit-filled house*(*hold*). Πνευματικός designates not a method of "spiritualistic" allegorization but rather marks the house and the sacrifices as objects of the creating and sustaining activity of the Holy Spirit. He actualizes God's electing grace, builds living stones into a Royal house, sanctifies the body of priests, and makes their sacrifices acceptable. *As* βασίλειον *denotes the community as the house of God the King, so* οἶκος πνευματικός *explains that in this Messianic Age the King's house is in reality the house*(*hold*) *infused with the Holy Spirit.*

Εἰς ἱεράτευμα ἅγιον, juxtaposed to οἶκος πνευματικός, introduces the *purpose and task of the elected people*: the Spirit-filled house(hold) is

---

in 1 P are both distinguished and left unrelated. To describe the activity of vv. 5 and 9 as an "amtliches Tun" performed by "Amtsträger" who derive their "office" from their Holy Baptism is to draw implications far exceeding the expression of the author himself.

[1] If, despite the absence of an explicit statement on the part of 1 P, one were to attempt to depict, on the basis of the implications of 1 P, the relationship between ἱεράτευμα and the inner-directed ministry, one might point out that a ministry within a community presupposes the assembly, the establishment of that community. The inner-directed ministry would then serve and implement the task and purpose of the community as a whole. Ministry and order secure the fellowship and unanimity necessary for the community as body of priests to accomplish its task—a witness to the world of the saving deeds of God through life and word. Thereby the ultimate goal of both inner and outer-directed ministries is attained—the glorification of God (2:12, 4:11). As valid and as theologically defensible as such a statement might be, however, it exceeds the explicit expression of Peter himself.

to be a holy body of priests which offers through Jesus Christ Spiritual sacrifices acceptable to God. Ἱεράτευμα depicts the community of the faithful as a *corporate and active body of priests,* as the continuation and yet also the consummation of Chosen People of God. Its appearance here is unique in the entire NT literature and not equateable with the other NT version of the EF in the Apocalypse where the variant and more individual form ἱερεῖς occurs. The NT statements on the subject of Christian priesthood are disparate and offer no uniform image of the priestly community or the believers as priests. Therefore the significance of this term is to be determined from its own context. According to this context this predicate for the body of the faithful was not construed by the author as an attribute analogous to a priesthood of Jesus Christ. Nor was this title conceived according to a theory of incorporation into the σῶμα Χριστοῦ whereby the members participate in the qualities of their Head. Neither theory is found in 1 P. Rather, the community, through its members' faith in Jesus Christ, is elect and holy and thereby ascribed the honorary titles pertinent to the Chosen People of God.

Priesthood and sacrifice are correlates. Insofar, ἀνενέγκαι πνευματικὰς θυσίας describes the activity proper to a body of priests. The term "body of priests" was not imported into the text to fit a preconceived notion of sacrifice on the part of the author. The addressees were not a "body of priests" because they sacrificed but sacrificed because they were a "body of priests." "To offer Spiritual sacrifices" is a terminological accommodation to the cultic inference of "body of *priests.*" "Spiritual" designates the sacrifices as under the influence of the Holy Spirit. The holiness which He imparts implies election as well as obedience to the holy will of the holy God. This obedience is comprehended in two keywords of 1 P's paraenesis, ἀναστροφή and ἀγαθοποιΐα. Inasmuch as these terms express in 1 P the holy and obedient behavior of the holy community, they determine the implication of "Spiritual sacrifices." Their missionary import and witness character indicate that the responsibility of the ἱεράτευμα is toward the world. To "offer Spiritual sacrifices" is to live a life of holy obedience *coram Deo* and a life of well-doing *pro hominibus.* This world-orientation of the body of priests is also implied by v. 9: the body is to proclaim the mighty deeds of God, the word of mercy and salvation.

This priestliness is not mediatorial in the strict sense but involves the one-way communication of God's word and deeds to man. This witnessing activity of the "body of priests" implied in the phrase "Spiritual sacrifices" is neither essentially confined to the Eucharistic oblation nor extended to potential suffering. Not derivative of the ministry of Jesus, ἱεράτευμα is not equated with the orders of authority. Ἱεράτευμα and its task applies not to individual servers or leaders but to the holy responsibility of the total elect community.

Verse 5 thus contains a definitive statement on the essence and responsibility of the believing community. With the elect community thus compared to the elect Stone Jesus, the way is prepared for the great collation of texts to follow in vv. 6-10, the well-known expressions of Israel's messianic hope and her self-awareness as the elect λαὸς τοῦ θεοῦ. All that had been anticipated aforetime under the Old Dispensation has now reached its culmination in the union between the Elect Stone and the Elect Race.

In this carefully composed and self-contained unit the relationship between the believers and Jesus is thus brought to its fullest expression. This is a relationship grounded in faith, expressed in the motions of "coming to Jesus" (2:4) and "obeying the word" (2:8). Those who come and obey are in effect the elect People of God, the subjects of His electing and sanctifying activity. In identifying themselves with Jesus Christ they are participants in the determinate counsel of God. As Jesus is the living Stone of messianic hope, so believers in Him likewise are stones made alive. As He is the elect and precious Stone of God, so they are the elect and precious race, the royal house of God, the body of priests, the holy nation, God's private property. As they come to Jesus in faith, the Spirit builds them and welds them together into *com-munity*. This notion of faith and process of *con-struction* and sanctification finds its final goal in the witness of an obedient holy God-pleasing life—the sacrifices which eventually lead to the glorifying of His Name.

Our analysis of vv. 4-5, and therewith vv. 4-10, has reached its conclusion. A study of these verses would be incomplete, however, until the relation and connection between this pericope and its immediate context was adequately accounted for. Though vv. 4-10 present a self-contained unit of thought, certain elements of both form and content indicate that this unit cannot be isolated from its context but rather forms an essential segment in the total continuity of thought. Insofar as this continuity can be established, final evidence will be gained to corroborate the correctness of the interpretation of vv. 4-10 offered here.

CHAPTER FIVE

CH. 2:4-10 IN THE GENERAL CONTEXT OF 1 P

The significance of 2:4-10 is then fully appreciated when it is seen as the appropriate climax to the entire initial paraenetic section 1:13-2:10. For here the exhortations to holiness of living and brotherly love and the thought of birth and nourishment from the Divine word are gathered together and substantiated in a final pericope describing the electedness, holiness, and union of the believing community with her elected Lord.

It has been seen that the context within which 2:4-10 falls is paraenetic in character and involves two major sections, 1:13-2:3 and 2:11ff. Though the themes of proclamation of the word and witness to the world unite our pericope with the following context, it is primarily the preceding section to which 2:4-10 join both thematically and formally. Therefore we can concentrate our attention on the section, 1:1-23.

A. The Preceding Context

The themes of election and holiness relate our pericope to the salutation, 1:1-2. This salutation contains a greeting of the Apostle Peter to the "elect non-residents of the Dispersion in Pontus, Galatia, Cappadocia, Asia, and Bithynia." In the opening words of the epistle election is specifically explicated according to its origin in the plan of God, its execution through the sanctification of the Spirit, and its purpose: obedience and the blood sprinkling of Jesus Christ.

Thereupon follows a hymn of praise and thanksgiving to God for the rebirth to a living hope through the resurrection of Jesus Christ, the author of salvation (1:3-9).[1] This salvation, its source and the time of its occurrence, continues the author, was the object of the

---

[1] This is the first of numerous hymnic and liturgical fragments in 1 P; cf. Bultmann, "*Bekenntnis- und Liedfragmente*"; Boismard, *Quatre Hymnes*. J. Coutts, "Eph. 1:3-14 and 1 P 1:3-12," *NTS* 3 (1957), 115-27, finds in 1 P and Eph. reflections of a liturgical prayer connected with baptism.

prophets' search. Yet this Evangel of Christ's sufferings and glory was not theirs but "yours," proclaimed to "you" by those preaching through the power of the Holy Spirit (1:10-13). That is, the rebirth of a living hope is the consequence of both the resurrection of Jesus Christ and the evangelical preachment. The hope of the final revelation of Jesus and the consummation of salvation is grounded upon present reality (ἀναγεννήσας [aorist], 1:3; νῦν, 1:12).[1]

On the basis of this fact (Διό, 1:13) the author brings the first of a series[2] of imperatives[3] which continues through the end of the epistle. In fact, one is justified in saying that these imperatives of 1 P supply the formal structure of the entire writing.[4] The first exhortation addresses the hearers/readers to concentrate upon the coming hope (1:13) and as obedient children to lead a holy life (1:14-17).

This imperative follows as a consequence of the embracing reality expressed in 1:3-12: the experience of Divine grace and mercy and its proclamation. However, it is also followed by a supporting indicative explaining that the addressees have been made free to such a holy life, have been redeemed, by the precious blood of Christ the holy, spotless lamb, slaughtered, raised, and glorified (vv. 18-21).

The next imperative "love one another earnestly" (v. 22) is also a consequence of the previous indicative, "since you have purified yourselves (v. 21a) as well as the thought supported by the following indicative "you have been born anew through the imperishable word of God" (v. 23).

This interdependence of imperative and indicative, i.e. imperative

---

[1] This argues against Preisker's suggestion, *op. cit.*, p. 156, that only from 1:22 (perfect tense: "have purified") onward is a reflection upon a change of state observable.

[2] 1 P 1:13, 14, 15, 17, 22; 2:1, 2, 12f., (14), 16, 17 (four imperatives), 18; 3:1, 3, 5, 7 (*bis* ?), 8, 9, (10, 11), 14 (*bis*), 15, 16; 4:1, 7, 8, 9, 10, 11, 12, 13, 15, 16; 5:2, 3, 5, 6, 7, 8 (*bis*), 9, 14.

[3] Here in 1 P, as in other NT documents, the participle is used also as an imperative. Daube, in Selwyn, *op. cit.*, has demonstrated this use of the participle to have been determined by late Hebrew usage. Functioning as an imperative, the participle denotes a custom, habit, or rule and appears restricted to codes and quotations from or allusions to codes. Similarities with Jewish catechisms and mutual affinites of the imperatival function of the participle have led Daube to postulate an "early Christian code of behaviour within the new community" (p. 488; cf. 467–88).

[4] So Schelkle, *op. cit.*, p. 5. Some authorities, in fact, are inclined toward seeing 1 P as a composition of various general and specific categories of admonition; cf. Schneider, *Petrus*; Wikenhauser, *op. cit.*, pp. 356-65.

based upon indicative and then substantiated by a following indicative, sets the pattern for the whole of the epistle. The specific sequence of imperative followed by indicative[1] marks the difference from Paul who normally followed a reverse procedure (indicative followed by imperative).[2]

The first sequence of imperative and indicative (1:13-21) centers in an exhortation to *holiness*[3] and mentions both the source and goal of the holy way of life: the Divine holiness, the spotlessness of Christ, and the glorification of God. The terminology of this and the following sections and the specific allusion to Lev. 19:2 suggest the influence and use of traditional material and patterns centering in the concept of holiness.[4]

The next group of verses, 22-25, with the perfect participle ἡγνικότες (v. 22a) continue this theme and lead into a related idea concerning brotherly love. The pattern is the same as in 1:13ff.: allusion to the foregoing / imperative / OT citation. Likewise, the relation of imperative and indicative is the same as in vv. 17-19: imperative ("love one another!," v. 22b = v. 17b) / supporting indicative ("since you have been reborn . . .," v. 23a = v. 18b) / qualification of the indicative in negative and them positive terms ("not from corruptible seed but from incorruptible," v. 23b = vv. 18a, 19).

In the continuity of thought 1:22-25 embodies a transition from the thought of holiness and love to a statement concerning the word, its creative and nourishing character (1:23-2:3). The origin of purity (v. 22) and rebirth (v. 23) is traced back to the word of God: "You have been reborn not of corruptible seed, but of incorruptible, through the living and abiding word of God."[5]

---

[1] 2:18-20 / 21-25; 3:3-4 / 5; 3:8-9b / 9c; 3:13-17 / 18-22; 4:1a / 1b / 1c-6; 4:8a / 8b; 4:12-16 / 17-19; 5:4ab / 4c; 5:7a / 7b.

[2] So E. Lohse, *op. cit.*, p. 86.

[3] As Schelkle, *op. cit.*, p. 45, has emphasized, ἅγιος and the concept of holiness have been given in 1 P "tragende Bedeutung." Cf. sim. E. Lohse, *op. cit.*, p. 78; Schneider, *Petrus*, pp. 51ff.

[4] Cf. the evidence gathered by Carrington, *op. cit.*, and Selwyn, *op. cit.*, esp. pp. 363-466. Both conclude that Peter, along with other NT authors, was making use of a common "Holiness Code" (HC). Cf. also van Unnik, *De verlossing*, pp. 45ff., who sees the OT book of Leviticus as having exerted an influence upon the formulation of 1 P. For affinities between this material and paraenetic sections in the literature of Qumran and Jewish Proselytism cf. the literature listed *infra*, p. 213, n. 2.

[5] ζῶντος, καὶ μένοντος are best understood as modifying λόγου and not θεοῦ. It is not the life and abiding of God but that of the Divine word which is the point being stressed.

The interpretation which the author gives the Isaiah quotation (Is. 40:6-8), a thought cited to illustrate the antithesis between the transigence of man and the permanence of the word of God, lends a concluding application to this point concerning birth through the word. He uses a verb occurring earlier in v. 12 as participial substantive: τὸ ῥῆμα τὸ εὐαγγελίσθην (v. 25), cp. τῶν εὐαγγελισαμένων (v. 12). This comment concluding the first section 1:13-15 shows: (1) The exhortation to a holy way of life and love (vv. 13-22) has been framed within an indicative explaining the hearers'/readers' new eschatological existence as an immediate product of their confrontation with the "evangelized" word of God (vv. 23-25, 12). (2) This new existence has been effected through the resurrection of Jesus Christ (v. 21; 3). The substance of this evangelized word and the instrument of the new existence is the resurrected Lord Jesus Christ (vv. 19-21, 23, 24, 25; 3, 11f.). The weight of this fact thus accounts for the substitution of κύριος for θεός (LXX reading of Is. 40:7) in v. 24. This also suggests that the λόγος in v. 23 is none other than Jesus Christ;[1] for ῥῆμα is undoubtedly another term for the λόγος ζῶντος θεοῦ καὶ μένοντος.[2] In effect, the Evangel produces confrontation with *The* word. (3) Confrontation with this word has led to faith (v. 21; 8), hope (v. 13; 3, 9), rebirth (v. 23; 3), and obedience (v. 14, 22; 2). (4) Peter thus directs his hearers/readers to the fact of their new Being. His imperative is grounded in the eschatological reality of a new existence.

Insofar, v. 24 appears to epitomize and conclude the sections 1:3-12 and 13-24, both of which end with the thought of confrontation with and birth through the Evangel. As the following deductive particle οὖν and the new concrete imperatival participle ἀποθέμενοι indicate, from this point the author proceeded to draw explicit conclusions.

---

[1] Cf. the recurrent use of διά with Christ: 1:3, 20, 2:5, 3:21, 4:11, and the connection of ζῶντος with Jesus Christ again in 2:4b.

[2] So Schlatter, Petrus, p. 89: "ῥῆμα tritt an die Stelle von λόγος weil nicht nur an den Akt des Sprechens, sondern auch an den Inhalt der Botschaft gedacht ist." This thought is corroborated by v. 25 ("And this is the word which was proclaimed to you") which implies that κυρίου was intended as an objective genitive. The change from λόγος to ῥῆμα might also be seen as an accomodation to the formulation of Is. 40:7. Cf. also Jn. 12:15 where Is. 40:9 is applied to Jesus; further, Is. 40:10 in Apoc. 22:7, 12, and Is. 40:13 in Rom. 11:34, 1 Cor. 2:16 which together with 1 P, Jn. and Jac. 1:10f. point to a common Christian identification of this Isaianic context with Jesus Christ. Thus this term would seem to designate Jesus Christ in particular in this context rather than baptismal confession and preaching in general, *contra* M. H. Scharlemann, "Why the *Kuriou* in 1 Peter 1:25?" *CTM* 30/5 (1959), 352–56.

In 2:1 he encourages his hearers/readers to desist from every kind of evil and guile, from hypocrisy, envy, and slander in particular. These are the vices which disturb and hinder φιλαδελφία.[1] The last of these evils, however, is a "word vice" inconsistent with the new life through the word. Thus the author has not departed from the previous section of thought but draws implications from the preceding indicative. This is even clearer in the following verse.

In v. 2, ὡς ἀναγέννητα βρέφη picks up the thought of rebirth (ἀναγεννημένοι, 1:23) and λογικός recalls the λόγος of 1:23. The particle ὡς implies, as elsewhere, that the injunction which follows applies to the addressees from a particular point of view.[2] The author is not comparing them to newly-born babies; he is rather giving encouragement on the basis of the fact that they *are* newly-born infants.[3] This verse provides the positive counterpart to v. 1 and together vv. 1-2 reflect conclusions drawn from both the holiness-love and rebirth-word themes of 1:13-22, 23-25.

Development of the rebirth-word theme may be seen in the following factors:

(1) The positive injunction of 2:2 has been phrased according to the analogy of birth: "While eliminating the hindrances to φιλαδελφία and a wholesome sharing of the word (such as guile and hypocrisy, v. 1), make use of and yearn for the 'guileless' Logos-milk through which you have taken on new existence as newly-born babies."

(2) Likewise, in keeping with the analogy of birth, the object for which the hearers/readers should yearn is depicted as "milk." According to 1:23, 25 and customary Christian usage,[4] implied here

---

[1] Cp. φιλαδελφίαν ἀνυπόκριτον with ὑποκρίσεις (1:21, 2:1).

[2] Cf. *supra*, p. 36, nn. 1–5.

[3] ἀρτιγέννητα βρέφη, literally "newly-born embryos," has been held to reflect the act of baptism recently exercised upon converts who thus are termed "new-born babies" (so Beare, *op. cit.*, p. 88). Evidence for the use of this word as a *terminus technicus* for the newly-baptized is not prevalent. Though such a connotation is not unlikely, in 1 P a more immediate point of contact is 1:23ff. where rebirth is described as a *regeneration* through the imperishable word; "denn im Blick auf das ewige Wort Gottes sind alle Menschen ebengeborene" (F. Büchsel, *TWNT* I, 671).

[4] Cf. 1 Cor. 3:1f. and the comments of H. Schlier, *TWNT* I, 644. According to Schlier, in both instances γάλα is used as "a picture for the basic elements of the divine teaching, the elementary Christian instruction." Cf. further, Barn. 6:17; Od. Sol. 8:17, 19:1ff., 35:6; Ign. Trall. 5:1; Act. Jn. 45. For γάλα as "initial teaching" cf. also Philo, *Congr.* 19, *De Agric.* 2; Epictetus, *Disserationes* III 24:9. Cf. 1 Th. 2:7 for the picture of nursing children as an analogy for the "sharing of the Gospel."

is the identification of γάλα with ῥῆμα and λόγος.[1] The identification of the Evangel as τὸ δὲ ῥῆμα κυρίου (1:24f.) and λόγος ζῶντος θεοῦ καὶ μένοντος (1:23) and the explication of its contents as τὰ εἰς Χριστὸν παθήματα καὶ τὰς μετὰ ταῦτα δόξας (1:11) leave no doubt as to the basic point of reference, namely the crucified and resurrected Lord.[2] This is demonstrated also by the following prepositional phrase ἐν αὐτῷ (2:2), the clause εἰ ἐγεύσασθε ὅτι χρηστὸς ὁ κύριος (2:3) and the relative pronoun introducing v. 4.

(3) ἄδολον provides the positive counterpart to πάντα δόλον (2:1): "remove all guile . . . seek the guileless."

(4) The relationship between γάλα and λόγος is expressed explicitly in the adjective λογικός. Many of the translations and interpretations of this word fail to maintain this correspondence.[3] Walther Grundmann attempts to preserve this connection with the translation "dem Worte entsprechend, worthaftig."[4] However, as Beare has noted, perhaps there is no better word in English than "spiritual."[5] The phrase "Logos-milk" has been coined here in order to avoid the unhappy formulation "milk of the Word" (Authorized Version) and to maintain the point of reference. As Beare has aptly stated, "It (λογικός) is that which is proper to the Logos, and to the life which is mediated through the Logos."

Thus Peter's directive is that his hearers/readers apply themselves to and make earnest use of the Divine nourishment of the word to which they owe their new birth.

The purpose and goal is that they may "grow up for the coming salvation"[6] (for they have already "tasted that the Lord is good,"

In our passage γάλα is not an alternative to βρῶμα (cp. 1 Cor. 3:2) but is itself a designation for that which is bestowed in the Evangel; sim. Schlier. Selwyn, *op. cit.*, p. 154: "The sustinence given by the Gospel, which causes growth, is the property relevant here."

[1] So recently, W. Grundmann, "Die νήπιοι in der urchristlichen Paränese," *NTS* 5 (1958/59), 188-205, p. 189.

[2] Cf. Schelkle, *op. cit.*, p. 56.

[3] "Rational, reasonable" (so Vulgate, Hort, Schlatter, Cerfaux, *BAG*); "metaphorical" (so *M-M*); "spiritual" (so Selwyn, Beare) "geistig," "übersinnlich" (so Hauck; G. Kittel, *TWNT* IV, 145; Schelkle).

[4] Grundmann, *op. cit.*, p. 189; sim. Bengel, Bigg, Perdelwitz, Spörri, Brandt, *op. cit.*, p. 25).

[5] Beare, *op. cit.*, p. 89. Unlikely, however, is any affinity between λογικός so translated and πνευματικός ("of the Holy Spirit") in 2:5.

[6] Implied is that they grow in faith and thus be prepared for the consummating salvation about to arrive. The textual genuineness of εἰς σωτηρίαν is attested by both the numerous εἰς constructions in 1 P and the futuric aspect of σωτηρία (cf. 1:3, 4, 7, 11; 2:8; 1:5, 9, 10).

v. 2c-3). The image of new birth and feeding thus continues in v. 3. Again the structure recurs: imperative followed by an indicative in the form of an OT verse (cf. 1:24f.). With this citation the author associates the object of nourishment with the κύριος and thereby shows that in his train of thought κύριος, γάλα, ῥῆμα, and λόγος relate to one and the same subject: Jesus Christ.[1]

In v. 3, εἰ, as observed by all commentators, is used in a *sensum reale*: "since," "seeing that," as in 1:17.[2] 'Εγεύσασθε continues the analogy of feeding and is best understood in the sense, "since you have already been introduced to the goodness of the word of the Lord."[3] The thought is an adaptation of LXX Ps. 33:6: γεύσασθε καὶ ἴδετε ὅτι χρηστὸς ὁ κύριος.[4] That this psalm figured significantly in the terminology and thought of 1 P is seen in the extensive allusions made to it throughout the epistle (cf. esp. the long citation of vv. 13-17 in 1 P 3:10-12).[5]

---

[1] Grundmann, *op. cit.*, pp. 189f.: "Dieses Wort legt Zeugnis ab von der Güte des κύριος . . . wer sie im Hören des Wortes geschmeckt hat, d.h. wer aus ihr seine menschliche Existenz neu empfangen hat, trägt Verlangen nach dem weiteren Hören des Wortes."

[2] Selwyn, *op. cit.*, p. 157, also calls attention to the argumentation of Eph. 4:17-24 and to the compilation of similar classical and NT examples by G. B. Winer, *A Grammar of the Idiom of the New Testament* Prepared as a Solid Basis for the Interpretation of the New Testament, 7th edition enlarged and improved by G. Lünemann, English edition prepared by J. H. Thayer, Andover, 1899, p. 562.

[3] Cp. the similar line of thought in Heb. 6:4-6. Selwyn, *ibid.*, suggests the meaning "if you have taken the initial step of adherence to Christ." This idea of initiation is brought out even more strongly in the Heb. passage and may reflect part of the context of a baptismal setting; cf. G. Bornkamm, "Das Bekenntnis im Hebräerbrief," *ThBl* 21 (1942), 56ff., [reprinted in *Studien zu Antike und Urchristentum, Gesammelte Aufsätze* II, 188-203].

[4] Perdelwitz, *op. cit.*, p. 66, overlooked this fact and attempted to defend the reading χριστός in place of χρηστός on the basis of a supposed itacism. The textual witness (Mosquensis, Angelicus, a few minuscules), however, is very weak. Furthermore, according to Holzmeister, *op. cit.*, p. 237, while there are examples of the itacism ι for η occurring increasingly after A. D. 150, the proposed exchange of an η for an original ι finds few parallel examples. One would also have to question the sense of the statement, "since you have *tasted* that the Kyrios is Christ."

[5] Cf. also the manifold parallels between 1 P and ψ 33 assembled by Bornemann, *op. cit.*, pp. 146-50. Bornemann's conclusion, however, that 1 P is thus best understood as a baptismal homily based on the text of ψ 33 fails to comprehend Peter's use of OT material. OT citations and allusions made by the author are never the objects of his exegesis. The point of departure is never an OT text but the situation of his addressees, i.e. the reality of their

Important here is the fact that Peter has altered the original imperative mood of γεύσασθε to the indicative: εἰ ἐγεύσασθε. This "tasting of the goodness of the Lord" is not a consequence of the new birth nor is it an anticipated action yet to be undertaken as in ψ 33. Rather it is the *basis* of the preceding imperative ("yearn for the Logos-milk") and hence identified with the process of new birth.[1] Insofar, this adapted citation "rounds off" the picture of new birth and feeding drawn in 1:23-2:3.[2] The object of nourishment, the Logos-milk, is identified with the goodness of the *Kyrios*. Thereby both initial rebirth and ensuent growth are traced to confrontation with and continuation in this word. Paramount in the message of the author is that this word originates and centers in the *Kyrios*, and the weight which this fact receives is indicated by the emphasized position of ὁ κύριος at the end of the verse concluding the second section (1:22-2:3) and πρὸς ὅν at the beginning of the next section, 2:4-10.

Thus this thought of a relationship to the Lord, clothed in the language of ψ 33, forms a transition from the theme of rebirth and nourishment in the word to that of election.

At first glance this transition is by no means obvious, for the change in analogy from new birth-milk-feeding to stone-building appears as an abrupt alteration of metaphor. Accordingly, the occasion for the inclusion of the statements in 2:4-10, and, in particular, the term ἱεράτευμα, has been sought in at least two more comprehensive and more general entities: (1) baptism and (2) the

---

new life through Christ. This is the object of interpretation; the OT and other Christian sources or traditions are introduced to illustrate this fact. ψ 33:6 has not been used as text but as illustration for the text proper—rebirth through the word.

[1] Bengel and Schlatter, *ad loc.*, suggest that this psalm verse occasioned the analogy of feeding in vv. 2-3. More likely is the suggestion that the author is following a widespread tradition and pattern into which he has introduced this psalm; cf. Carrington, *op. cit.*, pp. 30ff.; Selwyn, *op. cit.*, pp. 369ff.; Grundmann, *op. cit.*, pp. 188ff.

Recurrence of ψ 33 in 1 P 3:10ff. and elsewhere as well as in Heb. 12:14 (= ψ 33:15) and 1 Cl. 22:2, 23:1, 28:1 suggest the use of this psalm in early Christian paraenesis. Selwyn, *op. cit.*, p. 157, conjectures that this psalm "was already in use in the Church of Asia Minor, perhaps as part of a 'catechumen-document' or of a 'persecution-document' or as a baptismal hymn." For the occurrence of Ps. 33(34) in Jewish paraenetic material cf. also G. Klein, *Der Älteste Christliche Katechismus und die Jüdische Propaganda-Literatur*, Berlin, 1909, pp. 137ff.; H. Kosmala, *Hebräser - Essener - Christen*, Leiden, 1959, pp. 128f. (Qumran).

[2] So Schlatter, *Petrus*, p. 92.

holiness paraenesis. Neither, however, can adequately and sufficiently account for this inclusion. Though both the sacrament of baptism and the holiness paraenesis figure significantly in the thought and expression of this epistle, and though both relate ultimately to the theme of election presented in 2:4-10, there is no textual evidence that the EF derived from a baptism tradition, a Christian Holiness Code or "neo-Levitical" conception of the Church.

Excursus 6

ἱεράτευμα, *Baptism, and a "Neo-Levitical" Community*

1. *Baptism*

Though opinion might vary concerning the precise size of the role which baptism, its explication and/or its celebration played in 1 P, scholars are united in recognizing this sacrament as one of the fundamental "Bezugspunkte" or points of reference in this epistle. Beside the presence of a type of "baptismal jargon" (e.g. ἀναγεννήσας, 1:3; ἀναγεννημένοι, 1:23; ἀρτιγέννητα βρέφη, 2:2) including an explicit reference to and explanation of baptism in 3:21, the theological content of this document with its discussion of rebirth through the resurrection of Jesus Christ and an encounter with the word (1:3, 23ff.), and the use of a paraenesis which would be especially relevant to initiants in the faith leave little doubt as to the influence which this sacrament had upon the formation and formulation of 1 P.

Indeed, even terminology within 2:4-10 (e.g. φῶς, v. 9) and its immediate context ("newly-born babies," 2:2) as well as the themes of election and holiness reflect definite points of contact with the NT conception of baptism.

The point is, however, that no matter how germane and pertinent the thought and the statements of vv. 4-10 might be to the event of baptism, there is no textual evidence for a postulation such as Käsemann's that "das allgemeine Priestertum aller Gläubigen wird hier also aus der Taufe abgeleitet."[1] Though Käsemann is certainly correct in rejecting a typical Protestant misconception of ἱερατευμα whereby an individualization and a private "priestly" relation between the individual and God is imagined, the rebuttal contained in this pericope against such a view is primarily not that of a corporate conception of baptism but a corporate conception of the *Gottesvolk* as βασίλειον and ἱεράτευμα. These two factors are indeed not mutually exclusive; rather theological reflection shows them to

[1] *Amt und Gemeinde*, p. 123, cf. also Dabin, *op. cit.*, pp. 293-320.

belong together. But this reflection is not explicit in the text of 1 P.

It can hardly be questioned that ἱεράτευμα and the accompanying epithets were applied to the believing community *qua* community of the baptized. But on the basis of 1 P it cannot be stated that such predicates were derived immediately from baptism. Such a statement would involve a short circuit. Overlooked in this case would be the factor of election which is the theme that occasioned reference to the EF. This is the bond and the intermediate step between the Christian appropriation of the EF, the predicates for Israel, and the event of baptism. The EF in 2:5 and 9 is not a direct product of or a direct allusion to the event of baptism or a baptismal rite. It is rather an application to a community which had undergone that rite. Insofar, there is a relation of ἱεράτευμα and the EF to baptism, but it is no more than indirect and implicit. The idea of baptism as the "ordination to the general priesthood of believers" or the "anointing or coronation of kingship and priesthood"[1] may be theologically defensible, but not on the basis of 1 P.

Later coordinations of baptism and the EF made among the Church Fathers within a theology of baptism or an ecclesiology represent a more developed stage of reflection than that found in 1 P.[2] To equate these two stages would be exegetically unsound.[3]

2. *A Holiness Code and a "Neo-Levitical" Community*

Although mutual dependence upon common paraenetic sources intimately related to baptism is very likely the best explanation for many affinities between 1 P and other NT documents, it is quite doubtful that our pericope assumed its position in 1 P according to the scheme which the theory of a "Holiness Code" (HC) proposes.

One of the proponents of this theory, Selwyn, suggests, namely, that 1 P 2:4-10 contained a "section on worship" which formed a regular part of the earliest stage of this pattern, a "neo-Levitical torah on holiness."[4] This suggestion is unlikely for at least two reasons. First, the pattern which 1 P seems to be following is not based upon the scheme "Baptism—its basis and nature in the Word; the new life: its renunciations; the new life; its faith and worship,"

---

[1] Cf. e.g. recently Richardson, *op. cit.*, p. 337, and primarily, of course, Luther, *op. cit.*

[2] Cf. e.g. Tertullian, *De baptismo* 17 (MPL I, 1206; CSEL XX, 214-15); *De exhortatione castitatis* 7, 3 (MPL II, 922; CSEL LXX, 137-39); *De monogamia* 12 (MPL II, 947).

[3] In this sense cf. Botte, *op. cit.*, p. 26: "Tout d'abord, ce symbolisme de l'onction n'est pas exprimé dans les paroles qui accompagnent le rite lui-même. C'est une explication littéraire, si je puis dire, très belle et très naturelle; mais aucun *rituel* (italics Botte) ancien ne nous permet de la prendre à la lettre. Toutes les anciennes formules sont vagues et ne font aucune allusion à ce sacerdoce."

[4] Selwyn, *op. cit.*, pp. 374, 404-06, 460; cf. also Carrington, *op. cit.*, pp. 28f.

as Selwyn and Carrington maintain. Rather, 1 P develops the scheme: birth through the Word (1:23-25), nourishment from the Word and growth (2:2-3).[1] On the one hand, the texts taken to indicate a general "worship" section[2] are for the most part scattered passages which do not belong to or follow en total sequence postulated. Only 1 P, Jac., Col., and Eph. even remotely suggest the influence of a common pattern and here the similarities of a supposed "worship section" are quite vague. On the other hand, we have seen that the θυσίαι in 1 P 2:5 refer not to a cultic act of worship but to a way of life. Its presence, moreover, is due to the appearance of the term ἱεράτευμα rather than dictated by an overall pattern.

Secondly, the designation of the congregation as a "neo-Levitical" community is incongruent with its predication as ἱεράτευμα. To a first-century Christian who would have understood under the term "Levitical" someone or something belonging to the progeny of Levi and the hieratical institution, the mere use of terminology from the book of Leviticus or emphasis upon the ideas of holiness, separation from uncleanness, and love would hardly have conveyed the idea that he were a "neo-Levite." He would have had to be identified as such, *expressis verbis*, and in 1 P exactly this was not done. Rather, not a Levitical predicate but an epithet for Israel *in toto* was selected to describe the New Covenant Folk. This choice would in no way be explainable had Peter intended to identify his readers as neo-Levites.

To find this conception of a neo-Levitical community we must turn from 1 P to the sectaries of Qumran and Damascus. Here in a text such as C. D. III, 19-IV, 4 this idea came to direct expression:

> But God in His wonderful mysteries made conciliation for their trespasses and pardoned their impiety 'and He built them a sure house' in Israel, the like of which has not stood from ancient times even until now. They that hold fast to it are destined for eternal life and all glory of man is theirs; as God swore to them by the hand of the prophet Ezekiel, saying: 'The priests and the Levites and the sons of Zadok, who kept charge of My sanctuary when the children of Israel strayed from Me, they shall approach Me to minister unto Me, and they shall stand before Me to offer Me fat and blood.' The priests are 'they that turned (from impiety) of Israel' who went out from the land of Judah; and the Levites are they that joined themselves with them; and the Sons of Zadok are the elect of

[1] Cf. Grundman, *op. cit.*, pp. 189–96.

[2] 1 P 1:17, 14, 2:4, 9; Jac. 1:27; Rom. 12:1f.; Col. 3:16f. Eph. 5:17-20: Jn. 4:23f.; Heb. 13:15f.; Phil. 2:10f.; 1 Cor. 3:16f.; 2 Cor. 6:16f.; 1 Th. 5: 16-18, 20 Selwyn, *ibid.*, pp. 400-06).

Israel, 'the men called by name' who shall arise in the end of days.[1]

Here is truly a community which regarded itself as the legitimate continuation of the hieratic dynasty and institution. Whether these titles are to be understood as applying to the entire community or to the leaders in particular,[2] it is clear that the group is being described with Levitical terminology. This text is typical for the sectaries insofar as it indicates the pre-eminence which was attributed the concept of priesthood. The literature found at Qumran is replete with indications that in organization and ordinance, in personal behavior and public worship, in peace and war, in every facet of life the self-awareness of this community was determined by the sacerdotal image.[3]

Yet all evidence of this massive sacerdotal conception points to a derivation from one central source: the cultic institution of temple worship and the Levitical priesthood. No trace has yet been found of any consideration of the priesthood of Israel as prescribed in Ex. 19:6.

This is a point which cannot be overemphasized: as far as the evidence shows, Ex. 19:6 played absolutely no role in the Qumranic literature. This fact alone would advise a cautious attitude regarding a comparison of 1 P 2:4ff. and 1QS such as that undertaken by David Flusser. Flusser, comparing 1 P 2:4-6 with 1QS VIII, 4-11 (IX, 3-6), has concluded that the former represents a quotation from a Hebrew prototype resembling the latter.[4] However, the absence of the EF in 1QS, the literal dependence upon the EF in

---

[1] Translation according to Chaim Rabin, *The Zadokite Documents*, I. *The Admonition* II. *The Laws*, 2nd rev. ed., Oxford, 1958, pp. 12-14. Rabin substantiates his proposed reading "the Levites are" (CD. IV, 3) by noting the same etymology followed in Eth. Jub. 3:16 based upon Gen. 29:34, Num. 18:2, 4 (p. 14, n. 2 *ad* 4:3).

[2] Cf. G. Molin, *Die Söhne des Lichtes*, Wien, 1954, p. 143; Maier, *op. cit.*, II, 47.

[3] Priests were recognized as the leaders of the congregation and ascribed first rank (1QS VI, 4ff.; VIII, 1ff.; CD X, 4ff.; XIII, 2, XIV, 3-8; 1QS28a II, 22; 1QS28b 4; 4Qtest. 14-19; 4Qflor. I, 19). They taught the Law (1QS V, 9; CD X, 4, XII, 22; XIV, 6-8; 1QS28b III, 22-25; 1QpMic. I, 5; 1QpHab. II, 7-10, XI, 4f.). They served as judges (1QS IX, 7; CD IX, 13ff.). They led the worship (1QS I, 16ff.; 1QM II, 2ff.; 1QS28b IV, 22). They blew the trumpets and led the armies in the Final Battle (1QM VII, 10-17; X, 3; XIII, 1; XV, 4-6, XVII, 10). Furthermore, the awaited Messiah was to be a priestly Messiah (1QS IX, 11; CD XII, 23; XIV, 19; 1QS28a II, 19). The community *in toto* also shared a priestly responsibility: to live a holy and pure life and achieve reconciliation for the world (1QS V, 5f.; VII, 6f.; 1QM II, 1-5; 1QS 28a, I, 3) which way of life was oblation pleasant to God (1QS VIII, 9f.; IX, 3-5). And the defects which kept one from entering the congregation were extensions of priestly disqualifications (1QS28a II, 3-9; 1QM VII, 3-6).

[4] Flusser, *op. cit.*, esp. p. 235.

1 P, and the texts of the two sections compared make this theory most unlikely.

From the outset we can see with Flusser certain similarities between the two texts: mention of a house (1QS VIII, 5; IX, 6/1 P 2:5b); a priestly entity ("a holy of holies for Aaron" VIII, 5f., 8; IX, 6/ "a holy body of priests" 2:5c); the offering of sacrifice (VIII, 9; IX, 4f./ 2:5d) acceptable to God (VIII, 6, 10; IX, 5/2:5d); and allusion to Is. 28:16 (VIII, 7f./2:4b, 6bc). Though Flusser does not expressly do so, we might consider further the mention of holiness (VIII, 5f., 8; cp. 11, 20f., IX, 2, 6/2:5c) and election (VIII, 6/2:4b, [5]) and the Holy Spirit (IX, 3/2:5b,d) or stress upon witness and service for the world (VIII, 6, 10; IX, 4/2:5d) and a holy way of life (IX, 5; cp. VIII, 26; IX 2/2:5d; cp. 1:14-17, 2:12).

Nevertheless, these affinities represent no more than a similarity of concepts and themes and hardly a literal textual dependence. Direct dependence would presume a similar word order and this is not the case. Even acknowledging that IX, 3-6 is an abbreviated doublet of VIII, 5-10, Peter's word order does not follow even that of the latter.[1] According to Flusser's theory, 1 P 2:4ff. has translated a Hebrew version of the 1QS text. Thus he assumes that οἶκος πνευματικός rendered בֵּת קוֹדֶשׁ and ἱεράτευμα ἅγιον, קוֹדֶשׁ קוֹדָשִׁים לְאַהֲרוֹן (VII, 5f., 8f.). Aside from the fact that οἶκος and ἱεράτευμα both related to the EF, can one seriously contend that οἶκος πνευματικός is an accurate version of בֵּת קוֹדֶשׁ or ἱεράτευμα of מְעוֹן קוֹדֶשׁ קוֹדָשִׁים? Certainly it is obvious from the latter in particular that these two are entirely different entities! "Body of priests" designates a community of priestly functionaries; "holy of holies" is a technical term for the innermost sanctuary of the temple.

In the case of Is. 28:16 Flusser maintains that 1 P did not translate the verse from the "Hebrew prototype" but rather followed the LXX version.[2] Hardly! If Peter were rendering in Greek a Hebrew prototype why should he suddenly interrupt his "translation" and rely upon a LXX formulation? Furthermore, are we really to believe that Is. 28:16 in 1 P 2:6 followed the LXX but that the truly LXX formulation ἱεράτευμα in v. 5 did not?

The major oversight of this theory is the failure to see the dependence of 1 P 2:5 and 9 upon the EF and the LXX version of Ex. 19:6. 1QS VIII, 4-11 has no relation to the EF but reflects solely the sphere of the Jerusalem temple and the Aaronic priesthood (cf. IX, 7). The difference cannot be smoothed over by assuming that the typical image of the sect as two divided houses (Israel and Aaron) "has been resolved in the Christian passage into two independent images which can be combined but need not be."[3]

[1] This is clear even from the order of Flusser's table: οἶκος πνευματικός = VIII, 5, 9; ἱεράτευμα ἅγιον = VIII, 8, 5-6; ἀνενέγκαι πνευματικὰς θυσίας = VIII, 9; εὐπροσδέκτους θεῷ = VIII, 6; 2:6bc = VIII, 7f.

[2] *Ibid.*, p. 235.

[3] *Ibid.*, p. 234.

Our examination has shown that these "images" belong essentially together. The statement that the "whole complex of ideas and phrases . . . was transposed into a new language and a new *milieu*"[1] in no way accounts for these radical and non-reconcilable differences. Rather, our observations show that the point of contact between 1 P 2:4ff. and 1QS VIII, 4-11 was not in an idea of priesthood or a "spiritual temple" but in the mutual allusion to Is. 28:16 representing an eschatological "stone" tradition of which both 1QS and 1 P made use. The *novum* of 1 P is not specifically in its language or *milieu* but in its combination of two originally unrelated traditions, this λίθος complex and the EF. Therefore Eduard Lohse, for one, is justified in rejecting Flusser's theory as untenable.[2]

Neither in 1QS VIII, 4-11 nor CD. IV, 3f. nor as yet in any other text found at Qumran can be located any trace of the EF or a priesthood of Israel in this original sense. Therefore, if J. T. Milik's use of the term "priesthood of all believers" as a description of the state of affairs depicted in CD. IV, 3f.[3] is permissable, then it could no longer be brought into any connection with Ex. 19:6, for this would imply an affinity between two texts which are far from similar and between conceptions of priesthood which have nothing in common. For similar reasons it is difficult to agree with Matthew Black who in his recent study, *The Scrolls and Christian Origins*, states in regard to Apoc. 1:6 that "Christians are 'kings and priests' unto God because they are the direct heirs of the ancient priestly tradition of Israel *through* Qumran"[4] (italics mine). To the contrary, the tradition upon which Apoc. 1:6 as well as 1 P 2:5,9 depended fails to support any theory of "a close resemblance and affinity between Qumran and the Primitive Church."[5] Contrary to Black who cites Selwyn approvingly, 1 P 2:4ff. cannot be used as demonstration of the suggestion that the Church, by conceiving herself as sacerdotal in character, a priestly movement, a "neo-Levitical or priestly community," was following in the footsteps of the Qumran sectaries.[6]

However the theories of a priestly tradition and its significance

---

[1] *Ibid.*

[2] E. Lohse, *op. cit.*, p. 80.

[3] *Ten years of Discovery in the Wilderness of Judea* (Translated by J. Strugnell from the original French: *Dix ans de Découvertes dans le Désert de Juda*, Paris, 1957) (*SBT* 26), London, 1959, p. 105, n. 1.

[4] M. Black, *The Scrolls and Christian Origins*, London, 1961, pp. 80f.

[5] *Ibid.*

[6] *Ibid.* Furthermore, inasmuch as οἶκος πνευματικός relates to the EF and not to the λίθος complex, Black is operating with a faulty assumption when he suggests that this phrase means "spiritual temple" and that exact parallels can be found in the Qumran texts, supposedly employing the same OT *testimonia* (elsewhere, *ibid.*, p. 42, in this respect he points to 1QS V, 6; VIII, 8; IX, 3). Cf. further Dabin, *op. cit.*, pp. 320-56, esp. 335, who relates the ideas of a "royal priesthood" and "le lévitisme chrétien."

for Qumran and the NT are to be evaluated,[1] it is evident that ἱεράτευμα in 1 P did not have its prototype in the clericalism of the community at Chirbet Qumran. Ἱεράτευμα did not relate to the Levitical system nor did it specify the neo-progeny of Levi. Rather, it constitutes a predicate for Israel *in toto* and in 1 P designates the New Chosen People of the Spirit.

As is obvious throughout 1 P, the author in composing his message made use of various sources. He drew water from various wells in different regions. The resultant mixture cannot be attributed to a single spring or solely one source. While baptism and a holiness paraenesis in particular figure significantly in the composition of 1 P, neither was the parent of the reference to the EF in 2:5 and 9. That which accounts for its presence here is the election theme which was joined to a previous section treating holiness and the pattern of birth and growth in the word. To see the mode of combination of 2:4-10 with the preceding we return to our consideration of 1:13-2:3.

B. The Relation with 2:4-10

A striking feature of the section of 1:13-2:3 is the large number of similarities with phrases, motifs, and patterns employed in the initiation rites and the related paraenesis of Qumran and Jewish Proselytism.[2] Such similarities make it probable that the paraenesis —possibly a baptism paraenesis—which Peter developed in this section was to an appreciable extent influenced by, if not dependent

---

[1] Cf. E. Stauffer, "Probleme der Priestertradition," *ThLZ* 81/3 (1956), 135-50; Molin, *op. cit.*, pp. 143ff.

[2] In general cf. Grundmann, *op. cit.* For the affinity between Qumran and the NT in respect to the concept of holiness cf. D. Barthelémy, "La sainteté selon la communauté de Qumrân et selon l'Évangile," *La Secte de Qumran et les Origines du Christianisme. Communication aus IXes Journées bibliques Louvain, Sept.* 1957, ed. J. van der Ploeg, Paris, 1959, pp. 203-16 and F. Nötscher, "Heiligkeit in den Qumranschriften." *RQ* 6 (1960), 163-81; RQ 7 (1960), 315-44. An impressive list of similarities between 1 P and Jewish Proselytism has been assembled by van Unnik, *De verlossing*, esp. pp. 36-87. Both W. Nauck, *Die Tradition und der Charakter des ersten Johannesbriefes*, Tübingen, 1957 and O. Betz, "Die Proselytentaufe der Qumransekte und die Taufe im Neuen Testament," *RQ* 2 (1958), 213-34, offer much evidence for the relationship between the initiation rites of Qumran and Proselytism and the NT sacrament of Holy Baptism. Both studies refer to 1 P as does a further investigation of Betz' treating the image of birth in Qumran, "Die Geburt der Gemeinde durch den Lehrer," *NTS* 3 (1956/57), 314-26; cf. also E. Sjöberg, "Neuschöpfung in den Toten-Meer-Rollen," *StTh* 9/2 (1955/56), 131-36.

upon, patterns of thought shaped earlier in these quarters.[1] The pattern of "conversion, separation, and union" found by D. Barthélemy in 1QS V, 1f. or the scheme of birth (through the word) and growth noted by Grundmann and Otto Betz in the paraenesis connected with the initiation rites of Qumran, Proselytism, and the NT could, in general, be seen reflected in 1 P 1:13ff.: members of the community are to *turn* from their former way of life (vv. 14-17), to *separate* themselves from all evil (2:1), so that they might be *united* together (2:5). Again, the image of birth (1:23-25, 2:2) and growth (2:2) is employed.

On the other hand, 2:4-10 as a whole is a unique arrangement of thought having no parallels in earlier literature. And the combination here effected—the relationship drawn between Jesus and the believing community—provides the clue concerning the Petrine *novum* involved in 1:13-2:3 and the mode in which Peter finally joined this first section and 2:4ff.

As in 2:4ff., so throughout 1:13-2:3 a factor given paramount importance is the *relationship between the believers and Jesus.*[2] This is evident in each verse where an imperative is corroborated by a subsequent indicative. The hearers/readers are to turn from their former way of life and lead an obedient life as God-fearers (vv. 14-17) because they have been redeemed by Jesus the holy sacrifice Who is responsible for their faith in God (vv. 18-21). Sanctifying themselves in obedience, they are to practice unhypocritical brotherly love (v. 22) because they have been reborn not through corruptible seed (just as they have not been redeemed with corruptible wealth, v. 18) but through the imperishable word of God (v. 23, cp. v. 19), the word "evangelized" to them (vv. 23-25, cp. v. 12). Therefore they are to abstain or separate themselves from hypocrisy (2:1, cp. 1:22) and guile (2:1) and as newly-born babies to yearn for this word-milk, that they might grow to salvation

---

[1] These were important links in the transmission and influences in the formation of the HC eventually taken over by the early Church.

[2] The opening lines of Schlatter's treatment of the characteristics of 1 P in *Die Theologie des Neuen Testament II. Die Lehre der Apostel*, Tübingen, 1910, p. 186, emphasize this fact: "Für den Petrinischen Brief besteht die Religion in der Verbundenheit mit Jesus . . . (Der Brief) leitet alles, was er den Gemeinden über ihre Aufgaben sagt, aus dem ab, was Jesus für sie ist. Die Verbundenheit mit Christus wird nicht durch einen mystischen Vorgang hergestellt, sondern ist durch den Ausgang seiner Geschichte begründet, durch sein Kreuz, seine Auferstehung, seine Erhöhung, seine Wiederkunft."

(2:2, cp. 1:22-25). For the word which gave them birth is that which nourishes and affords growth—the word of Jesus the κύριος (2:3).

Emphasis upon this relationship continues then in 2:4ff. By coming to Him in faith they have been made alive as He has been made alive (v. 4). They have been elected by God as He was elect (v. 4, 5). They grow, are built, are united into a community (v. 5). They have become precious (v. 7) because they have believed in Him, the Precious One (v. 4, 6, 7); they have obeyed the word (v. 8). Thereby they participate in God's mighty deeds of salvation and have been made heirs of the covenant of mercy (vv. 9f.). Proclamation of this word is now their task, for through Jesus Christ they have become the Covenant People, a Spiritual house and a holy body of priests which is to offer herself to God.

Thus, in support of each concrete exhortation the author followed with a statement describing some aspect of the believers' relationship to Jesus. The images used vary from those pertaining to holiness and redemption to those related to birth, baby-likeness, feeding, and growth. While the images themselves derive from the traditional Christian and pre-Christian sources followed, the believers-Jesus relationship developed by way of these sources is the contribution of the author of 1 Peter.

The second novel feature is the connection made between the word-birth-growth pattern and the unit centering in the concept of election, 2:4-10. For though a Christian re-interpretation of the word-birth-growth theme is not peculiar to 1 P (cf. esp. Jac. 1:18-22, 1:10f.),[1] its combination with a section on election is not met again in the NT literature.

These two novel features of 1 P are not unrelated. To the contrary, it was precisely this alternation of imperative and indicative, this correspondence between what the community is to do and what has been done to her in and through Jesus Christ, which leads up to and is climaxed by the indicative statement in 2:4-10. Fitting into the general pattern of imperative followed by indicative, this pericope offers a final indicative statement to this first paraenetic section, 1:13-2:10. Corresponding with the intention of all preceding indicatives, this extensive explanation of the Church's election through Jesus Christ, her holiness, and her corporateness serves as a grand

---

[1] Cf. also 1 Cor. 3:1-3, 6-10f.; Eph. 4:12, 5:16; Heb. 5:14-6:20.

resumé of the basis and *Ausgangspunkt* of all the exhortation of this initial section.

As far as the mechanics of combination are concerned, it was phrases from ψ 33 which provided the formal transition from 2:3 to 2:4. ψ 33:9 was cited in altered form (καὶ ἴδετε was omitted and the imperative γεύσασθε converted into the indicative ἐγεύσασθε) in 2:3, completing the thought of 2:2. ψ 33:6, also in altered form, provided the initial words of 2:4.[1] In place of the original προσέλθατε πρὸς αὐτὸν appeared πρὸς ὅν προσερχόμενοι. The verb was changed from an aorist imperative to a present participle (indicative, not imperative) and the pronoun αὐτόν, to ὅν which then referred back to κύριος (v. 3). Thereby a continuation was given to v. 3,[2] and with the thought of "coming to the λίθος (= κύριος)" an introduction was afforded to the statement concerning Jesus in v. 4b.

This introduction is more a formal transitional device than a logical beginning to v. 4, for the idea of "coming to a stone" makes little sense. The attempt to find a more reasonable explanation in the rites of the Mystery cults[3] therefore is understandable, though unnecessary. Peter was not disinclined to build his bridges in a more formalistic manner. This we have already seen to have been the case in the next verse (v. 5), where a certain syntactical disjunction testifies to the formal combination of two originally separate elements: a λίθος complex (v. 5a) and an EF reference (v. 5b-d).

Two further elements possibly figuring also in the connection of vv. 4-10 with the foregoing are the verb οἰκοδομεῖσθε in v. 5a and the midrashic note in v. 8.

As Grundmann has pointed out, the image of "building" was a part of a common NT birth-growth pattern.[4] The texts which he cites (1 P 2:4f., 1 Cor. 3:10ff., and Heb. 6:1ff.) have little in common terminologically, however. Striking, nevertheless, is the mutual occurrence of οἰκοδομεῖσθαι / ἐποικοδομεῖσθαι in 1 P 2:5 and

---

[1] It is interesting to note that the citation from ψ 33:14-17 in 1 P 3:10-12 served much the same summarizing and climaxing purpose as did the pericope introduced also by a thought from ψ 33 in 2:4.

[2] Another example of the practice of continuing the train of thought through an additional reference to a quoted text is found in 1:16-17. Verse 17 (πατέρα . . . ἐν φόβῳ . . . ἀναστράφητε) picks up the theme from Lev. 19:3 (ἕκαστος πατέρα αὐτοῦ καὶ μητέρα αὐτοῦ φοβείσθω . . .), the continuation of Lev. 19:2 cited in v. 16.

[3] Cf. e.g. Perdelwitz, *op. cit.*, pp. 67-70.

[4] Grundmann, *op. cit.*, p. 191.

1 Cor. 3:10, 12, 14. If it may be assumed from 1 P 1:22-2:2 that Peter was acquainted with such a pattern, then perhaps we may also see this scheme as the inspiration of οἰκοδομεῖσθε in 2:5a. The likelihood of this possibility is strengthened by a Petrine midrashic note in 2:8b, which again reflects a concern on the part of the author to integrate the λίθος complex with the word-birth-growth analogy: "they *stumble* by having not believed (obeyed) the *word*."

This method of combining separate complexes resulted in a certain choppiness of thought and syntax, but this did not detract appreciably from the overall sense. What Peter thereby accomplished was a general continuity of thought which extended over a variety of independent complexes subsumed under the comprehending themes of holiness, birth-growth, and election. The final product testifies to the success of his endeavor.

In *conclusion*, 2:4-10, though a self-contained unit organized under a separate theme, relates directly to its immediate context and participates in an important manner in the general development of thought. This section, or elements thereof, was not intended as an explication of a baptismal office of ministry, nor was the EF explicitly derived from or related to the event of baptism, but rather primarily to that of election. Verses 4-6 do not represent a translation of an earlier Hebrew Qumranic prototype nor were they occasioned by the idea of the Church as a "neo-Levitical" community. Rather they are part of an original Petrine conception of the believing community as the Elect and Holy People of God. In this first portion of 1 P this pericope assumed a key position. It is united with its preceding context by the golden thread running through the entire first segment of 1 P: the bond between the faithful community and her glorified Lord. And as a statement on the election, corporateness and holiness of the believing community it points both backward to the holiness paraenesis in 1:13ff. and the birth-growth theme of 1:22ff., and forward to the social exhortation of 2:12ff. Here in 2:4-10 the injunction to a holy life, brotherly love, growth in the word, and witness to the world receives its most detailed support. Here the fundamental indicative for the entire epistle has been spoken.[1]

[1] For a very similar though, in view of its more precise and developed form, later expression of this idea of the community's election for holiness cf. Eph. 1:3-14, esp. 3f., 11, 14. Cf. further 1 Th. 4:7.

You are to lead a holy life of obedience, well-doing, and witness and can lead this life because He in Whom you believe, as a holy and perfect sacrifice, has redeemed you from your former polluted way of life. He has given you a second birth, nourishment, and growth. In reality you are the elect and holy eschatological community of God because He to Whom you come in faith is the Messiah, the raised, elect Stone of God through Whom you too receive life and election and the Spirit of holiness. Thus your task as the Spirit's royal house and the holy body of priests is to offer through this same Jesus Christ Spiritual sacrifices acceptable to God. For that which is written concerning the Stone also applies to you. His honor belongs to you as His believers in contrast to those who disbelieve the word about Him and stumble in rejection. Through Him you have become the objects of God's election and the people of His possession whose task is the proclamation of the saving acts of Him Who has turned your darkness to light, your rejection to acceptance and your alienation to inheritance as the λαὸς τοῦ θεοῦ.

SUMMARY AND CONCLUSIONS

1. The form and content of 1 P 2:4-10 reveal that this section was an attempt to describe via the motif of *election* the character and responsibility of the eschatological People of God, her bond with Jesus Christ, her infusion with the Spirit, her holiness, and her task of witness through the holy life and the proclamation of the saving deeds of God. The composition and structure reflect a combination of separate bodies of OT passages having the elect messianic/eschatological λίθος and the chosen People of God as their subjects. Of the materials used, particularly the λίθος complex and the EF show connections with Christian and pre-Christian traditions of interpretation which influenced the nuance of these elements in 1 P. Nevertheless, the overall combination, arrangement, and interpretation of these traditional elements here is unique in the NT and indicative not of an earlier source such as a *Testimonia* collection or Christian hymn but rather of the designing hand of the author of 1 P. Though forming a self-contained unit, this section is no excursus from the general train of thought but integrates directly with the thought of its preceding and succeeding context. According to the paraenetic pattern of imperative and indicative employed by the author, this pericope supplies the climaxing indicative statement to the paraenetic segment 1:3-2:10. Its explication of the two thoughts which figure so determinatively in 1 P, the election and holiness of the believing community, make it ultimately the fundamental indicative of the entire epistle.

2. A popular notion involved in the explication of this pericope is the assumption that vv. 5 and 9, in particular the references to the EF, were related to a Levitical conception of priesthood. The evidence has shown this assumption to be erroneous and a basic cause of many misconceptions concerning this text.

(a) NT statements concerning the priestly character of either Christ, Christians, or the corporate Church derive from and develop basically two sources:[1] the Levitical priesthood and Ex. 19:6. These sources are independent. In the OT the Levitical institution

[1] Excluding the Melchizedek tradition reflected in Ep. Heb.

had no relation to the statement of Ex. 19:6 "you shall be a kingdom of priests" and, vice versa, Ex. 19:6 was never brought into connection with the Levitical priesthood—either positively or negatively. This is equally the case in the NT. Where terms pertaining to "priest-ness" are employed, either the EF (1 P 2:5, 9; Apoc. 1:6, 5:10) or the Levitical priesthood (Rom. 15:16; Heb. *passim*; Apoc. 20:6 and *passim*) is followed; a mixture of priestly images in individual contexts is nowhere present.

(b) Ἱεράτευμα, deriving from Ex. 19:6, in no way relates to the Levitical image. It is most improbable that ἱεράτευμα and the EF belonged to an idea of the Church as a "neo-Levitical community" or to a Levitical Holiness Code. Though in 1 P the EF and elements of a possible Holiness Code fall within the same paraenetic section, their juxtaposition is due to a combination based upon a theme of holiness and not an idea of priesthood. The suggestion that the EF was cited as a "proof passage" for a Levitical conception of priesthood[1] represents a basic misunderstanding of the EF tradition and the function of Ex. 19:6 in 1 P.

(c) Since the idea of Christ's priesthood is developed according to the Levitical pattern whereas ἱεράτευμα relates to Ex. 19:6, and since no connection is made in 1 P between Christ's priesthood and ἱεράτευμα (an idea of the priesthood of Christ is nowhere developed in 1 P), there is no basis for the common assumption that in 1 P the community is a body of priests by virtue of participation in the priesthood of Christ.[2]

(d) Since ἱεράτευμα in no way relates to the Levitical priesthood, there is also no basis for the assumption that the use of ἱεράτευμα in vv. 5 and 9 implies a polemic against the Jewish cultic institution. In the first place, nowhere in the Scriptures or pre-Christian tradition is the EF posed as an alternate or antithesis to the Levitical priesthood. Secondly, 1 P 2:4-10 does not present an anti-Judaic polemic. The ascription of the honorific predicates of Israel to the believing community represents the unfolding of an eschatological event and not an engagement in polemics.

---

[1] So Best, *op. cit.*, p. 298.

[2] Kinder, *op. cit.*, p. 11, has also called attention to the difference in sources: "Alles, was das levitische Priestertum enthielt, mündet ein in das Priestertum Christi und nicht in das der Christen." But this distinction does not receive its full significance when Kinder maintains that "das Priestertum der Christen (including 1 P 2:5, 9) lebt aus dem Priestertum Jesu Christi" (*ibid.*, p. 13).

(e) 1 P 2:5 does not depict the "spiritualization" of Levitical cultic concepts but the application and interpretation of a completely different entity whose Spiritual quality originates solely in the creative and preserving work of the Divine Spirit.

(f) The ἱεράτευμα and its task cannot be compared to the mediatorial activity of the Levitical priesthood. Implied in the description of its task, "to offer Spiritual sacrifices," is a responsibility of witness toward the world. Mediation in the strict "two way" sense is not suggested, but rather a "one way mediation," as it were, of God's will, through holy obedience and well-doing, to all that is non-Church.

(g) Inasmuch as NT statements on the priesthood of Christ and Christians—including 1 P for the moment under the latter category—derive from and develop two mutually exclusive sources and concepts of priesthood, it is impossible to think in terms of "a single NT image of priesthood." The term ἱεράτευμα is unique in the NT and inequatable with the other text-form of the EF appearing in the Apoc. It is likewise incomparable with other statements on priesthood developed according to the image of the Levitical institution. All attempts to gather these disparate images under a single roof are from the outset destined to misinterpret 1 P 2:4-10.

3. Thus, attempts to explain ἱεράτευμα on the basis of the current first century view of the Levitical priesthood are pointless. The significance of this word and of the verses in which it appears was determined rather by the import of the EF which was the source and basis of both. The survey of the origin and history of this formula has shown that Ex. 19:6, from the OT to the NT, embodied a designation of a corporate body of people, Israel *in toto,* as the private and special possession of God. The two basic and correlative characteristics of this community were her *electedness* and her *holiness*. This was the fundamental import of this formula, as is seen in the various references to Ex. 19:6, and in this same sense it found a place in the thought of 1 P. Here those people who believe in Jesus the elect messianic Stone of God are named with the name of God's elect and holy nation: His Royal Residence, His Body of Priests.

4. The formation, election, and sanctification of this community is an eschatological salvific event. This act of salvation and "recreation," according to 1 P, involves the consummation of all that God had planned for His Israel. The focal point of this event is

Jesus Christ. People become participants in the event of salvation and re-birth in that they hear His word and confess Him to be the κύριος. They who believe in Jesus as the Elect and Precious One of God are gathered together as the Elect and Precious People. Through Jesus Christ, i.e. on the basis of His life and death as the spotless Lamb, those who come to Him in faith are made holy. They become the possession of His Spirit. This Spirit transfigures the βασίλειαν and the ἱεράτευμα of the Old Dispensation into a House-(hold) in which He resides, into a Body of Priests which He sanctifies.

5. To ask whether these entities "house(hold)," "body of priests," "sacrifices" are real or unreal is to pose a false and irrelevant question. Certainly the community is not literally a stone edifice with walls and a ceiling. Certainly she is not a corporation of sacerdotal functionaries. Is Jesus really a stone, a petrified inorganic specimen? The question is absurd as long as reality is sought in the literalness of the words. Of course Jesus is not a stone—and yet He *is* a stone. *He is the Stone* of messianic/eschatological hope. This identification posits Jesus as the Messiah, the Bringer of the Eschaton. Those who are reborn through His word and come to Him in faith are living stones as He is the living Stone, i.e. they too are made alive, elected, and given a share in this eschatological event. The reality of what this community is (living stones, house-(hold), body of priests, chosen race, holy nation, people of God's possession) and what she does (the leading of a God-pleasing life of witness and the proclamation of His mighty deeds) is grounded in the reality concerning Him to Whom this community commits herself: Jesus as the Christ, the eschatological Bringer of the Spirit. Insofar, to ask whether this folk is "really" a house or a body of "real" priests or whether it offers "real" sacrifices is to suggest a criterion of literalness and reality which has no place here. Only eschatologically is this people "really" what she is said to be. This eschatological event is epitomized in the factors of election through the Messiah and sanctification through the activity of the Spirit.

6. This salvation-event, this election, involves the formation of a corporate body of believers, a community. What Krister Stendahl has noted concerning the significance of election in the NT can be seen with especial clarity in 1 P: "Election in Christ not only constitutes a new society; its meaning is to be found in the new

society, and not in the status of individuals."[1] The predicates for this new elected society are collective and corporate, applicable only to *a people, a community* and not to individuals. It is in this sense that they were used in 1 P 2:4-10.

7. This coincides with both the text-form and the interpretation of Ex. 19:6 given in vv. 5 and 9. Ἱεράτευμα means "body of priests." It does not mean "priesthood" which is rather the equivalent of ἱερατεία, a more static and more abstract term in comparison with the *nomen actionis* ἱεράτευμα. βασίλειον does not mean "royal" in v. 9 but is an independent substantive signifying "royal residence or dwelling place." In v. 5 this substantive is interpreted as the "house-(hold) of the Spirit." Both terms are corporative and have been interpreted by the author of 1 P in this sense. It is semantically inadmissable to attempt to reduce either of these words to an individual-distributive classification and thereby to suggest that each individual believer is being depicted as a "king" and a "priest." This is contrary to the law of logic, points out Dabin, followed so carefully even among the Fathers: *"a collectivo ad distributivum non valet illatio."*[2] As the other corporate predicates, both βασίλειον and ἱεράτευμα are only ascribable to the community *qua* community and only relevant in this context *qua substantiva corporativa.*

8. Just as βασίλειον bears no implication of "royal rule, kingly freedom, or royal dignity and status," so ἱεράτευμα, though it denotes a people close to God, does not imply *in se* the abolition of mediation or the conferment of "priestly rights and prerogatives." The significance of ἱεράτευμα lies not in its cultic connotations, but together with βασίλειον, in its designation of the electedness and holiness of the Divine Regent's Community.

9. Ἱεράτευμα, connoting both active as well as corporate character, was the appropriate term with which the task and function of the elect and holy community should be associated: "to offer through

---

[1] "The Called and the Chosen, An Essay on Election," *The Root of the Vine: Essays in Biblical Theology*, ed. A. Fridrichsen, Westminster, 1953, p. 69.

[2] Dabin, *Sacerdoce . . . moderne*, p. 36. Dabin points out that the Fathers did not attempt to interpret the collective form ἱεράτευμα in the light of the distributive term ἱερεῖς in the Apoc. but cited both together as the two possible alternative versions of Ex. 19:6 presented in the inspired Scriptures. Best, *op. cit.*, p. 296, apparently thinks little of this careful distinction. He suggests that ἱεράτευμα means no more than "a group of priests and contains no suggestion that priesthood belongs to the group as group." Insofar, he overlooks the entire semantical question regarding ἱεράτευμα.

Jesus Christ Spiritual sacrifices acceptable to God." This task, described in cultic terms accommodated to the implications of "body of *priests*," does not indicate participation in the Eucharaistic oblation or in a destiny of suffering but rather consists in the exercise of a holy life of obedience and well-doing *coram Deo* and *pro hominibus*.

10. This activity is basically a witness orientated toward the world and complements a second aspect of the community's responsibility, the proclamation of the word of salvation and mercy. No connection has been made in 1 P between this responsibility to the world and the inner-directed ministry discussed in 4:7-5:5. 2:4-10 speaks neither for nor against a particular ministry or office in the Church. However, 4:7-5:5 indicates that the same community called a ἱεράτευμα also was charged with a charismatic ministry and ordered according to a certain sense of office. Therefore, it can only be concluded that the task of the ἱεράτευμα and that of the particular ministry were not mutually exclusive but inclusive, not contradictory but complementary. But they were also not identical. The task of the Chosen People described in 2:4-10 is a corporate witness directed to the world; that outlined in 4:7ff. involves an individualized service to the Christian brother.[1]

11. The community to which these words of 2:4ff. apply is a baptized community. Nevertheless, there is no evidence for the theory that references to the EF was occasioned by the event of baptism. The EF did not belong to a type of baptismal paraenesis. 1 P affords no support to the suggestion that baptism is to be considered as a "coronation to kingship" or an "ordination to priesthood." To repeat, it was the theme of election which accounted for the appearance of the EF in 1 P, and nothing else. This election theme explicates the essence of the baptized congregation and only via this motif is the EF related to Holy Baptism.

12. 2:4-10 centers in the motif of election and not in an idea of priesthood. This latter thought would involve the inadmissable isolation of one expression from the total context of thought. It

[1] Kinder, *op. cit.*, p. 19, n. 18, considers incorrect a division which would denote "das Amt, Dienst an der Gemeinde . . . das allgemeine Priestertum (under which he includes 1 P 2:4-10) aber Dienst der Gemeinde an der Welt." He holds that "das NT sagt von dem christlichen Priestertum auch gewichtige innergemeindliche Funktionen und Bestätigungen aus." Such inner-directed functions are not evident in 1 P 2:4ff., however, and there is no reason for the rejection of such a distinction or division here.

would incorrectly ascribe pre-eminence to a term which is only one of several related predicates and would lead inevitably to an unbalanced interpretation of this pericope. Admittedly, ἱεράτευμα figures significantly in v. 5, but then so does βασίλειον, or more specifically, its interpretative correspondent οἶκος πνευματικός. *Ἱεράτευμα is not used to present a theory on priesthood but to serve the motifs of election and holiness.* As a dynamic term, it is appropriate as a link with the community's holy way of life. As a member of the historical Covenant Formula, it is particularly expressive of the Church's electedness.

13. Neither of these two thoughts basic to 1 P 2:4-10, election and holiness, relate to the ideas commonly associated with the notion of the universal priesthood or the priesthood of all believers. That associations with Holy Baptism, the priesthood of Christ, and the particular ministry of the Church have been suggested by sundry representatives of various persuasions of the Church Catholic is indeed reflective of a long and time-honored tradition of interpretation. Nevertheless, according to the available evidence such associations are not traceable to the thought and intention of the author of 1 P but only to a subsequent period.[1]

According to one modern Lutheran theologian, the Danish systematician Regin Prenter, "vom allgemeinen Priestertum wird gesprochen, wenn *jedes Mitglied* (my italics) des Volkes ganze oder zum Teil priesterliche *Rechte* (my italics) und Funktionen ausüben kann."[2] If this is to be acceptable as a valid definition of the idea of the priesthood of believers, then this idea will have to seek a *locus* other than the text of 1 P 2:4-10 which depicts not the rights and privileges of individuals but rather the electedness and holiness of the corporate People of God.[3]

---

[1] For possible NT texts cf. Apoc. and Ep. Heb., *supra*, pp. 169-74; for pertinent sub-Apostolic literature cf. *supra*, p. 14, n. 2. Hans Freiherr von Campenhausen, "Die Anfänge des Priesterbegriffs in der alten Kirche," SEÅ 4 (1939), 86-101 [reprinted in *Tradition und Leben*: *Kräfte der Kirchengeschichte*, Tübingen, 1960, pp. 272-89], concludes that the first explicit development of this idea of an "*allgemeines Priestertum*" is to be found in the second Christian century.

[2] *RGG* V, 581.

[3] This is not to suggest that such a definition is inconsonant with the classical conception of a priesthood of all believers as formulated by Luther. To the contrary, Prenter's statement coincides with the various elements stressed also by Luther: (1) "the equivalent spiritual authority and dignity of each Christian; (2) the Christian's unobstructed approach to God and His

The emphases of systematic theologians, Protestants in particular, upon the rights, privileges, and authority of individual Christians and their citation of 1 P 2:5 and 9 as Biblical support, though understandable in the light of their own historical and theological positions, and the failure of exegetes to criticize the incoherences of such argumentation, unfortunately have led to a thorough misunderstanding and misappreciation of the original significance and purpose of 1 P 2:4-10. If the import of 1 P 2:4-10 is that suggested by this study, then perhaps it is not too much of an overstatement to suggest that the success of the exit from the dead end involved in these verses and the significance which this pericope assumes in the dialogue concerning the nature and task of the Church will be measured by the degree to which these thoughts regarding the electedness and holiness of the eschatological People of God receive their just due.

Word; (3) the priestly office of offering oneself to one's God; (4) the commission of proclamation given to the Christian within a certain defined area" (cf. Brunotte, *op. cit.*, p. 200).

Rather, this is to point out that the historical situation which occasioned Luther's polemic against the then current understanding of priesthood and his stress upon the ideas of individual equality and individual authority was far different from the situation which occasioned the words written by the author of 1 Peter.

Furthermore, this is to imply that there has been long overdue an appreciation of this text of 1 Peter over against the historical situation of the Church in the first century rather than in the sixteenth.

ABBREVATIONS

Angelos	*Angelos. Archiv für neutestamentliche Zeitgeschichte und Kulturkunde.* Leipzig
AT	Altes Testament, Ancien Testament
ATD	*Das Alte Testament Deutsch. Neues Göttinger Bibelwerk.* Göttingen
Aufl.	Auflage
BFChrTh	*Beiträge zur Förderung christlicher Theologie.* Gütersloh
BWANT	*Beiträge zur Wissenschaft vom Alten und Neuen Testament.* Leipzig, Stuttgart
BZ	*Biblische Zeitschrift.* Freiburg (Neue Folge: Paderborn)
CSEL	*Corpus Scriptorum ecclesiasticorum Latinorum.* Editum consilio caesareae vindobonesis. Vienna. 1866ff.
CTM	*Concordia Theological Monthly.* St. Louis
EB	*Die Heilige Schrift in Deutscher Übersetzung. Echter Bibel.* Würzburg
EF	Exodus Formula (= Ex 19:6)
ENT	A. Schlatter, *Erläuterungen zum Neuen Testament.* Stuttgart
EphLov	*Ephemerides Lovanienses.* Louvain
esp.	especially
EstBi	*Estudios Biblicos.* Madrid
EvTh	*Evangelische Theologie.* München
ExpT	*The Expository Times.* Edinburgh
FRLANT	*Forschung zur Religion und Literatur des Alten und Neuen Testaments.* Göttingen
Gk. Frag.	A Greek Fragment relating to Testament Levi 11:4-6, located in a 10th Century A.D. Mt. Athos Manuscript of the Testaments of the Twelve Patriarchs
HAT	*Handbuch zum Alten Testament.* Tübingen
HBK	*Die Heilige Schrift für das Leben erklärt. Herders Bibelkommentar.* Freiburg
HCAT	*Kurzer Hand-Commentar zum Alten Testament.* Leipzig, Freiburg
HCNT	*Hand-Commentar zum Neuen Testament.* Leipzig, Freiburg
HNT	*Handbuch zum Neuen Testament.* Tübingen
hrsg.	herausgegeben von
HTKNT	*Herders Theologischer Kommentar zum Neuen Testament.* Freiburg
ICC	*The International Critical Commentary of the Holy Scriptures of the Old and New Testament.* Edinburgh
imper.	imperative
imperf.	imperfect
JBL	*Journal of Biblical Literature and Exegesis.* Philadelphia
JLW	*Jahrbuch für Liturgiewissenschaft.* Münster
JQR	*The Jewish Quarterly Review.* Philadelphia
JTS	*The Journal of Theological Studies.* Oxford
KAT	*Kommentar zum Alten Testament.* Leipzig

KEK	*Kritisch-exegetischer Kommentar über das Neue Testament.* Begründet von H. A. W. Meyer. Göttingen
KJV (AV)	The King James Version (Authorized version)
LCL	*The Loeb Classical Library.* London
Lit.	Literature
MPL	*Patrologiae cursus completus. Series Latina.* Ed. J. P. Migne. 221 vols. Paris. 1844-64.
MT	Massoretic Text
NF	Neue Folge
NR	Neue Reihe, Nieuwe Reeks
n.s.	new series
NT	New Testament, Neues Testament
NovTest	*Novum Testamentum.* Leiden
NTD	*Das Neue Testament Deutsch. Neues Göttinger Bibelwerk.* Göttingen
NTS	*New Testament Studies.* Cambridge
OT	Old Testament. Oude Testament
OTS	*Oudtestamentische Studien.* Leiden
par. memb.	*parallelismus membrorum*
pass.	passive
pl.	plural
pll.	parallel(s)
pss.	passages
R.	Rabbi
RB	*Revue Biblique.* Paris
Rbb.	Rabbinic
resp.	respectively
RHE	*Revue d'Histoire Ecclésiastique.* Louvain
RQ	*Revue Qumrân.* Paris
RSPhTh	*Revue des Sciences Philosophiques et Théologiques.* Paris
RSV	The Revised Standard Version
SBT	*Studies in Biblical Theology.* SCM Press. London
SEÅ	*Svensk Exegetisk Årsbok.* Uppsala
sim.	similarly
SJT	*Scottish Journal of Theology.* Edinburgh
s.l.	sub loco
StTh	Studia Theologica. Lund
s.v.	sub voce
Syn.	Synoptics
T.	Targum
Test.	Testament (of the Twelve Patriarchs)
ThBl	*Theologische Blätter.* Leipzig
ThEx NF	*Theologische Existenz heute.* Neue Folge. Herausgegeben von K. G. Steck und G. Eichholz. München.
ThLZ	*Theologische Literaturzeitung.* Leipzig
ThR	*Theologische Rundschau.* Tübingen
TS	*Theological Studies.* Baltimore
TThZ	*Trierer Theologische Zeitschrift.* Trier
ThZ	*Theologische Zeitschrift.* Basel
transl.	translated by
VT	*Vetus Testamentum.* Leiden
WA	*D. Martin Luthers Werke.* Kritische Gesamtausgabe. Weimar. Hermann Böhlau. 1883ff.

WMANT	*Wissenschaftliche Monographien zum Alten und Neuen Testament.* Neukirchen
WUNT	*Wissenschaftliche Untersuchungen zum Neuen Testament.* Tübingen
ZAW (*BZAW*)	*Zeitschrift für die alttestamentliche Wissenschaft* (*Beihefte* zur . . .) Giessen, Berlin
ZKNT	Kommentar zum Neuen Testament, herausgegeben von Th. Zahn, Leipzig
ZNW	*Zeitschrift für die neutestamentliche Wissenschaft und die Kunde der alten Kirche.* Giessen, Berlin

Abbreviations of the Biblical and related literature are given according to *BAG* (*vide infra*) with the following exceptions or additions:

Act.	Acts of the Apostles
Act. Jn.	Acta Johannis
Apoc.	Apocalypse of St. John
Auc. Heb.	Author of the Epistle to the Hebrews
Barn.	Barnabas
Cant.	Canticles
1, 2 Chr.	1, 2 Chronicles
Dan.	Daniel
Did.	Didache
(Ep.) Heb.	Epistle to the Hebrews
Ign. Eph.	Ignatius to the Ephesians
Ign. Magn.	Ignatius to the Magnesians
Ign. Smyrn.	Ignatius to the Smyrnaeans
Ign. Trall.	Ignatius to the Trallians
Jac.	Jacobus, James
Jn.	John
1, 2, 3 Jn.	1, 2, 3 John
Od. Sol.	Odae Salomonis
1, 2P	1, 2 Peter
Ps(s). Sol.	Psalm(s) of Salomon
Sap.	Sapientia Salominis
T(arg).	Targum
T. Jer(us) I, II	Targum Jerushalmi I, II
T. Onkelos	Targum Onkelos
Test. 12. Patr.	Testament(s) of the Twelve Patriarchs
Tob.	Tobit

Abbreviations of the writings of *Philo* are given according to *Philonis Alexandrini opera quae supersunt*, ed. Cohn-Wendland (for full bibliography *vide infra*).

Abbreviations of the literature discovered in the region west of the Dead Sea are given according to *Discoveries in the Judean Desert*, ed. Barthelémy-Milik et al. I-II. (for full bibliography *vide infra*).

Abbreviations of the *Greek Literature*, authors and works, epigraphical and papyrological publications are given according to *A Greek-English Lexicon*, ed. Liddell-Scott-Jones (for full bibliography *vide infra*).

Abbreviations of the *Rabbinic literature* are given according to the Soncino edition of the Babylonian Talmud (for full bibliography *vide infra*).

All further abbreviations of cited works are contained in the following bibliography and are given in () following the respective work.

BIBLIOGRAPHY

1. TEXTS AND TRANSLATIONS

Old and New Testament

Biblia Hebraica. Ed. R. Kittel, P. E. Kahle *et al.* 9th ed. Stuttgart. 1954.

Novum Testamentum Graece. Ed. Eb. Nestle, Erw. Nestle *et* K. Aland. 24th ed. Stuttgart. 1960.

Septuaginta. Ed. A. Rahlfs. I-II. 5th ed. Stuttgart. 1952. (LXX)

Other Bible Versions

Bible in Aramaic, The. Ed. A. Sperber. I. *The Pentateuch According to Targum Onkelos.* Leiden. 1959. *III. The Latter Prophets According to Targum Jonathan.* 1962.

Biblia Sacra iuxta Latinam Vulgatam Versionem. Ed. A. Gasquet. I-II. Rome. 1929.

Hebräische Pentateuch der Samaritaner, Der. Ed. A. Freiherr von Gall. Giessen. 1918.

Neofiti 1. Biblioteca Apostolica Vaticana. Rome.

Old Testament in Greek, The. According to the text of the Codex Vaticanus supplemented from other Uncial MSS. Ed. A. E. Brooke and N. McLean. Vol. I, Part II. Exodus and Leviticus. Cambridge. 1909.

Origenis Hexaplorum quae supersunt sive veterum graecorum in totum Vetus Testamentum fragmenta. Ed. F. Field. I-II. Oxford. 1861-74.

Apocrypha and Pseudepigrapha

Apocrypha and Pseudepigrapha of the Old Testament, The. Ed. R. H. Charles. I-II. Oxford. 1913. (*AP*)

Jubilees, The Book of. Transl. R. H. Charles from his edition of the Ethiopic Text (The *Ethiopic Version of the Hebrew Book of Jubilees.* Edited from 4 MSS. and compared with the MT, Samaritan, Greek, and Vulgate. Oxford. 1895). London. 1902.

Testaments of the Twelve Patriarchs, The Greek Versions of the. Ed. R. H. Charles from nine MSS together with the Variants of the Armenian and Slavonic Versions and some Hebrew Fragments. Oxford. 1908. (*Testaments*)

Qumran Literature

Discoveries in the Judean Desert. I. *Qumran Cave I.* Ed. D. Barthelemy and J. T. Milik. Oxford. 1955. (*DJD*)

——. III. *Les 'Petites Grottes' De Qumrân* (*2Q, 3Q, 5Q, 6Q, 7Q-10Q, Le rouleau de cuivre*). Ed. M. Baillet, J. T. Milik, R. de Vaux. Oxford. 1962.

Megilloth Midbar Yehuda. The Scrolls from the Judean Desert. Ed. A. M. Habermann, with Vocalization, Introduction, Notes and Concordance. Jerusalem. 1959.

Scriptures of the Dead Sea Sect, The. Transl. T. H. Gaster. London. 1957.

Texte vom Toten Meer, Die. I. Übersetzung. II. Anmerkungen. Hrsg. J. Maier. München/Basel. 1960.

Zakokite Documents, The. I. The Admonition. II. The Laws. Ed. C. Rabin, with a translation. 2nd revised ed. Oxford. 1958.

Rabbinic Literature

Mechilta de-Rabbi Simon b. Jochai. Ed. D. Hoffmann. Frankfurt/Main. 1905.

Mechilta D'Rabbi Ismael. Ed. H. S. Horovitz and I. A. Rabin. Frankfurt/Main. 1931.

Mekhilta D'Rabbi Sim'on b. Jochai. Fragmenta in Geniza Cairensi Reperta. Ed. J. N. Epstein and E. Z. Melamed. Jerusalem. 1955.

Mekilta de-Rabbi Ishmael. A Critical Edition on the Basis of the Manuscripts and Early Editions with an English Translation, Introduction, and Notes by J. Z. Lauterbach. I-III (*The Schiff Library of Jewish Classics*). Philadelphia. 1949.

Leviticus. Sifra. Torah Kohanim. Hrsg. E. H. Weiss. Wien. 1852. Reprinted in New York, 1946.

Psalms, Midrash on the. Midrash Tehillim. Transl. W. G. Braude from the Hebrew and Arabic (*Yale Judaica Series* 13/1-2). New Haven. 1959.

Sefer Mekilta of Rabbi Ishmael to the Book of Exodus. Ed. M. Friedmann. Vienna. 1870. Reprinted in New York, 1948.

Talmud, Babli. Babylonian Talmud. (b)

Talmud, The Babylonian. Ed. I. Epstein. 18 Vols. London. 1933-48. (*Soncino*).

Talmud, Jerushalmi, Palestinian Talmud. (p)

Tannaitischer Midrasch zu Exodus, Ein. Übersetzt und erläutert von J. Winter und A. Wünsche. Leipzig. 1909.

Jewish-Hellenistic Literature

Flavii Josephi Opera. Ed. B. Niese. *Editio Minor*. I-VI. Berlin. 1888-95.

Philo. Ed. and transl. F. H. Colson and G. H. Whitaker. I-XI. (*LCL*). London. 1949-54.

Philonis Alexandrini opera quae supersunt. Ed. L. Cohn et P. Wendland. I-VI. Berlin. 1896-1915. VII/1-2: Indices (incomplete), J. Leisegang. 1926-30. (*C-W*)

Werke Philos von Alexandria in Deutscher Übersetzung, Die. Hrsg. L. Cohn, I. Heinemann, M. Adler. I-VI. Breslau. 1909-38.

Ancient Near Eastern and Greek Texts and Inscriptions

Ancient Near Eastern Texts relating to the Old Testament. Ed. J. B. Pritchard. I-II. 2nd corrected and enlarged edition. Princeton. 1955.

Sylloge Inscriptionum Graecarum. Ed. W. Dittenberger. I-IV. 3rd edition. Leipzig. 1915-24.

2. CONCORDANCES GRAMMARS LEXICONS

Bauer, W. *Griechisch-Deutsches Wörterbuch zu den Schriften des Neuen Testaments und der übrigen urchristlichen Literatur*. 5. Aufl. Berlin. 1958. (*WNT*)

——, Arndt, W. F., and F. W. Gingrich. *A Greek-English Lexicon of the New Testament and Other Early Christian Literature*. A Translation and adaptation of W. Bauer's 4th Revised and Augmented Edition, 1952. Illinois/Cambridge. 1957. (*BAG*)

Blass, F. *Grammatik des neutestamentlichen Griechisch*. Bearbeitet von A. Debrunner. 9. Aufl. Göttingen. 1954. (*Bl-D*)

Evangelisches Kirchenlexikon. Kirchlich-theologisches Handwörterbuch. Hrsg. H. Brunette und O. Weber. I-IV. Göttingen. 1955ff. (*EKL*)

Frisk, H. *Griechisches Etymologisches Wörterbuch*. I. Heidelberg. 1960.

Gesenius, W. *Hebräisches und Aramäisches Handwörterbuch über das Alte Testament*. Bearbeitet von F. Buhl. 17. Aufl. Leipzig. 1915.

Hatch, E., and H. A. Redpath. *A Concordance to the Septuagint and the other Greek Versions of the Old Testament (Including the Apocryphal Books)*. I-II. Oxford. 1897. (*H-R*)

Jastrow, M. *A Dictionary of the Targumim, the Talmud Babli and Yerushalmi, and the Midrashic Literature*. I-II. New York. 1886-1903. Reprinted in New York, 1950.

Kasowski, C. H. *Thesaurus Thosephthae. Concordantiae Verborum Quae in Sex Thosephthae Ordinibus Reperiuntur*. Jerusalem. 1932.

Kretschmer, P., ed. *Rückläufiges Wörterbuch der griechischen Sprache*. Ausgearbeitet von E. Locker, Göttingen. 1944.

Liddell, H. G., and R. Scott. *A Greek-English Lexicon*. A New Edition revised and augmented throughout by H. S. Jones with the assistance of R. McKenzie. 9th ed. Oxford. 1940. (*L-S-J*)

Lisowsky, G. *Konkordanz zum Hebräischen Alten Testament*. Unter verantwörtlicher Mitwirkung von L. Rost. Stuttgart. 1958.

Mayser, E. *Grammatik der Griechischen Papyri aus der Ptolemäerzeit*. I-II. 2. Aufl. Berlin. 1936.

Moulton, J. H., and G. Milligan. *The Vocabulary of the Greek New Testament Illustrated from the Papyri and Other Non-Literary Sources*. London. 1952. (*M-M*)

Moulton, W. F. and A. S. Geden. *A Concordance to the Greek New Testament according to the Texts of Westcott and Hort, Tischendorf, and the English Revisers*. 3rd ed. Edinburgh. 1897.

Passow, F. *Handwörterbuch der griechischen Sprache*. I-II. 4. Aufl. Leipzig. 1831.

Religion in Geschichte und Gegenwart, Die. Handwörterbuch für Theologie und Religionswissenschaft. Hrsg. K. Galling. I-VI. 3. Aufl. Tübingen. 1957-62. (*RGG*)

Schmoller, A. *Handkonkordanz zum griechischen Neuen Testament* (Text nach Nestle 15-16. Aufl.). 7. Aufl. Stuttgart. 1938.

Schwyzer, E. *Griechische Grammatik*. I-III. München. 1953.

Theologisches Wörterbuch zum Neuen Testament. Begründet von G. Kittel, hrsg. G. Friedrich. Stuttgart. 1933ff. (*TWNT*)

Winer, G. B. *A Grammar of the Idiom of the New Testament*. Prepared as a Solid Basis for the Interpretation of the New Testament. 7th edition enlarged and improved by G. Lünemann. English edition prepared by J. H. Thayer. Andover. 1899.

3. MONOGRAPHS COMMENTARIES ARTICLES

Aalen, S. *Die Begriffe 'Licht' und 'Finsternis' im Alten Testament, im Spätjudentum und im Rabbinismus*. Oslo. 1951.

——."'Reign' and 'House' in the Kingdom of God in the Gospels," *NTS* 8 (1962), 215-40.

Abel, M., O.P. *Les Livres des Maccabées*. 12e ed. Paris. 1949.

Albright, W. F. *From the Stone Age to Christianity*. 2nd ed. New York. 1957.

Allegro, J. M. "Fragments of a Qumran Scroll of Eschatological Midrashim," *JBL* 77 (1958), 350-54.

——."Further Messianic References in Qumran Literature," *JBL* 75 (1956), 174-87.

Arndt, W. "A Royal Priesthood," *CTM* 19 (1948), 241-49.
Asmussen, H. *Das Priestertum aller Gläubigen*. Stuttgart. 1946.
Asting, R. *Die Heiligkeit im Urchristentum* (*FRLANT* NF 29). Göttingen. 1930.
Baltzer, K. *Das Bundesformular* (*WMANT* 4). Neukirchen. 1960.
Barthelémy, D., O.P. "La sainteté selon la communauté de Qumrân et selon l'Évangile," *La Secte de Qumrân et les Origines du Christianisme. Communication aux IXes Journées bibliques Louvain, Sept.* 1957, ed. J. van der Ploeg. Paris. 1959. Pp. 203-16.
Baudissin, W. W. Graf. *Die Geschichte des alttestamentlichen Priesterthums*. Leipzig. 1889.
Bauer, J. B. "Könige und Priester, ein heiliges Volk (Ex. 19,6)," *BZ* 2 (1958), 283-86.
Beare, F. W. *The First Epistle of Peter*. 2nd revised ed. Oxford. 1958.
Beer, G. *Exodus* (*HAT* 1/3). Mit einem Beitrag von K. Galling. Tübingen. 1939. (Beer-Galling)
Behm, H. *Der Begriff des allgemeinen Priestertums*. Schwerin/Mecklnb. 1912.
Bengel, J. A. *Gnomon Novi Testamenti*. 3rd ed. Tübingen. 1773.
Bentzen, A. *Introduction to the Old Testament*. I-II. 4th ed. Copenhagen. 1958.
Best, E. "Spiritual Sacrifice. General Priesthood in the New Testament," *Interpretation* 14/3 (1960), 273-99.
Betz, O. "Felsenmann und Felsengemeinde (Parall. zu Mt. 16:17-19 in den Qumranpsalmen)" *ZNW* 48 (1957), 49-77. (*Felsenmann*)
——."Die Geburt der Gemeinde durch den Lehrer," *NTS* 3 (1956/57), 314-26. (*Geburt der Gemeinde*)
——.Offenbarung und Schriftforschung in der Qumransekte (*WUNT* 6). Tübingen. 1960.
——."Die Proselytentaufe der Qumransekte und die Taufe im Neuen Testament," *RQ* 1 (1958/59), 213-34.
Beyerlin, W. *Herkunft und Geschichte der ältesten Sinai-traditionen*. Tübingen. 1961.
Bickermann, E. "Ein jüdischer Festbrief vom Jahre 124 v. Chr.," *ZNW* 32 (1933), 233-54.
Bigg, C. *A Critical and Exegetical Commentary on the Epistles of St. Peter and St. Jude* (*ICC* 16). 2nd ed. Edinburgh. 1902.
Billerbeck, P. (H. L. Strack-) *Kommentar zum Neuen Testament aus Talmud und Midrasch*. I-IV. München. 1922-28. V-VI. 1955-61. (*Str-B*)
Blinzler, J. "IEPATEYMA. Zur Exegese von I Petr. 2,5 u. 9," *Episcopus: Festschrift für Kardinal Michael von Faulhaber*. Regensburg. 1949. Pp. 49-65.
Boccaccio, P., S.J. "Integer Textus Targum Hierosolymitani Primum Inventus In Codice Roma Vaticano," *Biblica* 38 (1957), 237-39.
Boismard, M.-E., O.P. "Une Liturgie baptismale dans la Prima Petri. I. Son influence sur Tit., I Jo. et Col.," *RB* 63/2 (1956), 182-208. II. Son influence sur l'épître de Jacques," *ibid.*, 64/2 (1957), 161-83.
——.*Quatre Hymnes baptismales dans la première épître de Pierre* (*Lectio Divina* 30). Paris. 1961. (*Quatre Hymnes*)
Bornemann, W. "Der erste Petrusbrief - eine Taufrede des Silvanus?," *ZNW* 19 (1919/20), 143-65.
Bornkamm, G. "Das Bekenntnis im Hebräerbrief," *ThBl* 21 (1942), 56ff. Reprinted in *Studien zu Antike und Urchristentum. Gesammelte Aufsätze*. München. II. 188-203.
——."Formen und Gattungen im Neuen Testament," *RGG* II, 999-1005.

Botte, B. "L'idée du sacerdoce des Fidèles dans la tradition. I. L'Antiquité Chrétienne," *La participation . . .* (*vide infra*). Pp. 21-28.

Bousset, W. *Die Offenbarung Johannis* (*KEK* 16). 6. Aufl. 1906.

Brandt, W. "Wandel als Zeugnis nach dem 1. Petrusbrief," *Verbum Dei Manet in Aeternum: Festschrift für Otto Schmitz*, ed. W. Foerster. Witten. 1953. Pp. 10-25.

Braumann, G. "Zum traditionsgeschichtlichen Problem der Seligpreisungen Mt V 3-12," *NovTest* 4 (1960), 253-260.

Braun, F. M. O.P. "Les Testaments des XII Patriarches et le Problème de leur Origine," *RB* 67 (1960), 516-49.

Braun, H. *Das Leiden Christi* (*ThEx* NF 69). München. 1940.

Bruce, F. F. "Qumran and Early Christianity," *NTS* 2 (1955/56), 176-90.

Brunotte, W. *Das Geistliche Amt bei Luther*. Berlin. 1959.

Buber, M. *Königtum Gottes*. 3. Aufl. Heidelberg. 1956.

Büchsel, F. ἀρτιγέννητος, ἀρτιγεννάω, *TWNT* I, 671-74.

Bultmann, R. "Bekenntnis- und Liedfragmente im ersten Petrusbrief," *CN* 11 (in honorem A. Fridrichsen) (1947), 1-14. (*Bekenntnis- und Liedfragmente*)

——."Paulus," *RGG* IV (2. Aufl. 1930), 1019-45.

——.*Theology of the New Testament*. I-II. New York. 1951, 1955. Transl. by K. Grobel from the original German: *Theologie des Neuen Testaments*. Tübingen. 1948-53. (*TNT*)

Campenhausen, H. von. "Die Anfänge des Priesterbegriffs in der alten Kirche," *SEÅ* 4 (1939), 86-101. Reprinted in *Tradition und Leben: Kräfte der Kirchengeschichte*. Tübingen. 1960. Pp. 272-89.

Casel, O., O.S.B. "Die λογικὴ θυσία der antiken Mystik in christlich-liturgischer Umdeutung," *JLW* 4 (1924), 37-47.

Carrington, Ph. *The Early Christian Church*. I-II. Cambridge. 1957.

——.*The Primitive Christian Catechism*. Cambridge. 1940.

Caspari, W. "Das priesterliche Königreich," *ThBl* 8 (1929), 105-10.

Cerfaux, L. "Regale Sacerdotium," *RSPhTh* 28 (1939), 5-39. Reprinted in *Recueil Lucien Cerfaux*. II. (*Bibliotheca Ephemeridum Theologicarum Lovaniensum* 6/7). Gembloux. 1954. 283-315.

——.*La Théologie de l'Église suivant S. Paul* (*Unam Sanctam* 10). Paris. 1942.

——."Un Chapitre du Livre des Testimonia," *EphLov* 14 (1937), 69-74.

——."Vestiges d'un florilège dans 1 Cor. 1:18-3:24," *RHE* 27 (1931), 23ff.

Charles, R. H. *A Critical and Exegetical Commentary on the Revelation of St. John* (*ICC* 18/1-2). Edinburgh. 1920. (*Revelation*).

Cody, A. "When is the Chosen People Called a Goy?," *VT* 14/1 (1964), 1-6.

Cohen, A. *Psalms* (*Soncino Books of the Bible*, ed. A. Cohen). London. 1945.

Congar, Y. M.-J., O.P. *Lay People in the Church*. A Study for a Theology of Laity. London. 1957. Transl. by D. Attwater from the original French: *Jalons pour une théologie du laicat*. Paris. 1952. (*Lay People*)

——.*Der Laie. Entwurf einer Theologie des Laientums*. Stuttgart. 1957. Transl. from the same French original by the Gemeinschaft der Dominkaner in Walberberg. (*Der Laie*)

——.*The Mystery of the Temple* or the Manner of God's Presence to His Creatures from Genesis to the Apocalypse. Westminster. 1962. Translated by R. F. Trevett from the original French: *Le Mystère du Temple* (*Lectio Divina* 22). Paris. 1958. (*Temple*)

——.*Das Mysterium des Tempels*. Salzburg. 1960. Translated by A. H. Geldern from the original French: *Le Mystère du Temple*.

Coutts, J. "Ephesians 1. 3-14 and 1 Peter 1. 3-12," *NTS* 3/2 (1956/57), 115-27.

Cranfield, C. E. B. *The First Epistle of Peter*. London. 1950.

Cross, F. L. *I Peter: A Paschal Liturgy*. London. 1954.

Cullmann, O. *Early Christian Worship* (SBT 10). London. 1953. Translated by A. S. Todd and J. B. Torrance from the second edition of the German *Urchristentu mund Gottesdienst*, Zurich, 1950, with an extra chapter on "Jesus and the Day of Rest" from the French translation of Part 2, which appeared under the title *Les Sacrements dans L'Evangile Johannique*, Paris, 1951.

Dabin, P., S.J. *Le Sacerdoce Royal des Fidèles dans les Livres Saints*. Paris. 1941.

——.*Le Sacerdoce Royal des Fidèles dans la tradition ancienne et moderne* (*Museum Lessianum* 48). Bruxelles/Paris. 1950. (Where this work rather than the preceding work bearing a similar title is meant, "*Sacerdoce . . . moderne*" is used).

Dahl, N. A. *Das Volk Gottes* (*Skrifter utgitt av Det Norske Videnskaps-Akademi i Oslo*. II. Historisk-Filosofisk Klasse. No. 2). Oslo. 1941.

Danell, G. A. "The Idea of God's People in the Bible," *The Root of the Vine: Essays in Biblical Theology*, ed. A. Fridrichsen. Westminster. 1953. Pp. 23-36.

Danielou, J., S.J. *The Dead Sea Scrolls and Primitive Christianity*. Baltimore. 1958. Translated by S. Attanasio from the original French: *Les Manuscrits la Mer Morte et les Origines du Christianisme*. Paris. 1957.

——.*Sacramentum Futuri*. Etudes sur les Origines de la Typologie Biblique. Paris. 1950.

——.*Théologie du Judéo-Christianisme* (*avant Nicée*). Tournai. 1950. (*Théologie*)

Deissmann, A. *Licht vom Osten*. 4. Aufl. Tübingen. 1923.

Delling, G. *Der Gottesdienst im Neuen Testament*. Berlin. 1952.

Dennefeld, L. *Les Grands Prophetes* (*La Sainte Bible* VII). Paris. 1952.

Dibelius, M. "Der himmlische Kultus nach dem Hebräerbrief," *ThBl* 21 (1942), 1-11. Reprinted in *Botschaft und Geschichte* II. Tübingen. 1956. 160-76.

Dibelius, M. *An die Kolosser, Epheser, an Philemon* (*HNT* 12). Dritte neubearbeitete Aufl. von H. Greeven. Tübingen. 1953.

——.*Die Pastoralbrief* (*HNT* 13). Dritte neubearbeitete Aufl. von H. Conzelmann. Tübingen. 1955.

——."Zur Formgeschichte des Neuen Testaments (ausserhalb der Evangelien)," *ThR* NF 3 (1931), 207-42.

Diez Macho, A., M.S.C. "The recently discovered Palestinian Targum: Its Antiquity and Relationship with the other Targums," *Congress Volume Oxford 1959* (*Supplements to Vetus Testamentum*, VII). Leiden. 1960. Pp. 222–45.

——."Una copia de todo el Targum jerosolimitano en la Vaticana," *EstBi* 15/4 (1956), 446f.

Dodd, C. H. *According to the Scriptures*. The substructure of New Testament Theology. London. 1952.

Driver, S. R. *An Introduction to the Literature of the Old Testament*. 9th ed. Edinburgh. 1913.

Duhm, B. *Das Buch Jesaia* (*HAT* 3/1). Göttingen. 1892.

Dunin-Borkowsky, St. von. "Die Kirche als priesterliche Gesellschaft," Esser-Mausbach, *Religion, Christentum, Kirche* II. Kempten. 1921. 413-28.

Dupont, J. "ΛΑΟΣ ΕΞ ΕΘΝΩΝ," *NTS* 3 (1956/57), 47-50.

——."L'Utilisation apologétique de l'A. T. pour la prédication et l'apologétique chrétienne," *EphLov* 26 (1953), 289-327.
Dupont-Sommer, A. *Les écrits esséniens découverts près de la Mer Morte.* Paris. 1959.
Eastwood, C. *The Priesthood of All Believers.*. An examination of the Doctrine from the Reformation to the Present Day. London. 1960.
——.*The Royal Priesthood of the Faithful.* An Investigation of the Doctrine from Biblical Times to the Reformation. London. 1963. (*Royal Priesthood*)
Eissfeldt, O. *Einleitung in das Alte Testament.* 2. Aufl. Tübingen. 1956.
Elliger, K. *Die Einheit des Tritojesaja* (56-66). Stuttgart. 1928.
Ellis, E. E. *Paul's Use of the Old Testament.* Edinburgh. 1957.
Eppel, R. *Le Piétisme Juif dans les Testaments des Douze Patriarches* (*Etudes d'Histoire et de Philosophie Religieuses.* Publiées par la Faculté de Théologie Protestante de l'Université de Strasbourg 22). Paris. 1930.
Feine, P. - J. Behm, *Einleitung in das Neue Testament.* 12., völlig neu bearbeitete Auflage von W. G. Kümmel. Heidelberg. 1963.
Fitzmyer, J. A. "4Q Testimonia and the New Testament," *TS* 18/4 (1957), 513-37.
——."The Use of Explicit Old Testament Quotations in Qumran Literature and in the New Testament," *NTS* 7 (1960/61), 297-333.
Flew, R. N. *Jesus and His Church.* A Study of the Idea of the Ecclesia in the New Testament. 2nd ed. London. 1943.
Flusser, D. "The Dead Sea Sect and Pre-Pauline Christianity," *Scripta Hierosolymitana* 3 (1958), 215-66.
Fohrer, G. "Der Vertrag zwischen König und Volk in Israel," *ZAW* 71 (1959), 1-22.
Fraeyman, M. "La spiritualisation de l'idée du temple dans les épîtres pauliniennes," *EphLov* 33 (1947), 378-412.
Fransen, I. "Une homélie chrétienne: la première Épître de Pierre," *Bible et Vie Chrétienne* (1960), 28-38.
Gall, A. von. βασιλεία τοῦ Θεοῦ. Eine religionsgeschichtliche Studie zur vorkirchlichen Eschatologie (*Religionswissenschaftliche Bibliothek* 17). Heidelberg. 1926.
Galling, K. *Die Erwählungstradition Israels* (*BZAW* 48). Giessen. 1928.
Ginsberg, L. *The Legends of the Jews.* I-VII. Philadelphia. 1913ff.
Grant, F. C. *Ancient Judaism and the New Testament.* New York. 1959.
Grelot, P. "Notes sur le Testament Araméen de Levi (Fragment de la Bodleian Library, colonne a)," *RB* 63 (1956), 391-406.
Grundmann, W. "Die νήπιοι in der urchristlichen Paränese," *NTS* 5 (1958/59), 188-205.
Gunkel, H. *Der erste Brief des Petrus* (*Schriften des Neuen Testaments* 3). 3. Aufl. Göttingen. 1917.
Hamer, J., O.P. *L'Église est une communion* (*Unam Sanctam* 40). Paris. 1962.
Hanhart, E. "Fragen um die Entstehung der Septuaginta," *VT* 12/2 (1962), 139-63.
Harris, J. R. *Testimonies.* I-II. Cambridge. 1916, 1920. (*Testimonies*)
Hatch, E. *Essays in Biblical Greek.* Oxford. 1889.
Hauck, F. *Die Katholischen Briefe* (*NTD* 3/2). Göttingen. 1933. (*NTD* 4/3. 7-8. Aufl. 1958).
Haufe, Ch. M. *Das Allgemeine Priestertum im Katholizismus der Gegenwart.* Dissertation: Leipzig (typewritten). 1961.
Holzmeister, U., S.J. *Commentarius in Epistulas SS. Petri et Judae Apostolo-*

rum. I. Epistula Prima S. Petri Apostoli (*Cursus Scripturae Sacrae* 3/13). Paris. 1937.

Hommes, N. J. *Het Testimoniaboek*. Studien over O. T. Citaten in het N. T. en bij de Patres, met critische Beschouwingen over de Theorieën van J. Rendel Harris en D. Plooy. Dissertation: Amsterdam. 1935.

Hort, F. J. A. *The First Epistle of St. Peter I*:1-11:17. London. 1898.

Horst, F. "Heilig und profan im AT und Judentum," *RGG* III, 148-51.

Hoskier, H. C. *Concerning the Text of the Apocalypse*. I-II. London. 1929.

Jeremias, J. "Der Eckstein," *Angelos* 1 (1925), 65-70.

——."Eckstein - Schlusstein," *ZNW* 36 (1937), 154-57.

——.*Golgotha* (*Angelos* 1). Leipzig. 1926.

——.γωνία and cognates, *TWNT* I, 792f.

——.*Jesus als Weltvollender* (*BFChrTh* 33/4). Gütersloh. 1930.

——."κεφαλὴ γωνίας - 'Ακρογωνιαῖος," *ZNW* 29 (1930), 264-80.

——.λίθος, *TWNT* IV, 272-83.

Joest, W. "Allgemeines Priestertum der Gläubigen," *EKL* III, 330-32.

Jonge, M. de. *The Testaments of the Twelve Patriarchs*, A study of their text, composition and origin. Dissertation: Leiden. Assen. 1953.

Jülicher, A. *Einleitung in das Neue Testament*. Siebte Aufl. neubearbeitet von E. Fascher. Tübingen. 1931.

Junker, H. "Das allgemeine Priestertum des Volkes Israel nach Ex. 19:6," *TThZ* 56 (1947), 10-15.

Käsemann, E. "Amt und Gemeinde im Neuen Testament." A lecture given in Herborn on 13 October 1949 and printed among his collected essays in *Exegetische Versuche und Besinnungen* I. 2. Aufl. Göttingen. 1960. 109-34. (*Amt und Gemeinde*)

——."Das Formular einer neutestamentlichen Ordinationsparänese," *Neutestamentliche Studien für Rudolf Bultmann*. Berlin. 1954. Pp. 261-68. Reprinted in *Exegetische Versuche* I, 101-08.

——."Liturgische Formeln im NT," *RGG* II, 883-96.

——."Ein neutestamentlicher Überblick (1949/50)," *Verkündigung und Forschung* (1951), 191-218.

——."Eine urchristliche Taufliturgie," *Festschrift für Rudolf Bultmann*. Stuttgart. 1949. Pp. 133-48. Reprinted in *Exegetische Versuche* I, 34-51.

——.*Das wandernde Gottesvolk* (*FRLANT* NF 37). 4. Aufl. Göttingen. 1961.

Kahle, P. E. *The Cairo Geniza*. 2nd ed. Oxford. 1959. (*Cairo Geniza*)

——.*Die Massoreten des Westens*. I-II. Stuttgart. 1930. (*Massoreten des Westens*)

——."Das palästinische Pentateuchtargum und das zur Zeit Jesu gesprochene Aramäisch," *ZNW* 49 (1959), 100-116. (*Palästin. Pentateuchtargum*)

Ketter, P. *Die Apokalypse* (*HBK* 16/2). 3. Aufl. Freiburg. 1953.

——.*Der erste Petrusbrief* (*HBK* 16/1). Freiburg. 1950. (*Petrusbrief*)

——."Das allgemeine Priestertum der Gläubigen nach dem 1. Petrusbrief," *TThZ* 56 (1947), 43-51. (*Priestertum*)

Kiddle, M., and M. K. Ross. *The Revelation of St. John* (*Moffatt Commentary*). London. 1940.

Kinder, E. "Das allgemeine Priestertum im Neuen Testament," *Schriften des Theologischen Konvents Augsburgischen Bekenntnisses* 5. Berlin. 1953. Pp. 5-23.

Kirk, K. E. "The Apostolic Ministry," *The Apostolic Ministry. Essays on the History and Doctrine of Episcopacy*, ed. K. E. Kirk. London. 1946.

Kittel, G. λογικός, *TWNT* IV, 145-47.

Klein, G. *Der Älteste Christliche Katechismus und die Jüdische Propaganda-Literatur*. Berlin. 1909.
Klijn, A. F. J. "Die Wörter 'Stein' und 'Felsen' in der syrischen Übersetzung des Neuen Testaments," *ZNW* 50 (1959), 99-105.
Kluge, O. *Die Idee des Priestertums in Israel-Juda und im Urchristentum*. Leipzig. 1906.
Knopf, R. *Die Briefe Petri und Judä* (*KEK* 12). 7. Aufl. Göttingen. 1912.
Koch, K. "Priestertum in Israel," *RGG* V, 574-578.
König, E. *Das Buch Jesaja*. Gütersloh. 1926.
——.*Geschichte der alttestamentlichen Religion*. 2. Aufl. Gütersloh. 1915.
Kosmala, H. *Hebräer - Essener - Christen* (*Studia Post-Biblica*, ed. P. A. H. de Boer 1). Leiden. 1959.
Kraemer, H. *A Theology of Laity*. London. 1958.
Krafft, E. "Christologie und Anthropologie im ersten Petrusbrief," *EvTh* 10 (1950/51), 120-26.
Kuenen, A. *Historisch-kritische Einleitung in die Bücher des Alten Testaments*. I-III. 1887-94. Transl. by Weber and Müller from the original Dutch: *Historischkritisch Onderzoek naar het ontstaan en de verzameling van de boeken des Ouden Verbonds*. I-III. Leiden. 1861-65.
Küng, H. "The Ecumenical Council in Theological Perspective," *Dialog* 1/3 (1962), 40-49. Inaugural Address at the University of Tübingen (24 November 1960). Translated by J. W. Kleiner.
Kuhn, K. G. "Der Heiligkeitsbegriff im rabbinischen Judentum," *TWNT* I, 97-101.
Kutscher, E. Y. "The Language of the Genesis Apocryphon: A Preliminary Study," *Scripta Hierosolymitana* 4 (1958), 1-33.
Llopart, E. M. "La Protovetlla Pasqual Apostolica," *Liturgica I. Cardinali A. Schuster in Memoriam*. Montserrat. 1956. Pp. 387-524.
Lohmeyer, E. *Die Briefe an die Kolosser und an Philemon* (*KEK* 9/2). 9. Aufl. Göttingen. 1953.
——.*Die Offenbarung des Johannes* (*HNT* 16). 2. Aufl. 1953. (*Offenbarung*)
——."Vom urchristlichen Abendmahl," *ThR* 9 (1937), 168-228; 273-312.
Lohse, B. "Priestertum in der christlichen Kirche," *RGG* V, 578-81.
Lohse, E. "Paränese und Kerygma im 1. Petrusbrief," *ZNW* 45 (1945), 68-69.
Love, J. P. "The First Epistle of Peter," *Interpretation* 8/1 (1954), 63-87.
Manson, T. W. *Ministry and Priesthood: Christ's and Ours*. London/Richmond. 1959.
——."The O. T. in the Teaching of Jesus," *BJRL* 34 (1951/52), 312-32.
Marti, K. *Das Buch Jesaja* (*HCAT* 10). Tübingen. 1900.
Martin, R. P. "The Composition of I Peter in Recent Study," *Vox Evangelica*. Biblical and Historical Essays by Members of the Faculty of the London Bible College, ed. R. P. Martin. London. 1962. Pp. 29-42.
McCarthy, D. J. *Treaty and Covenant*. Rome. 1963.
McKelvey, R. J. "Christ the Cornerstone," *NTS* 8 (1961/62), 352-59.
Michel, O. *Der Brief an die Römer* (*KEK* 4). 12. Aufl. Göttingen. 1962.
——.οἶκος and cognates, *TWNT* V, 122-61.
——.*Paulus und seine Bibel*. Gütersloh. 1929.
Milik, J. T. A review of M. de Jonge's *The Testament of the Twelve Patriarchs*, *RB* 62 (1955), 297-98.
——.*Ten Years of Discovery in the Wilderness of Judea* (*SBT* 26). London. 1959. Transl. by J. Strugnell from the original French: *Dix ans de Découvertes dans le Désert de Juda*. Paris. 1957. (*Ten Years*)
——."Le Testament de Lévi en araméen. Fragment de Grotte 4 de Qumrân

(Pl. 4)," *RB* 62 (1955), 398-406.
Miller, D. G. "Deliverance and Destiny," *Interpretation* 9 (1955), 413-25.
Mitton, C. L. "The Relationship between I Peter and Ephesians," *JTS* n.s. 1/1 (1950), 67-73.
Moe, O. "Der Gedanke des allgemeinen Priestertums im Hebräerbrief," *ThZ* 5 (1949), 161-69.
Molin, G. *Die Söhne des Lichtes*. Wien. 1954.
Moran, W. L. "A Kingdom of Priests," *The Bible in Current Catholic Thought*, ed. J. L. McKenzie. New York. 1962. Pp. 7-20.
Moule, C. F. D. "The Nature and Purpose of I Peter," *NTS* 3 (1956/57), 1-11.
——."Sanctuary and Sacrifice in the Church of the New Testament," *JTS* n.s. 1/1 (1950), 29-41.
——."Some Reflections on the 'Stone' Testimonia in Relation to the Name Peter," *NTS* 2 (1955/56), 56-59.
Mowinckel, S. *Le décalogue*. Paris. 1927.
Muilenburg, J. *The Book of Isaiah* (*The Interpreter's Bible* V). New York. 1956.
——."Covenantal Formulations," *VT* 9 (1959), 343-65.
Nauck, W. "Probleme des frühchristlichen Amtsverständnisses (1 Petr. 5. 2f)," ZNW 48 (1957), 200-220. Printed earlier in condensed form in *ThLZ* 81 (1956), 351f.
——.*Die Tradition und der Charakter des 1. Johannesbriefes*. Tübingen. 1957.
Niebecker, E. *Das Priestertum der Gläubigen*. Dissertation: Münster. Paderborn. 1936.
Nötscher, F. "Heiligkeit in den Qumranschriften," *RQ* 2 (1960), 163-81; 315-44.
Noth, M. *Amt und Berufung im Alten Testament* (Rektoratsrede an der Rheinischen Friedrich-Wilhelms-Universität zu Bonn 1958. *Bonner Akademische Reden* 19. Bonn. 1958). Reprinted in *Gesammelte Studien zum Alten Testament* (*Theologische Bücherei* 6). 2. Aufl. München. 1960. Pp. 309-33.
——.*Die Gesetze im Pentateuch* (*Schriften der Königsberger Gelehrten Gesellschaft*. Geisteswissenschaftliche Klasse 17/2). Halle (Saale). 1940. Reprinted in *Gesammelte Studien*. Pp. 9-141.
——.*Das System der zwölf Stämme Israels* (*BWANT* 4/1). Stuttgart. 1930.
——.*Überlieferungsgeschichte des Pentateuch*. Stuttgart. 1948.
——.*Das zweite Buch Mose: Exodus* (*ATD* 5). 2. Aufl. Göttingen. 1961.
Oesterley, W. O. E., and T. W. Robinson. *An Introduction to the Books of the Old Testament*. London/New York. 1934.
Ordonez, V. "El Sacerdocio de los Fieles," *Revista Espanola de Teologia* 64 (1956), 359-79.
Otzen, B. "Die neugefundenen herbräischen Sektenschriften und die Testamente der zwölf Patriarchen," *StTh* 7/1-2 (1953), 125-57.
Participation Active des Fidèles au Culte, La. Cours Conférences des Semaines Liturgiques. Tome XI. Louvain. 1934.
Perdelwitz, R. *Die Mysterienreligionen und das Problem des 1. Petrusbriefes* (*Religionsgeschichtliche Versuche und Vorarbeiten* 11/3). Giessen. 1911.
Philonenko, M. *Des interpolations chrétiennes des Testaments des Douze Patriarches et les Manuscrits de Qumrân* (*Cahiers de la Revue d'Histoire et de Philosophie Religieuses* no. 35). Paris. 1960.
Plooy, D. *Studies in the Testimony Book* (*Verhandelingen der Koninklijke Akademie van Wetenschappen te Amsterdam*. Afdeling Letterkunde. NR. 32/2). Amsterdam. 1932.

Preisker, H. *Das Ethos des Urchristentums*. 2. Aufl. Gütersloh. 1949.
Prenter, R. "Allgemeines Priestertum," *RGG* V, 581f.
——."Die göttliche Einsetzung des Predigtamtes und das allgemeine Priestertum bei Luther," *ThLZ* 86/5 (1961), 321-32.
Prigent, P. "Quelques Testimonia messianiques," *ThZ* 15 (1959), 419-30.
——.*Les Testimonia dans le Christianisme primitif. L'Épître de Barnabé I-XVI et ses Sources* (*Etudes Bibliques*). Paris. 1961. (*Testimonia*)
Procksch, O., and K. G. Kuhn. ἅγιος, *TWNT* I, 87-116.
Rad, G. von. βασιλεύς, *TWNT* I, 563-69.
——.*Das formgeschichtliche Problem des Hexateuch* (*BWANT* 4/26). Stuttgart. 1938. Reprinted in *Gesammelte Studien zum Alten Testament* (*Theologische Bücherei* 8). München. 1961. Pp. 9-86. (*Hexateuch*)
——.*Old Testament Theology*. I. Edinburgh/London. 1962. Transl. by D. M. G. Stalker from the original German: *Theologie des Alten Testaments. I. Die Theologie der geschichtlichen Überlieferungs Israels*. München. 1957.
Reuss, J. *I. und II. Timotheus, Titus, Philemon, Hebräer, Die Katholischen Briefe*, und E. Schick, *Die Apokalypse* (*EB* NT 3). Würzburg. 1959.
Richardson, A. *An Introduction to the Theology of the New Testament*. New York. 1958.
Rost, L. "Jubiläenbuch," *RGG* III, 960f.
Scharlemann, M. H. "Why the Kuriou in 1 Peter 1:25?" *CMT* 30/5 (1959), 352–56.
Schelkle, K. H. *Die Gemeinde von Qumran und die Kirche des Neuen Testaments*. Düsseldorf. 1960.
——.*Jüngerschaft und Apostelamt*. Freiburg. 1957.
——.*Die Petrusbriefe, der Judasbrief* (*HTKNT* 13). Freiburg. 1961. (*Petrusbriefe*)
Schlatter, A. *Die Briefe des Petrus, Judas, Jakobus, der Brief an die Hebräer* (*ENT* 9). Stuttgart. 1910-50. (*Briefe*)
——.*Die Briefe und die Offenbarung des Johannes* (*ENT* 10). Stuttgart. 1950.
——.*Opfer - ein Verzicht?* Vier Reden von Adolf Schlatter. (*Das Gott wohlgefällige Opfer*, 1926). Hrsg. R. Frick. Bad Salzuflen. 1958. (*Opfer*)
——.*Petrus und Paulus nach dem 1. Petrusbrief*. Stuttgart. 1937. (*Petrus*)
——.*Die Theologie des Neuen Testament*. II. *Die Lehre der Apostel*. Tübingen. 1910. (*TNT*)
Schlier, H. *Der Brief an die Epheser*. 2. Aufl. Düsseldorf. 1958.
——.γάλα, *TWNT* I, 644f.
Schmidt, K. L. βασίλειος, *TWNT* I, 593.
Schmidt, W. *Königtum Gottes in Ugarit und Israel* (*BZAW* 80). Dissertation: Berlin. Berlin. 1961.
Schmitz, O. *Die Opferanschauungen des späteren Judentums und die Opferaussagen des Neuen Testaments*. Tübingen. 1910.
Schneider, J. *Die Briefe des Jakobus, Petrus, Judas, und Johannes* (*NTD* 10). 9. Aufl. Göttingen. 1961. (*Petrus*)
——."Erwählung im NT," *RGG* II, 613f.
——.προσέρχομαι, *TWNT* II, 680-82.
Schrenk, G. ἐκλεκτός, *TWNT* IV, 186-97.
——.γραφή, *TWNT* I, 749-54.
——.ἱεράτευμα, *TWNT* III, 249-51.
Schunck, K.-D. "Makkabäerbücher," *RGG* IV, 620-22.
——.*Die Quellen des I. und II. Makkabäerbuches*. Halle. 1954.
Schweizer, E. *Church Order in the New Testament* (*SBT* 32). London. 1961. Transl. by F. Clarke from the original German: *Gemeinde und Gemeinde-*

ordnung im Neuen Testament. Zürich. 1959.
——."πνεῦμα, πνευματικός im NT," *TWNT* VI, 394-449.
Scott, R. B. Y. "A Kingdom of Priests (Ex. 19:6)," *OTS* 8 (1950), 113-119.
Scott, W. F. M. "Priesthood in the New Testament," *SJT* 10/4 (1957), 399-415.
Seeberg, A. *Der Katechismus der Urchristenheit*. Leipzig. 1903.
Seidensticker, Ph., O.F.M. *Lebendiges Opfer* (*Röm.* 12.1) (*Neutestamentliche Abhandlungen*, hrsg. M. Meinertz. 20 1/3). Münster. 1954.
Sellin, E. *Einleitung in das Alte Testament*. 9. Aufl. bearbeitet von L. Rost. Berlin. 1959. (*Sellin-Rost*)
Selwyn, E. G. *The First Epistle of St. Peter*. 2nd ed. London. 1955.
Sevenster, G. "Het Koning- en Priesterschap der Gelovigen in het Nieuwe Testament," *NThT* 13 (1958), 401-17.
Sjöberg, E. "Neuschöpfung in den Toten-Meer-Rollen," *StTh* 9/2 (1955), 131-36.
Slotki, I. W. *Isaiah* (*Soncino Books of the Bible*, ed. A. Cohen). London. 1949.
Smits, C., O.F.M. *Oud-Testamentische Citaten in het Nieuwe Testament* (*Collectanea Franciscana Neerlandica* 8/I-III). s'Hertogenbosch. 1952-57.
Soden, H. von. *Briefe des Petrus* (*HCNT* 3/12). 3. Aufl. Freiburg in Breisgau. 1899.
Sommerlath, E. "Amt und allgemeines Priestertum," *Schriften des Theologischen Konvents Augsburgischen Bekenntnisses* 5. Berlin. 1953. Pp. 40-89. Reprinted as a separate volume under the same title in Berlin, 1954.
Spörri, Th. *Der Gemeindegedanke im ersten Petrusbrief*. Gütersloh. 1925.
Stade, B. *Die Geschichte des Volkes Israels*. I-II. Berlin. 1887-88.
Stählin, G. *SKANDALON*: *Untersuchung zur Geschichte eines biblischen Begriffes* (*BFChrTh* 2/24). Gütersloh. 1930.
Stauffer, E. "Probleme der Priestertradition," *ThLZ* 81/3 (1956), 135-50.
Stendahl, K. "The Called and the Chosen: An Essay on Election," *The Root of the Vine*: *Essays in Biblical Theology*, ed. A. Fridrichsen. Westminster. 1953. Pp. 63-80.
Steuernagel, K. *Lehrbuch der Einleitung in das Alte Testament*. Mit einem Anhang über die Apokryphen und Pseudepigraphen. Tübingen. 1912.
Stibbs, A. M. *The First Epistle General of Peter* (*The Tyndale New Testament Commentaries*). Grand Rapids. 1959.
Storck, H. *Das Allgemeine Priestertum bei Luther* (*ThEX* NF 37). 1953.
Strack, H. L. *Introduction to the Talmud and Midrash*. New York. 1959. Translation on the basis of the author's revised copy of the fifth German edition: *Einleitung in Talmud und Midrash*. Berlin. 1920.
Strathmann, H., and R. Meyer. λαός, *TWNT* IV, 29-58.
Streeter, B. H. *The Primitive Christian Church*. New York. 1929.
Sundberg, A. C. "On Testimonies," *NovTest* 3 (1959), 268-81.
Thornton, T. C. G. "I Peter, a Paschal Liturgy," *JTS* n.s. 21/1 (1961), 14-26.
Torrance, T. F. *Royal Priesthood* (*SJT Occasional Papers* 3). Edinburgh. 1955.
Unnik, W. C. van. "Christianity According to I Peter," *ExpT* 68/3 (1956), 79-83.
——."The Teaching of Good Works in I Peter," *NTS* 1/2 (1954), 92-110.
——.*De verlossing I Petrus* 1:18-19 *en het probleem van den eersten Petrusbrief* (*Mededeelingen der Nederlandsche Akademie van Wetenschappen*. Afdeeling Letterkunde. NR. 5/1). Amsterdam. 1942. (*De verlossing*)
Vajta, V. "Der Christenstand als 'königliches Priestertum,'" *Welt-Luthertum von Heute*: *A. Nygren Festschrift*. Stockholm. 1950. Pp. 350-73.
Vaux, R. de. "Fouilles de Khirbet Qumrân. Rapport préliminaire sur les 3e,

4e et 5e campagnes," *RB* 66 (1956), 533-77.
Vielhauer, Ph. *OIKODOME: das Bild vom Bau in der christlichen Literatur vom Neuen Testament bis Clemens Alexandrinus*. Dissertation: Heidelberg. Karlsruhe. 1940.
Vollmer, H. *Die alttestamentlichen Citate bei Paulus*. Freiburg. 1896.
Volz, P. *Jesaia II* (*KAT* 9: *Jes*. 40-66). Leipzig. 1932.
Wand, J. W. C. *The General Epistles of St. Peter and St. Jude*. London. 1934.
——."The Lessons of First Peter," *Interpretation* 9 (1955), 387-99.
Wendland, H.-D. "Heilig und Profan im NT," *RGG* III, 151.
——."Opfer im NT," *RGG* IV, 1647-51.
Wendland, P. *Die urchristlichen Literaturformen* (*HNT* 1/3). Tübingen. 1912.
Wenschkewitz, H. *Die Spiritualisierung der Kultusbegriffe Tempel, Priester und Opfer im Neuen Testament* (*Angelos* 4). Leipzig. 1932.
Wernberg-Møller, P. "Reflections on the Biblical Material in the Manual of Discipline," *StTh* 9 (1955), 40-66.
Wikenhauser, A. *Einleitung in das Neue Testament*. 4. Aufl. Freiburg i. Br. 1961.
Wildberger, H. *Jahwes Eigentumsvolk* (*Abhandlung zur Theologie des Alten und Neuen Testaments* 37). Zürich. 1960.
Windisch, H. *Die Apostolischen Väter. Der Barnabasbrief* (*HNT* Ergänzungsband 3). Tübingen. 1920.
——.*Die Katholischen Briefe* (*HNT* 15). 2. Aufl. Tübingen. 1930. Dritte, stark umgearbeitet Aufl. von H. Preisker. 1951. (*Windisch-Preisker*)
Winter, P. "Eine vollständige Handschrift des palästinischen Targums aufgefunden," *ZNW* 48 (1957), 192.
Wohlenberg, G. *Der erste und der zweite Petrusbrief und der Judasbrief* (*ZKNT* 15). Leipzig/Erlangen. 1915. 3. Aufl. 1929.
Woude, A. S. van der. *Die Messianische Vorstellung der Gemeinde von Qumran*. Assen. 1957.
Wright, G. E. "Erwählung im AT," *RGG* II, 610-12.
Zahn, T. *Die Offenbarung des Johannes* (*ZKNT* 18/1-2). Leipzig, 1924.
Zeitlin, S. "The Book of Jubilees. Its Character and Its Significance," *JQR* n.s. 30 (1939/40), 1-31.

INDEX OF PROPER NAMES

INDEX OF PASSAGES

OLD TESTAMENT

NEW TESTAMENT

APOCRYPHA AND PSEUDEPIGRAPHA OF THE OLD TESTAMENT

ANCIENT NEAR EASTERN TEXT

QUMRAN LITERATURE

RABBINIC LITERATURE